THE COMPLETE BOOK OF

FLY~FISHING

THE COMPLETE BOOK OF

FLY~FISHING

A Worldwide Guide to the Fish, the Waters, the Flies, and the Challenge

General Editor MALCOLM GREENHALGH
Consultant ED JAWOROWSKI

The Reader's Digest Association, Inc.
Pleasantville, New York • Montreal

CONTENTS

A Reader's Digest Book
Edited and produced by
Mitchell Beazley, an imprint of
Reed Consumer Books Limited

Executive Editor   Samantha Ward-Dutton
Executive Art Editor   Emma Boys

Senior Editor   Penelope Cream
Senior Art Editor   Kathy Gammon
Editors   Casey Horton
                          Cathy Lowne
                          Claire Musters
Designer   Lisa Pettibone

Design Concept   Luise Roberts
Production   Rachel Staveley
Picture Researcher   Jenny Faithfull
Illustrators   Stuart Carter
                          Mick Loates
                          Denys Ovenden
                          Gill Tomblin
Maps   Hardlines

Library of Congress Cataloging in Publication
Data has been applied for.

ISBN 0-7621-0026-5

Reader's Digest and the Pegasus logo
are registered trademarks of
The Reader's Digest Association, Inc.

Printed and bound in China

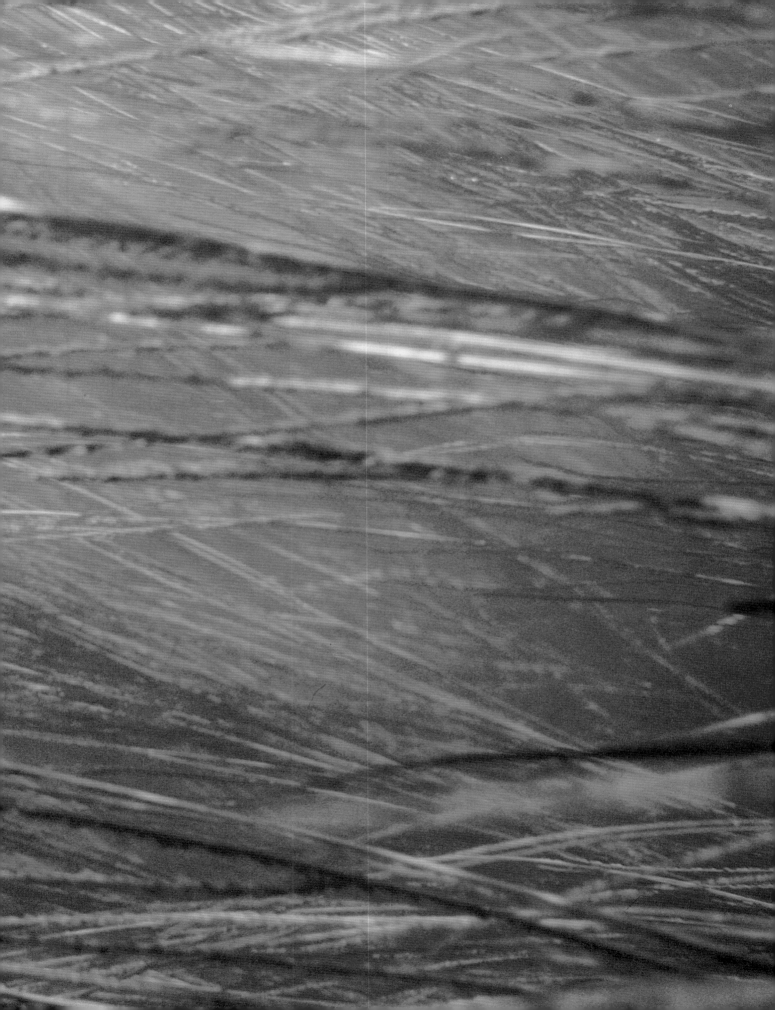

FOREWORD

DAVE WHITLOCK

Welcome to the world of fly-fishing! This book celebrates that fascinating world and has a very special place reserved for each of you who accepts our invitation to be part of it. Whether you are nine, 19, or 99, your best years as a fly-fisher lie ahead.

I began fly-fishing when I was nine years old, and each of my 55 years since has become better and better. Fly-fishing improved my health, my crippled body, and my outlook on life. It gave me something to enjoy and to strive for every day.

When you take up fly-fishing you can become part of a wonderful world, one in which men and women who fly-fish can be recognized by their willingness to share their knowledge, favorite fly-fishing places, tackle, flies, and time. I have witnessed fly-fishers willingly sharing a special fly, fishing technique, or spot with a complete stranger who needed some assistance. That generosity of spirit must remain, for us all, an integral part of the sport.

There are limitless plateaux in fly-fishing. All the world's fish, streams, lakes, seas, and oceans can be enjoyed with a fly-rod. For a true fly-fisher, any body of water encountered or heard of – a water near your home, or one halfway around the world – holds a fascination. There is always the puzzle to solve of the type of fish that live there, what the fish eat, and how best to imitate their food with a fly. Then there is the thrill as the fish comes to your fly, the excitement as you hook, play, and capture it, that special feeling as you slip the barbless hook from the jaw of the fish and return it to the water to continue its natural life and mission. No matter how successful a day is, the next day will be just as special, so that each day brings its own new thrill; the sport is always challenging, surprising, enriching, and fulfilling.

A fly-fisher, to be best rewarded, must understand a fish's world and become nearly invisible and silent among the natural scenes. When I fly-fish I escape into a private world that is free of pain, finances, taxes, or family or business problems. An almost hypnotic love affair connects me with the water, air, land, weather, and nature's natural rhythms. This oneness is not only pleasing to my mind and heart, but also makes me realize how special Earth and its wild places are.

At such moments only my fly exists as it sails to meet the water and the fish, moving from a gentle stroke of my arm and my hand, with the long delicate rod, looping fly-line, and leader. The fish senses its arrival and moves up to intercept it as a living food. It captures the fly, and I, in turn, am captured, fixed to a wild creature. What a feeling it is to be part of that natural scene. The fish takes my fly, or I tire it and bring it to me, but in either event it soon swims free. Then we each resume the hunt.

Fly-fishing is the ultimate practice of meditation: it clears and relaxes our minds and bodies of life's stresses. It makes us all nicer people. Once you fly-fish, killing and eating your catch becomes less and less desirable, even if no one tells you that catch and release is accepted practice. It just naturally evolves. Because you have learned about the fish's life and worth, recognized what a special, beautiful, living creature it is, you respect it too much to harm it. Fly-fishers, almost to the last person, become active in the conservation and preservation of fish habitats and the world environment. It is almost something magical in the activity that does this.

Fly-fishers are also moved to share the sport with others. Usually they are moved to teach it, write prose or poetry about it, or take up camera, wood, clay, or paint and brush to express their feelings about it in some visible, tangible form, in order to share their pleasure. No other sport has accumulated such a large body of writing, sculpture, philosophical thought, poetry, art, science, and photography, created by its own followers. This book is a perfect example of the fly-fishers' urge to express their love of fly-fishing. Many of the world's most avid and knowledgeable fly-fishers have contributed their expertise and love to put this book of fly-fishing together.

We have begun by describing the beauty of the world's fish and their waters, and continued with details of how the fish live and feed, the challenge that fly-fishing presents, and the methods taken to choose and present the fly. Finally, we introduce you to some of the secret, favorite places of the fish around the world.

In this book you will read about a sport, a philosophy, and a lifestyle. Here are ideas, gifts, and pleasures that are such an essential part of fly-fishing. Welcome to the celebration!

The distant peaks are tinged
with the pink and gold of
a lone fly-fisher's dawn.

THE ESSENCE OF FLY-FISHING

MALCOLM GREENHALGH

Dawn was just starting to break as I reached the river on a beautiful day in early June. In the east the summits of the angular hills stood out as blue-gray silhouettes against a background of rose pink. And in the belts of dense woodland flanking the terrace slopes on either side of the river the early birds were ignoring the worm; instead they were belting out the near deafening cacophony of their dawn chorus. I tackled up the trout fly-rod in the semi-darkness, at the same time drinking in the sights, sounds, and sweet fresh aroma of late spring, and anticipating a long day – a very long day – of pleasurable toil. For I intended to fish through the day to the evening rise, more than 18 hours away.

The river pool by which I sat was flat and unruffled by wind. Not one fish stirred. But as a constant background to the vibrant birdsong there were the rippling, tinkling notes of the run into the pool from beneath a line of still, black alders, and a quite separate low rushing sound of the pool tail as it flowed under the ancient gritstone packhorse bridge. I listened as I tied a new point to my leader, holding the ends of the fine monofilament against the now fiery red eastern sky to make the tying of the four-turn water knot that bit easier. Then I turned to the dry-fly boxes. Later in the day big *Danica* mayfly duns would be hatching, and spinners falling. But not at dawn. What would the trout be devouring in the next hour or so? Midges? Of course. Midges! I chose a size 20 Gray Midge, carefully knotted it to the end of the leader, and then gave it a light dressing of floatant. Now I was ready. All that remained was a little co-operation from the real midges and the trout.

Away in the distance the church clock struck four and, almost immediately, the flat pool became a boiling cauldron as trout after trout slashed and crashed at the surface, breakfasting on the sudden and huge hatch of insects. But midges? Carefully I cast my midge imitation over the nearest rise – but the trout ignored my offering. So too did the second, and third, and the fourth. I did what the majority of fly-fishers do in these circumstances. I lost all sense of reason and began to bombard the trout with a host of randomly selected flies.

Within 20 minutes my hat was festooned with wet dry flies, the river still had as many trout in it as it had before I started trying to catch them, and the trout were all feeding as keenly as ever.

Even worse: I was no longer enjoying myself, and I was casting badly. Then – it was now fully light – I spotted the problem. In fact, I was stupid not to have made an effort to spot it much earlier. The trout were not feeding on midges as I had expected. Instead they were gorging themselves like the proverbial pigs on a small fly which was now flying in clouds over the water. I caught one and examined it.

The fly that the trout were taking was a small species of mayfly, with a body length matched by a size 18 dry-fly hook. There were three tails – long, pale gray tails. The body was quite distinct: a slender, segmented off-white abdomen and a pronounced dark, almost black, thorax. The wings were opaque and milky white.

It was clear that what I was witnessing was a hatch of some species of "anglers' curse." However, all the hatches of anglers' curse that I had seen before were an afternoon event, and the flies tinier than the one I was holding now. It was closer to a size 26 hook. The afternoon anglers' curse is a fly that trout love but fly-fishers hate, because during a hatch the flies are so abundant and so tiny. Imitating them is not easy; getting a trout to take an imitation can be almost impossible.

Alas I had no flies in my boxes that would imitate this new species of "dawn curse." Hastily I collected a few specimens in a plastic film canister and went back to try and catch a trout. Try! Imagine, on perhaps 200 casts, your fly drifting downstream over rising trout and being ignored on every cast. It was that bad. One small foolish trout did save the dawn session by grabbing a small black dry fly. Its throat was crammed with the dawn curse.

I missed the evening rise. Instead I went home and checked my reference books. Yes, there was a species of anglers' curse that hatched at dawn, but it had been recorded from relatively few rivers and rarely in large numbers. Then I set to tying some imitations, using my specimens as models. A size 18 hook equalled body length. The three tails were matched by stiff fibers from a blue dun hackle. For the off-white abdomen I stripped the fibers from the stalk of a white hackle and wound that around the hook-shank; it made a lovely segmented abdomen. Three turns of peacock herl produced a most realistic thorax. For the wings I chose two white cock hackle

points. And for the gray legs of the insect I substituted a wound blue dun hackle. Once I had tied half a dozen of my new flies, I went to bed.

I awoke before the alarm clock and when the church bell was tolling four o'clock I was back by the river with my Morning Curse tied to a new fine leader point. I did not have long to wait. As on the previous day, in the half-light of dawn flies began to hatch and trout to rise. I noticed a particularly large boil made by a fish just downstream of the alders in the neck of the pool. Carefully I lengthened line and dropped my new fly a short way downstream of the fish. I watched the white wings of the fly as they drifted downstream. They dragged a little across the flow. I stripped some more line from the reel, then made a couple of false casts to shake any moisture from the fly, and flicked the fly up above the trout, at the same time making a reach upstream so that the slack line would prevent any unnatural drag of the fly. Again I watched the white wings drift downstream and then, suddenly, disappear in a swirl. I tightened the line and a couple of minutes later was privileged to slip a most beautiful, red-spotted and butter-yellow-bellied brown trout back into the flow.

That experience embraced all the magic of fly-fishing: a beautiful and spectacular fish that is not so easily caught; the food of the fish; a fly that matches that food item; the bits and pieces of fly-fishing tackle; the tying of the fly to the leader; spotting the fish; the cast; the anticipation; a feeling of elation when fish takes fly, and the excitement of playing the fish; a deep sense of reverence, of admiration for the fish; a sense of becoming a part of nature itself.

This magic is what this book is all about.

Malcolm Greenhalgh

THE CONTEMPLATIVE RECREATION

ED JAWOROWSKI

The true-life experience related on the previous pages summarizes the essence of fly-fishing: the familiar paradigm of participation in the natural and eternal rhythms of fish and water. Yet this is not always the gentle sport, for it wears a thousand faces.

If nature conducts symphonies on trout streams, she orchestrates vibrant sound and light productions along the edge of the ocean. Daybreak: swirls in the water; amid the combers terns wheel erratically, gulls squawk harshly, fish splash viciously as bait leap futilely skyward or race onto the sand in frantic attempts to avoid the savage maws of their predators.

And I am there too. Not as a voyeur, but as a participant, operating in the chain, stalking the predator next on the scale below me, by imitating its prey still farther down the scale. This too requires me to make observations calculations, and to fit my range of skills to problem solving. What forage? What imitation? Where to cast? Depth and speed of retrieve? Why the jacks or tunas or bluefish disdain what I believe should be more desirable offerings, meaty eight-inch prey, and focus their attention on diminutive sandeels or anchovies, barely two inches long, puzzles me. Then as suddenly as it began, the surface settles, the swirls are gone. The bait has moved on, along with the gamefish I'm seeking. Are they simply sated, digesting their surfeit, or awaiting the next change of tide or passage of the next bait school before resuming feeding?

Such mysteries of nature play out endlessly, not only in the trout's rhythmic rise and the bluefish's savage attack, but in the silent search of the bonefish on the tropical flats, the ominous stalking of the pike amid shallow northern weed beds, or the ambush of the pavon in underwater jungles.

For many of us, an additional fascination lies in the technique and intensive nature of this sport. It demands highly refined tackle, finely honed skills, awareness of limnology, entomology, physics, biology, chemistry, oceanography, and a dozen other sciences, plus the wide range of practical skills – casting, knots, fly-tying. No implacable goddess called luck rules here, just cause and effect. Of paramount importance perhaps, is the attempt at least to understand, because casual, unexplained success is what Colonel E W Harding, in *The Fly Fisher and the*

Trout's Point of View, called "Dead Sea fruit to the palate of enjoyment". Fly-fishers don't stand on the sidelines, coldly detached. Close to the natural realm, today's fly-fishers participate in the animal world, ennobling their activity by retaining the option to kill but, more often, choosing not to. To subdue is enough: contact is conquest.

We have pushed back the frontiers. How would Dame Juliana or Walton or Cotton feel, seeing the sport as we know it today? I think they would revel in it as we do. For they were not voyeurs either, observing only in idle distraction. They sought to understand, to become a part of it all. The "contemplative man's recreation," as Walton dubbed it, requires study, learning, mastery of skills, and flawless execution, then as now. Only participation can produce appreciation. We have carried our activity to its logical conclusion, preserved the traditions, and explored its essence; we have not only pushed, but expanded its frontiers until it encompasses every stream, river, lake, and ocean of the world.

Whether on freshwater (left) or saltwater (above), successful fly-fishing depends on making so many right decisions: which fish, what fly, a good knot, the appropriate rod and line, the right cast… the list is almost endless.

Ed Jaworowski

THE FLY-FISHERS' FISH

The first written account of fly-fishing comes from the 2nd century AD. In *de Animalium Natura*, the Roman author and traveler Claudius Aelianus described how people fishing on the River Astraeus in Macedonia normally used bait to catch fish, but that bait did not work when the fish were eating natural flies floating on the surface. The anglers tried impaling these flies on their hooks, but found that the flies shrivelled up and the fish ignored them.

"Instead," wrote Aelianus, "they fasten red wool round a hook and tie to the wool two wax-colored feathers that grow under a cock's wattles. Then they throw their fly on to the water, and the fish becomes very excited, and comes straight at it, anticipating a succulent mouthful." And what fish? Aelianus calls them "fish with speckled skins." We call them brown trout.

Brown trout and grayling dominated fly-fishing for the next 1700 years. In 1496 Wynkyn de Worde published the first printed book on fishing, *The Treatise on Fishing with an Angle*. "Salmon," de Worde told his readers, "will be rarely taken on fly, as you might take trout and grayling." In 1624 Juan de Bergara published *El Manusrito de Astorga*, describing fly-fishing in northern Spain. The work starts: "God and Our Lady willing. This is a book on how to tie and dress feathers in order to fish for trout."

In his first edition of *The Compleat Angler*, published in 1653, Izaak Walton plagiarized de Worde's *Treatise*, but Charles Cotton added a supplement to the second edition in 1776, *Being instructions How to angle for a trout or grayling in a clear stream*. Again, anglers fly-fished for trout and grayling. Species such as salmon and pike were not fly-fishers' fish because they were too big to be landed on the primitive tackle used. A fixed line about as long as the rod was tied to the rod-tip and, if a big fish zoomed off, the line or rod would usually break. But by 1682 salmon had been added to the list of fly-fishers' fish. In his book, *The Experienced Angler*, Colonel Robert Venables told the world that "The salmon takes the artificial fly very well, but you must use a troll [a reel], or he, being a strong fish, will hazard your line." When rod, reel, and line improved, pike were also added to the list of fly-fishers' fish.

In the 19th century, emigrants from Europe took fly-fishing to North America: brook and lake trout, rainbow trout, steelhead, and five species of Pacific salmon joined the list, along with muskellunge, pickerel, largemouth and smallmouth bass, and shad. And by the end of the 19th century saltwater species were joining freshwater fish as suitable quarry for the fly-fisher. Theodore Gordon, considered by many to be the father of dry-fly-fishing in North America, was catching striped bass on fly in 1912.

Throughout the 20th century salmonids have retained their preeminence for freshwater fly-fishers. However, with the availability of inexpensive travel a wealth of saltwater fish has also opened up for the fly-fisher. This section deals with the most popular, and often most spectacular, of the fly-fishers' fish, described by fly-fishers who know their quarry well.

FRESHWATER FISH

MALCOLM GREENHALGH

To the non-fly-fisher a river is a river and a lake is a lake. For fish and, therefore, for fly-fishers, there is a great variety of rivers and lakes. There are big rivers and lakes; and tiny ones. Their size, temperature, and other unique characteristics determine what fish live in each, and where you are likely to find them.

Rivers
Most major river systems start as tiny trickles in mountains and grow as they flow down to the sea. Their character changes and, as their character changes, so do the fish species. Throughout the world, big rivers can be divided into zones.

Trout zone   This is the uppermost reach of a river, where the water is cool (rarely above 10°C [50°F] in summer) and very turbulent, with an extremely high concentration of oxygen. At this point the river has a steep gradient and unstable boulder bed (the term "free-stone river" is often used for this higher reach) and virtually no aquatic vegetation. The fish community is dominated by trout and juvenile salmon.

Grayling zone   Downstream the gradient lessens and the river meanders in a less turbulent manner over a bed of shingle. Oxygen levels remain very high and in summer water temperatures rarely exceed 15°C (59°F). In the deeper pools a bed of coarse sand may support weeds, including water-buttercups. Trout are still abundant, but in large parts of Europe, northern Asia, and northeast America grayling become a co-dominant species.

Pike, barbel, and bream zones   Farther downstream the river leaves the mountains and begins to flow through a broader lowland valley that is often intensively farmed. Fertilizers and treated sewage are washed into the river, so the water is much richer and it supports more aquatic plants. Because of the less turbulent flow, aquatic plants can root easily in the silt and mud of the riverbed. Oxygen levels tend to be lower, although rarely lethal to fish. Temperatures may exceed 20°C (68°F) in summer – a temperature bordering on the lethal for salmon, trout, and grayling. In Europe these lower reaches have been named after the

two most common fish occurring there: bream and barbel. However, neither of these are fly-fishers' fish. For fly-fishers throughout Europe, northern Asia, and North America the lower reaches are better called the "pike zone", for it is here that river pike are at their most abundant and, in North America, largemouth and smallmouth bass and "panfish" occur.

Salmon may migrate through these lower reaches to spawning grounds in the trout and grayling zones. Shad may also run from the sea to spawn in these lower river reaches.

Estuary zone   Below the bream zone the river eventually reaches its destination and empties into the sea in the estuary zone.

Smaller, shorter rivers   The short free-stone streams that flow from mountains straight into the sea – such as many North American rivers flowing west from the Rockies, the rivers of Greenland and Iceland, those in the west and north of the British Isles, and in Scandinavia – are usually "trout zone" in nature. The fish populations are dominated by species of trout and salmon, and sometimes char, grayling, and whitefish.

The short rivers known as chalkstreams that flow from springs situated at the foot of chalk hills are in a class of their own. Always cool, with temperatures lower than 10°C (50°F) in summer and with a fairly constant flow, they are often excellent trout streams.

Lakes
From the fish's point of view the most important features of lakes are the amount of oxygen in the water, the temperature of the water, and productivity (how much aquatic plant life the lake water can support).

Productivity is the basis of the food chain that feeds invertebrate fish prey, and leads to forage-fish and the larger fish that fly-fishers try to catch. Productivity depends on the concentration of mineral nutrients that are dissolved in the water. Nutrients in the form of treated or untreated sewage and agricultural by-products such as artificial fertilizers and animal slurry increase the productivity of the lake.

Unproductive lakes   Unproductive, or oligotrophic, lakes are usually found in barren mountainous areas or in the Arctic tundra. In such places there are very few people and very little agriculture. Trout, char, or whitefish are the dominant fish, although salmon, sea trout, steelhead, or other migratory species may run through the lake to spawn in lake feeder-streams. Fish growth rates are usually very slow. In some oligotrophic Scottish lochs, for example, trout achieve an average length of only 12cm (5in) at three years, and in some lakes in Lapland and the Canadian North the average length of char is only 16cm (6in) at three years.

Productive lakes Productive, or eutrophic, lakes are usually found in lowland regions. The area around them is often intensively farmed, and the lakes are usually located close to towns and cities. Because oxygen levels fall too low for salmonids to survive in hot weather conditions, species such as trout and char tend to be scarce or absent in eutrophic lakes. Instead, in European eutrophic lakes, cyprinids (members of the carp family) become the dominant species and, although they are of relatively little interest to fly-fishers, they encourage populations of fast-growing pike. In eutrophic lakes pike often reach weights in excess of 10kg (22lb).

In North American eutrophic lakes a variety of "panfish" species, such as bluegills, which will take the fly keenly, become most abundant. These lakes are also the main habitat for smallmouth and largemouth bass, and for pike and muskellunge.

There is a middle range of productivity between oligotrophic and eutrophic lakes – the mesotrophic lakes. For freshwater fly-fishers these lakes are perhaps the most important, because they have high levels of oxygen in the water and sufficient food sources to produce fast-growing trout and char. The lakes of the Minipi system in eastern Canada, which produce phenomenally huge brook trout, and the great loughs of Ireland,

A beautiful stretch of river with loose boulders, little weed, an erratic turbulent flow, and superb fly-fishing for trout. When it reaches the lowlands, this river will be completely different in character... and fish stocks.

which have fast-growing brown trout, are all mesotrophic. Other mesotrophic lakes include those in Tasmania, New Zealand's Lake Taupo, where naturalized brown and rainbow trout reach immense sizes, and those Irish loughs that produce big brown trout.

PACIFIC SALMON

JIM TEENY

The salmon and steelhead that run the rivers draining into the North Pacific basin include some of the most spectacular of fly-fishers' fish. They are among the largest of the freshwater fly-rod quarry species – beautiful fish, fish that often run in schools numbering in the thousands. If they are to fall for the fly-fishers' art, a high level of planning, water craft, and skill are required. What is more, to catch them you will travel to some of the world's most beautiful and magnificent rivers.

SOCKEYE

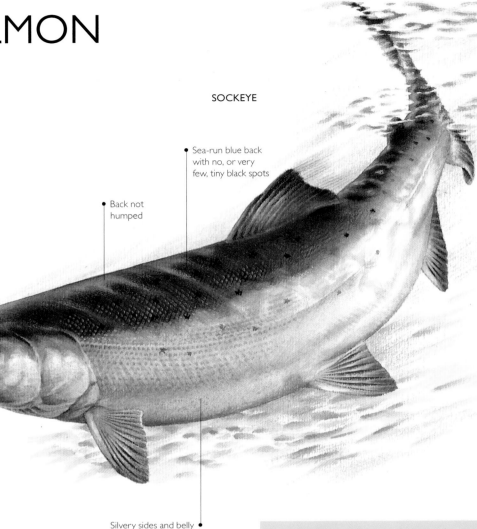

Sea-run blue back with no, or very few, tiny black spots

Back not humped

Silvery sides and belly

SOCKEYE OR RED SALMON

Oncorhynchus nerka

The blue-green back and silvery sides of the ocean-feeding sockeye fade rapidly as the fish leaves the sea on its spawning run. In males the sides become a bright brick red, the head a dull green. Females tend to be duller, often with olive-green sides. In males the jaws elongate, becoming hooked and full of sharp teeth. In all stages of its development the sockeye generally lacks black spots, although there may be a very few spots visible on the dorsal fin or top of the back.

Juvenile sockeye spend between one and three years in freshwater before heading to the ocean, and they may spend up to two years feeding at sea. The size of mature sockeye remains relatively constant at 2–3.5kg (4–8lb). Any fish over 4.5kg (10lb) should be considered a trophy fish. Exceptional specimens weighing up to 6.8kg (15lb) have been reported.

Depending on the area, sockeye run from June through to October. Although they are quite small fish, pound for pound they are possibly the strongest and most spectacular of all the Pacific salmon.

In the lower tidal reaches of rivers salmon will come to the surface to chase and take a fly. Further upstream, in pure freshwater, the best time to get the fish to take the fly is soon after they have arrived, because the longer they are in freshwater the more difficult it is to tempt them to feed.

An important feature of the natural history of sockeye salmon, as in all Pacific salmon, is the timing of the runs. These vary from river to river, so when planning a fishing trip, make sure it coincides with the run in that river.

Distribution In North America the sockeye is found from the Columbia River north through Alaska, and in northeastern Asia from northern Japan north to Arctic Russia. Unlike other Pacific salmon, the sockeye favors rivers with large shallow lakes on their courses, which serve as nurseries for the juveniles.

FOOD, FLIES, AND FISHING

In the sea Pacific salmon grow quickly on a diet of planktonic crustaceans, lesser fish, shrimp, prawns, and squid. In some inshore waters of British Columbia and Alaska, fly-fishers usually fish for feeding salmon with bait such as dead herring. Flies are not generally used because the salmon are feeding too deep. However, flies are used when Pacific salmon return to rivers to spawn. When they return they have stopped feeding, so it is impossible to catch them on an imitation of their food. Fortunately, they will take a fly. The reason for this is unclear, but it is likely to be a combination of curiosity, aggression, and perhaps memory – the memory of food devoured far out at sea.

You can use an enormous variety of hair-winged and feather-winged wet flies, streamers, and floating flies such as Bombers to goad the salmon into striking. Brightly colored wet flies are most popular, especially those with flashy materials, such as Flashabou, in the dressing.

SPAWNING COLORATION OF SOCKEYE

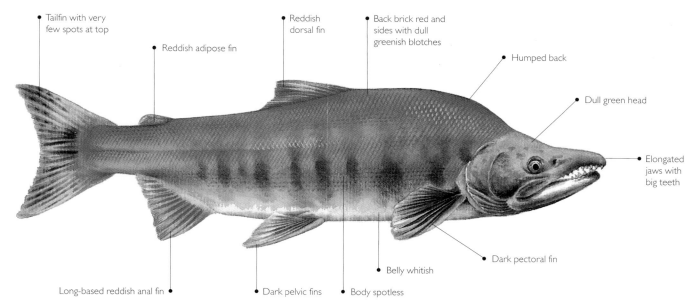

- Tailfin with very few spots at top
- Reddish adipose fin
- Reddish dorsal fin
- Back brick red and sides with dull greenish blotches
- Humped back
- Dull green head
- Elongated jaws with big teeth
- Long-based reddish anal fin
- Dark pelvic fins
- Body spotless
- Belly whitish
- Dark pectoral fin

The change from the short-snouted, humpless, silver sea sockeye to the colorful spawning sockeye takes only a few weeks as the fish return to the river. The changes in coloration and body structure of Pacific salmon on their return to freshwater are related to reproductive success.

The scarlet and green colors of spawning sockeye help to prevent them from interbreeding with other salmon species, because sockeye will not spawn with salmon of other colors that may be living in the same river, and vice versa.

 Catching Salmon in Freshwater 146–7

 Salmon Flies 108–9

 Atlantic Salmon 24–5 • Bristol Bay, Alaska 178–9 • British Columbia 180–181

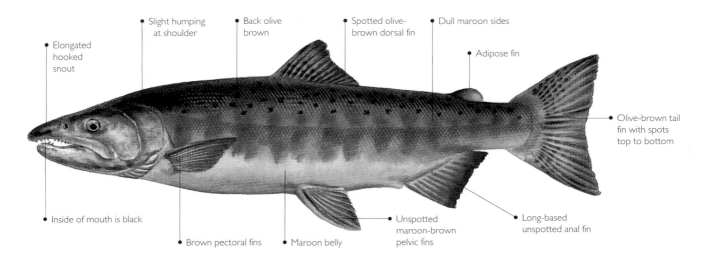

Elongated hooked snout

Slight humping at shoulder

Back olive brown

Spotted olive-brown dorsal fin

Dull maroon sides

Adipose fin

Olive-brown tail fin with spots top to bottom

Inside of mouth is black

Brown pectoral fins

Maroon belly

Unspotted maroon-brown pelvic fins

Long-based unspotted anal fin

CHINOOK OR KING SALMON
Oncorhynchus tshawytscha

All members of the salmon family can be identified by the presence of an adipose fin: a small, fleshy fin on the back between the dorsal and tailfins. All Pacific salmon can be separated from Atlantic salmon by their much longer-based anal fins and the size of the mouth. In Atlantic salmon the mouth extends to a point no farther back than the center of the eye, whereas in Pacific salmon the jaw extends to a point behind the rear of the eye.

On its re-entry into freshwater the chinook has its sea colors of blue-gray back and silvery sides. This fades quickly, and the fish becomes browner overall, with an olive-brown back and dull maroon sides. The inside of the mouth becomes black. At the same time, the upper and lower jaws of the male elongate and become slightly curved at the tip.

At all stages of the chinook's life the black spotting on its body is characteristic: there are many spots scattered over the back, and over the dorsal, adipose, and tailfins.

The chinook is a very sought-after trophy fish, offering a great challenge on any tackle and an exceptional challenge on a fly-rod. It is the largest of all the Pacific salmon, although the size attained by an individual fish depends largely on the length of time it was feeding in the ocean.

Most juvenile chinook go to sea after 12–18 months in freshwater and return after one to seven years at sea. So while the average fish returning to freshwater may weigh about 10kg (22lb) – having spent two years at sea – some Alaskan fish that have been out in the ocean for four to five years will average around 25kg (55lb). The largest recorded (probably a seven-year-old ocean fish) weighed 57kg (126lb). There are two distinct runs, one in spring and one in the fall.

Distribution Chinook run rivers throughout the west coast of North America, from California to Point Hope, Alaska, and the north Pacific coast of Russia. They have been successfully introduced to the Great Lakes and waters in South America.

CHERRY OR YAMAME SALMON
Oncorhynchus masu

There are both sea-run and freshwater resident populations of this small, locally distributed salmon. In the sea it is a silvery fish with a dark blue back, silver sides, and white belly; in freshwater it has an olive-brown back lightening to gray sides and a whitish belly. Freshwater cherry salmon retain about nine oval gray parr markings along each side of the body throughout their life. There are also dark brown spots along the sides.

The cherry is the smallest salmon. The parr of sea-run cherry salmon go to the ocean at the age of one year and return about three years later at lengths of 50–60cm (20–23in) and weights of 2–3kg (4–6lb). Freshwater cherry salmon mature at 25–30cm (9–12in), and weigh up to 1kg (2.2lb).

Peak runs from the sea occur between the months of July and September.

Distribution Cherry salmon are confined to northern Japan and to Russian rivers draining into the Sea of Okhotsk.

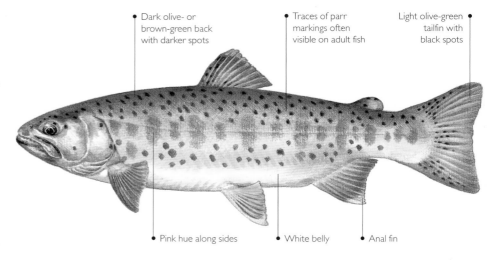

Dark olive- or brown-green back with darker spots

Traces of parr markings often visible on adult fish

Light olive-green tailfin with black spots

Pink hue along sides

White belly

Anal fin

Dark blue back

Dark blue-black dorsal fin

Purple-blue sheen; no black spots

Blue-black adipose fin

In all Pacific salmon the jaw extends behind the eye (not in Atlantic salmon)

Dark tailfin

Dark pectoral fins

Silvery sides

Silver belly

Dark pelvic fins

Dark, long-based anal fin

CHUM OR DOG SALMON

Oncorhynchus keta

In the ocean, chum salmon are silvery fish with a purple-blue sheen that darkens on the back. However, on their return to the river this quickly fades and is replaced by a darker olive-green. A maroon band runs along the body just above the belly, from which irregular maroon bars or bands extend up the sides. These bars are often blue-gray to the rear of the anal fin. The sexes are similar in color, but in the male the shoulders become slightly humped and the ends of the upper and lower jaws more hooked. The complete lack of spotting on body and fins is a sure way of separating the chum from all other Pacific salmon.

Young chum salmon go to sea soon after hatching and return to the rivers after three to five years of feeding in the ocean. The longer they stay at sea the bigger they grow. Most are in the 4–7kg (9–15lb) range; the record is 15kg (33lb).

Chum run their spawning rivers from July onward, sometimes as late as December. Because they are very aggressive salmon that hit flies hard and, once hooked, display a tremendous amount of strength, they have recently become very popular with fly-fishers.

Distribution Chum salmon can be found throughout the Pacific river systems, from Oregon north through Washington State and from the province of British Columbia to Alaska, where

the largest fish are to be found. They also run the rivers of Kamchatka, in Russia.

This fly-caught coho shows clearly the larger mouth of Pacific salmon compared with Atlantic salmon. This is its spawning color.

KOKANEE

Oncorhynchus nerka

The kokanee is the land-locked form of sockeye salmon. Its color is similar to that of the sea-going form. When feeding in the lakes it is silvery, and could be confused with rainbow trout that may also be present in the lake. Kokanee have few if any spots, while rainbow trout have many. Kokanee have an anal fin with a long base; in rainbow trout the base of the anal fin is very short. At the beginning of the spawning season the kokanee's head becomes green and its body red. The average length is 25–30cm (10–12in), exceptionally up to 45cm (18in). Maximum weight is usually about 1.5kg (3lb 5oz).

Although Kokanee feed and grow in lakes, they spawn in lake feeder-streams.

Distribution Kokanee are found naturally in lakes in Idaho, Oregon, Washington, Alaska, and British Columbia, and have been stocked in lakes and reservoirs throughout California, Nevada, Colorado, Wyoming, and Utah.

Blue back with few (often no) black spots

Blue-gray dorsal fin

Silvery sides

Blue-gray tailfin

Mouth angled upwards

Gray pectoral fin

White belly

Light gray pelvic fin

Long-based anal fin

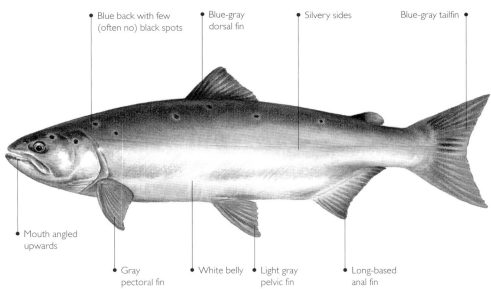

PINK OR HUMPY SALMON

Oncorhynchus gorbusca

At sea the pink salmon has a blue-gray back and silver-gray sides, but as it returns to the rivers to spawn its color darkens to a dull brown or olive-brown, often with red-purple markings, especially on the tail. Most noticeable is the change of body shape, which, while occurring to some extent in all cock Pacific salmon, is seen at its most grotesque in pink salmon. The body becomes steeply humped just behind the head. The jaws elongate, become strongly curved at the tips, and filled with long, sharp teeth. Females tend to be duller, and have less of a humped body.

At all stages there are a few large spots on the back and dorsal fin, and oval black blotches over the entire tailfin. The color of the flesh is very pale pink (red in other salmon), which has earned this salmon its common name "pink."

The fry of pink salmon go to sea soon after hatching and, as adults, return to spawn when two years old. They are the smallest of the North American salmon, and are mainly in the 1–2kg (2–4lb) range, with occasional specimens

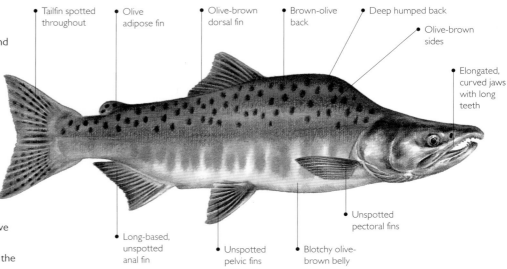

- Tailfin spotted throughout
- Olive adipose fin
- Olive-brown dorsal fin
- Brown-olive back
- Deep humped back
- Olive-brown sides
- Elongated, curved jaws with long teeth
- Long-based, unspotted anal fin
- Unspotted pelvic fins
- Blotchy olive-brown belly
- Unspotted pectoral fins

weighing up to 4kg (9lb). Despite their small size, pink salmon take the fly well, fight hard, and provide a lot of action for the fly-fisher.

Runs start in July and last until October, the precise times depending on the area. The largest runs occur in even-numbered years.

Distribution The pink salmon is found in rivers that drain into the Pacific from Oregon (there are very few), and from the state of Washington northward to Alaska. They also occur east of Alaska through the Aleutian Islands, and south through Russia to Korea.

COHO OR SILVER SALMON

Oncorhynchus kisutch

At sea the coho salmon has a blue back, which lightens on the sides to bright silver. Within a few days of its return to the river it starts to gain its spawning dress: brown on the back and bright maroon-red along the sides, lightening on the belly. The inside of the mouth becomes gray. Females tend to be lighter overall. At the same time the jaws elongate and become hooked at the tip. The amount of spotting is characteristic at all stages of the species' development: there are tiny black spots on the back, on the base of the dorsal fin, and on the upper half of the tailfin.

Young coho spend one year in the river before going to sea for one to three years. The longer they remain at sea, the larger they are when they return. Most run in the range of 3–5kg (7–11lb), with fish that have spent three years at sea weighing up to 9kg (14lb). The record fish weighed in at 14kg (31lb).

Coho usually run the rivers from late summer throughout the fall. They are a highly sought-after gamefish, renowned for the aggressive way they take the fly and, once they are hooked, for their leaping acrobatics.

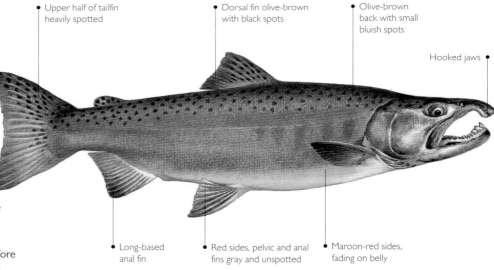

- Upper half of tailfin heavily spotted
- Dorsal fin olive-brown with black spots
- Olive-brown back with small bluish spots
- Hooked jaws
- Long-based anal fin
- Red sides, pelvic and anal fins gray and unspotted
- Maroon-red sides, fading on belly

Distribution The coho occurs in rivers from Monterey Bay, California, north to Alaska and across the Bering Straits, and from Russia south to northern Japan. It has also been introduced into the Great Lakes.

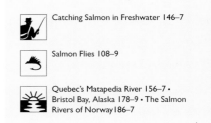

Catching Salmon in Freshwater 146–7

Salmon Flies 108–9

Quebec's Matapedia River 156–7 • Bristol Bay, Alaska 178–9 • The Salmon Rivers of Norway 186–7

STEELHEAD

JIM TEENY

The steelhead is a migratory rainbow trout, but it is so like the Pacific salmon, rather than a resident freshwater trout, that it is logical to treat the two populations separately. This approach will be applauded by all those who have fished for steelhead, because steelhead are perhaps the most powerful of all fly-fishers' salmonids.

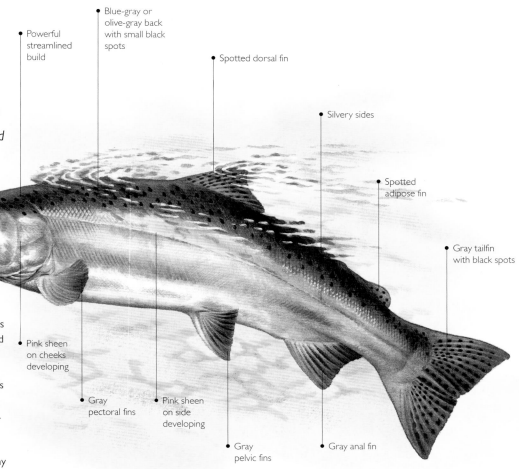

- Powerful streamlined build
- Blue-gray or olive-gray back with small black spots
- Spotted dorsal fin
- Silvery sides
- Spotted adipose fin
- Gray tailfin with black spots
- Pink sheen on cheeks developing
- Gray pectoral fins
- Pink sheen on side developing
- Gray pelvic fins
- Gray anal fin

STEELHEAD

Oncorhynchus mykiss

As the steelhead enters the river from its time spent feeding in the Pacific, often over 1000km (620 miles) from where it hatched from an egg, it is a veritable "bar of silver" with a blue-gray back and shimmering silver sides. Slowly, as the spawning time approaches, a pink sheen appears on the gill cover and along the sides, revealing the steelhead's shared family relationship with the colorful rainbow. In males the sheen becomes rose purple. Males also develop hooked jaws.

A steelhead fresh-run from the sea can be distinguished from all fresh-run salmon by the many tiny spots over the back, sides, and dorsal and tailfins, and by the short-based anal fin (long-based in all Pacific salmon).

Juvenile steelhead spend up to three years in the river before going to feed in the ocean. They may then return after 18–24 months of sea-life weighing up to 4kg (9lb); after 30–36 months of sea-life weighing up to about 10kg (22lb); after 42–48 months of sea-life weighing up to about 13kg (29lb); and after 60 months (exceptional) of sea-life weighing up to 19.5kg (43lb).

A run of steelhead occurs in at least one river on every day of the year.

 Catching Salmon in Freshwater 146–7

 Salmon Flies 108–9

 Steelhead in British Columbia 180–1

FOOD, FLIES, AND FISHING

At sea steelhead are mainly fish-eaters, but on their return to freshwater they cease feeding, so their aggression must be exploited if they are to take the fly. Fresh-run fish are normally the most aggressive, and it is important for success that there are fish in the pools fresh from the sea. They will strike at a large variety of flies, the most effective size and color seeming to vary from one river to the next. You should carry wet flies or streamers in sizes 2–10 and in black, purple, orange, pink, and bright green. Most steelhead are caught by casting the fly down and across the stream and then letting it swing across the current. In the summer and fall months it is also worth tying dry flies, such as Bombers, especially when the rivers are low and the fish are becoming reluctant to take the wet fly.

Distribution Steelhead occur naturally in rivers of the west coast of North America – from California to Alaska – and in Russia's Commander Islands and the Kamchatka Peninsula. They have been introduced to places as far distant as Tierra del Fuego, New Zealand, northern Europe, and North America's Great Lakes.

ATLANTIC SALMON

DICK SHELTON

Atlantic salmon have been the object of valuable fisheries at least since the 12th century, and the use of salmon as symbols by the Picts is evidence that the special status of this "king of fish" has been recognized since the Dark Ages. At that time, fly-fishing for salmon (first recorded in the 17th century) was largely for the pot. Today, a sporting salmon fisher is often just as inclined to release the catch in order to contribute to future generations as to kill it for the table.

"Horns" at corner of tailfin

Gray adipose fin

Gray dorsal fins

Gray tailfin

Dark blue-gray back

Gray anal fin

Gray pelvic fins

Mouth toothless or almost so

Sides silvery with blue and pink sheen and black spots

Belly silvery-white

Gray pectoral fins

ATLANTIC SALMON
Salmo salar

The appearance of sea-run salmon varies greatly, depending on how recently they entered freshwater. Immediately after river-entry, they have the bright silver livery of a pelagic marine predator, with a blue-green back, silver sides, and white underside. Small round and cross-shaped black spots are present above the lateral line.

With longer river residence the silvery sheen is lost. Hens become darker and cocks develop red and orange mottling and a pronounced hook (kype) to the mouth. The growth of the kype is part of a general increase in connective tissue, which includes enlargement of the adipose and dorsal fins and a marked thickening of the skin.

After spawning, Atlantic salmon are known as "kelts." Most kelts die, but a few, mostly hen fish, "mend," regaining their silvery sheen and returning to sea. These kelts may be distinguished from fresh-run fish by their emaciation, and by the protrusion and looseness of their vents.

Strictly speaking, the term "salmon" refers only to multi-sea-winter (MSW) fish: those that

have spent more than one winter feeding in the ocean. One-sea-winter fish (1SW) are known as "grilse." In practice, fly-fishers tend to report any fish over 3.6 kg (8lb) as a salmon irrespective of the number of sea winters recorded on its scales.

Very large fish may still be caught in the rivers of northern Norway – the world record is 36kg (79.38lb) from the Tana River – and in the Kola

ATLANTIC SALMON
MALE IN SPAWNING LIVERY

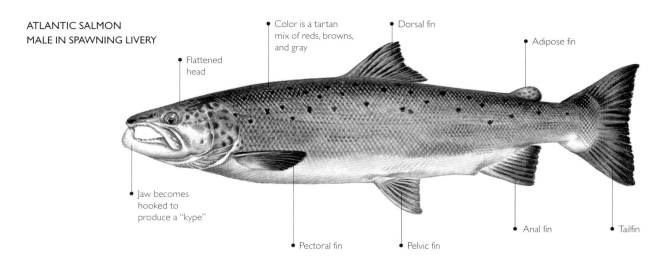

Color is a tartan mix of reds, browns, and gray

Dorsal fin

Adipose fin

Flattened head

Jaw becomes hooked to produce a "kype"

Pectoral fin

Pelvic fin

Anal fin

Tailfin

SEBAGO SALMON

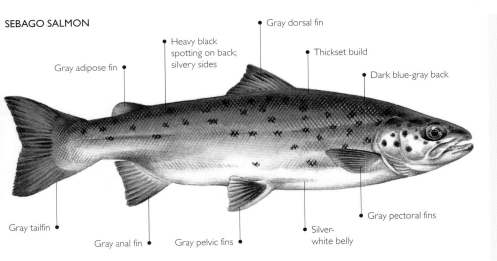

Gray adipose fin

Heavy black spotting on back; silvery sides

Gray dorsal fin

Thickset build

Dark blue-gray back

Gray tailfin

Gray anal fin

Gray pelvic fins

Silver-white belly

Gray pectoral fins

SEBAGO PARR

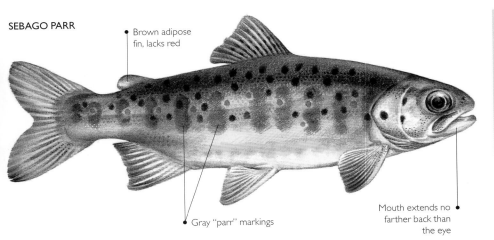

Brown adipose fin, lacks red

Gray "parr" markings

Mouth extends no farther back than the eye

In brown trout parr, the adipose fin is often red, and the mouth extends back beyond the eye. If you catch a parr, do not handle it, but shake it gently from the hook

THE TIMING OF SALMON RUNS

In river systems subject to severe icing, salmon tend to enter rivers in late summer and fall. Salmon runs of short-spate rivers farther south also tend to occur in the same period because of the absence of good holding pools capable of retaining fish safely during hot, low-water conditions. In larger rivers in the middle of the fish's range, river entry may take place at any time. Generally speaking, the earlier-running fish tend to head for cooler, often upper catchment, spawning sites, and later-running fish for the lower ones. Within each spawning population, older sea-age fish tend to run before younger ones.

FOOD, FLIES, AND FISHING

At sea, salmon feed on planktonic crustaceans and on a wide variety of small fish. When close to the coast, returning adults are known also to take terrestrial insects blown offshore. The return migration of adult salmon is set in train by hormonal changes associated with the earliest stages of sexual maturation. As maturation progresses, rising sex hormone levels suppress the fish's appetite. By the time they are in freshwater, swallowing and retaining food in the gut have effectively ceased, and this is the basis of the general rule that adult salmon do not usually feed during their riverine spawning migration.

Fortunately for fly-fishers, there is much more to feeding behavior than swallowing and retaining food in the gut. These are only the final stages in a series of relatively instinctive responses to the range of visual, mechanical, and olfactory stimuli associated with a potential prey. When salmon are fresh from the sea, much of normal feeding behavior remains, and the fly-fisher's ability to catch them is correspondingly high. Radio-tracking studies have shown that catchability declines as the season progresses, even for fresh-run fish, although the response to potential prey remains. Catchability also increases sharply after salmon have been "woken up" and stimulated to move upstream by a flood.

Peninsula, localities at the northern edge of the geographic range of Atlantic salmon. However, very large "portmanteau" salmon are currently rare at temperate latitudes. The British fly-caught record is Miss Clementina Morison's massive cock fish of 27.7kg (61lb) from the Lower Shaws beat of the Deveron. This fish was caught on a Brown Wing Killer in October 1924, some two years after Miss Georgina Ballantyne trolled a 29kg (64lb) cock fish from Glendelvine on the Tay. Although more than 50 per cent of multi-sea-winter fish are hens, the very largest salmon, and in big rivers more than half the grilse, are cocks.

Land-locked salmon, or "sebago", are silver but spottier and more thickset than those that go to sea, and tend not to weigh above 1.8 kg (4lb) Sebago are also known as *ouananiche* (Lake St John) and *blanklax* (Lake Vänern, Sweden).

Atlantic salmon are sometimes confused with large sea trout. Generally speaking salmon are readily distinguished by the pronounced wrists by which they may be tailed, their more forked tails, their more streamlined appearance, and their larger scales (10–13 from adipose fin to lateral line in salmon, 13–16 in sea trout).

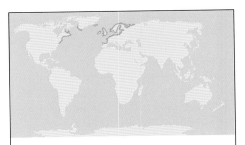

Distribution The modern spawning distribution of the Atlantic salmon extends from the rivers of Maine and northern Spain in the south to southern Greenland and Northern Russia in the north. Its ocean distribution extends from the North American and European coasts to the highly productive subpolar waters of Labrador, Greenland, and the Norwegian Sea.

 Reading Rivers 112–13 • Reading Lakes 114–15

 Salmon Flies 108–9

 Quebec's Matapedia River 156–7 • The Salmon Rivers of Norway 186–7 • Iceland 196–7

TROUT

ANDY WALKER

Of all fish, trout are the ones most closely associated with fly-fishing. Without trout the sport of fly-fishing might never have been brought into existence, for fly-fishing evolved as a way of catching trout using imitations of the natural flies on which they feed. Today, catching a trout on a delicate dry fly is one of the fly-fishers' greatest challenges, and the sight and sound of a big trout swirling at the surface to suck down a dry fly is one of the biggest thrills of fly-fishing.

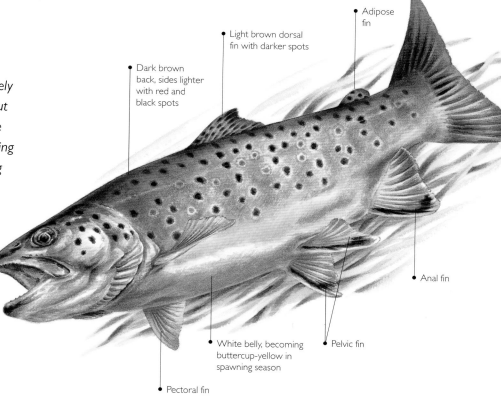

Adipose fin

Light brown dorsal fin with darker spots

Dark brown back, sides lighter with red and black spots

Anal fin

White belly, becoming buttercup-yellow in spawning season

Pelvic fin

Pectoral fin

BROWN TROUT

Salmo trutta

The body of the brown trout is slender and streamlined, usually four-and-a-half to five times as long as it is deep. The dorsal fin has 8–10 rays and the unrayed adipose fin is usually tinged with red. There are 116–135 scales along the lateral line. The brown trout's body color varies remarkably from one area to another, so that even among those that live entirely in freshwater, some are highly silvered with black spots, while others are much darker and may have prominent red, yellow, and brown spots. Some trout are dark green on the back, merging to golden yellow on the underside; others are basically dark brown. The tailfin is a uniform dark color that verges on black, although in some individuals there may be a very few spots close to the upper or the lower margin.

In some lakes the different trout strains can be identified by their color. For example, the gillaroo found in many Irish loughs is a heavily spotted, bright red fish. By contrast the sonaghan of Lough Melvin is a small gray trout with black fins.

Some brown trout run to sea, returning to the rivers in summer prior to spawning in the fall. These sea-run (anadromous) brown trout, or sea trout, are characteristically highly silvered when they are fresh from the sea, but gradually darken with time in freshwater. They therefore become progressively more difficult to distinguish from those brown trout that have remained in freshwater, although they can sometimes be told apart by their generally larger size.

Sea trout adopt a similar life-cycle to Atlantic salmon, but are coastal rather than oceanic and may revisit freshwater several times, even overwintering there, without spawning. Wholly freshwater forms may also be migratory to some extent, descending from spawning streams into lakes or rivers as fry or parr, and then returning to spawn when they become sexually mature. However, some individuals spend their entire lives in short sections of hill streams, confined to areas between waterfalls. Brown trout therefore appear to be more adapted to life in freshwater and less adapted to life at sea than are Atlantic salmon.

The size to which brown trout grow depends on the amount of available food. In tiny streams or impoverished mountain lakes they may mature when only 10cm (4in) long or 10g (½oz) in weight. Fish-eating brown trout, such as the dollaghan of Lough Neagh and the deep-swimming, char-eating trout of the glacial lakes of Scandinavia and Scotland, are often 80cm (31½in) long and weigh 6kg (13lb). The "average" fly-fisher's trout from the productive Irish lakes or the European chalkstreams would be in the 1–1.8kg (2–4lb) class. However, in areas where brown trout are not native but have been introduced, such as North America, brown trout weighing more than 5kg (11lb) are commonly caught on fly. The world record fly-caught brown trout weighed 16.3kg (35lb 15oz). It was caught in a lake in Patagonia in 1952.

Distribution Brown trout are native to Europe, northwest Asia, and North Africa, where the mean air temperature does not exceed 27°C (80°F) in July, or drop below -17°C (0°F) in January. Since the mid 19th century, these trout have been introduced to all continents except Antarctica. Although closely related to Atlantic salmon, brown trout are better adapted to life in freshwater. Native stocks of sea trout are found in the north from Iceland to the White Sea and as far south as the Bay of Biscay.

 Reading Rivers 112–13 · Reading Lakes 114–15

 Food and Flies 82–99 · Freshwater Baitfish 104–5

 Scotland's Wild Trout Lochs 190–1 · Trout Fishing New Zealand 184–5 · Great Trout Loughs of Ireland 194–5

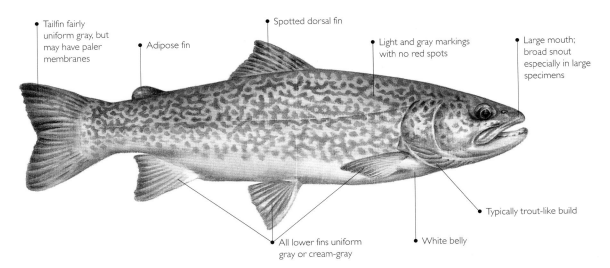

Tailfin fairly uniform gray, but may have paler membranes

Adipose fin

Spotted dorsal fin

Light and gray markings with no red spots

Large mouth; broad snout especially in large specimens

All lower fins uniform gray or cream-gray

White belly

Typically trout-like build

MARBLED TROUT

Salmo (trutta) marmorata

Although considered by some to be a distinct subspecies of brown trout, there is increasing evidence to suggest that the marbled trout, or "marmorata" as it is called in its home range, is a species in its own right. It can be identified by its much broader, almost pike-like snout, and by its general coloration: a distinctive blue-gray, with wavy vermiculation or marbling. Marbled trout grow large on their preferred diet of fish. At three years of age they may weigh 1.8kg (4lb); at five years 5kg (11lb). There are several records of marbled trout weighing in excess of 10kg (22lb).

Distribution Marbled trout were once found in most rivers draining into the Adriatic Sea, but the effects of pollution and the consequences of introducing non-native brown and rainbow trout into these rivers almost resulted in the extinction of this remarkable fish. Today it survives only in Slovenia's Soca River. Here there is an intensive hatchery program and the fly-fishing is very carefully regulated, the result of which is that the marbled trout is thriving once again.

CUTTHROAT TROUT

Oncorhynchus clarki

A close relation of, and superficially similar to the rainbow trout, the cutthroat trout has a speckled tail, 150–180 scales along the lateral line, and 8–11 rays in the dorsal fin. The main feature that distinguishes it from all other trout is the red slashes on either side of the throat, from which it gets its common name.

Despite its relatively narrow distribution, in the last five million years several very distinct subspecies of cutthroat trout have evolved. Taxonomists currently name 14, and at least three others are under review. Four of the major subspecies are described below.

The coastal cutthroat (*O. c. clarki*) is a rather dull, heavily spotted trout. Some coastal cutthroats migrate to sea outside the breeding season. The sea-run individuals have a silvery body, the residents a coppery hue.

The west slope cutthroat (*O. c. lewisi*) is a brighter fish, with a general yellow or orange color. There is a mass of black spots on the tail and on the back.

The Yellowstone cutthroat (*O. c. bouvieri*) is a yellow-olive fish that, close to the breeding season, become quite red. Large black spots are scattered across the body, and are highly concentrated on the tail.

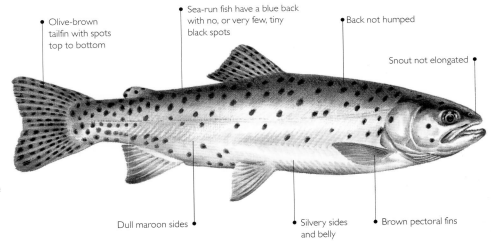

Olive-brown tailfin with spots top to bottom

Sea-run fish have a blue back with no, or very few, tiny black spots

Back not humped

Snout not elongated

Dull maroon sides

Silvery sides and belly

Brown pectoral fins

The Lahontan cutthroat (*O. c. henshawi*) is a yellow-brown trout with black spots scattered fairly evenly over the body.

Most cutthroat trout are small fish, weighing 1–1.8kg (2–4lb), depending on the subspecies and on the water in which they reached maturity. Lakes Tahoe and Pyramid (in the states of California and Nevada respectively) produced huge record cutthroats to 14.3kg (31½lb) and 18.6kg (41lb) respectively. Unfortunately the cutthroat is now extirpated from these locations.

Distribution The coastal cutthroat occurs in coastal streams from Alaska as far south as northern California. The west slope cutthroats are found in lakes and rivers in parts of Idaho, Montana, southeastern British Columbia, and southwestern Saskatchewan. The Yellowstone cutthroat is centered on Yellowstone, with other closely related subspecies found through much of the Rocky Mountain interior. The Lahontan cutthroat and four other closely related subspecies occur on the southeast side of the Rockies.

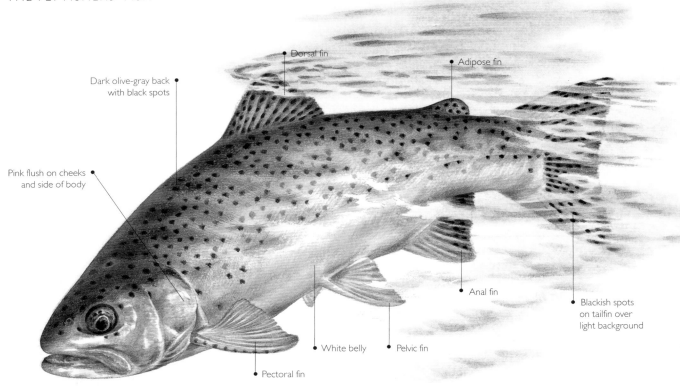

Dark olive-gray back with black spots

Dorsal fin

Adipose fin

Pink flush on cheeks and side of body

Anal fin

Blackish spots on tailfin over light background

White belly

Pelvic fin

Pectoral fin

RAINBOW TROUT

Oncorhynchus mykiss

The rainbow trout can be distinguished immediately from the brown and marbled trout by its overall speckled tail. There are 140–160 scales along the lateral line and 10–13 rays in the dorsal fin. The background color of the body shows great variation. In most river populations it is yellow-brown or pale olive; in lake populations it is more silvery. Some rainbow trout are heavily spotted with black, others, especially lake forms, are relatively unspotted. The name "rainbow"

comes from the iridescent purplish sheen of the band that runs lengthwise along the side of the fish and also on the gill cover. This coloration is especially strong just prior to breeding.

Growth rate and size depend partly on the food supply available to the trout, and also on the strain of rainbow trout. Trout of the same strain stocked at the same size from the same hatchery have been known to lose weight in impoverished lakes, but to more than double their size in one year in productive lakes. Rainbows from rivers where the maximum size is 20–25cm (8–10in)

have quickly grown to 35–50cm (14–20in) when they have been introduced into a productive lake.

In British Columbia's Kootenay Lake there are two forms of rainbow trout. One feeds solely on invertebrates and grows to an average weight of 1.8kg (4lb), while a second strain feeds on land-locked sockeye salmon ("kokanee") and can attain weights in excess of 20kg (44lb).

Distribution Rainbow trout occur naturally only in the rivers and lakes draining westward from the Rocky Mountains, from Alaska south to Mexico. However, they have been introduced to temperate lakes and rivers throughout the world.

The steelhead is the sea-going migratory form of the rainbow trout, but because of its similarity in structure and behavior to the Pacific salmon it is described with that group and featured on p23.

A school of rainbow trout: note how the pink gill cover and sides stand out on each fish.

GOLDEN TROUT
Oncorhynchus aguabonita

Like the rainbow and the cutthroat trout, the golden trout has a speckled tailfin. It has 160–210 scales along the lateral line and 10–14 rays in the dorsal fin.

Golden trout are, as the name suggests, the most brightly colored of all trout. The back is usually yellow- or green-brown and the underparts are a bright golden yellow. Bands of rose-red run the full length of the trout's belly and along either side of its body.

These trout are usually not large, although in lakes with small populations some larger specimens may be found. Most river trout are a maximum length of 20cm (8in): few lake specimens exceed the 500g (18oz) mark. The record came from a trout that weighed 5kg (11lb), which was caught in a lake in Wyoming in 1948.

Distribution Golden trout are natives of the Kern River catchment in California. They have been introduced to other rivers that are located in the Sierra Nevada.

FOOD, FLIES, AND FISHING

Trout everywhere feed at the surface of lakes and rivers on flies that are washed or blown in from terrestrial sources, or that hatch from immature, aquatic stages. Under the surface they feed on various crustaceans such as scuds and crayfish, mollusks such as snails and small bivalves, and on the larvae, nymphs, and pupae of insects, such as midges, stoneflies, mayflies, and caddisflies. In lakes, many trout feed on tiny zoöplankton – crustaceans that are often only one or two millimeters in length. Larger trout are often active predators of other fish, including their own species, and are not averse to eating frogs or even voles. These fish can grow to specimen sizes, although they may then be less likely to be caught by the fly-fisher. Sea-run trout tend to be opportunistic feeders, taking whatever the saltwater can offer, such as shrimp, prawns, crabs, and smaller baitfish.

The most primitive form of trout fly-fishing involves the use of real flies. This is still practiced commonly in Ireland and in the west of Scotland where the big mayfly, *Ephemera danica,* is used during a hatch of real mayflies, and grasshoppers and crane flies (daddy-long-legs) during summer and fall when these may drop naturally onto the water. Two natural insects are used on the one hook, and it is said in the west of Ireland that the "fly" is more attractive to the trout if a yellow gorse flower is impaled on the hook between the two insects.

However, most trout are caught by fly-fishers fishing artificial flies that imitate what the trout are eating. A wide range of wet flies imitates the underwater food of trout, from the nymph, larva, and pupa stages of aquatic insects to large fish and crayfish prey. Dry flies that float on the surface are tied to match the features of insects such as mayflies and caddisflies that the trout may find on the surface. For sea-trout fishing in saltwater there are special marine shrimp and baitfish imitations.

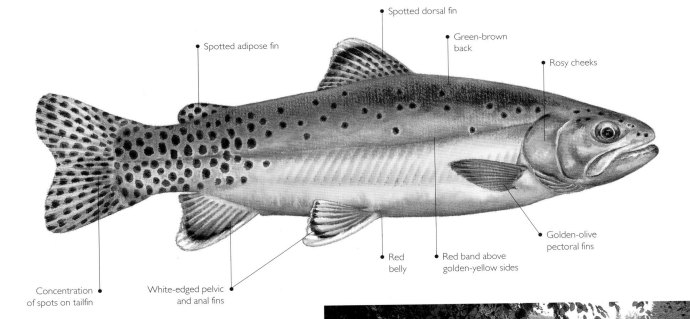

Spotted dorsal fin

Spotted adipose fin

Green-brown back

Rosy cheeks

Red belly

Red band above golden-yellow sides

Golden-olive pectoral fins

Concentration of spots on tailfin

White-edged pelvic and anal fins

Rainbow trout have been successfully introduced to many European rivers, and now breed freely in some Alpine streams.

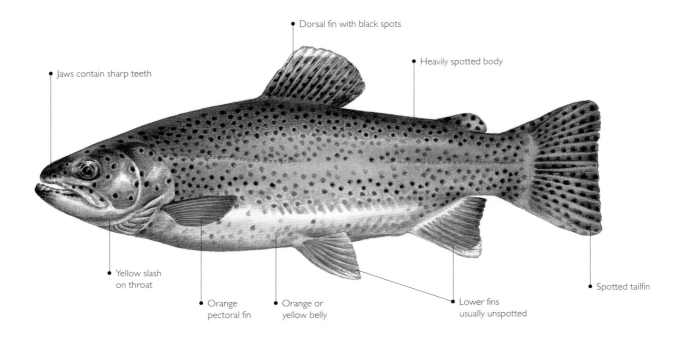

Dorsal fin with black spots

Heavily spotted body

Jaws contain sharp teeth

Yellow slash
on throat

Orange
pectoral fin

Orange or
yellow belly

Lower fins
usually unspotted

Spotted tailfin

GILAE AND APACHE TROUT

Oncorhynchus gilae

The gilae trout and apache trout (*O. apache*) are considered by some taxonomists as separate species; others prefer to keep both as one species and treat them as two subspecies, the gilae trout (*O. g. gilae*), and the apache trout (*O. g. apache*). Like all American *Oncorhynchus* trout, both have spotted tailfins. The gilae has 130–164 scales in the lateral line, the apache 142–170; both have 10–12 rays in the dorsal fin.

The gilae has a brown back, yellow-brown sides, and a warm golden-yellow color on the belly. Oval gray-brown parr markings may be retained on the sides into adulthood (other species of trout tend to lose them after a year or so and well before they become adults). The apache is duller than the gilae, olive-brown on the sides, and olive-yellow on the belly. Both gilae and apache have yellow slashes on either side under the lower jaw.

Gilae and apache trout rarely grow to more than 20–25cm (8–10in) in rivers; in lakes apache trout have been recorded at over 50cm (20in), and weighing over 1.5kg (3lb 5oz).

Distribution The native range of the gilae trout is the upper reaches of the Gila River and tributaries of the Salt River (Arizona/New Mexico). Apache trout are native to the Little Colorado, Salt, and San Francisco rivers of Arizona. Unfortunately the introduction of rainbow trout and transference of gilae to other streams has resulted in hybridization, so few rivers now have pure gilae and apache stocks.

THE PRECAUTIONARY PRINCIPLE

Throughout the world an increasing proportion of the trout caught by fly-fishers is carefully returned to the water alive. This practice of catch and release is important in the conservation of wild trout. The concern is that many wild trout populations are in need of protection from overfishing, genetic pollution from stocking of tame inbred hatchery strains and competition, and the dangers of inbreeding resulting from the introduction of non-native species (for example, rainbow trout in gilae or apache trout streams, and brown trout in marbled trout rivers). The conservation of wild trout is up to fly-fishers, and part of that conservation is to return wild trout to river, lake, or sea, so that they can eventually spawn and give rise to the next generation. So the future of all fly-fishers' fish is in our hands. We should also be constantly aware of the need to protect and promote clean water and healthy fish stocks.

A fly-fisher plays a wild rainbow trout in New Zealand's Wilderness River.

CHAR

ANDY WALKER

*Char are among the most beautiful of fish.
With their light spotting or marbling on
a dark background they are "trout in
negative." The other feature that makes
char such a fascinating group of fish is
that they occur in some of the northern
hemisphere's wildest places. To catch
a wild, sea-run Arctic char or dolly
varden you must go to a wild
northern river. To catch
a wild "laker" you must
take your fly-rods to
the wilds of Canada.*

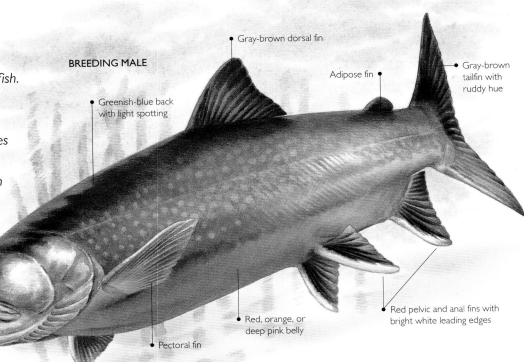

BREEDING MALE

Gray-brown dorsal fin

Adipose fin

Gray-brown tailfin with ruddy hue

Greenish-blue back with light spotting

Red pelvic and anal fins with bright white leading edges

Red, orange, or deep pink belly

Pectoral fin

ARCTIC CHAR

Salvelinus alpinus

Coloration varies from dark blue to dark green on the back and sides, gradually changing to silver or off-white on the belly, or the flanks. The belly and the underfins may be intensely red, with enamel white leading edges. The sides are usually spotted with orange or red. Close to the spawning season, males tend to be brighter than females. However, some forms are fairly drab even when spawning, so the mature males and females are difficult to tell apart. Sea-run Arctic char are pale overall and silvery when they return to freshwater, but their creamy-white belly, lower fins, and spotting redden as the breeding season approaches.

Long-lived, slow-growing individuals in some Arctic populations can live for 30 years. The largest recorded sea-run char of 15.9kg (35lb) was caught close to the island of Novaya Zemlya in the Barents Sea. Lac Léman in Switzerland is reported to have produced land-locked char of 12–14kg (27–31lb). Before the days of intensive exploitation, the Austrian Fuschersee and Hintersee yielded large specimens of 8–10kg (18–22lb), and Lake Vattern in southern Sweden is also known to have produced char weighing 4–5kg (8–11lb). Many lake and river systems of North America also produce big Arctic char: here the record, from the Tree River in Canada, weighed 14.5kg (32lb). (But you shouldn't expect to catch this size of char whenever you go fishing.) Sea-run Arctic char usually run to 1–3kg (2–6lb), non-migratory (land-locked) char up to 2kg (4lb).

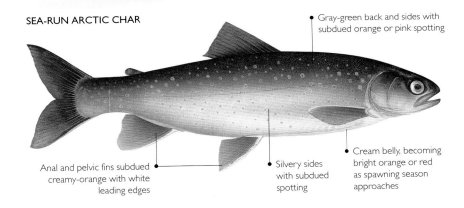

SEA-RUN ARCTIC CHAR

Gray-green back and sides with subdued orange or pink spotting

Anal and pelvic fins subdued creamy-orange with white leading edges

Silvery sides with subdued spotting

Cream belly, becoming bright orange or red as spawning season approaches

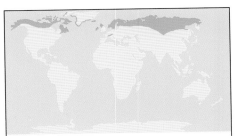

Distribution The Arctic char is a circumpolar species that is very well adapted to the rigorous environment of northerly freshwaters and the Arctic Ocean. Sea-run populations that go to sea to feed and return to the river to spawn occur in rivers southwards to the approximate limit of sea ice in winter. South of this limit only non-migratory, land-locked resident populations occur.

FOOD, FLIES, AND FISHING

Young char feed mainly on zoöplankton, benthic crustaceans, and insect larvae, while older ones tend to have a diet of baitfish. The biggest char resident in freshwater come from lakes with huge baitfish populations, such as whitefish and kokanee. So, catch smaller freshwater char on imitations of what they are feeding on, but catch big char on baitfish imitations. Sea-run populations eat baitfish such as capelin, sandeels, sculpins, and crustaceans. Fresh-run sea char can be caught at first on fish and crustacean imitations, but later require smaller and more delicate tactics. During the upstream migration, brightly colored streamer or wet-fly patterns fished close to the bottom work best.

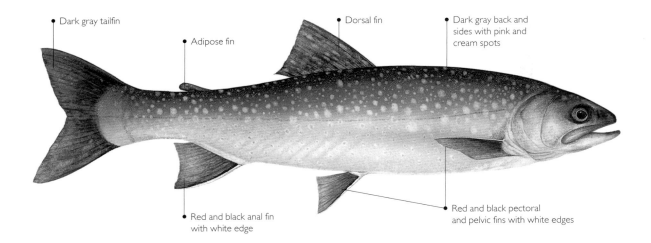

Dark gray tailfin

Adipose fin

Dorsal fin

Dark gray back and sides with pink and cream spots

Red and black anal fin with white edge

Red and black pectoral and pelvic fins with white edges

DOLLY VARDEN

Salvelinus malma

The dolly varden is very closely related to the Arctic char. Immature fish are green-brown spotted with red, and have pale bellies. They also have up to 12 blackish, oval parr markings on the sides. Those that remain in freshwater become darker, but those that go to sea develop an olive- or brown-green back and silver sides and belly, which are covered with faint red or orange spots. When sea-run fish return to the river to spawn, their coloration brightens. The spots become an intense red and the belly bright orange or red. The lower fins are orange or red with clear white margins. Adult females are somewhat duller than the males of the species.

Sea-run dolly varden average 50cm (20in) in length and weigh about 1kg (2lb). Any fish that is over 3kg (6lb 6oz) should be considered a trophy fish. The record, from the Wulik River, Alaska, scaled 7.9kg (17lb 5oz).

Distribution This is a northern Pacific basin fish, occurring in North America from Puget Sound northward through Alaska to the MacKenzie River, and in Asia from Vladivostok and Hokkaido north to Chaunsk Bay at the western end of Russia's Chukokst Peninsula.

BROOK TROUT

Salvelinus fontinalis

Brook trout are very beautiful fish. They have cream to greenish spots along the flanks that are mixed with red spots and ringed with blue haloes. The top of the back may be marbled with wavy lines; the sides of the belly of mature males are often bright orange or red, grading to a sooty appearance underneath. The underfins are often bright orange with prominent white edges backed by a black strip. Mature females and juveniles tend to have less spectacular colors.

Although the brook trout usually has the shortest life-span of all char, the maximum age of the sea-run form in the Koksoak River in Quebec is 12 years. And in a high-altitude lake in California, stocked brook trout have been found that have lived to the age of 24 years.

By the age of three, most brook trout weigh about 1.5kg (3lb), and in most lakes or rivers anything in excess of this figure should be considered a specimen fish. In Quebec, the Broadback River, and the Rupert, Nemiscau, and Assinica Lakes have all produced fish of over 4.5kg (10lb). Similarly, some of the lakes in southern Patagonia (Argentina and Chile), such as Lago General Paz and Lago Fontana, contain very large

Dark tailfin

Dark olive-green back with lighter vermiculations and spots

Dark olive-green dorsal fin with lighter vermiculations

Sides lighter than back

Anal and pelvic fins orange or red with a black line separating white leading edges

Creamy-orange belly

specimens. The world rod-caught record is a fish weighing 6.57kg (14lb 1oz), which was taken in the Nipigon River in Ontario.

Distribution The brook trout thrives in cool, clear water, and high summer water temperatures have long been recognized as a limiting factor to their distribution. They are native to streams and lakes in eastern North America and most common in the Canadian provinces of Newfoundland, Quebec, Ontario, Labrador, New Brunswick, and Nova Scotia, although they also occur westward into northern Manitoba. In the United States, they are common in Maine, Vermont, New Hampshire, and upper New York. They are found also in headwater streams along the Appalachian Mountains south to the states of Tennessee and Georgia. The brook trout has been introduced around the world for fishing purposes and is naturalized in Europe, Asia, New Zealand, Australia, southern Africa, and South America (notably in Chile and Argentina).

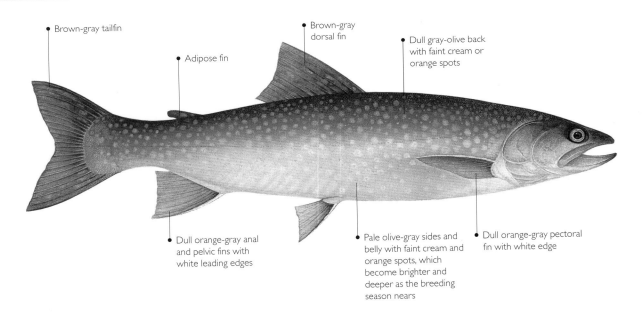

LAKE TROUT
Salvelinus namaycush

Very deeply forked tailfin

Adipose fin

Dorsal fin

Powerful, streamlined build

Anal fin

Brown or red-brown pelvic fin with white leading edge

Very pale gray or olive-gray markings on darker background

Brown or red-brown pectoral fin with white leading edge

The overall coloration is lighter than that of most other salmonids, and is usually a greenish-gray, but it can range from silver to almost black. The whole body is covered with large spots, which again are pale in color: often whitish, gray, or golden, but never red. The anal and paired fins have whitish leading edges, and the top of the back is often vermiculated, although less so than in the brook trout. The body is elongated and slender. The tailfin has a very deep fork, while the dorsal fin is set farther back than in the other char.

Mature males may develop dark, iridescent bands, which distinguish them from females.

The lake trout is highly prized as a trophy fish because it grows to great size. Age at maturity varies from 4–13 years, at lengths of 28–65cm (11–26in) and weights of 0.5–2.5kg (1–5lb). However, lake trout have great longevity and keep on growing throughout their long lives. While a specimen of 46.3kg (101lb 15oz) taken in Lake Athabaska by commercial fishermen is the world record for the species, the recognized rod-caught record is a much smaller fish of 28.6kg (63lb) from Lake Superior. However, a lake trout weighing 39.5kg (87lb), caught in Lake Bennett in the Yukon Territories, does appear to have been authentic.

Distribution The lake trout is native only to northern North America, but has been introduced into other parts of the United States, and also into Argentina, Peru, Bolivia, Finland, Sweden, Switzerland, France, and New Zealand.

Brown-gray tailfin

Adipose fin

Brown-gray dorsal fin

Dull gray-olive back with faint cream or orange spots

Dull orange-gray anal and pelvic fins with white leading edges

Pale olive-gray sides and belly with faint cream and orange spots, which become brighter and deeper as the breeding season nears

Dull orange-gray pectoral fin with white edge

BULL TROUT
Salvelinus confluentus

Overall, the bull trout is a rather dull char, somewhat resembling the lake trout. However, it lacks the lake trout's deeply forked tail and has slightly more colorful spots — cream or very dull orange instead of gray-white. The fins are also dull orange-gray, the lower ones with white margins. As the spawning season approaches the adults gain some color, the belly and spots usually becoming a dull orange, and the lower fins rusty-orange. This is potentially a long-lived fish, some individuals not maturing until 8–10 years of age and lengths of 60cm (24in) or more. The largest reported bull trout weighed 14.5kg (32lb).

Distribution The bull trout occurs in rivers draining into the Pacific Ocean from northern California north as far as southern Alaska.

 Reading Rivers 112–13 •
Reading Lakes 114–15

 Food and Flies 82–99 •
Freshwater Baitfish 104–5

 The Minipi Watershed 154–5 •
Finland 188–9

GRAYLING

ROSS GARDINER

The grayling is the perfect river fly-fishers' fish. It takes artificial flies boldly and fight hard to regain its freedom. It is also beautiful, subtly attired, and gentle, and is sometimes called "the lady of the stream."

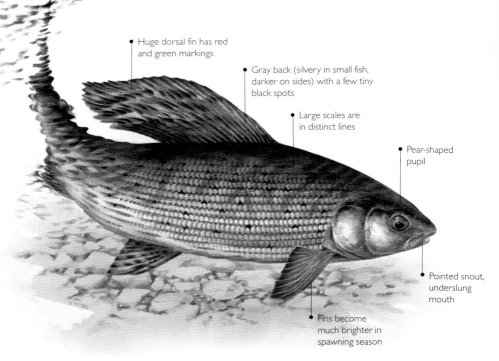

Huge dorsal fin has red and green markings

Gray back (silvery in small fish, darker on sides) with a few tiny black spots

Large scales are in distinct lines

Pear-shaped pupil

Pointed snout, underslung mouth

Fins become much brighter in spawning season

EUROPEAN GRAYLING

Thymallus thymallus

Features that distinguish grayling from other salmonids include the large sail-like dorsal fin and very large scales. The mouth is underslung and the eyes pear-shaped. Both of these characteristics are adaptations for feeding on the bottom of pools. The color is often silvery or gray. Mature fish are usually darker, particularly the males around spawning time. Males can also be identified by their larger and trailing dorsal fin. In mature fish the dorsal fin is often brightly colored with a prominent reddish-purple edge.

Grayling can grow quickly and reach 30–40cm (12–16in) at three years. In later life growth is often slower, and the maximum size is 1.4–1.8kg (3–4lb) at 40–50cm (16–20in). Males grow a little faster and reach larger maximum sizes than females. In northern Scandinavia and Russia, grayling may continue growing steadily to much larger sizes, despite slow growth rates initially of perhaps 5cm (2in) a year in early life. They can reach 60cm (2ft) and weigh more than 3kg (7lb).

Distribution The grayling is a species of the central and northern countries of Europe, Aisa, and North American. It occurs in rivers and cold lakes. The lake populations often, but not always, depend on streams to provide spawning and nursery areas.

FOOD, FLIES, AND FISHING

Grayling feed mainly on insects and crustaceans. Although tackle (weight number 4–6 outfits) and artificial flies are similar to those used for trout, the behavior of the grayling distinguishes it from the trout in three ways. First, grayling are usually found in schools, whereas trout are often isolated or are independent. Second, when feeding on flies at the surface, trout usually lie "on the fin" just below the surface of the water. Grayling don't: they swim from the bottom to take food at the water's surface. Third, trout can be very selective, and your artificial fly must sometimes be a very precise imitation of the natural fly. Grayling are not selective: they will often take a wide variety of artificial flies.

ARCTIC GRAYLING

Thymallus arcticus

MONGOLIAN GRAYLING

Thymallus brevirostris

The Arctic grayling is very similar in appearance to the European grayling, but it has an even larger dorsal fin. It reaches a length of about 30cm (12in) when three years old. The Arctic grayling's diet includes small mammals.

A third species, the Mongolian grayling (*T. brevirostris*), is very distinct, with a large mouth and well-developed teeth. The Mongolian grayling is reported to grow to a large size – up to 5kg (11lb).

Distribution Arctic grayling are found in North America and Asia. The Mongolian grayling is restricted to land-locked basins in northwestern Mongolia and the adjacent area of Russia.

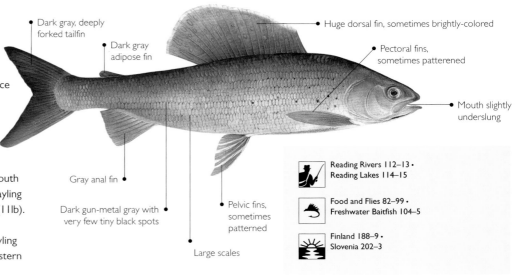

Dark gray, deeply forked tailfin

Dark gray adipose fin

Huge dorsal fin, sometimes brightly-colored

Pectoral fins, sometimes patterned

Mouth slightly underslung

Gray anal fin

Dark gun-metal gray with very few tiny black spots

Pelvic fins, sometimes patterned

Large scales

Reading Rivers 112–13 • Reading Lakes 114–15

Food and Flies 82–99 • Freshwater Baitfish 104–5

Finland 188–9 • Slovenia 202–3

WHITEFISH

ROSS GARDINER

The whitefish (Coregoninae) are the oldest branch of the living salmonids. They are typically salmonid in appearance, with large scales and no spots or other clear markings on a silvery-white body. Their teeth are small or are absent. Some might question whether it is worth fly-fishing for them.

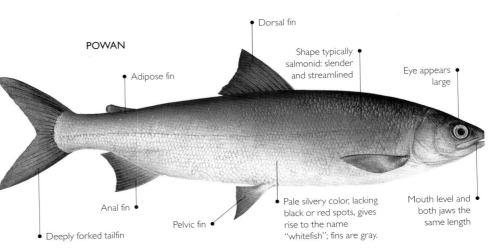

POWAN

Dorsal fin

Shape typically salmonid: slender and streamlined

Eye appears large

Adipose fin

Mouth level and both jaws the same length

Pale silvery color, lacking black or red spots, gives rise to the name "whitefish"; fins are gray.

Anal fin

Pelvic fin

Deeply forked tailfin

There are three reasons why whitefish are worth bothering about. First, some whitefish are quite large, so they provide excellent sport. Second, most whitefish are not very easy to catch, despite the fact that they take a fly well, so they provide a challenge. Third, they take a variety of forms, which is quite bewildering and makes them fascinating fish.

Three genera of whitefish are currently recognized: *Prosopium*, *Stenodus*, and *Coregonus*.

Prosopium

The several species of *Prosopium* (round whitefish) found in Asia and North America are the most primitive of the whitefish. They have a rounder body form and, unlike other whitefish, their young have parr markings. Most primitive of all is the mountain whitefish (*Prosopium williamsoni*), found in streams and lakes in some parts of the Rocky Mountains. With the exception of having a small dorsal fin, it is strikingly similar in behavior and appearance to the grayling. It grows to an average of about 450g (1lb) and a maximum of 1.8kg (4lb). It is a good sport fish.

Stenodus

This genus contains only one species, the inconnu (*Stenodus leucichthys*), which is found in Asia and North America. The inconnu has a large overslung mouth and predatory feeding habits, so it can grow quickly to a large size. Fully grown fish average 50–60cm (20–23in) in length, and 2.3–4.5kg (5–10lb) in weight. The record, which came from Alaska's Kobuk River, scaled 10.4kg (23lb). Both sea-run and freshwater-resident forms occur. It is a valuable sport fish.

Coregonus

This genus includes the ciscoes and various other whitefish of Europe, Asia, and North America. *Coregonus* whitefish are so complex that even now taxonomists cannot decide whether they should be considered as one species or as separate species.

The pollan, or Arctic cisco (*C. autumnalis*) is a slender silvery fish. It has a quite remarkable distribution in several Irish lakes and in the Arctic regions of Asia and North America. Several other ciscoes of North America may also be of the same species. To be certain of identification examine the mouth, which is level, with neither jaw extending beyond the other. This is not a big fish; 25cm (10in) is about average for an adult aged three years.

The houting, schelly, or powan are just three of the names given to the species *C. lavaretus*, which is found in many British and mainland European lakes. The houting, being a sea-run form, still occurs in rivers running into the Baltic Sea, but has been largely lost from North Sea rivers. The lake whitefish of North America is closely related, if not the same species. The upper jaw is longer than the lower, and the mouth is on the underside of the snout. Lake forms average 20cm (8in), but sea-run houting may attain more than 30cm (12in).

The vendace (*C.albula*) occurs throughout much of northern Europe and in two lakes in northern England (Bassenthwaite and Derwentwater). Recent genetic work suggests that the least cisco (*C. sardinella*) of North America and Asia and the vendace may be different races of the one species. The lower jaw is curved upwards and is extended, so that the mouth opens on the upper side of the snout.

FOOD, FLIES, AND FISHING

Inconnu are predatory fish, and will take baitfish imitations or general streamers. The majority of other whitefish feed mainly on insects and crustaceans, so flies that imitate these are essential. Most species have a very small mouth and, while they can suck down large, fragile insects, they readily reject imitations tied on large iron hooks. To catch whitefish you will often need flies tied on much smaller hooks than you might use to catch trout, char, or grayling.

SCHELLY, VENDACE, AND HOUTING

In the schelly the upper jaw overlaps the lower.

In the vendace the lower jaw extends a little beyond the upper.

In the houting the upper jaw is greatly extended, producing a long snout.

Different species of whitefish can often be identified by mouth shape

 Reading Rivers 112–13 • Reading Lakes 114–15

 Food and Flies 82–99 • Saltwater Baitfish 104–5

 Yellowstone National Park 172–3

HUCHEN, TAIMEN, AND LENOK

MALCOLM GREENHALGH

The members of the salmon family are the most widely popular of freshwater fish. Many fly-fishers have caught a trout in their time, as well as salmon and char. But few fly-fishers have ever seen the three species described here.

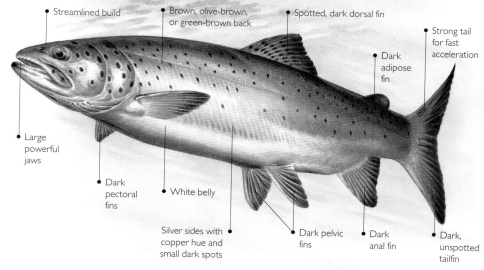

Streamlined build · Brown, olive-brown, or green-brown back · Spotted, dark dorsal fin · Strong tail for fast acceleration · Dark adipose fin · Large powerful jaws · Dark pectoral fins · White belly · Silver sides with copper hue and small dark spots · Dark pelvic fins · Dark anal fin · Dark, unspotted tailfin

HUCHEN

Hucho hucho hucho

The presence of an adipose fin confirms that huchen, taimen, and lenok are members of the salmon family. Huchen also have the streamlined salmonid shape, but with a slightly larger head and more slender form than the salmon and trout. Huchen have a green-brown back, silvery sides with a copper hue, and white belly. They can grow to a large size. At five years they may reach 75cm (30in) in length; at 10 years, 1.2m (4ft); and at 15 years, over 1.5m (5ft).

Unfortunately the huchen has declined recently, mainly through pollution and the building of impassable dams across rivers. Today, many fish are raised in hatcheries and are used to stock the rivers, but very few grow to old age and to the great sizes that they did 50 and more years ago.

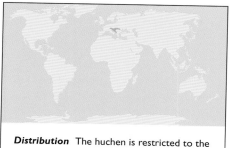

Distribution The huchen is restricted to the River Danube and its tributaries.

FOOD, FLIES, AND FISHING

Huchen and taimen feed mainly on fish, including grayling and nase, usually between dusk and dawn – which is the best time to catch them. Large fish-imitating flies or streamer patterns are ideal, fished on a sinking line where the current is deep and strong. Use at least 5kg (11lb) test leaders. The lenok feeds predominantly on invertebrates such as water-bred mayflies, stoneflies and caddisflies, and crustaceans. It is readily caught on imitations using river trout fly-fishing outfits and techniques.

TAIMEN

Hucho hucho taimen

The taimen is considered a subspecies of the huchen, which it resembles, except that it is a slightly more slender and a grayer fish. It also has conspicuous red or red-brown anal and tailfins. Most adults are 12kg (26lb), with rare specimens weighing up to 70kg (154lb).

Distribution Taimen occur in Siberia from the Volga in the west to the Amur River in the east.

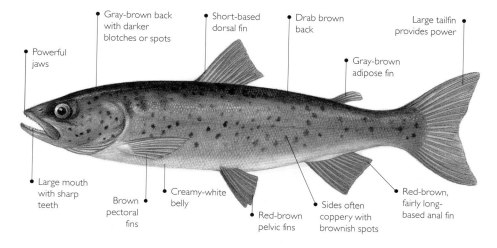

Powerful jaws · Gray-brown back with darker blotches or spots · Short-based dorsal fin · Drab brown back · Large tailfin provides power · Gray-brown adipose fin · Large mouth with sharp teeth · Brown pectoral fins · Creamy-white belly · Red-brown pelvic fins · Sides often coppery with brownish spots · Red-brown, fairly long-based anal fin

LENOK

Brachymtstax lenok

This is a trout-like salmonid, similar to a rainbow trout in general color – olive-brown with black spots on the back, gray-white below, and red-pink blotches on the sides. The gray pelvic fins have a white leading edge. The mouth is diagnostic, being very small, ending in front of the eye. It averages 1–2kg (2–4lb), exceptionally 4–5kg (9–11lb).

Distribution Lenok occur across Asiatic Siberia east to Korea and south to northern China.

Reading Rivers 112–13

Freshwater Baitfish 104–5

Slovenia 202–3 (for huchen)

LARGEMOUTH BASS

DAVE WHITLOCK

Largemouth bass are powerful and ferocious predators. While they will take your fly at all depths, the surface fly will quickly become your favorite, for the largemouth surface strike is among the most exciting experiences in fly-fishing.

LARGEMOUTH BASS
Micropterus salmoides

The largemouth is the largest member of a group of fish known as black bass, which also includes the smallmouth. These fish have an olive or green back and a pale cream belly, separated by a vivid black lateral line from the eye to the base of the tail. The double dorsal fin of largemouth bass is divided into two separate sections, the front one spiny and the rear one soft rayed. In other black bass, the spiny and soft rayed segments are connected. As its name suggests, the mouth is very large and, when closed, the jaw extends well beyond the eye.

Most largemouth bass reach maturity in three years, when they will usually weigh 450–900g (1–2lb). The smaller males seldom exceed 900g–1.8kg (2–3lb), but females will frequently reach 2–4.5kg (4–10lb). The world record (all angling methods) stands at 10. 09kg (22lb 4oz); the fly-fishing record at 7.8kg (16lb 2oz).

Largemouth bass prefer still and slow-flowing waters, with water temperatures in the range of 18–29°C (65–85°F). They are especially attracted to waters that are laden with surface and subsurface structures, such as aquatic vegetation, rocks, stumps, roots, logs, fallen trees, boat docks, bridges, and duck blinds.

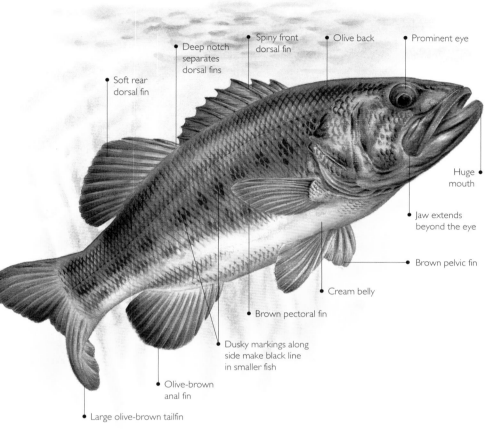

- Soft rear dorsal fin
- Deep notch separates dorsal fins
- Spiny front dorsal fin
- Olive back
- Prominent eye
- Huge mouth
- Jaw extends beyond the eye
- Brown pelvic fin
- Cream belly
- Brown pectoral fin
- Dusky markings along side make black line in smaller fish
- Olive-brown anal fin
- Large olive-brown tailfin

Distribution Largemouth bass are native to North America, and because they are such exciting and adaptable game fish, they have been introduced into Mexico, South America, Puerto Rico, Cuba, Europe, Asia, and Africa.

FOOD, FLIES, AND FISHING

Bass are mainly ambush feeders: the structure of the mouth and body enables them to be quick, maneuverable, and accurate predators. Largemouth bass prefer to eat large insects, minnows, crayfish, shrimp, leeches, worms, small birds, mammals, and reptiles. Flies that imitate these foods are usually referred to as bass bugs. These, and flies that simply suggest live food, will be eagerly attacked by largemouth when they are accurately cast and then very slowly and seductively puppeteered over, through, or past the largemouth's places of ambush.

Because bass bugs are quite heavy flies, and because largemouths often live in very snaggy water, fine tackle is not adequate. Fly-tackle in the range of numbers 6–10 weight, with surface and sinking tip fly-lines, and leaders testing 3.5–5.4kg (8–20lb) are ideal, with the heavier of these used for casting the largest bass bugs, and fighting larger bass in the most structure-laden habitats. Accuracy is far more important than distance when fly-casting for largemouth bass.

The huge mouth of a largemouth bass. The fly is a big deerhair Bass Bug which "pops" when brought through the surface.

 Reading Rivers 112–13 · Reading Lakes 114–15

 Freshwater Baitfish 104–5

SMALLMOUTH BASS

BOB CLOUSER

The smallmouth bass is a member of the black bass family and, because of its pugnacity and willingness to take a fly, is one of the most important freshwater gamefish found in North America. Once hooked, this fish fights harder than any other fish of comparable size. It is rightly widely acclaimed as the finest member of the bass family to catch on the fly-rod.

• Stout, deep body

Two components of the dorsal fin are separated by only a shallow notch; the front part of the fin has 10 sharp spines

• Brown tailfin

Long-based brown anal fin has three sharp spines

Back and sides are olive-or bronze-brown with dark blotchy bars running down the sides

Jaw does not extend beyond eye

Sandy-brown pectoral fins

Sandy-brown pelvic fins

• White belly

SMALLMOUTH BASS

Micropterus dololmieui

The smallmouth bass has a stout, thickset body with an overall brownish or bronze cast and dark blackish-olive vertical bars running down the sides. The upper jaw does not extend beyond the eye, as does that of its close relative the largemouth bass. The dorsal fin has a very shallow notch, while the tail sports a black band with a white outer edge and, nearer to the body,

an orange cast. This tail coloration is most prominent on young smallmouth species.

The fish's growth rate and size depend on the amount of available food, the water temperature, and the length of the growing seasons. It can grow to a length of 23cm (9in) in two years, 30cm (12in) in four years in fertile rivers, and 45–50cm (18–20in) in 7–10 years. Most smallmouth caught by fly-fishers usually weigh from 1.8kg (4lb), with exceptional trophy fish up to 5.4kg (12lb).

FOOD, FLIES, AND FISHING

The first food of young smallmouth is zoöplankton. The fish then turn to a diet of insect larvae, crayfish, and various baitfish. If you want to catch smallmouth you should imitate their natural food in the river or lake you are fishing.

If they are feeding on crayfish or other large bottom-dwelling invertebrates, use a good weighted imitation and bounce it across the bottom. If you find that the smallmouth are taking baitfish, choose a good imitation – whether a Sculpin, Minnow, or Fry – or a general streamer pattern. In deep water or very cold conditions use a weighted pattern; in shallow, snaggy, or warm water an unweighted one. And fish the fly with long fast pulls allowing the fly to pause briefly between strips. If you see smallmouth feeding at the surface, then you will almost always catch them on Poppers, Hairbugs, or Floating Minnows.

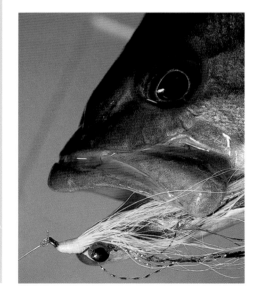

Distribution The smallmouth loves rocky places in both lakes and rivers. Until 1869, its native range was largely confined to the Lake Ontario and Ohio River drainage systems. This range widened in the 1870s as a direct result of the growth of the American railroad system. Fly-fishers interested in the fish began to put brood stock in buckets and hang them in the water tenders of the steam locomotives, transporting them in this way into other watersheds all over the country. As a result the smallmouth now has a wide distribution; it is found in nearly every state in the United States and throughout southern Canada.

Compared with that of the largemouth bass (page 37), the mouth of the smallmouth bass is quite dainty, but the smallmouth will still take big flies, like this lead-eyed streamer.

PIKE

BARRY REYNOLDS AND JOHN BERRYMAN

Pike are the biggest and the toothiest predators found in temperate and sub-Arctic freshwater habitats of the Northern Hemisphere. They offer one of the greatest challenges to the river and lake fly-fisher.

Dorsal fin well back on body

Large tailfin

Dark olive or brown-green back and sides with lighter (cream or rich yellow) markings

Anal fin is close to tailfin and opposite dorsal fin to provide powerful acceleration

White belly

Pelvic fins

Huge jaws with long, sharp fangs

Pectoral fins, like all fins, brown or olive with darker markings

NORTHERN PIKE

Esox lucius

With their long, streamlined bodies, and the power-generating dorsal and anal fins positioned well back on the tail, pike are built for rapid acceleration. Their wide, powerful jaws are designed for seizing large, active prey. Most northern pike have cream to white underbellies and sides that range from pure silver (the rare "blue" color phase) through light and dark shades of green and brown, with lighter green or yellow spots and flecks. The fins also vary in color from shades of green-brown to red. In North America, to distinguish them from muskellunge, check the northern's dark background with lighter spots. Check too that there are no long teeth in the upper jaw. Another characteristic is that the lower jaw usually exhibits 10 sensory pores.

Males are always shorter than females of the same age, so all big northern pike will be females. Males rarely grow heavier than 4.5kg (10lb),

whereas females frequently reach 14kg (30lb) or, rarely, even more. In Ireland, northern pike have been recorded to 41kg (90lb), in Russia and Scotland to more than 32kg (70lb), in Scandinavia, Germany, Poland, and Britain to more than 23kg (50lb). In North America the northern pike approach 23kg (50lb).

Distribution This species occurs in rivers, canals, and lakes in North America and Eurasia (except offshore islands) from about 40° to 70°N. It occurs in brackish water in the Baltic.

MUSKELLUNGE

Esox masquinongy

Although the muskellunge (often called the "muskie") is quite similar in appearance to the northern pike, with its pale belly and its overall green-brown coloration, it generally has a light background color on which there are darker spots or bars. Well-developed, long, sharp teeth are present in both the upper and the lower jaws, and the lower jaw exhibits 12 to 20 sensory pores (typically about 16).

As in northern pike, female muskies grow faster than males, and attain larger sizes – at the age of three years, females are about 63cm (25in) long. Muskies appear to live longer than northerns, and reach larger sizes. The accepted angling record stands at 70kg (154lb

3oz), but there are authenticated reports of fish weight as much as 50kg (110lb).

Distribution The muskellunge is a North American fish occurring naturally in the northeast corner of the United States east of the Mississippi

River, and the south-southeast portion of Canada. Although stocking programs in the United States do exist, they have not met with much success and therefore muskellunge are still something of a rarity outside their native range.

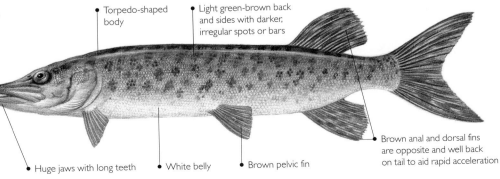

Torpedo-shaped body

Light green-brown back and sides with darker, irregular spots or bars

Brown anal and dorsal fins are opposite and well back on tail to aid rapid acceleration

Huge jaws with long teeth

White belly

Brown pelvic fin

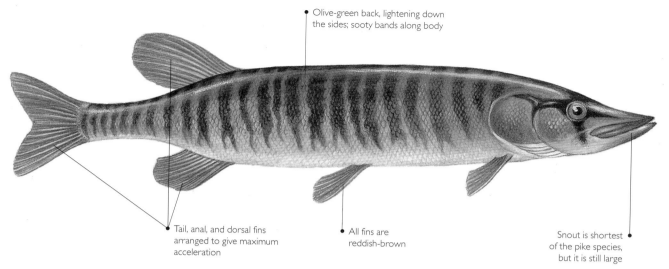

Olive-green back, lightening down the sides; sooty bands along body

Tail, anal, and dorsal fins arranged to give maximum acceleration

All fins are reddish-brown

Snout is shortest of the pike species, but it is still large

REDFIN PICKEREL

Esox americanus

This is a small pike with a proportionally shorter snout than other species. The back is olive-green and the sides a lighter olive. There are 10–13 dark, wavy vertical bands down the sides. The maximum length is about 40cm (15in) and weight about 0.5kg (1lb 4oz). This is a super-lightweight fish.

Distribution The redfin pickerel is found throughout the catchments of the Great Lakes and the Mississippi River south to Florida.

FOOD, FLIES, AND FISHING

Pike and muskies are mainly stillwater fish, which can be caught in lakes, canals, and the slowest of river pools. Both are lurkers and dashers, using their impeccable camouflage to hide among cover – brush, weeds, lily-pad beds, undercut banks, and inlets to bays – from where they dart out like torpedoes at unsuspecting prey. They go for smaller fish including panfish, smallmouth and largemouth bass, chub, minnows, shad, walleye, ciscoe, roach, bream, and trout – in fact any fish they can catch and swallow. And although the preferred size of prey is roughly 30 per cent of their size, there are several records of pike choking to death while trying to devour prey of their own size. Besides fish, they will also feed on ducklings, small turtles, small mammals, freshwater crayfish, and even large insects that breed in or near water, such as damselflies and green drakes.

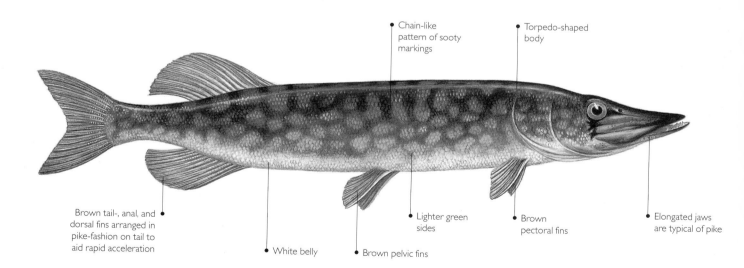

Chain-like pattern of sooty markings

Torpedo-shaped body

Brown tail-, anal, and dorsal fins arranged in pike-fashion on tail to aid rapid acceleration

White belly

Lighter green sides

Brown pelvic fins

Brown pectoral fins

Elongated jaws are typical of pike

CHAIN PICKEREL

Esox niger

This is a small pike, with its anal and dorsal fins set well back for acceleration, a characteristic spade-shaped mouth, dark green back, lighter green flanks, and white belly. There is a diagnostic chain of lace-like sooty markings along the sides. Average length is about 50cm (20in); weight about 1kg (2lb). Years ago there were records of much larger specimens of 4.5kg (10lb). This is a lovely, although often underrated, fly-fishers' fish. Light rods and lines and small baitfish imitations contrast with the heavier gear that is needed to catch pike.

Distribution The chain pickerel is found throughout eastern North America.

 Reading Lakes 114–15 • Handling Fish 144–5

 Freshwater Baitfish 104–5

SHAD

MALCOLM GREENHALGH

Shad are members of the herring family. They feed and grow in the sea but enter fresh or brackish water of rivers to spawn. They occur along the coasts of North America, and the coasts of northwest Europe, and in the Mediterranean. All shad have deep, keeled, laterally flattened silvery bodies covered with scales that come off easily when handled. The belly has a characteristic serrated or toothed outline when looked at side-on.

Dark dorsal fin

Furrows on gill cover

Thin, transparent fatty membranes over eyes

Deep blue back, shading to silver on belly; dusky spots on sides

Deeply forked, dark tailfin with leaf-like scales at base

Large head; lower jaw fits into notch in upper jaw

Dark pectoral and pelvic fins

Deep body, laterally flattened

Long-based, dark anal fin

TWAITE SHAD

Alosa fallax

In twaite shad the back is deep blue, shading to a gold tinge on the sides, and silver below. There are usually 6–10 dusky black splodges running in a line along the sides of the body (sometimes these are not very distinct). Most twaite shad attain a maximum length of 40cm (16in) and weight of 1kg (2lb); exceptionally they reach 50cm (20in) and 1.75kg (4lb).

Distribution The twaite shad is the most common of the European shad, occurring around the coasts of the British Isles and western Europe, and also east to southern Norway and the Gulfs of Bothnia and Finland, and south to the Mediterranean Sea.

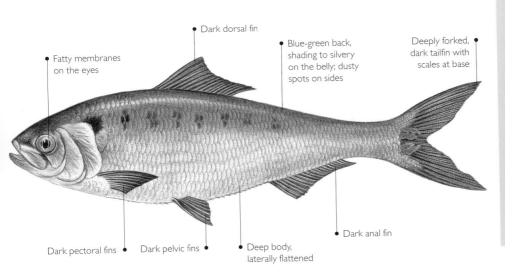

Fatty membranes on the eyes

Dark dorsal fin

Blue-green back, shading to silvery on the belly; dusty spots on sides

Deeply forked, dark tailfin with scales at base

Dark pectoral fins

Dark pelvic fins

Deep body, laterally flattened

Dark anal fin

FOOD, FLIES, AND FISHING

Shad are usually caught when they return from the sea to the rivers in spring (they are difficult to locate at sea). They stop feeding for the few weeks that they are in freshwater, but they can be caught on fairly small flies fished close to the bottom. Bright, tinsel-bodied attractor flies are most effective. Shad are very soft-mouthed and must be played gently if they are not to throw the hook.

Shad generally strike better early and late in the day or during periods of subdued light. They tend to stay in the deeper channels when moving upstream, generally at night, and to rest during the day. Early in the run, when the waters are higher and cooler, a very rapid hand-over-hand retrieve can be deadly with a sinking or sinking-tip line. Later, as temperatures rise and the fish approach spawning time, they are less aggressive and respond better to a slow down-and-across swing on a shallow sinking or a floating line.

AMERICAN SHAD

Alosa sapidissima

This species is very similar to the twaite shad, with its blue-green back, silvery-white underside, overall golden cast, and row of up to five dusky black splodges down the sides. This is the largest shad, attaining a maximum length of 75cm (30in) and weight of 4kg (9lb), although most that are caught will be in the 1.5–3kg (3–7 lb) class.

Distribution Native to the Atlantic coast of North America, from Florida to Canada, this shad was introduced into the Sacramento River, California in 1871. It has spread along the Pacific coast north to Alaska and south into Mexico.

Reading Rivers 112–13 •
Reading Estuaries and Tidal Creeks 116–17 •
Tides 132–3

SALTWATER FISH

ED JAWOROWSKI

Mastering saltwater fly-fishing demands knowledge of habitats that are as diverse as sweeping inlets, calm bays, pounding surf, shallow flats, and deep oceanic blue waters. In their concern with tackle, the latest developments in technique, and tricks for catching a variety of game species, fly-fishers often overlook the obvious and important first step: locating fish.

Appreciating the diverse water types along the whole of the littoral zone and offshore blue waters is the starting point for saltwater fly-fishing success. Fly selection and fishing techniques must be adapted to fit in with this information.

The term habitat, implying a residence, can itself be misleading when it comes to saltwater, since, as a rule, ocean gamefish do not have permanent homes. It is true that juvenile fish may, for a time, derive nourishment and protection from fertile and sheltered estuaries, but they soon move to the twin rhythms of tidal forces and baitfish migrations. That is precisely why, in addition to understanding the various types of food and the behavior of the target fish, fly-fishers must familiarize themselves with the range of resting, traveling, and feeding habitats. Recognizing the differences between these habitats is crucial to the flyfisher's success.

Consider some of the habitats frequented by marine fish: rivers and estuaries, bays, lagoons, ocean surf, rips, flats (along with the channels that run through them and the mangrove jungles that border them), the deep blue water beyond the horizon, and rock piles, reefs, and the artificial structures provided by abandoned wrecks, offshore lighthouses, bridges, piers, and jetties. Some structures offer spots from which to ambush prey, or to draw and hold baitfish, which in turn lure gamefish predators to them.

Tides can create feeding habitats but, equally, can cause them to vanish. There are also seasonal variations; what provides a good habitat at one time of a day, or year, may be worthless at another. The variables are vast as each fish is taken into account: as striped bass react to turbulence, so tarpon respond to wind; bonefish and tuna are sensitive to temperature, while changing salinity may affect the behavior of bluefish. And where snook require the security of mangroves, groupers prefer the safety that they are offered by the bottom structure of the reef.

While accounting for all these variables may seem a daunting task, the endless fascination of the sport does depend on this very complexity. Fly-fishing is a highly technique-intensive endeavor; it is very much like a chess game played between two masters, and fly-fishing in saltwater is especially complex, because of the sheer vastness of the seas and oceans and the sheer variety of their inhabitants. Its rewards will be realized by all those who are able to sense the pulse and the rhythm of life in the sea.

Once, on a bonefish flat in the Bahamas, on a falling tide, my guide and I located a huge school of fish that was moving out of dense and inaccessible mangroves where the fish had been feeding. Well fed and intent on reaching the shelter of deeper water, they refused all our offerings. We calculated the tide for the next day and determined to intercept this same school some hours earlier as it moved into the mangroves.

On the following day we did much better with the fish that were now intent on feeding and were, apparently, more secure in the deepening water.

Similarly, on another occasion, at low tide along a rugged sea cliff outside Gloucester harbor, Massachusetts, there were no fish in evidence. Experience told us that higher water would improve our chances. We left the area and returned three hours later, when the crashing waves from the rising tide generated more turbulence. We caught fish at will.

These examples illustrate the importance of reading the water, recognizing the effects of different habitats on different species, and incorporating that knowledge into a saltwater fly-fishing plan. Such plans are critical to success.

Tropical saltwater habitats, like this mangrove-fringed flat, hold a wide variety of marine fish that will all take an appropriate fly. So too do cooler temperate seas: don't neglect them.

STRIPED BASS

ED JAWOROWSKI

The striped bass is the premier gamefish of the east coast of the United States, the target of more fly-fishers than any saltwater fish in its range. In addition to taking flies readily, stripers fight strongly, grow to appreciable size, and large specimens can make long runs. They provide wonderful sport in a variety of coastal shallow-water habitats.

Gray-blue back

Silver sides with black stripes running along body

Two dorsal fins, front one supported by sharp spines

Large head

Light gray pelvic fins

Dark gray tailfin

Long-based, dark anal fin opposite rear dorsal fin produces rapid acceleration and powerful swimming

White belly

Light gray pectoral fins

STRIPED BASS

Morone saxatilis

The fusiform body has a fairly large head, well-separated dorsal fins, and a wide, powerful tail that can drive the fish with ease through turbulent surf and swift rips. Color varies with habitat: the back generally has an olive cast, ranging to bluish and nearly black. The sides are silvery, marked by seven or eight black horizontal stripes that blend into a white belly.

While stripers run to more than 23kg (50lb) and commercial harvesters have netted fish topping 45kg (100lb), fly-fishers commonly fish for "school" bass in the 2–7kg (5–15lb) range, and consider any fish over 14kg (30lb) as a trophy fish. Studies reveal that the majority of large bass – 9kg (20lb) or heavier and 10 years old or more – are females and therefore brood stock that most fly-fishers release, despite their being fine table fare.

Striped bass may ambush prey from the cover of structures (such as jetty walls and reefs) or actively feed in open water. Large schools in densely huddled masses may savage small minnows, or big individuals may chase solitary large prey, stunning them with a smack of their broad tails. Sometimes, a school may resemble a cornfield, the fish virtually standing on their heads to feed on sandeels or clams.

Fishing in some Chesapeake Bay tributaries resembles largemouth bass fishing, amid fallen timber in nearly still waters. In the fall, along mid-Atlantic beaches, fly-fishers look for stripers charging into the wash at the edge of the surf, chasing pods of mullet that hug the beach during their southern migration. Waters swirling around rock jetties are always prime locations, as are creeks draining marshes. Channels flowing past bridge abutments, where bass intercept small fish and crabs washed by the tide, also provide excellent opportunities.

Bass can be caught in bright sunlight, but low light is best – at dawn, dusk, on overcast days, and particularly at night. Striped bass see well at night, although their color perception is then poor; the darkest nights are generally the most productive for the fly-fisher.

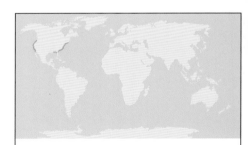

Distribution The striper's east-coast range extends from the Gulf of St Lawrence as far south as northern Florida. It also occurs in the waters of the Hudson, Delaware, Roanoke, and other rivers far from the sea, and roams the northern shores of the Gulf of Mexico. Late 19th-century transplants proliferated into a successful Pacific fishery on the west coast of the US, from central California northward. The striper winters in coastal rivers and spawns in freshwater in spring when water temperatures are 15–20°C (60–69°F). It also acclimatizes readily to varying conditions and inhabits large freshwater impoundments across the US.

A fly-caught striper almost ready for release. Note the conspicuous stripes that give this species its name.

FOOD, FLIES, AND FISHING

Striped bass are catholic in taste and feed on a wide range of baitfish, sandeels, silversides, anchovies, menhaden, herring, mullet, mackerel, and eels, as well as decapods, shrimp, crabs, squid, and a variety of seaworms. Most fly-fishers employ 9 or 10 weight rods, 275–290cm (9ft–9ft 6in) long, prepared with floating, slow- and fast-sinking line options. Simple leaders, with little tapering, can range from as long as the rod for surface fishing to as short as 60cm (2ft) for deeper water. Although bass lack sharp teeth, they have rough mouths, so a 30cm- (12in-) long, heavy mono bite tippet is recommended when angling for the largest specimens. Fly selection, although normally less important than presentation, can be critical, particularly in terms of size and, occasionally, color. A good assortment should take into account the size and behavior of local natural baits. Imitations should range from 5–25cm (2–10in) or more, with 10cm (4in) a good standard. Hook sizes may run from 4 through 4/0, and white, yellow, chartreuse, and black are the most useful colors. Experiment to determine the fish's preferred rate and speed of retrieve, direction of swing, and depth, as these may vary from tide to tide. As a rule, slow retrieves, sometimes painstakingly slow, work best.

 Reading Harbors and Jetties 118–19 • Reading Beaches and Bays 120–1 • Tides 132-3

 Mollusks: Clams and Squid 100 •Saltwater Crabs 101 • Saltwater Shrimp and Prawns 102–3 •Saltwater Baitfish 106–7

 Cape Cod 160–1

EUROPEAN BASS

GARY COXON

The bass (or seabass) is Europe's finest saltwater fly-fish. The "loup de mer" or "wolf of the sea", as the French describe it so well, is a hunter of lesser fish, shrimp, and crabs. It will take a well-presented fly boldly. When hooked it fights with the tenacity of a wolf! And it is a most beautiful fish.

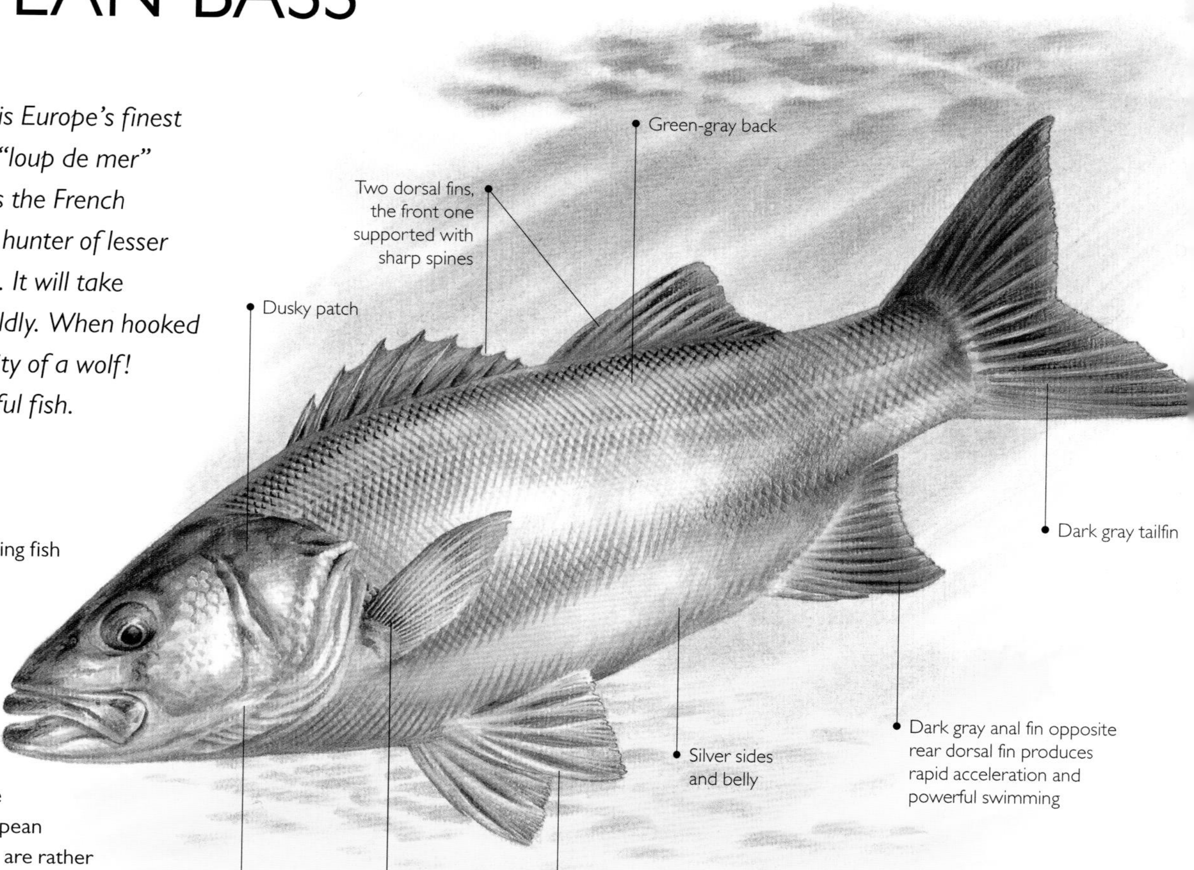

EUROPEAN BASS

Dicentrarchus labrax

The European bass is a striking fish with bright silver flanks and slate-gray back. The large head and mouth, powerful jaws, broad shoulders, and streamlined build give the bass power and speed, and contribute to its reputation as the ultimate sporting quarry for the European saltwater fly-fisher. Its scales are rather small in comparison with those of many other marine fish. The front dorsal fin has eight or nine sharp spines, the anal fin has three spines, and there are two razor-sharp flattened spines at the rear of the gill cover, so extreme care is needed when handling these fish.

Juvenile bass up to approximately 1kg (2lb) are often referred to as "school bass" because they live in schools and hunt as a pack. As they grow

Labels on illustration:
- Green-gray back
- Two dorsal fins, the front one supported with sharp spines
- Dusky patch
- Dark gray tailfin
- Large head
- Pale gray pectoral fins
- Pale gray pelvic fins
- Silver sides and belly
- Dark gray anal fin opposite rear dorsal fin produces rapid acceleration and powerful swimming

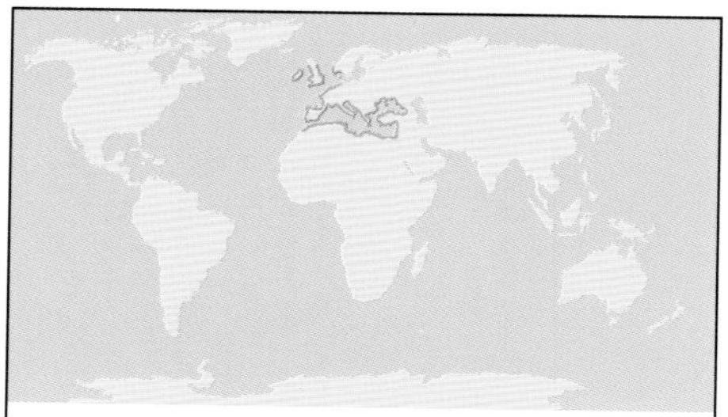

Distribution European bass range as far south as the Mediterranean, along the coasts of Spain and France, through the English Channel, and as far north as Scotland. The European bass is essentially a summer and fall quarry (June–October), reaching its northern range when sea temperatures exceed about 12°C (54°F).

and mature they tend to live more separate lives, although they will congregate in feeding hot-spots when an abundance of food attracts them to a particular area.

When searching for European bass, consider a wide range of inshore habitats; for example, tide races around headlands, fierce breakers off a storm beach, wide sandy estuaries, narrow muddy creeks, and harbors and marinas. Any or all of them might hold feeding bass that are prepared to take your fly.

Mature fish usually weigh between 2 and 3kg (4 and 7lb), but large specimens may reach 6kg (13lb) or more.

Reading Estuaries and Tidal Creeks 116–17 •
Reading Harbors and Jetties 118–9 •
Reading Beaches and Bays 120–1 • Tides 132–3

Mollusks: Clams and Squid 100 •
Saltwater Crabs 101 • Saltwater Shrimp and
Prawns 102–3 • Saltwater Baitfish 106–7

FOOD, FLIES, AND FISHING

There is little in the sea that swims or crawls that the European bass does not view as food. It will feed on tiny crustaceans such as sandhoppers and the maggots of seaweed-flies washed out from the tideline. At the other extreme, bass will hunt quite large fish, such as herring and mackerel. They seem to prefer medium-sized prey, including the fry of other saltwater fish species, sandeels, prawns, shrimp, and crabs.

Although they are opportunistic feeders they can become very preoccupied with one particular food and may ignore all others. Therefore, while you will often catch bass on quite general shrimp- or fry-imitating flies, there will be times when you will need to identify a particular prey and closely match it. For example, bass feeding on sandeels will often take only sandeel imitations.

BLUEFISH

D MITCHELL

Bluefish are nomadic saltwater predators found seasonally in most temperate and semi-tropical oceans. Enduring a wide range of temperatures and salinity, they inhabit both inshore and offshore waters. In both locales their feeding frenzies are legendary. Fast and formidable, aggressive and acrobatic, bluefish are among the most sought-after of all saltwater gamefish.

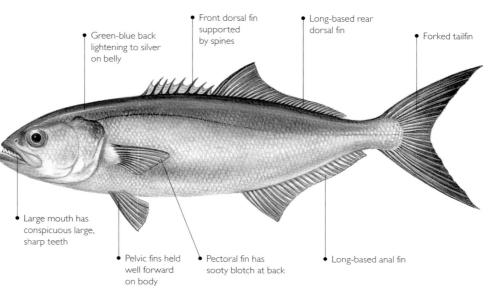

Green-blue back lightening to silver on belly

Front dorsal fin supported by spines

Long-based rear dorsal fin

Forked tailfin

Large mouth has conspicuous large, sharp teeth

Pelvic fins held well forward on body

Pectoral fin has sooty blotch at back

Long-based anal fin

BLUEFISH

Pomatomus salatrix

Adult bluefish are bluish-gray or greenish-gray above with white flanks and belly. Juveniles have bright silvery flanks. The body is long and slightly flat-sided, but nevertheless brawny, except at winter's end or immediately after spawning. The mouth is rigged with razor-sharp teeth, making this a fish to be handled only with the utmost care. Even after being subdued, a bluefish is capable of

The fly is removed from a bluefish caught from a New England beach.

clamping down its jaws in a vise-like grip, so you must also use a wire trace ahead of the fly. The head is fairly large, with the lower jaw jutting slightly beyond the upper. Bluefish have two dorsal fins: the one nearest the head is small and low, and contains strong spines; the second is softer, taller, and long, running nearly back to the tail. It is closely matched in size and shape by the anal fin. The tail is forked. The pectoral fin has a dark patch at the base. Bluefish slime has a strong odor.

Young bluefish, called "snappers", spend their first year feeding in shallow bays and estuaries. Bluefish have a life-span of about 12 years and can grow to more than 1m (3ft) in length and

9kg (20lb) in weight. They tolerate water temperatures ranging from 9–30°C (48–86 °F). Large adults often occupy cooler habitats, while smaller fish prefer warmer waters near the shore. Bluefish are known by many nicknames, including blues, tailors, choppers, slammers, and gators. Fish of 1–3kg (2–6lb) are referred to as harbor blues.

Distribution This is a subtropical species with somewhat local distribution, but is often abundant where it does occur: the eastern US coast south to the Florida Keys, around southern Africa, and off the eastern and western coasts of Australia. Small numbers occur also in the Mediterranean Sea and off the Atlantic coast of South America.

FOOD, FLIES, AND FISHING

Bluefish prefer schooling baitfish, especially oily ones such as menhaden. Streamer patterns are effective, as are sliders brought waking across the surface. In daylight, especially at dusk and dawn, poppers bring explosive strikes; bright flies with hot orange and chartreuse in the dressing will outfish dull ones, and moderate-to-fast retrieves are preferred over slow. At night, use a dark fly, but move it more slowly.

 Reading Estuaries and Tidal Creeks 116–17 · Reading Harbors and Jetties 118–19 · Tides 132–3

 Mollusks: Clams and Squid 100 · Saltwater Crabs 101 · Saltwater Shrimp and Prawns 102–3 · Saltwater Baitfish 106–7

 Cape Cod 160–1

BONEFISH

DICK BROWN

Bonefish live in shallow, warm seas — especially in the southwestern Atlantic and mid-oceanic atolls of the Pacific. They belong in the same league as tarpon and inhabit the same waters as permit, sharing heritage and habitat with two of the sport's other great inshore quarry. Their camouflaged, streamlined bodies and blazing speed make them perfect flats predators.

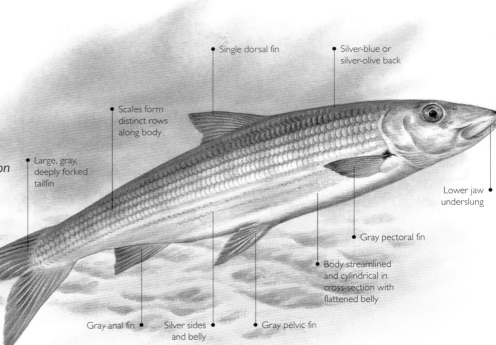

Single dorsal fin

Silver-blue or silver-olive back

Scales form distinct rows along body

Large, gray, deeply forked tailfin

Lower jaw underslung

Gray pectoral fin

Body streamlined and cylindrical in cross-section with flattened belly

Gray anal fin

Silver sides and belly

Gray pelvic fin

BONEFISH

Albula vulpes

Bonefish are members of the Elopiformes order, which also includes the ladyfish family and the tarpon family. Ichthyologists recognize three species of bonefish, but fly-fishers pursue only one of these, *Albula vulpes*, which inhabits warm shallow coastal waters worldwide.

Bonefish sport powerful, deeply forked tails that are often tinged with silver and sometimes edged in neon blue. Dorsal, pelvic, and anal fins share this coloration, with the neon azure cast appearing rarely on the tip of the pectorals. Eight greenish-blue bars cross the back like saddles, providing camouflage from above over grass and broken bottoms. Hundreds of small shiny scales cover the sides: a 52cm (21in) specimen caught in the Bahamas in 1984 had 987 of them. With a slightly bluish-silver cast, this skin of mirrors reflects the colors and patterns around the bonefish and makes them almost invisible.

The bonefish mouth is on the underside of the head, slightly behind a long, conical snout used to detect its bottom-dwelling prey. Rows of tiny teeth rim the inside and are angled toward the back. Large plates containing dozens of closely fitted round teeth line the rest of the mouth. These blunt, pearl-shaped molars form a ceramic-hard mosaic layer that crushes the shells of the mollusks and crustaceans.

Albula nemoptera, the longfin bonefish, lives in thin water near river outlets around high islands in the western Atlantic and eastern Pacific. A longer conical snout, a considerably smaller body, and a long last ray on both its dorsal and anal fins distinguish *A. nemoptera* from *A. vulpes*.

The third bonefish species, *Pterothrissus belloci*, resides in very deep waters where fly-fishers never encounter it.

Bonefish are not huge. Most run to 2kg (5lb), with trophy fish reaching over 4.5kg (10lb). The record (which came from Bimini, in the Bahamas) weighed 6.8kg (15lb). However, what they lack in size, they make up for with their tremendous power. The bonefish burst speed has been estimated by researchers at about 42kmph (26mph), which puts it about halfway between trout and sailfish, and much faster than most gamefish that are sought by fly-fishers. But while this clinical raw speed is impressive, what makes fly-fishers rank bonefish so highly as gamefish is that they will run at these speeds for several hundred feet in only 15cm (6in) of water!

Bonefish often feed in the shallow water of tropical saltwater flats, heads down and tails sticking out of the water. If the sun is strong, the tails give off reflective flashes. Sometimes you can hear their tails splash in the water during a feeding frenzy. This wariest of sea-hunters, constantly on the move and always hungry, has become one of the greatest fly-rod gamefish.

Bonefish are one of the few fish species that you must see before you can catch them. If you fish the water by casting at random as you wade or sail across a flat, then you will catch nothing. Similarly, if you fish at night for them, where do you cast your fly without scaring them? Whether you are wading the shallows or being poled in a boat, spotting fish requires care and experience. If you are inexperienced, seek the help of a guide.

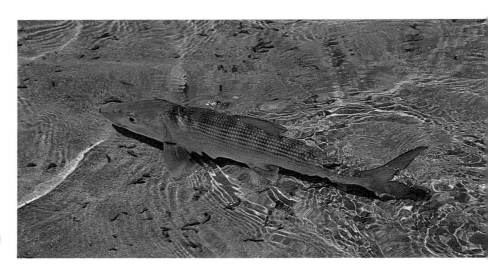

FOOD, FLIES, AND FISHING

Ravenous hunters, bonefish devour clams, shrimp, crabs, worms, urchins, and other bottom-dwellers. Larger fish favor crabs, toadfish, and mantis shrimps. Fast-sinking flies that mimic these bottom-dwelling prey are the best to use for catching bonefish in water of moderate depth, while lighter, slow-sinking patterns prove essential for stalking tailing fish in the shallowest flats. Bonefish tails, exposed and glistening out of the water, provide you with one of the easiest clues — and one of the most promising. When fish tail, they show you exactly where they are, and they tell you they are hungry. But tailing fish are also very wary and selective and this is the most nervous of all feeding conditions. Always cast the fly accurately and delicately.

Distribution Bonefish appear on the east coast of the Americas. They range in the north to the Bay of Fundy and in the south as far as Rio de Janeiro. They are also abundant in the central and south Pacific Ocean (e.g. Christmas Island and Hawaii) and in addition inhabit the Indian Ocean, and the waters off Africa.

Reading Flats 122–3 •
Tides 132–3

Mollusks: Clams and Squid 100 •
Saltwater Crabs 101 •
Saltwater Shrimp and Prawns 102–3

The Bahamas 162–3 • The Florida Keys 164–5 •
Yucatan and Belize 166–7

After a careful approach, a bonefish has been spotted (right). Check there is enough fly-line off the reel. Quickly work out where the fly must hit the water. Now cast…Any moment now!

The shadowy bonefish (left) must be spotted before you can cast to it.

TARPON

CAPTAIN BEN TAYLOR

*The tarpon, often referred to as the
"silver king", is among the most powerful
of inshore fish. Its scientific name means
"the big eye of the Atlantic." To subdue
a giant tarpon on a fly-rod is considered
by many to be one of the pinnacles
of fly-fishing achievement.*

TARPON

Megalops atlanticus

The tarpon is one of the oldest fish
on Earth. Its ancestors date back
some 125 million years, and it
is little removed today from
its ancestral roots, having
retained some prehistoric
characteristics that account for
its survival. It has a primitive lung – really
little more than an air sac – that enables the
fish to obtain oxygen from the air in difficult
environments, or during periods of extended
physical exertion. The lung allows fry and juvenile
fish to escape predation in waters that are
inhospitable for their natural enemies.
Throughout their lives tarpon frequently roll for
air while traveling or resting, revealing themselves
to fly-fishers as they do so.

The last ray of a tarpon's dorsal fin is
extended, resembling a whip. Characteristic
silver sides are a distinct contrast to the color
of the upper body, which ranges from dark blue
to almost black or olive-green. Fish that inhabit
mainly dirty water have tan or golden backs
and light cream flanks. These resident fish are
often lazy fighters but aggressive feeders.

The only marked difference between males
and females is size. Few males exceed 45kg
(100lb). During periods leading to the spawn, the
vent will provide a milt or an egg trace when fish
are captured, but there are no obvious coloration
or body profile differences between the sexes.

Tarpon have huge scales and might be
considered armored. Fish over 45kg (100lb) are
protected by layers of almost palm-sized scales.
However, the scales do not protect the fish from
the large sharks that follow their migrations.

Tarpon are laterally compressed fish, relatively
narrow from side to side, but large fish attain
a noteworthy girth, sometimes exceeding 1.3m
(4ft). The world record, for a fish caught in

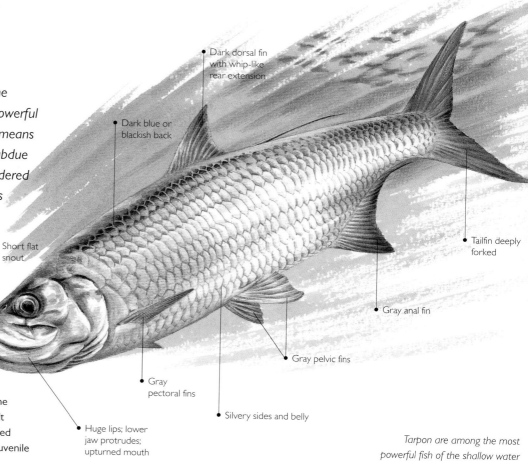

Dark dorsal fin
with whip-like
rear extension

Dark blue or
blackish back

Short flat
snout

Huge lips; lower
jaw protrudes;
upturned mouth

Gray
pectoral fins

Silvery sides and belly

Gray pelvic fins

Gray anal fin

Tailfin deeply
forked

*Tarpon are among the most
powerful fish of the shallow water
flats. The water erupts as the fish
rolls on the surface, revealing its
powerful jaws and sturdy body.*

Venezuela, is 129kg (283lb). Tarpon are known
to grow to over 160kg (350lb) and have a
potential 55-year life-span.

You will often find schools of very small fish
living around mangroves and in slow shallow
estuaries. These "baby tarpon" take the fly well:
at three years of age they average about 65cm
(26in) in length.

Fortunately, throughout most of their range
tarpon are not considered a worthwhile food
species. They would be easily harvested, because
large migrating schools often stall in shallow basins
providing comfortable water temperatures and
abundant forage. Their economic value as a sport
fish in many regions ensures that fly-fishers
release them, unless they are of record size.

Tarpon are born far offshore and float to the
coast on ocean currents. They make their way
to brackish and even stagnant freshwater, where
they live for several years before returning to sea.
Juveniles often reside all year in estuaries and
rivers in the warmer portions of their range.
Mature adults, fish that are over 1.2m (4ft) long
and about seven years of age, are typically

migratory, seeking water temperatures of
75–90°F (24–32°C). Smaller fish are far more
tolerant of temperature variations.

Tarpon are lazy fish, and, while migrating, like
to be pushed by moving water. They may swim
in as little as 50cm (20in), and if the current flows
strongly they will allow it to push them before it.
In the best regions for fly-fishing, migrating fish
often use less than 3m (10ft) of water, but are
found lounging around wrecks or traveling at the
surface in 30m (100ft) or greater depths of water.

You will find huge tarpon in other coastal
habitats besides the flats. Estuaries, such as that
of Costa Rica's Rio Colorada, can be full of
tarpon; but here, in the murky water, you cannot
spot the fish and cast directly to them. Instead you
must search the water with your fly. You will
know when your fly has found a fish!

If you are in the Florida Keys between June
and September, take a look and listen at night
under the bridges when the tide is ebbing.
You may hear tarpon – not huge ones – churning
up the water as they feed. Cast a fly to them –
even a small tarpon seems huge in the darkness!

FOOD, FLIES, AND FISHING

Tarpon eat lesser fish and shellfish, and flies that imitate baitfish are ideal. Because a school of big tarpon need large quantities of food, the fish must migrate in search of new supplies.

Migrating fish are of greatest interest to fly-fishers, for they often travel close enough to the surface. This allows for the use of floating fly-lines. Resting fish or fish content with an abundance of food may reside in discolored water and hug the bottom. Here you must use a sinking line. Much coastal fishing is done in deeper channels or rivers, demanding the use not only of a sinking line but of a bushy fly of dust mop proportions. In clearer shallows, the fish prefer a smaller pattern if there is a lot of fishing pressure.

Fly-fishers face formidable problems setting hooks in a tarpon's jaw. A tarpon's mouth is shaped much like the cargo door of a transport airplane. The lower jaw hinges to meet the upper lip. You must allow the fish to turn away with the fly in order to put some portion of its maw between fly-fisher and hook point. The mouth is

huge and the fly must be well inside the mouth before you set the hook. But even when you have waited before striking, and felt the fish's weight through rod and line, you have another problem. Much of the tarpon's mouth is hardened, so the fish might grind shellfish or squash the bones, fins, and spines of a baitfish. And most hooks will not penetrate this armor. You must use a very sharp and strong hook, good timing, and firm strike if you hope to hold on for more than a jump or two. More tarpon are lost because the hook never went in than are lost for all other reasons combined.

Finally, the tarpon's rough, hard mouth can quickly grind through a fine fly tippet too, so to land a tarpon you will have to master the use of shock leaders.

While never a routine catch, tarpon respond well to flies. If you have not fished for tarpon before, seek a competent guide in the prime South Florida and Central America fisheries, and you can expect to hook fish. However, landing the fish will be largely up to you and your skill.

Distribution Tarpon occur in subtropical and tropical waters on both sides of the Atlantic. The best fly-fishing is in estuaries and rivers and along shorelines, from Florida through the Gulf of Mexico, along Central America and South America to Venezuela.

Reading Estuaries and Tidal Creeks 116–17 • Reading Harbors and Jetties 118–19 • Reading Flats 122–3

Saltwater Baitfish 106–7

The Bahamas 162–3 • The Florida Keys 164–5 • Yucatan and Belize 166–7

PERMIT

LEFTY KREH

For years it was thought that permit couldn't be caught on a fly. True, in the 1960s a few were caught: Joe Brooks caught one in the Bahamas. I cast to every permit I could find and only one took my fly. Most experienced saltwater fly-fishers of the time believed that there was no logical way to catch permit. Now we know better, but the permit remains one of the most difficult fish to catch on a fly – and catching your first will provide you with a memory to cherish.

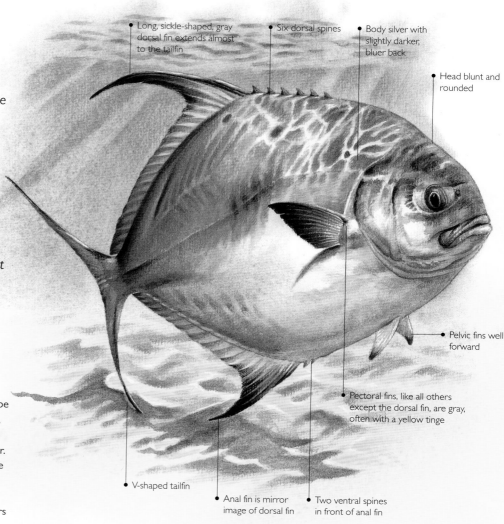

Long, sickle-shaped, gray dorsal fin extends almost to the tailfin

Six dorsal spines

Body silver with slightly darker, bluer back

Head blunt and rounded

Pelvic fins well forward

Pectoral fins, like all others except the dorsal fin, are gray, often with a yellow tinge

V-shaped tailfin

Anal fin is mirror image of dorsal fin

Two ventral spines in front of anal fin

PERMIT

Trachinotus falcatus

If you lift a permit from the water it appears to be an almost round, silvery fish. It has a blunt head, and the long, sickle-shaped dorsal, anal, and tailfins that are indicative of a powerful swimmer. There are six dorsal spines set just in front of the dorsal fin. The silvery sides and slightly darker bluish back and fin edges provide a camouflage that makes it difficult for inexperienced fly-fishers to spot swimming permit – even large ones. This is because the silver sides reflect the background over which the fish are swimming: white over white sand, dark blue-green over turtle grass, and so on.

What you will see, if you look carefully at a permit swimming through shallow water, is a slightly darker line or Y-shape on the water, caused by the dorsal and tailfin edges. Permit have a wobbling, or back and forth swimming motion, much like that of a shark. In fact, on several occasions I thought a small shark was approaching, only realizing too late it was a permit!

Permit prefer water depths from 60–150cm (24–60in) on the flats and temperatures from 20–26.5°C (68–80°F). These conditions also offer the best fly-fishing. Permit will often follow underwater ridges on the flats, trying to trap bait and crabs against the wall of a ridge. They also like to "lay up," or suspend just below the surface on calm days in white sand depressions on the flats.

Permit tend to travel in the same direction when feeding on the flats. If you see one moving along a certain path, most others will probably be too. Catching permit is never a sure thing, but the techniques and fly patterns used now mean that most people who employ a good guide and have some perseverance can catch a permit on fly. Del Brown has caught more permit (more than 300) on a fly than the total catch of almost any other six fly-fishers – proof that if you do things correctly, you can score consistently.

Most permit run to about 9kg (20lb), with trophy fish around 14kg (30lb); exceptional specimens reach around 27kg (60lb).

A beautiful silvery specimen permit with the artificial crab that deceived it still in its mouth. Catching such a fish is a pinnacle of fly-fishing achievement.

Distribution Most permit fly-fishers agree that the best place to catch a permit is on the flats around the Florida Keys. The Central American flats, particularly the Yucatan Peninsula and some areas in Belize and Venezuela, hold many schools of smaller permit. There are also large permit, but not in the numbers found near Key West. Many World War II wrecks in the Gulf of Mexico also hold large numbers of permit. Small numbers occur around northern Australia, Papua New Guinea, and some Pacific islands.

FOOD, FLIES, AND FISHING

Permit love to eat crabs, and the introduction of crab flies has been one part of the development of successful fly-fishing for permit. Good crab flies are weighted on one end, so that they tilt to one side when they strike the surface and dive quickly, imitating a crab that appears to be fleeing from a permit.

For smaller permit, use a size 2 or 1/0 hook, but on larger permit, a 2/0 is recommended. The technique devised by Del Brown and Captain Steve Huff is the one that you must try. This, with the development of crab flies, made permit catchable. You sight a permit while poling the flats and throw the weighted crab pattern as close as possible to the fish. Many will spook, but don't worry. Allow the fly to sink quickly to the bottom and don't move it – moving the fly drastically will reduce your chances. Let the fly sink, and then leave it alone when a big permit is close by. If the permit swims away, make another cast, repeating the process described above.

The best tackle for larger permit is a 9- or 10-weight fly rod and line. The reel should have a good, smooth drag and hold at least 180m (600ft) of 13.5kg (30lb) test backing.

A school of permit in deeper water. When these fish move over a flat to feed they usually travel along the bottom, in a looser school.

 Reading Flats 122–3 •
Tides 132–3

 Mollusks: Clams and Squid 100 •
Saltwater Crabs 101 •
Saltwater Shrimp and Prawns 102–3

 The Bahamas 162–3 •
The Florida Keys 164–5 •
Yucatan and Belize 166–7

BARRACUDA

JOHN A KUMISKI

One of the finest and most fearless fly-fishers' fish of the tropical reef and lagoon, barracuda provide wonderful sport on light tackle. As they are played to the boat, their fast surface runs and high leaps get your adrenaline going; once in the boat their teeth are awesome.

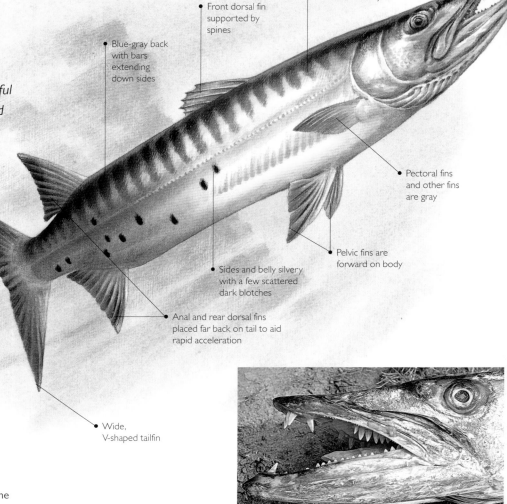

- Slender and streamlined body
- Front dorsal fin supported by spines
- Blue-gray back with bars extending down sides
- Pectoral fins and other fins are gray
- Pelvic fins are forward on body
- Sides and belly silvery with a few scattered dark blotches
- Anal and rear dorsal fins placed far back on tail to aid rapid acceleration
- Wide, V-shaped tailfin

BARRACUDA

Sphyraena barracuda
Although several species of barracuda occur worldwide, the great barracuda is the fish of most interest to the fly-fisher. This species reaches lengths of nearly 2m (6ft). In appearance, it somewhat resembles the pike, having a long, slender body, a wide V-shaped tail, pointed head, and a large mouth armed with powerful jaws and razor-sharp teeth. Silvery sides blend into a darker back and a white belly, and there are usually vertical gray or black blotches running down the sides.

Barracuda are sexually mature at around two years, at a length of about 60cm (2ft). Some individuals may live for a long time. Scale analysis of specimens over 1.2m (4ft) in length reveals that mature specimens are probably at least 14 years old. The current IGFA all-tackle world record for great barracuda weighed 35.55kg (78lb) and was taken at Christmas Island in April 1992. All the IGFA fly-rod, tippet-class world records except one were caught in the Florida Keys. The largest fly-rod record barracuda caught – the 6kg (13lb) tippet class – weighed 17.12kg (37½lb).

Barracuda may be found on shallow flats, along mangrove shores, around markers, over wrecks, under floating debris, near reefs, or near any structure. They make superb fly-rod targets.

Barracuda eat other fish almost exclusively. If barracuda lack popularity with many saltwater fly-fishers it is not because of their lack of fighting ability, but because of their habit of attacking hooked fish that are being played.

Do barracuda pose any danger to the fly-fisher? Documented cases of unprovoked barracuda attacks on humans are extremely rare.

However, like many other fish that leap when hooked, barracuda don't watch where they are going and occasionally land in boats. Fishermen have suffered serious cuts by leaping barracuda.

When handling barracuda to remove the hook, care must be used around the head of the creature. Even small barracuda have enough teeth to inflict a nasty cut. Big ones routinely chop through fish such as bonito and mackerel. Imagine what they could do to your fingers.

Finally, caution must be used when reviving fish of any type where barracuda are present. Biologist Jim Whittington of the Florida Department of Natural Resources was reviving a snook he had tagged when a large barracuda flashed up and removed the mid-section from the fish. A badly shaken Whittington held the snook's head in one hand and the tail in the other. The barracuda had the middle portion. Fortunately, Whittington still had all his fingers.

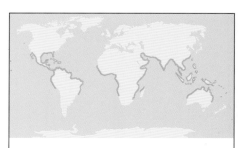

The barracuda's head is pointed and the lobe on the lower jaw is an extra streamlining feature. The mouth has flat, razor-sharp teeth.

Distribution Barracuda are found in all the world's tropical oceans except parts of the western Pacific and Indian Oceans. Although smaller specimens school, the larger fish live alone. Barracuda prefer water temperatures of 23–28°C (74–82°F).

FOOD, FLIES, AND FISHING

After being hooked barracuda make lightning runs and often spectacular leaps that may end 10m (30ft or more) from where they left the water. They lack stamina, however, so fairly light tackle – a standard 7- or 8-weight – is all that's needed. The "standard" barracuda fly is a needlefish imitation, most often tied on a 1/0 hook, from 15–30cm (6–12in) in length. Bright colors such as fluorescent pink, orange, or chartreuse seem to work best. A 15cm (6in) length of single strand wire trace must be attached to the hook eye with a haywire twist to keep the barracuda's teeth from severing the leader. Other types of flies work sometimes, too. Although streamer flies are most popular, a popping bug will garner savage and spectacular surface strikes. Because of the barracuda's teeth, you only catch one fish per fly. Various techniques are used to take barracuda. On the flats, or when lying close to a structure such as a piece of reef or wreck, they present quite a challenge. The standard procedure is to spot your target from as great a distance as possible, make a long, accurate cast beyond and in front of the fish, and rapidly strip the fly past the fish so that it sees the fly. If all goes according to plan, the fish is suddenly on the end of your line. They move astonishingly fast! More frequently though, the fish will follow the fly without taking until it sees you, at which point it turns off. More often than not if it doesn't strike on the first cast it won't strike at all. Another technique involves casting the fly in front of the fish and immediately pulling it out of the water, then making another cast to the same spot. Do this four or five times, then make a normal cast and high-speed retrieve. The idea here is to aggravate the barracuda into striking.

A school of barracuda: note the pointed snout, the large eye, and the ventral barring that camouflages the fish deep in the waters of the ocean.

SNOOK

RUSTY CHINNIS

Snook are one of the great tropical saltwater fly-fishers' fish. They grow big but live close to the shore. They take the fly well, but you need a careful approach and good cast to hook one. And when hooked they fight hard — very hard!

Snook form a group of fish in the genus *Centropomus*, of which the common snook is the most wide ranging and makes up the majority of the recreational catch. Other species are of less importance to the fly-fisher, but are caught occasionally. They include the sword-spine snook, *C. ensiferus*, the smallest species reaching only 30cm (12in) in length; the tarpon snook, *C. pectinatus*, so-called because of the upturned jaw that resembles that of a tarpon; and the fat snook, *C. parallelus*, the second-largest snook, reaching approximately 45cm (18in), which, in Florida, is found in the Lake Okeechobee drainage southward through the Keys.

COMMON SNOOK

Centropomus undecimalis

This is a long-bodied fish, and the females often become thick around the mid-section as they mature. Colors vary, but the back is generally brown or olive-green, graduating to silver on the lower sides and belly. The pectoral and pelvic fins, as well as the dorsal lobe of the tail, have a yellow cast. The head accounts for approximately one-third of its length and features a long, concave snout. The most distinctive feature is a pronounced black lateral line running from just behind the gill plate to the tip of the tail. Snook mature at around three years and 1.4–1.8kg (3–4lb). The all-tackle record is 24.27kg (53lb 10 oz). The largest snook taken on a fly weighed 13.7kg (30lb 4oz) and was landed on a 9kg (20lb) class tippet by Rex Garrett at Chokoloskee Island, Florida in 1993.

 Reading Estuaries and Tidal Creeks 116–17 • Reading Flats 122–3

 Saltwater Baitfish 106–7

 The Florida Keys 164–5

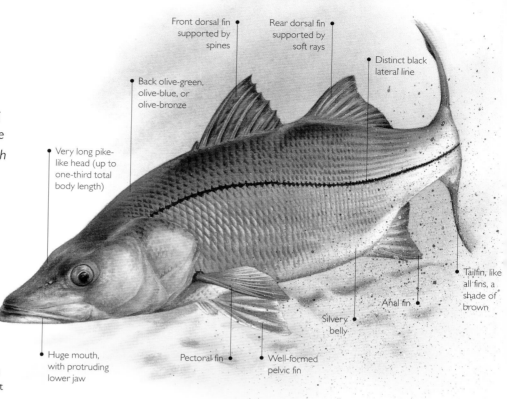

Front dorsal fin supported by spines

Rear dorsal fin supported by soft rays

Distinct black lateral line

Back olive-green, olive-blue, or olive-bronze

Very long pike-like head (up to one-third total body length)

Tailfin, like all fins, a shade of brown

Anal fin

Silvery belly

Huge mouth, with protruding lower jaw

Pectoral fin

Well-formed pelvic fin

FOOD, FLIES, AND FISHING

Snook are carnivores, with a diet that consists mainly of small fish. They also feed on crustaceans such as shrimp and crabs. Snook will hit a variety of flies, from small minnow imitations to larger, heavily dressed baitfish patterns. Yellow, yellow and red, red and white, and chartreuse and white are favorite colors. Popular snook patterns include Lefty's Deceiver, Blanton's Sar-Mul-Mac, Hansen's Glass Minnow, and Clouser's Deep Minnow.

Deer hair creations tied as poppers, divers, and sliders are also widely used and can be very effective at times. Yellow, and combinations with yellow, are time-tested favorites. When casting poppers allow the fly to sit still for several seconds after hitting the water, and then alternately pop the fly and let it sit still until the rings it creates disappear.

The most important consideration when rigging for snook is a shock tippet that can withstand their rasp-like mouths. Generally, 13.6kg (30lb) test monofilament leader will suffice. A number 7–9 weight outfit can be used, depending on where you are fishing. Snook are intelligent and must be approached with appropriate caution. To be effective, casts must often extend to 18m (60ft) and beyond, especially on shallow flats.

Distribution Snook are native to the coastal waters of the tropical and subtropical western Atlantic Ocean. Large populations extend from the central coasts of Florida to southeastern Brazil, and inhabit inshore waters in the Caribbean Sea. On the Pacific Coast a related species, the black snook, ranges from the Gulf of California to northern Peru. The areas of highest abundance are in southern Florida, south of a line from Tampa Bay on the west coast to Cape Canaveral on the east coast. Snook are highly tolerant of varying salinity levels, but are very sensitive to changes in water temperature, which limit their distribution. At temperatures at or near 16°C (60°F) snook become sluggish; if the sea temperature falls to 10°C (50°F) they die.

This is a lovely snook that is almost ready for release. Notice how huge the mouth is when it is held open.

JACKS AND TREVALLIES

PHILL WILLIAMS

The jacks and trevallies comprise a highly predatory and very wide-ranging family of fish. And, because they take artificial flies well and scrap hard, they include some of the world's best-known and most sought-after gamefish. All three species are confined to tropical and subtropical oceans within a preferred water temperature of 20–30°C (68–86°F).

CREVALLE JACK

Caranx hippos

This is a powerful fish. Its upper body is gray-blue, becoming paler on the flanks and silvery beneath. Distinguishing marks include a black spot on both the gill cover and the base of the pectoral fin, and scales on an area in front of the ventral fins (the remainder of the body is scaleless). It grows to a maximum of around 32kg (70lb).

   Distribution The crevalle jack is an Atlantic species, with similar species occurring in the Pacific and Indian Oceans.

GIANT TREVALLY

Caranx ignobilis

A blunt-headed, rather stocky, powerful-looking fish. The upper body is usually dark greenish-gray, giving way to silver below. It lacks distinguishing dark spots on the fins and gill cover. However, like the crevalle jack it has a patch of scales in front of the ventral fins on its otherwise scaleless body. Its maximum weight is around 91kg (200lb).

   Distribution The giant trevally occurs in the Indo-Pacific and has a fairly widespread distribution. The largest concentrations are around Hawaii, northern Australia, parts of southeast Asia, and particularly off Kenya.

THREADFIN TREVALLY

Alectis ciliaris

The threadfin trevally has a deep, even angular body profile but retains the lateral body flattening common to the family. The upper body is usually bluish-green, becoming silvery below. Juveniles may have darker, wavy vertical bands on their flanks. The first four to six rays of the single dorsal and anal fins are long and threadlike, and can be particularly noticeable in juvenile fish. Adult fish reach a maximum weight of around 27kg (60lb).

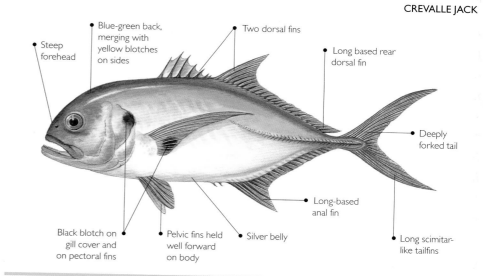

CREVALLE JACK

- Steep forehead
- Blue-green back, merging with yellow blotches on sides
- Two dorsal fins
- Long based rear dorsal fin
- Deeply forked tail
- Long-based anal fin
- Long scimitar-like tailfins
- Silver belly
- Pelvic fins held well forward on body
- Black blotch on gill cover and on pectoral fins

GIANT TREVALLY

- Steep forehead
- Back very dark greenish-gray
- Small, spiny front dorsal fin
- Long-based rear dorsal fin
- Distinct keel along tail
- Scimitar-shaped tail
- Long-based anal fin
- Long, pointed pectoral fin
- Long, pointed pectoral fin
- Lower body silvery; body lacks spots
- Pelvic fin well formed; all fins gray
- Blunt snout

   Distribution The threadfin trevally (also known as the African pompano) is one of the most widely distributed jacks. It occurs throughout the world's tropical and subtropical seas, where its usual habitat is deep-lying rocky and reefy terrain.

 Reading Harbors and Jetties 118–19 •
Reading Beaches and Bays 120–1 •
Reading the Open Sea 124–5

 Mollusks: Clams and Squid 100 •
Saltwater Crabs 101 •
Saltwater Baitfish 106–7

 Yucatan and Belize 166–7

FOOD, FLIES, AND FISHING

These three species feed mainly on baitfish, so flies imitating baitfish are most effective. It is vital that you use sound tackle, because when these fish are hooked they invariably head for obstructions in which the line will snag and break. Therefore in shallow water, where the fish may be in the evening or after dark, use a powerful rod (number 12 weight outfit). All three species may feed to great depth in deeper water, and here you may have to chum to bring them within casting range. Once hooked at the surface, they will run fast and deep.

BARRAMUNDI

ROD HARRISON

Although not an enormous fish, the barramundi is a spectacular one, hitting the fly with a violent smash and then plowing through the waves with heart-stopping leaps. It also has an unusual Australasian distribution; to catch one most fly-fishers must travel a long way.

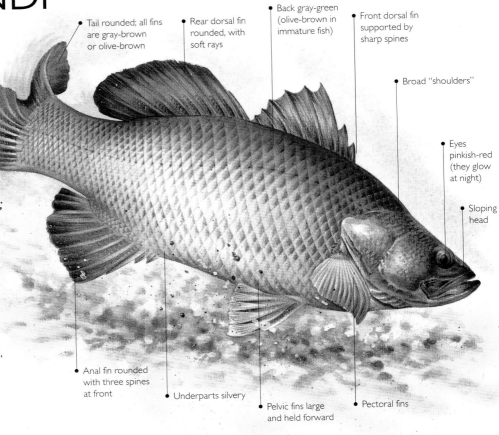

Tail rounded; all fins are gray-brown or olive-brown

Rear dorsal fin rounded, with soft rays

Back gray-green (olive-brown in immature fish)

Front dorsal fin supported by sharp spines

Broad "shoulders"

Eyes pinkish-red (they glow at night)

Sloping head

Anal fin rounded with three spines at front

Underparts silvery

Pelvic fins large and held forward

Pectoral fins

BARRAMUNDI

Lates calcifer

The barramundi has a noticeably steep-sloping head and broad "shoulders" just in front of the first of two separate dorsal fins. The rear dorsal, anal, and tailfins are rounded. The back is gray-green with a hint of bronze. The lower body is silver when the fish is in saltwater, but when it enters brackish lagoons and river mouths the color becomes browner.

Barramundi is an Australian aboriginal word meaning "fish with big scales." Scales on a mature fish can be over 5cm (2in) in diameter and glisten with metallic tones – silver on fish that have been in saltwater and gilded on freshwater residents. The eyes are a conspicuous pinkish-red.

All barramundi are born as males, and as sexual maturity is reached, at around three years of age and at a weight of 6kg (13lb 4oz), part of the stock becomes female. The barramundi is fast growing, but never becomes large. A trophy barramundi is 23kg (50lb).

The barramundi is primarily a fish-eater and, while always an opportunist, it does have specific feeding times. In freshwater, peak periods occur after dark, while in tidal zones the hour either side of low water is prime feeding time.

During feeding periods schools of barramundi will herd baitfish in open water, especially waters around creek junctions. When good conditions for observations occur in tidal waters, barramundi can be observed cruising among the mangrove fringes. This calls for some creative casts, and as long as the fly-fisher has the element of surprise, the presentation is met with an explosive response. Resting barramundi are cover-oriented and have an affinity for snags and rockbars.

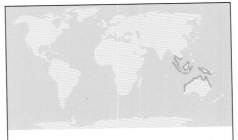

Distribution The barramundi is distributed throughout the Indo-Pacific region, from the eastern coast of Australia, westward through Indonesia and Thailand to the Bay of Bengal. The fish inhabits the coastal saltwater zone as well as freshwater.

Spawning takes place in tidal waters around the start of the Southeast-Asian monsoon season (December). The newly hatched barramundi then begin an upstream journey, moving in some instances several hundred miles inland. Taking up residence in rivers, creeks, and swamps, they remain in those waters – some of which become isolated in the dry seasons – until they reach maturity. When wet season rains raise river levels the barramundi then move downstream to spawn.

FOOD, FLIES, AND FISHING

Feeding barramundi tend to give themselves away by an audible "chop" when taking baitfish. This is not the barramundi chopping food, it is the noise their jaws make as they ingest the baitfish whole. Alert fly-fishers can capitalize on this by casting to the sound.

A wide array of streamer type flies will take barramundi. Best results come from subsurface fishing with weight patterns such as the Pink Thing, Ed Givens' Barred and Black, and Clouser's Minnow. However, don't neglect surface presentation. It is a memorable experience when barramundi detonate on a noisemaker deer-hair bug such as the Dahlberg.

 Reading Harbors and Jetties 118–19 • Reading Beaches and Bays 120–1 • Reading the Open Sea 124–5

 Mollusks: Clams and Squid 100 • Saltwater Crabs 101 • Saltwater Shrimp and Prawns 102–3 • Saltwater Baitfish 106–7

COBIA

TOM EARNHARDT

The cobia is a hard, rugged fish that takes a fly readily and, when hooked, fights hard close to the surface. Fly-fishers have developed a special love for this great fish — one of the most exciting that can be caught on fly-rod and line.

COBIA

Rachycentron canadum

The cobia is a powerful fish with an elongated and streamlined body that is round in cross-section. The large head is flattened; the large mouth lacks teeth but is rough and leathery. Be careful when handling a cobia. It may be toothless, but it has crushers in its throat that will mangle your fingers if you are foolish enough to put them there.

The long anal fin extends from the vent almost to the tailfin. The dorsal fin is even longer, extending over half the body length. In front of the dorsal fin are eight to nine dorsal spines that can fold back into a groove. The back and fins are a dark, almost blackish-brown, the sides a paler silvery-gray with dark brown bands running the length of the body. The belly is white with a patch of orange between anal and pelvic fins.

The cobia attains an average weight of 16kg (35lb) at the age of four to five years but it can grow to more than 45kg (100lb). Most of the cobia caught on fly will average 9–18kg (20–40lb).

Cobia are often found feeding around buoys, pilings, offshore oil rigs, wrecks, floating debris, and artificial or natural reefs. They will often move around structures in a counter-clockwise direction as they search for prey, so position yourself accordingly. Make sure that your cast will allow you to retrieve the fly in front of the cobia as it follows its counter-clockwise route. Keep your eyes open for large turtles and rays, as cobia often swim close behind them.

In spring and early summer cobia often come inshore to shallow bays and inlets where they gorge on crabs. Spot one feeding, cast out your Merkin Crab, and hold on.

Fishing tackle has been smashed and fly-fishers injured by a cobia flailing about in a boat. Always land cobia in a large landing net. They are then usually very docile and can be released easily, without injury either to them or to you.

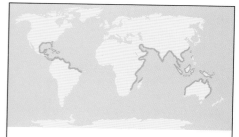

Large, powerful tailfin

Body round in cross-section

Long-based brown dorsal fin

Short bony spines in front of dorsal fin

Dark brown back

Flat head

Long-based anal fin

Side silvery with dark brown bands

Orange patch on belly

Brown pectoral and pelvic fins close together

Mouth toothless but leathery; protruding lower jaw

Superficially, a cobia that is swimming up to the surface might well be mistaken for a small shark.

FOOD, FLIES, AND FISHING

Cobia eat shrimp, crabs, and lesser fish including eels and menhaden, which they take in their mouth and then crush with their "crushers" before swallowing them. Streamers and Lefty's Deceivers in sizes 2/0–4/0 and in a variety of colors are most often used, although cobia will also take large popping bugs and hair-bodied flies such as the Dahlberg Diver. The Merkin Crab is also becoming popular: tied onto a size 2/0 hook, it is a deadly cobia fly in any water.

Distribution Cobia are found on the east coast of the Americas from Maryland south through Florida and Texas, Mexico, and Belize, as far south as Brazil. On the west coast they are found only off the shores of Central America. Elsewhere cobia occur around many islands in the Pacific and Indian Oceans, around Papua New Guinea, and off northern Australia and parts of East Africa.

 Reading Harbors and Jetties 118–19 • Reading Beaches and Bays 120–1 • Reading the Open Sea 124–5

 Mollusks: Clams and Squid 100 • Saltwater Crabs 101 • Saltwater Shrimp and Prawns 102–3 • Saltwater Baitfish 106–7

 Yucatan and Belize 166–7

ROOSTERFISH

NICK CURCIONE

The ultimate prize, at least for the inshore Pacific fishery, is the roosterfish. When hooked it makes line-blistering runs and ranks as one of the strongest-pulling fish in the ocean. Aside from their appearance and tremendous fighting ability, the one quality that makes roosters such a prize catch is the fact that they are not easily enticed with artificial flies.

ROOSTERFISH

Nematistius pectoralis
Roosters are graced with a series of dark bluish-black bands that run diagonally along their sides from the gill plate to the prominently forked tail. Their most distinguishing feature, however, is the seven long flexible spines protruding from the first dorsal fin. When the fish is aroused the spines are erected. It is quite an adrenaline-pumping experience to see these projections suddenly spring from the surface of the water when a rooster starts tracking your fly.

Juvenile roosterfish run in the 1.3–2.2kg (3–5lb) class; "big moes" can top the 38kg (70lb) mark.

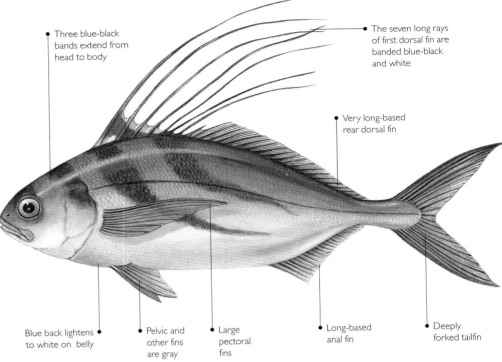

Three blue-black bands extend from head to body

The seven long rays of first dorsal fin are banded blue-black and white

Very long-based rear dorsal fin

Blue back lightens to white on belly

Pelvic and other fins are gray

Large pectoral fins

Long-based anal fin

Deeply forked tailfin

Distribution The roosterfish is limited primarily to the tropical seas of the eastern Pacific. Some of the most abundant populations are along the East Cape region of Baja and the Bat Islands off Costa Rica's north Pacific coast.

FOOD, FLIES, AND FISHING

Roosterfish are often found feeding in quite shallow water, chasing small baitfish just beyond the surf. They can be caught by casting directly to them: look for surface commotion caused by roosters tearing into pods of terrified baitfish. Roosters tend to be extremely wary and the slightest unnatural intrusion will spook them, so approach as unobtrusively as possible.

Baitfish imitations matching what the roosterfish are taking are ideal; if the roosters are breaking the surface and fly erupting in front of them, try a big popper. If you cannot see the fish feeding you may have to tease it to the boat by trailing a baitfish (hookless) where you think the roosters are lying. When it takes the bait, remove the bait quickly while the fly is cast straight in front of its nose.

All roosterfish have the characteristically striped body and the long, separate dorsal fin rays. If you want to take up one of fly-fishing's greatest challenges, try for a roosterfish.

REDFISH

TOM EARNHARDT

Because of their size and power, and their willingness to take a fly in water that is often only 30cm (12in) in depth, the redfish has become one of the most popular quarry species for saltwater fly-fishers on the east coast of North America.

Large black "eye" spot (may be two of these)

Long-based rear dorsal fin supported by soft rays

Front dorsal fin supported by spines

Broad tailfin

Short-based anal fin

Overall coloration gray-silver overlaid with copper or red

Pelvic and pectoral fins close together

Mouth is underslung

REDFISH

Sciaenops ocellatus

The redfish, which is also known as red drum and channel bass, has a long, sturdy body with broad "shoulders", a blunt snout, and a large, slightly underslung mouth where the upper jaw extends slightly beyond the lower one. The dorsal fin is double, the front portion having 9–10 sharp spines, and the rear portion consisting only of soft

The drab colors on the body camouflage the redfish – but note how the orange fins stand out.

rays. The overall coloration is of a red or copper hue masking a gray-silver background.

At the base of the tailfin there is a large black spot, and sometimes a second spot or, more rarely, there may be a series of black spots. These marks, which from a distance resemble eyes, will cause fish-eating birds of prey such as ospreys to attack the wrong end of the redfish, thereby facilitating the fish's escape.

By their third year most redfish average 60cm (24in) in length. They continue to grow rapidly before reaching maturity at weights of 4.5–7kg (10–15lb). Immature fish form the bulk of shallow

water catches. Larger adult redfish, scaling up to the 14kg (30lb) mark, but growing on to over 18kg (40lb), are mainly encountered in spring when they come inshore to shallow water.

Distribution Redfish occur along the east coast of North America, from the Gulf of Maine south as far as the Gulf of Mexico. Hot-spots are the waters around the barrier islands of South Carolina and Georgia, the Indian River area of Florida, and the flats along the Texas coast. The largest redfish – with bait-caught fish recorded to more than 41kg (90lb) – are found around the Outer Banks of North Carolina and in the waters of Virginia.

FOOD, FLIES, AND FISHING

Redfish eat crabs, shrimp, and small baitfish, with larger specimens taking bigger fish such as menhaden, mullet, and even flounder. Imitations include the Clouser's Minnow, Merkin Crab, Dahlberg Diver, and Cave's Wobbler. Redfish are also particularly susceptible to white flies with red or orange in the dressing. Flies should be fished on number 8–9 weight outfits in shallow water or, in the deeper waters of Virginia and North Carolina where redfish run big, a number 10–11 weight outfit. The most exciting fishing is in very shallow water, often less than 30cm (12in) deep.

 Reading Harbors and Jetties 118–19 •
Reading Beaches and Bays 120–1 •
Reading the Open Sea 124–5

 Mollusks: Clams and Squid 100 •
Saltwater Crabs 101 • Saltwater Shrimp and
Prawns 102–3 • Saltwater Baitfish 106–7

 The Florida Keys 164–5

MULLET
MALCOLM GREENHALGH

There are many species of mullet, and at least one can be found anywhere in the world in temperate or tropical inshore waters. They were once largely ignored by fly-fishers, who dismissed them as baitfish. Yet most species do grow to 2kg (4lb) or more. They will take a fly – although a different sort to most saltwater gamefish. And when hooked they are powerfully fast: so much so that today their reputation as fly-fishers' fish is rapidly growing.

GRAY MULLET (THICK-LIPPED)
Liza labrosus

This is one of the most common mullet species. Others can be separated from it by scaling, lip formation, tooth structure, and fin arrangement. For example, another very common species, the thin-lipped mullet (*L. ramada*), has a thinner upper lip, finer teeth, and shorter pectoral fins.

All mullet have a streamlined, torpedo-shaped body covered with large scales. There are two well-separated dorsal fins, the front one with four spines. The body is silvery-gray, sometimes with a buffish cast, the back is a darker blue-gray, the sides are silvery, and the belly is whitish.

Mullet schools will contain a wide range of individuals of varying ages and sizes, from 20cm- (8in-) long two-year-olds to mature four- and five-year-olds of 75cm (30in) or more in length and weighing at least 4.5kg (10lb). Trophy fish may reach weights of up to 6.5kg (14lb).

Distribution European gray mullet move north from the Mediterranean and Bay of Biscay as seawater temperatures reach 10–12°C (50–54°F) in summer, reaching Trondheim Fjord in Norway, the inner Baltic, and central Scotland. In fall, as sea temperatures drop, they retreat south. They are common in shallow muddy bays, estuaries, and harbors, moving in with the tide and out on the ebb.

GRAY MULLET (THIN-LIPPED)

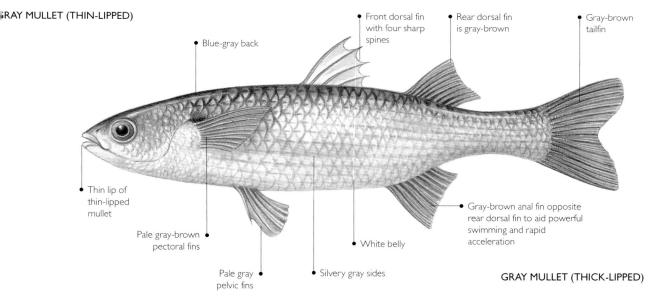

Blue-gray back

Front dorsal fin with four sharp spines

Rear dorsal fin is gray-brown

Gray-brown tailfin

Thin lip of thin-lipped mullet

Pale gray-brown pectoral fins

Pale gray pelvic fins

Silvery gray sides

White belly

Gray-brown anal fin opposite rear dorsal fin to aid powerful swimming and rapid acceleration

FOOD, FLIES, AND FISHING

Mullet graze algae from the seabed and suck in mud to filter out tiny shrimp and worms. Because the mullet's food is so tiny, many fly-fishers have considered them almost uncatchable on the fly. However, tiny weighted nymphs (hook size 16–18) presented in front of an advancing school of mullet can be hugely successful. In very shallow water Soft-hackled Spider wet flies sometimes score: Orange Partridge, Snipe & Purple, and Waterhen Bloa are worth trying. So, too, is a fly dressed to imitate lime-green *Enteromorpha* algae, of which mullet seem especially fond: use some sparse

strands of lime-green mohair or Icelandic sheep wool tied to a size 16 hook. This has caught many fish of more than 2kg (4lb). It is especially effective in estuaries where mullet can be seen rising to take wisps of *Enteromorpha* drifting in the flow.

Of course, these tiny flies must be fished on fine nylon: a leader of less than 2kg (4lb) breaking strain. Hooking a mullet is a challenge; playing one on such fine tackle really is exhilarating. However, my own records suggest that, of 10 mullet that will take the fly, only six will be hooked, and only one will be landed.

GRAY MULLET (THICK-LIPPED)

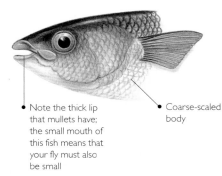

Note the thick lip that mullets have; the small mouth of this fish means that your fly must also be small

Coarse-scaled body

Reading Estuaries and Tidal Creeks 116–17 •
Reading Harbors and Jetties 118–19 •
Tides 132–3

ATLANTIC MACKEREL

PHILL WILLIAMS

Mackerel are one of the most important sea fish both for the fly-fisher and as a baitfish for large predatory species. There are about 45 members in the family Scombridae, *including some well-known gamefish such as the wahoo and tuna. The smaller mackerel are ideal fish for beginners learning saltwater fly-fishing, as they so readily take the fly, scrap so hard on very light tackle, and are so widespread through tropical and temperate seas.*

Dark pectoral fins

Dark front dorsal fin

Blue-green back with irregular black markings

Dark gray rear dorsal fin opposite anal fin to aid acceleration

Finlets on tail aid acceleration

Slender, forked brown-black tailfin

Pale gray pelvic fins

Whitish belly and lower sides with iridescent lines

Light gray anal fin

CHUB MACKEREL

Scomber scombrus, S. japonicus, S. australicus
The chub mackerel is a slender, streamlined fish that is built for speed and constant swimming. It exhibits the characteristic feature of all mackerel: a row of tiny soft finlets between the second dorsal fin and the tail, and between the anal fin and the tail. The upper body is dark green or green-blue with a series of darker wavy vertical stripes, and the underparts are pearl to silvery-white.

In particularly calm weather, mackerel might move to within casting range of the beach. They can also frequently be taken from such places as jetties, harbor walls, and rock marks throughout the summer months.

Mackerel find headlands, islands, offshore rocks, and shallow reefs attractive, especially when the tide is flooding or ebbing strongly.

Distribution Chub mackerel are found around the coasts of western Europe, including Iceland and the Mediterranean, the waters of western and southern Africa, the western and eastern seaboards of the United States, Hawaii, and the waters off Australia, New Zealand, and southeast Asia.

FOOD, FLIES, AND FISHING

Mackerel are schoolfish, although the larger ones will often be loners, or more prone to feeding deep down. Their main food is pelagic crustaceans and small fish, which they pursue with the vigor and intensity of predators that are many times their own size.

You can cast blind in areas known to have schools of mackerel, or locate them with an echo sounder. In early morning and late evening during calm weather, you may be able to see the schools at the surface. Use a light (number 5–7) outfit, with floating or intermediate line if the fish are on top, and a sinker if they are deep. Use any small fry imitation, or, in shallower water, a shrimp or prawn pattern.

The water is boiling where mackerel are feeding on small baitfish. Note that the gulls are also taking baitfish — they are good indicators of schools of baitfish and big predators.

Reading Harbors and Jetties 118–19 • Reading Beaches and Bays 120–1 • Reading the Open Sea 124–5

Mollusks: Clams and Squid 100 • Saltwater Crabs 101 • Saltwater Shrimp and Prawns 102–3 • Saltwater Baitfish 106–7

GARFISH

PHILL WILLIAMS

Garfish are one of the few fish of northern latitudes that can be caught on fly with a fair degree of ease. This is fortunate, as the region normally has strong tides and a predominance of bottom-feeding fish. They are voracious feeders, often close to the surface, and are readily caught once you have located a school — if you have chosen the right fly.

GARFISH
Belone belone

This is a long, streamlined fish with long, beak-like jaws, single dorsal and anal fins, and a metallic silver body. The upper back, like its bones, has an oxidized coppery-green hue. Other elongate fish with long beak-like jaws found elsewhere in the world have similarly colored green bones and upper body scales, suggesting some distant evolutionary link. Garfish grow to an average length of 75cm (30in) and weight of 1kg (2lb); exceptionally to 90cm (36in) and 1.5kg (3lb).

Garfish are fish of the open sea, although they frequently move within shore-casting range during the warmer summer months. They feed within the upper layers of the sea, where they will take any available small fish.

Distribution The garfish has a widespread distribution. It is found in the coastal waters around western Europe, from the Bay of Biscay north as far as southern Iceland and central Norway. Other, similar fish species occur throughout the world, but none of these has been exploited for fly-fishing.

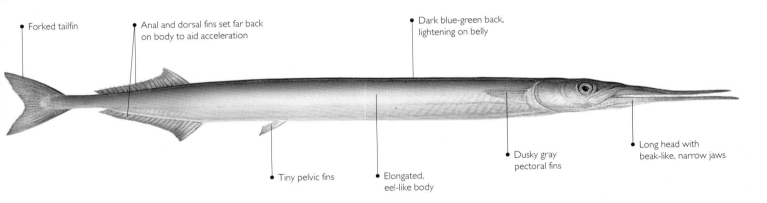

- Forked tailfin
- Anal and dorsal fins set far back on body to aid acceleration
- Dark blue-green back, lightening on belly
- Tiny pelvic fins
- Elongated, eel-like body
- Dusky gray pectoral fins
- Long head with beak-like, narrow jaws

The Channel Islands are a hot-spot for garfish during the summer. The biggest challenge in catching garfish here is locating the schools.

FOOD, FLIES, AND FISHING

Garfish eat small, slender fish such as herring fry ("whitebait") and sandeels. Therefore patterns that imitate these are ideal. The simplest would be a blue-and-white bucktail streamer dressed on a silver hook. Because of the narrowness of their mouths, a narrow hook gap is essential (flies tied to "shanks" with a tiny treble at the rear are becoming popular). If there is no surface activity, try a sinking line and experiment by allowing different sink-times to find the depth at which the garfish are feeding. If they are feeding at the surface, an intermediate line is ideal. Chumming is an effective way of bringing deep-feeding garfish to the surface. Garfish are great fun on light tackle (number 6–7 rods and lines).

Reading the Open Sea 124–5 • Tides 132–3

Mollusks: Clams and Squid 100 • Saltwater Crabs 101 • Saltwater Shrimp and Prawns 102–3

BILLFISH

TREY COMBS

Billfish manifest the attributes fly-fishers most admire in offshore gamefish. In their strength, beauty, great size, and jumping ability, they have no equal. Look closely at a live billfish. Both dorsal and ventral fins drop down and disappear into slots, and the pectoral fins fold into depressions against the body. The billfish's huge tail drives it at bursts of speed that often exceed 80kmph (50mph). Little wonder, then, that sailfish, marlin, and spearfish have historically put the "big" in big game fishing.

Peak of dorsal fin rays are of unequal length; in the similar striped marlin, first three rays are equal in length

Deep blue back with light blue stripes

Rear dorsal fin starts behind rear anal fin

Small rear anal fin

Scimitar-shaped tailfin

Front anal fin is like bluish rear fin

Silvery-white belly

Reduced pelvic fin

Bill-like upper mandible

Lower mandible has slight downcurve

Large pectoral fin folds flat

BLUE MARLIN

Makaira nigricans

The blue marlin, a deepwater tropical and subtropical species, attains the largest weight of any marlin. Females weighing over 907kg (2000lb) have been caught commercially; the males rarely weigh more than 136kg (300lb). Based on lateral line markings, some taxonomists divide blue marlin into Atlantic and Indo-Pacific species.

This billfish species is named for its deep blue back. It has a first dorsal fin that is never as tall as the depth of the body; and although these fish also carry bars along the sides of the body, the dorsal fin height distinguishes the blue from the striped marlin. Note that the term "billfish" refers to the bill or beak-like extension to the snout. Note also

the powerful streamlined shape of the body that is characteristic of all billfish.

Most marlin are well beyond the capacity of even the heaviest fly tackle. Therefore, most fly-fishers search the blue marlin's range for juveniles. On the Pacific side of the Americas, blues are regularly encountered in the range of 73–113kg (150–250lb), with a few individuals that are smaller and many that are larger.

Blue marlin are the most difficult billfish to take on a fly. They are erratic, incredibly aggressive,

lightning fast on the tease, and tremendously strong for their size. Following a series of jumps, they typically sound, often to depths of 183m (600ft) or more. With fly tackle, they are nearly impossible to get back from such depths, and they are likely to come up at the line and get their bills tangled with it.

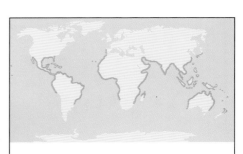

Distribution The species is rarely abundant anywhere in its range. Blues weighing about 45kg (100lb) often occur off Puerto Rico, Santo Domingo, the Virgin Islands between August and October, off the Bahamas in spring, off Hawaii's Kona Coast in June–July, off Mauritius in February, and on Venezuela's La Guaira Bank between November and February. Fly-fishers in the years to come will certainly find other locations.

A blue marlin: note especially the bright electric blue stripes down the back. Both blue marlin and black marlin weighing more than 453kg (1000lb) have been caught on rod and reel. These "grandees" of the sea continue to represent the ultimate challenge in offshore fishing.

LONGBILL SPEARFISH
Tetrapturus pfluegeri
SHORTBILL SPEARFISH
Tetrapturus angustirostris

Spearfish, slender sailfish-like gamefish of great beauty and jumping ability are the exotics of the billfish family. Rarely found, most are caught incidentally, which is a pity, because they are an extraordinary fly-rod species.

Both species have a long, nearly level dorsal fin with only the anterior part peaking above. This fin is proportionally higher than those of marlin, but shorter and more even than those found in sailfish. The coloring of both is deep blue above and silvery-white below. On the shortbill spearfish, the snout or bill is only slightly longer than the lower jaw; in the longbill the bill is at least twice the length of the lower jaw.

The largest spearfish caught in sport fishing, a longbill taken off the island of Madeira, weighed 41.19kg (90lb 13oz). Most spearfish weigh only half that much.

Distribution The longbill spearfish is found in the Gulf of Mexico and in the Atlantic Ocean from the Tropic of Capricorn north to New Jersey and Morocco. The shortbill spearfish has a large tropical Indo-Pacific range, extending south to New Zealand's North Island.

FOOD, FLIES, AND FEEDING

Billfish eat other fish: mackerel, small tuna, needlefish, sardines, octopus, and squid, so any large baitfish or squid imitation is ideal. Sailfish sometimes hunt in groups with individuals corralling baitfish by raising their dorsal fins and creating a living fence. A single sailfish races into the school and stuns bait with its bill. Sailfish holding below casually eat the baitfish that fall out of the school.

Because billfish are usually attracted with lures trolled at or near the surface, many fly-fishers assume they live most of their lives at this level. They don't. In fact, all species of billfish change depths dramatically to feed, and may spend days at depths far beyond the reach of sport boats. For example, during one exceptionally slow fishing week at Costa Rica's Flamingo Beach Resort, local hand-liners fishing at depths of 304m (1000ft) for grouper caught many Pacific sailfish that had been feeding on squid right on the bottom. These changes in depth accompany very significant changes in water temperatures. Sailfish have been successfully teased in and hooked on flies when ocean surface temperature held at 31°C (88°F). However, fish-finding sonar indicated that these billfish were cruising at least 30m (10ft) below the surface, and came to the surface only to investigate the trolled lure. It is known that when seasonal surface temperatures drop below a level that is comfortable for billfish, they move towards the Equator.

The method of catching billfish on fly was worked out by Dr Webster Robinson and his wife Helen, of Key West, Florida, who took a 33.79kg (74lb 8oz) Pacific sailfish on a fly in 1962. A hookless lure, a "teaser," is trolled across the surface to locate the sails. When the sailfish comes to the lure, the boat is slowed to a speed just fast enough to prevent the fish from gaining a firm hold. When the sailfish has been "teased" within casting range, the boat is taken out of gear and the cast made. The frustrated fish usually grabs the fly immediately.

Spearfish are known to chase down baitfish from behind and nip off their tails, afterwards consuming their prey more leisurely. As a result of this habit, a single-hook fly may result in short strikes. Tandem hook flies are desirable. The fly-fisher who wishes to fish only a single hook can cut the first hook off at the bend. Any good baitfish imitation will do.

SHORTBILL SPEARFISH

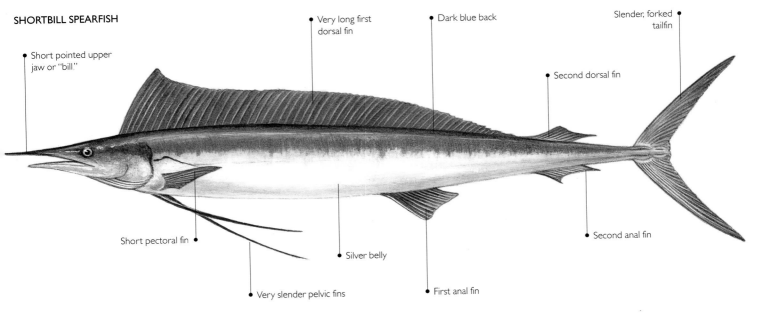

- Very long first dorsal fin
- Dark blue back
- Slender, forked tailfin
- Short pointed upper jaw or "bill"
- Second dorsal fin
- Second anal fin
- Short pectoral fin
- Silver belly
- First anal fin
- Very slender pelvic fins

BLACK MARLIN

Makaira indica

Even as a juvenile, the black marlin possesses great mass for its length. The "black" refers to the dark slate-gray dorsal color of the fish. No other marlin has such a short dorsal fin – less than 50 per cent of its greatest body depth. Only the black marlin has rigid pectoral fins that cannot be closed against the body.

The all-tackle world records, for men and women respectively, were 707.6kg (1560lb) and 691.7kg (1525lb). These records date back to the 1950s and came off Cabo Blanco, Peru. However, the food on which these colossal marlin fed disappeared when ocean currents changed. Today, the world's largest black marlin come from Queensland, Australia. Two of the largest weighed 600.1kg (1323lb) and 610.9kg (1347lb).

Distribution The black marlin, a tropical species distributed widely in the Pacific and Indian Oceans, often concentrates near reefs, islets, seamounts, and banks. One such area, now legendary for the September occurrence of its "grander" blacks, are the ribbons of coral off Cairns, Australia. Here the huge females congregate to spawn with the much smaller males.

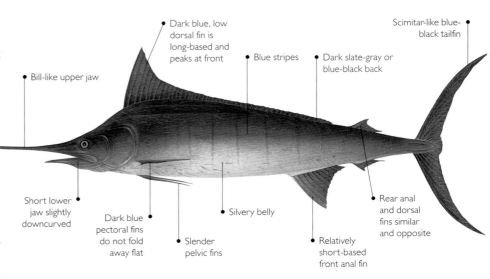

Bill-like upper jaw

Dark blue, low dorsal fin is long-based and peaks at front

Blue stripes

Dark slate-gray or blue-black back

Scimitar-like blue-black tailfin

Short lower jaw slightly downcurved

Dark blue pectoral fins do not fold away flat

Slender pelvic fins

Silvery belly

Relatively short-based front anal fin

Rear anal and dorsal fins similar and opposite

Dozens weighing over 435.5kg (1000lb) are hooked each year. Stories of blacks pushing the 907kg (2000lb) mark persist, but such fish have yet to be documented in the sport fishery. The young from this spawning appear as juveniles on the Great Barrier Reef near Townsville the following summer. The young blacks, averaging 13–22kg (30–50lb), prey on scad in this area for months.

Mixed with these juveniles are the occasional yearling and two-year-olds of 22–68kg (50–150lb). Juvenile blacks in the 45kg (100lb) range are found elsewhere, but never so dependably or abundantly. Some parts of the Indian Ocean, such as Mauritius, have a run of juvenile blacks in the winter and black marlin can sometimes be found off the Americas.

SAILFISH

Istiophorus platypterus

The sailfish, named for its huge, deep blue dorsal fin, ranges worldwide in tropical and subtropical waters. The fish's back is also slate-blue and the underside silvery-white. Faint bars are visible all along its flanks. When the fish is lit up these bars become bright blue, and the long pectoral fins turn to neon blue. Fly-fishers observe this when a sailfish is chasing a teaser.

When the fish has taken the fly and is under stress, the bars along the flank quickly turn copper in color. It is not unusual, during a prolonged fight on a fly-rod, for a sailfish to become entirely brown. Most captains will quickly revive and release such fish and will not allow them aboard for pictures.

Some taxonomists divide sailfish into two groups: the Pacific sailfish (*I. platypterus*) and the Atlantic sailfish (*I. albicans*). The Pacific form is noticeably brighter than the Atlantic and grows to double the Atlantic's size. However, most taxonomists now believe the sailfish to be a single species consisting of discrete races.

The smallest sailfish are found off the east coast of the United States, from Cape Hatteras to the Florida Keys, where they commonly weigh 11–22kg (25–50lb). Much larger Atlantic specimens, with some individuals well over 45kg (100lb), range off Africa's west coast, especially near Principe Island, Angola, and Nigeria. Sailfish of 22–45kg (50–100lb) and more are found off East Africa and around the volcanic island nations in the Indian Ocean. The largest occur in the Pacific off the Americas, from Mexico to Ecuador, and in Polynesia, including Fiji and Tonga. The all-tackle record sailfish is 100.24kg (221lb) for a fish that came from Ecuador. Fly records from Panama and Costa Rica are for fish in the 57–61kg (125–135lb) class, mainly because the captains in these countries have had years of experience with fly-fishers.

Distribution Sailfish can often be found close to land off reefs, ridges, and banks throughout the tropical Atlantic, Indian, and Pacific Oceans.

ATLANTIC SAILFISH

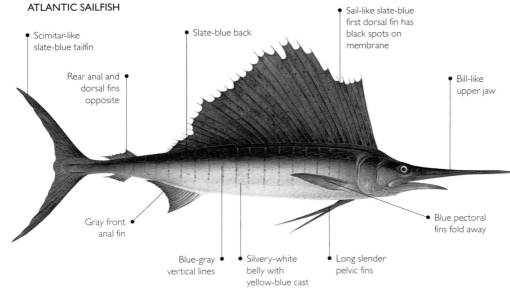

Scimitar-like slate-blue tailfin

Rear anal and dorsal fins opposite

Slate-blue back

Sail-like slate-blue first dorsal fin has black spots on membrane

Bill-like upper jaw

Gray front anal fin

Blue-gray vertical lines

Silvery-white belly with yellow-blue cast

Long slender pelvic fins

Blue pectoral fins fold away

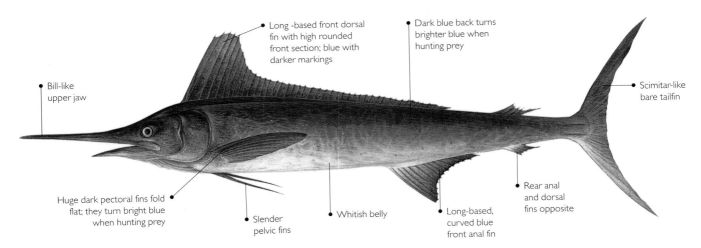

Long -based front dorsal fin with high rounded front section; blue with darker markings

Dark blue back turns brighter blue when hunting prey

Bill-like upper jaw

Scimitar-like bare tailfin

Huge dark pectoral fins fold flat; they turn bright blue when hunting prey

Slender pelvic fins

Whitish belly

Long-based, curved blue front anal fin

Rear anal and dorsal fins opposite

WHITE MARLIN

Tetrapturus albidus

Any fly-fisher watching an excited, or "lit up," white marlin coming down a swell after a teaser will never forget the experience. With its extremely long pectoral fins turning a pale neon blue, and its dorsal run of pale greenish-blue glowing brightly, it looks like a strangely beautiful bird flying directly at you – and if you don't get out of the way it will hit you. Viewed laterally, its rounded dorsal and ventral fins are characteristic, and set it apart from all other marlin. This is the smallest of the marlin, for which the all-tackle record, from Brazil, is 81.2kg (181lb). The average size is much smaller, 20–32kg (45–70lb).

Distribution The white marlin is a highly migratory species. Its range is confined almost entirely to the Atlantic Ocean and to the surrounding waters. Concentrations are found in the Gulf of Mexico off Mexico's Yucatan Peninsula, and in the Gulf Stream off the east coast of the United States to 45°N.

STRIPED MARLIN

Tetrapturus audax

A high, pointed dorsal fin, usually equal to its greatest body depth, identifies this gamefish. The stripes, a brilliant blue on the hunting fish, turn copper when the marlin is highly stressed, and fade in death. The free-swimming striped marlin has a deep blue back, and a blue or silvery-white belly. As with all marlin species, the females are larger and will, for a given length, show much more body depth. Striped marlin are the most challenging and spectacular of all offshore fly-rod gamefish. No other marlin jumps more.

The largest striped marlin are found off New Zealand, where individuals weighing over 136kg (300lb) are often caught. The all-tackle record is 224kg (494lb) for a fish that came from Tutukaka, New Zealand. Stripers in the Americas are much smaller. Those in Mexico and Central America are in the 29–79kg (85–175lb) class; fish over 90kg (200lb) are uncommon. Striped marlin off Colombia and Ecuador often exceed 97kg (200lb).

Distribution The striped marlin occurs in tropical and temperate waters throughout both the Pacific and the Indian Oceans. Several quite distinct populations are represented within this distribution.

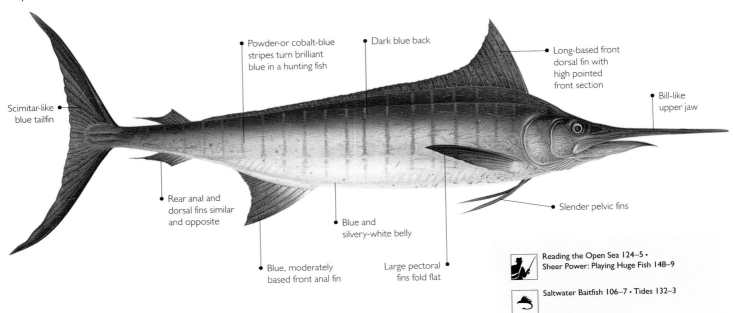

Powder-or cobalt-blue stripes turn brilliant blue in a hunting fish

Dark blue back

Long-based front dorsal fin with high pointed front section

Scimitar-like blue tailfin

Bill-like upper jaw

Rear anal and dorsal fins similar and opposite

Blue and silvery-white belly

Slender pelvic fins

Blue, moderately based front anal fin

Large pectoral fins fold flat

Reading the Open Sea 124–5 • Sheer Power: Playing Huge Fish 148–9

Saltwater Baitfish 106–7 • Tides 132–3

TUNA

TREY COMBS

Tuna are outstanding saltwater fly-fishers' fish. They take the fly readily and when hooked are fast, powerful fighters. There are many quite different species, each with its own special character.

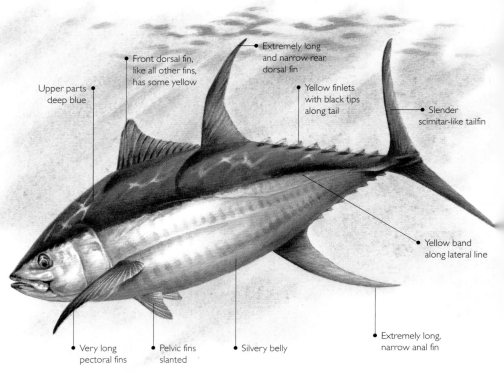

Upper parts deep blue

Front dorsal fin, like all other fins, has some yellow

Extremely long and narrow rear dorsal fin

Yellow finlets with black tips along tail

Slender scimitar-like tailfin

Yellow band along lateral line

Very long pectoral fins

Pelvic fins slanted

Silvery belly

Extremely long, narrow anal fin

YELLOWFIN TUNA

Thunnus albacares

Like all tuna, the yellowfin has a deep, muscular torpedo-like body, sickle-shaped fins, and a series of finlets running along the top and bottom of the tail, in front of the tailfin.

Adult yellowfin are best identified by the yellow, highly elongated second dorsal and anal fins. With their bright yellow finlets, nearly black back, and wash of bright yellow through the lateral line, they easily qualify as the most colorful of the tuna species.

Yellowfin have tremendous strength; many sport fishers believe them to be, pound for pound, the most powerful of tunas. They grow rapidly, a fish of the year weighing 2.3kg (5lb) or more and a yearling twice that amount. Like all the great tunas, yellowfin school by general age groups, because fish of the same size can comfortably swim at the same speed. The largest yellowfin in the world live in Mexico's Revilla Gigedo Islands. The islands are reached by long-range fishing boats from San Diego. Using stand-up fishing gear, each year fly-fishers take yellowfin of over 136kg (300lb). The record fish, caught off San Benedicto Island, weighed 176kg (388lb).

Arguably, large yellowfin represent the ultimate fly-rod challenges. They are rarely found in shallow water and never tire themselves out by jumping. They have tremendous speed, at least 65kmph (40 mph), and the first run can be at a depth of 304m (1000ft). A 36kg (80lb) yellowfin can make an initial run of 640m (2100ft) directly away from the fly-fisher. No drag setting can stop this run and still save the leader tippet.

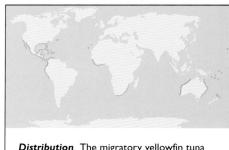

Distribution The migratory yellowfin tuna occurs worldwide in both tropical and temperate saltwater.

SKIPJACK TUNA

Katsuwonus pelamis

The skipjack tuna is a deepwater species that is found in both tropical and subtropical waters. It is possibly the strongest of all the gamefish for its size.

The back is dark purple-blue, blotched with lavender-blue. The lower body is silver with conspicuous longitudinal dark stripes that are characteristic only of skipjack.

Skipjack tuna weighing 14–18kg (30–40lb) can be caught in Hawaii and Mauritius. In most other areas where it is found, a skipjack of 9kg (20lb) must be considered exceptional.

Distribution The skipjack tuna is a widespread tropical and subtropical species that is found throughout the Atlantic, Indian, and Pacific Oceans.

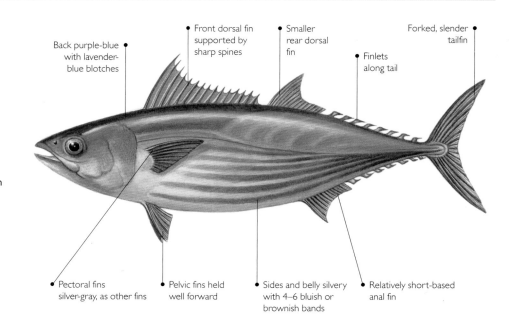

Back purple-blue with lavender-blue blotches

Front dorsal fin supported by sharp spines

Smaller rear dorsal fin

Finlets along tail

Forked, slender tailfin

Pectoral fins silver-gray, as other fins

Pelvic fins held well forward

Sides and belly silvery with 4–6 bluish or brownish bands

Relatively short-based anal fin

DOGTOOTH TUNA
Gymnosarda unicolor

Imagine a tuna with the speed, strength, and rapacious disposition to complement perfectly a mouth full of icepick-like teeth, and you have the basic makeup of the dogtooth tuna – or "doggie" as the Australians like to say. The upper parts of the fish are a purplish-black, the underparts are silver in color.

The largest dogtooth tuna taken on a fly weighed 11.99kg (26lb 7oz). Larger fish will certainly follow, because the species does grow to an immense size. The all-tackle record (from Korea) was a dogtooth weighing 131kg (288lb).

Distribution This is a migratory species native to the western Pacific and Indian Oceans. It periodically takes up residence off coral reefs.

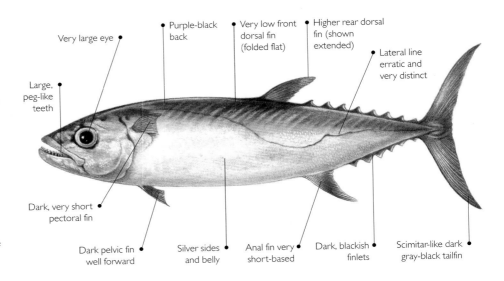

Very large eye • • Purple-black back • Very low front dorsal fin (folded flat) • Higher rear dorsal fin (shown extended) • Lateral line erratic and very distinct

Large, peg-like teeth

Dark, very short pectoral fin •

Dark pelvic fin well forward • Silver sides and belly • Anal fin very short-based • Dark, blackish finlets • Scimitar-like dark gray-black tailfin

BLACK SKIPJACK
Euthynnus alleteratus

The black skipjack, kawakawa, and little tuna are sometimes called "bonito," but they are not true bonitos, which belong to the genus *Sarda*.

The black skipjack's uppers parts are dark green-blue, with silvery flanks and belly. There are up to five black spots under the pectoral fin.

The all-tackle record weighed 12kg (26lb), for a fish caught off Baja California. The average size in Mexican waters is 4.5–5kg (8–10lb) and 1.8–2.3kg (4–5lb) in Central and South America.

Distribution It is found in tropical waters of the central and eastern Pacific, including coastal waters from California to Peru.

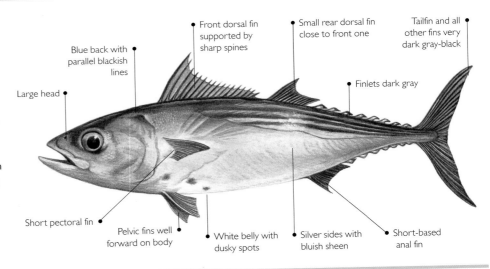

Blue back with parallel blackish lines • Front dorsal fin supported by sharp spines • Small rear dorsal fin close to front one • Tailfin and all other fins very dark gray-black

Large head • Finlets dark gray •

Short pectoral fin • Pelvic fins well forward on body • White belly with dusky spots • Silver sides with bluish sheen • Short-based anal fin

KAWAKAWA TUNA
Euthynnus affinis
LITTLE TUNNY (FALSE ALBACORE)
Euthynnus alletteratus

Kawakawa tuna have a dark green-blue back and silvery sides and belly. Most are 2.3–4.5kg (5–10lb), with the all-tackle record being 13kg (29lb) from Clarion Island, Mexico. The little tunny is very similar, but has a wavy black stripe along the back. Most little tunny are between 2.7–4.5kg (6–10lb), but fish of over 14kg (30lb) have been reported in Bermuda and in Algeria, where the all-tackle record was 15.9kg (35lb 2oz).

Distribution The kawakawa occurs in the Indian and Pacific Oceans, especially around the islands of Hawaii, Papua New Guinea, the Philippines, and Fiji. The little tunny occurs in the Atlantic from New England to Brazil and from South Africa to Spain and the Mediterranean Sea.

KAWAKAWA TUNA

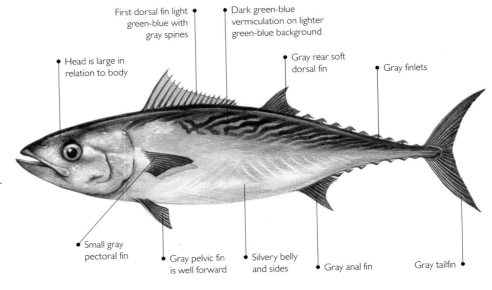

First dorsal fin light green-blue with gray spines • Dark green-blue vermiculation on lighter green-blue background • Gray rear soft dorsal fin • Gray finlets

Head is large in relation to body •

Small gray pectoral fin • Gray pelvic fin is well forward • Silvery belly and sides • Gray anal fin • Gray tailfin

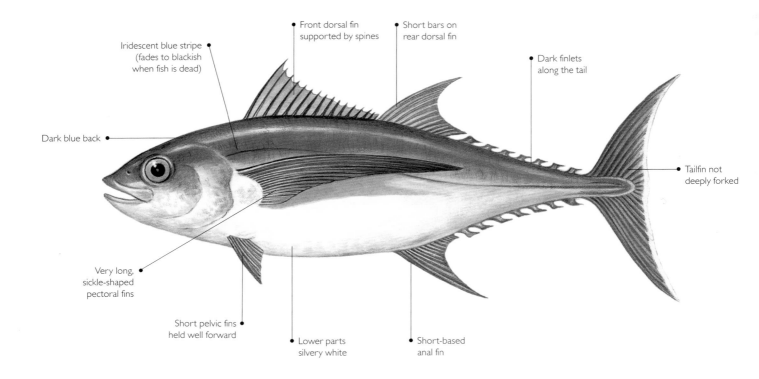

Iridescent blue stripe (fades to blackish when fish is dead)

Front dorsal fin supported by spines

Short bars on rear dorsal fin

Dark finlets along the tail

Dark blue back

Tailfin not deeply forked

Very long, sickle-shaped pectoral fins

Short pelvic fins held well forward

Lower parts silvery white

Short-based anal fin

ALBACORE

Thunnus alalunga

The albacore was nicknamed the "longfin tuna" because of the extremely elongated pectoral fin, which extends beyond the second dorsal fin. The upper body is black with a light blue stripe, and unmarked, silver-white underparts. The tailfin is diagnostically edged white.

The albacore probably reaches its maximum size of over 45kg (100lb) in the Hawaiian Islands. The all-tackle record of 39.9kg (88lb) came from the Canary Islands. Waters off California, South Africa, and Japan have produced albacore of over 32kg (70lb). Fly-fishers usually take the fish during seasonal migrations in temperate waters, where they can be found driving baitfish to the surface.

Distribution Albacore are highly migratory tuna that occur worldwide in both tropical and warm temperate oceans. They often migrate far to the north of the range that is tolerated by other tuna species. For example, off western North America, they will move as far north as British Columbia's Queen Charlotte Islands and the extreme southeasterly parts of Alaska.

BLACKFIN TUNA

Thunnus atlanticus

This species has a dark blue back, silver-white underparts, and blackish dorsal fins and anal fins, and finlets. The finlets have a yellow tinge. The pectorals do not extend as far back as the second dorsal fin.

Most blackfins weigh around 11kg (25lb), with fish of over 14kg (30lb) taken by fly-fishers fishing near south Florida's shrimp boats, where the blackfins feed on discarded portions of the catch.

The all-tackle record weighed 20.6kg (45lb 8oz) and came from Key West, Florida.

Distribution The blackfin tuna is a tropical and warm temperate species that occurs only in the western Atlantic Ocean, the Caribbean Sea, and the Gulf of Mexico.

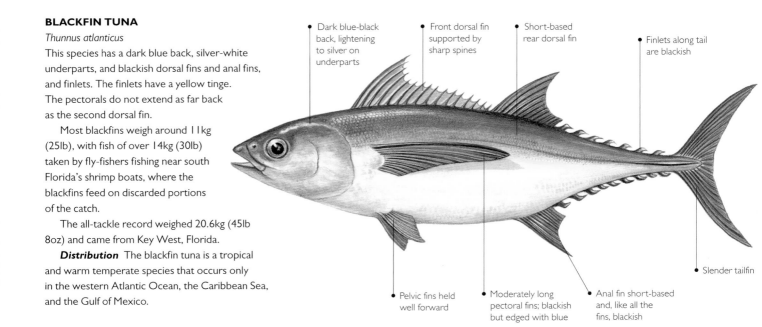

Dark blue-black back, lightening to silver on underparts

Front dorsal fin supported by sharp spines

Short-based rear dorsal fin

Finlets along tail are blackish

Pelvic fins held well forward

Moderately long pectoral fins; blackish but edged with blue

Anal fin short-based and, like all the fins, blackish

Slender tailfin

BLUEFIN TUNA

Thunnus thynnus

The bluefin tuna, a fish of mystery and legend, reaches colossal sizes during a highly migratory life in temperate and subtropical waters. It has a blue-black back, silver-white underparts, and diagnostic finlets, which are yellow edged with black.

Growth is extremely rapid; by the end of its first year a juvenile can measure 60cm (24in) long and weigh 4kg (9lb). Three years later the fish will top 27kg (60lb); as nine-year-olds they can hit 122kg (270lb); and a 14-year-old can top 318kg (700lb). It reaches a maximum size of at least 681kg (1500lb) off New England and the Canadian Maritime Provinces.

Bluefin over 91kg (200lb) overwhelm fly tackle, but smaller individuals do not. Records include fish of 45.8kg (101lb) and 58kg (128lb). Smaller bluefin weighing up to 18kg (40lb) are caught annually off the coasts of New Jersey, New York's Long Island, and New England.

Distribution The bluefin occurs in the northern Pacific and Atlantic Oceans, the Black and Mediterranean Seas, and the Gulf of Mexico.

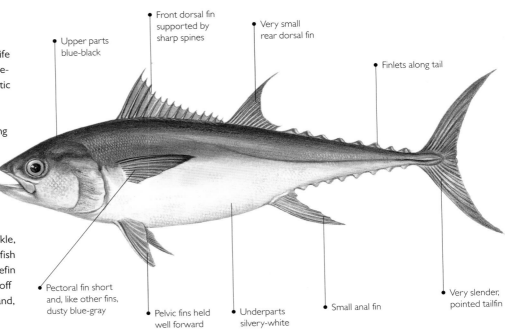

- Upper parts blue-black
- Front dorsal fin supported by sharp spines
- Very small rear dorsal fin
- Finlets along tail
- Pectoral fin short and, like other fins, dusty blue-gray
- Pelvic fins held well forward
- Underparts silvery-white
- Small anal fin
- Very slender, pointed tailfin

BIGEYE TUNA

Thunnus obesus

The upper body is black-blue, the lower silver-white. The first dorsal fin is yellow and the finlets yellow edged with black. The second dorsal and anal fins are very short (compared with the yellowfin) and the eye is very large.

The all-tackle record for the Atlantic is 170kg (375lb), and for the Pacific 197kg (435lb). But fly-fishers only rarely land fish this big; also the very large ones swim too deep for fly-fishing. Yearlings, weighing about 7kg (15lb), are caught most often.

Distribution The bigeye is found in most tropical and subtropical oceans.

LONGTAIL TUNA

Thunnus tonggo

The longtail tuna is found only in the central Pacific around the coasts of Australia and New Guinea. Australians call this species the "northern bluefin", because of its deep blue back. The finlets are yellow with gray edges, and the tail lobes are long.

The few catch records are in the 9kg (20lb) range; the all-tackle record is 35.8kg (79lb 2oz).

BONITOS

Regardless of the species, bonito remain highly popular gamefish with fly-fishers. They are fast, powerful, and eagerly strike the rapidly retrieved fly. Bonito school and feed on the surface, an activity that takes them from offshore to inshore bays and harbors. Averaging only about 2kg (4lb), they require no special tackle. There are four species, each found in a different part of the world's oceans: Atlantic bonito (*Sarda sarda*), Atlantic; Pacific bonito (*S. chiliensis*), Pacific coast from Canada south to Chile; Australian bonito (*S. australis*), southeast Australia and North Island, New Zealand; and the striped bonito (*S. orientalis*), the Indian Ocean, Western Australia, and tropical western Central America. Bonitos resemble slender tuna in build and structure; the upper body is blue-gray with darker longitudinal stripes, and the lower body is silver.

 Reading Harbors and Jetties 118–19 • Reading Bays and Beaches 120–1 • Reading the Open Sea 124–5

 Mollusks Clams and Squid 100 • Saltwater Crabs 101 • Saltwater Shrimp and Prawns 102–3 • Saltwater Baitfish 106–7

 Baja 182–3

FOOD, FLIES, AND FISHING

Tuna feed opportunistically and continually on fish, squid, and crustaceans, and any flies that match these will succeed, provided that you get them in front of the nose of the fish.

Smaller species and juveniles often feed at the surface and can be caught by conventional fly-casting. For example, thousands of surface-feeding skipjack often form immense schools. However, they will dive deep, out of range of your fly, if a fast-moving boat approaches. The boat must be stopped well away in a position toward which the skipjack are moving. Then you wait for the school to approach and drift with them, casting, hooking, and playing fish. Skipjack are usually fairly easy to catch, for they eagerly strike a variety of flies that match baitfish or squid. Other tuna must often be enticed to within casting distance, especially if huge baitfish and squid imitations (that cannot be conventionally cast) are being used to match the big natural foods being devoured. Chumming sometimes succeeds (if you are fishing for blackfins, anchor close to a shrimp boat that is attracting the tuna). Alternatively, tease the tuna to the surface close to the boat with hookless poppers.

It is worth repeating: tuna are very powerful fish. Make sure that your rods and reels are sound, the reels have plenty of backing, your leaders are spot on, and that every knot is tied perfectly.

SHARKS

PHILL WILLIAMS

Around 300 species of shark inhabit the seas, oceans, and lakes of the world. Many, such as the nurse shark, live on the bottom of shallow waters; others, including the potentially huge six-gilled shark, prefer to swim at great depth. What the fly-fisher requires are the more active hunting species of the upper water layers, reef edges, and shallows. The four species described here are ideal fly-fishers' fish in that they can be chummed to the fly easily or found feeding in shallow water. Get the fly to them and they will grab it, and, once hooked, will fight like tigers!

Asymmetric tailfin aids acceleration

Rear dorsal fin aids acceleration

Front dorsal fin slopes slightly backward, and aids maneuverability

Streamlined, torpedo-shaped body

Long snout

Small anal fin

Small pelvic fins

Coloration variable: dark gray to olive-brown with white belly; fins black tipped

Large pectoral fins for rapid maneuverability

Five gill slits

Underslung mouth

BLACKTIP SHARK

Carcharinus limbatus

The blacktip shark is a typically sleek-looking fish, with a build similar to that of a number of other shark species. Identification is made easy by the black tips of the pectoral fins. Body coloration is dark bluish-gray above with pale underparts and a whitish stripe along each flank. Blacktips are small sharks, and although specimens of up to 32kg (70lb) or more have been caught on bait, most of the ones you will catch on fly will be in the range of 5–15kg (11–33lb). The similar, but generally larger *C. maculipinnis* may also be seen, usually in deeper water. This species lacks the ridge along the centre of the back found in *C. limbatus*.

Distribution The blacktip shark is primarily an Atlantic species, occurring commonly from the Bahamas north of the Gulf of Mexico and from Madeira south to the Gambia. Lesser numbers are reported from Baja to Peru, and from a few localities in the Indian Ocean. Blacktips love coastal shallows, reef edges, and the margins of tropical flats. Here they can sometimes be spotted as they chase baitfish. They can then be caught by casting a fly to them without chumming. This makes them potentially one of the most receptive shark species for the fly-fisher.

BLUE SHARK

Prionace glauca

The blue shark is a beautifully proportioned, sleek fish. Its long snout and long pectoral fins are built for speed and agility. Blues can be recognized by their coloration, which is a deep indigo blue on the upper back, giving way to brilliant blue on the flanks, and a spotless white belly. As in all sharks, the males can be immediately distinguished by the presence of claspers on the inner edges of their pelvic fins.

Blue sharks vary in size throughout their range. In the North Atlantic, a fish 2.5m (8ft) in length or weighing 80kg (176lb) is a trophy fish, whereas in the Pacific and Indian Oceans they reach lengths of 3.8m (12ft) and weights of 150kg (330lb).

Distribution This is an abundant pelagic, open-oceanic fish found worldwide, in both tropical and subtropical waters. It will also foray into more temperate latitudes where warm-water currents provide their preferred temperatures of 10–22°C (50–72°F). They are often found in association with small schooling fish, such as mackerel and pilchard, on which they feed.

PORBEAGLE SHARK

Lamna nasus

The porbeagle is a powerful, stocky shark, with broad "shoulders" and a strong, conical head. A lateral keel at the rear of the tail extends to the base of the tailfin. Coloration is dark blue-gray or blue-brown on the back, lightening progressively to white-gray on the belly. Because this description applies equally to many other shark species, to confirm that the shark you have caught is a porbeagle check its teeth: they should have distinct cusps at the base. Also, the second (rear) dorsal fin should lie directly above the anal fin.

Most porbeagles grow to maximum lengths of 2–2.5m (6–8ft) and to weights of 150–230kg (330–510lb).

Distribution The porbeagle is found only in temperate belts of the oceans within a water temperature range of 10–20°C (50–68°F). It is a major sport fish off southwest Britain, North Island New Zealand, the northeastern United States and Oregon, where it favors reefy ground around islands and headlands.

FOOD, FLIES, AND FISHING

Most sharks are not easy to catch with flies. This is because they respond to scent over long distances, and to minute electrical impulses emitted by their prey species. Therefore, with few exceptions like bonnet heads and blacktips, sharks must be attracted by chumming.

This is part of the thrill of shark fishing – of watching the slick of chum drifting away on the current and of wondering if some sharks can detect it. Time passes: and then a long scimitar dorsal fin appears in the slick; then another. Slowly the sharks, attracted by the scent, approach on a zig-zag track. Nearer and nearer they come. Now you can see one – a blue, perhaps, of at least 36kg (80lb) – only 20m (65ft) away. You cast your fly out and swing it round in front of the advancing fish. There is a flash of white as the shark takes hold!

Pelargic sharks can be enticed to take the fly, but usually they have to be attracted to casting range by the use of "chumming."

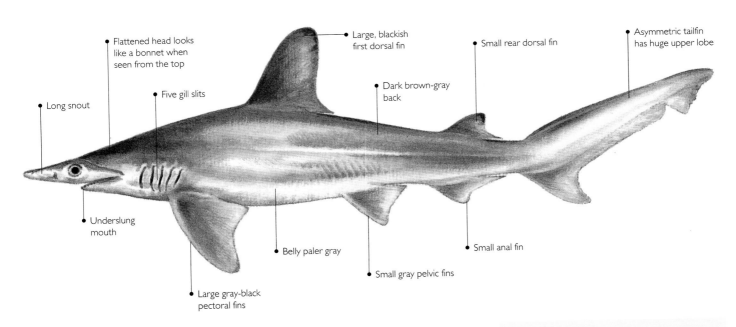

- Long snout
- Flattened head looks like a bonnet when seen from the top
- Five gill slits
- Large, blackish first dorsal fin
- Small rear dorsal fin
- Asymmetric tailfin has huge upper lobe
- Dark brown-gray back
- Underslung mouth
- Belly paler gray
- Small gray pelvic fins
- Small anal fin
- Large gray-black pectoral fins

BONNET HEADED SHARK

Sphyrna tiburo

This is a small shark that would be difficult to confuse with any other species because of the unique flattened and semi-circular head, which gives it its name. It is a sleek, fast-moving fish with a slender, gray-brown body (paler on the belly) that camouflages it on sandy backgrounds.

Most bonnet heads caught on fly will be in the 5–20kg (11–44lb) range; they grow exceptionally to 1.8m (6ft) in length and 45kg (99lb) in weight.

Distribution Worldwide warm-water sharks, bonnet heads are commonly found over shallow flats – and in the slightly deeper channels that separate them – where they feed on swimming crabs, shrimp, and small baitfish.

 Reading Harbors and Jetties 118–19 •
Reading Beaches and Bays 120–1 • Reading the
Open Sea 124–5 • Sheer Power 148–9

 Saltwater Baitfish 106–7

 The Florida Keys 164–5

DORADO

PHILL WILLIAMS

The dorado is sometimes called the mahi mahi, or the dorado dolphin, the latter because of its habit of swimming around becalmed ships like a real dolphin. But dolphins are mammals, not fish. Dorado are open-oceanic fish – active, high-speed predators of the upper layers of water. They are predominantly fish of the open blue water, although they are also attracted to current lines, upwellings, and similar features. They have everything: looks, power, acrobatics, and agility. In life, they are among the most strikingly beautiful creatures ever to come from the sea.

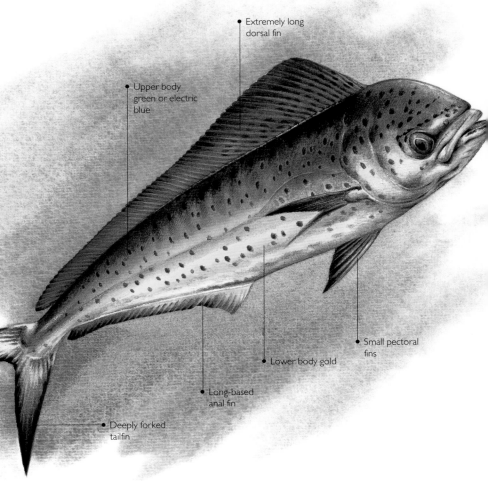

Extremely long dorsal fin

Upper body green or electric blue

Small pectoral fins

Lower body gold

Long-based anal fin

Deeply forked tailfin

DORADO

Coryphaena hippos

Dorado are sexually dimorphic fish, in which the head shape of adult bulls differs markedly from that of adult females and juveniles of both sexes. In the bull the forehead profile from the upper lip is steep and blunt, while in the female and immature fish (which are often called chicken dolphins) it is more gently rounded. The color gold dominates the upper flanks, sides, belly, and lower parts of the long, shallow, laterally compressed body. The coloration is the origin of the fish's name – *dorado* being the Spanish word for "golden."

The upper back, head, long single dorsal fin, and pectoral fins are either brilliant blue or green, according to location, with a scattering of darker spots over much of the upper body. Although they are aggressive predators, dorado do not have prominent teeth, so wire to the fly is not required.

Dorado are very fast-growing fish, with one estimate suggesting that they can add up to 14kg (30lb) in weight per year. A large dorado might measure around 2m (6ft), with a top weight pushing 45kg (100lb). The school fish tend to be modest in size. The big bulls tend to be loners.

Dorado often occur in mixed-sex schools that have a magnetic affinity towards surface cover, including areas of floating weed such as *Sargassum* weed, which can form long-wind-blown lanes that the dorado will patrol.

Despite its generally modest size, the dorado is in every sense the jewel in the off-shore fly-fishers' crown. It is a fish well able and willing to test every reserve of tackle quality, the fly-fisher's strength, skill, and staying power. The sound of the fly-line cutting the water as a sudden change of direction is made at speed is a lingering memory, as are the regular bouts of temper and acrobatics.

FOOD, FLIES, AND FISHING

Dorado have the pace and agility to track down and catch the flying-fish that often dominate their diet. They are also opportunistic feeders, taking other small baitfish species and squid where these are available.

Exploit the dorado's habit of sheltering under debris by bringing the boat to rest beside something like a floating log, then chum them up. When the frenzied pack gathers, looking for more handouts, it is time to introduce the fly.

Any large bright streamer type pattern, particularly if it contains yellow and/or red, will have fish actively competing to take it.

A fly reel with plenty of capacity and a good smooth dragging system is an absolute must.

Heavy mono is more than adequate to counter the abrasive action of the dorado's jaws. Once the fish is hooked, the action-packed fight might, however, turn out to be a long one on fly tackle, with many changes of direction to take the leader over the abrasive areas of the jaw.

It is good policy, therefore, to check for damaged areas in the leader after taking each fish, and to tie on a new leader at the first sign of any wear. The reel should have a good, smooth drag and hold at least 180m (600ft) of 13.5kg (30lb) test backing.

DORADO (MALE)

DORADO (FEMALE)

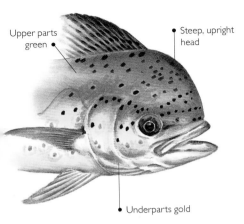

Upper parts green

Steep, upright head

Underparts gold

More shallow, rounded head

Pectoral fins are well forward on body of both sexes

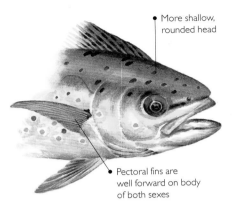

Tropical coral reefs, clear blue channels, and tiny atolls are where you will find the beautiful dorado. Head out in a boat to where the shallows suddenly plunge to oceanic depths and there you will find dorado.

 Reading the Open Sea 124–5 • Tides 132–3

 Saltwater Baitfish 106–7

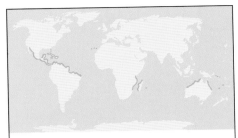

Distribution Dorado occur throughout the world's tropical and subtropical seas that have a temperature range of 20–30°C (68–86°F). There are particular pockets of abundance along the central seaboards of the Americas, Hawaii, and many tropical archipelagos, around Australia, and along the east African coast, but they are also common enough throughout the warmer oceans of the world. I have even seen them caught in Europe around the Canary Islands, although this is at the very edge of their range.

The general tendency is to start looking for dorado where the green water of the coastal shallows or fringing reef gives way to blue water depths. But dorado are not averse to making forays well inshore.

OTHER BIG GAMEFISH

PHILL WILLIAMS

Many families of saltwater fish contain one or more members that, by virtue of their specific fighting qualities, are classed as game species. Most, although not all, live in tropical or subtropical waters. The four different species described here are power-packed, explosive fish that will take your baitfish imitation and then zoom off at great speed into the distant horizon. Hold on tight!

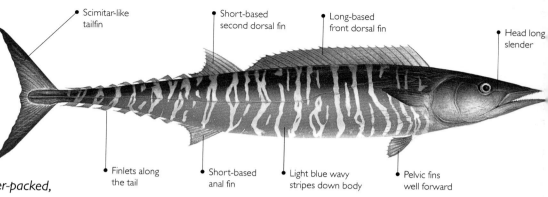

- Scimitar-like tailfin
- Short-based second dorsal fin
- Long-based front dorsal fin
- Head long slender
- Finlets along the tail
- Short-based anal fin
- Light blue wavy stripes down body
- Pelvic fins well forward

FOOD, FLIES, AND FISHING

All the four species are hunters of other fish, the identity of which will vary with location, water depth, and position in the water column. Use appropriately-sized fish imitations (I favor large Lefty's Deceivers or, when the fish are feeding close to the surface, big Poppers), a short length of wire between fly and mono leader, and a top-quality reel with plenty of backing. Fish such as these will quickly find flaws or knots in your tackle. And they are too great a prize to lose.

WAHOO

Acanthocybium solanderi

These are reputedly the fastest things with fins, capable of reaching speeds of 100kph (60mph) within a few body lengths. The name Wahoo probably comes from the Hawaiian island of Oahu, around which early explorers and mariners hunted this species for food.

Wahoo resemble a torpedo with two dorsal fins, a beak-like mouth, powerful tail, and a series of soft, rayed finlets. The upper body colour is a deep, electric blue with a series of alternate blue and gray wavy vertical stripes. The mouth and

teeth have a powerful bite, demanding a wire leader. Wahoo have a maximum growth potential of around 90kg (200lb).

Distribution Wahoo occur worldwide throughout tropical and subtropical waters within a preferred temperature range of 20–30°C (68–60°F). They can sometimes be found at more northerly latitudes, including the Bahamas and Canary Islands. They are usually open-oceanic loners, following the baitfish schools or working current lines. However, they can also be taken along reef edges, sometimes very close to the shore.

YELLOWTAIL

Seriola lalandi

A beautifully streamlined long fish with a short, low-profile first dorsal fin and long second dorsal fin, the yellowtail has just the one anal fin, no finlets, and a deeply forked tail. These structural features are designed for speed; when you hook a yellowtail it will make long, deep runs, and you will have to work hard to keep it out of snags in shallow water.

Coloration is greenish-blue on the upper parts, fading on the flanks before turning to off-white below, with an obvious yellow band running the full length of the body in the regions of the lateral line. The tail and the fins are also yellow. There is, too, a low-profile keel where the tail and the body meet. Yellowtails grow to a maximum weight of 70kg (150lb).

- Slender forked tailfin
- Very long-based rear dorsal fin
- Yellow stripe
- Blue-green back
- Long-based anal fin
- Yellow pelvic fin held forward
- Whitish underparts

Distribution Yellowtails occur in isolated populations around land masses washed by sea-water in the range of 15–18°C (58–64°F). There are four different species: California yellowtails (*S. lalandi dorsalis*) are found mainly along the coast

of California and western Mexico; southern yellowtails (*S. l. grandis*) around New Zealand and Australia; Cape yellowtails (no specific scientific name) around southern Africa; and Asiatic yellowtails (*S. l. auerovittata*) around Japan.

GREATER AMBERJACK
Seriola dumerili

This is a long, stocky, powerfully built fish with a small first dorsal fin, an elongated second dorsal, and a single anal fin. The upper body varies between bronze and olive-brown, becoming more silvery with a hint of bronze on the flanks and lower body. A diagonal brown stripe runs from the nose and past the eye to the first dorsal fin An amber lateral band usually runs from the eye to the tail, roughly along the course of the lateral line.

The amberjack can reach around 82kg (180lb). Small to medium-sized fish can be found in, or persuaded into, quite shallow water, particularly over reefs, along reef edges, and under floating debris and weedlines. Yet the biggest often spend their life at great depths, over submarine humps, ridges, reefs, and wrecks.

Amberjacks will take a big Popper when they are taking baitfish near the surface. But beware: once hooked they will usually dive deep, seemingly trying to snag the line and break free.

Distribution Despite its love of deep water, the amberjack is usually confined to coastal waters. It is found around the Caribbean, the eastern seaboard of south Mexico, Australia and Kenya, and throughout the remainder of the Indian Ocean and Australasia within its preferred temperatures of 20–30°C (68–86°F).

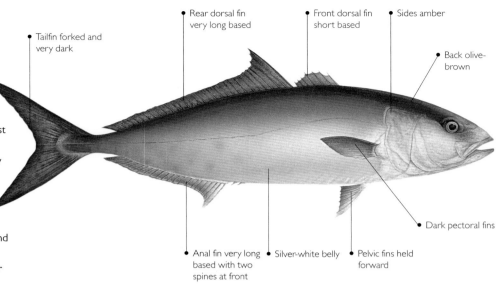

- Tailfin forked and very dark
- Rear dorsal fin very long based
- Front dorsal fin short based
- Sides amber
- Back olive-brown
- Anal fin very long based with two spines at front
- Silver-white belly
- Pelvic fins held forward
- Dark pectoral fins

A splendid great amberjack almost dwarfs its captor. This really is the fish of a lifetime.

QUEENFISH
Scomberoides commersonniaus

The queenfish's body is stout and laterally compressed, with a blunt facial profile, very long-based single dorsal and anal fins, and a large, deeply forked tail. There are up to seven very short spines in front of the dorsal fin and two in front of the anal fin. The tailfin is deeply forked. The upper body color varies between brilliant blue and green, giving way to silvery lower parts, which are sometimes tinged with gold. Above a prominent lateral line runs a series of between five and eight large dark spots. If the fish also has a row of five to eight spots below the lateral line, this is the closely related species *Scomberoides laysan*. Both species have a preference for water temperatures in the range 20–30°C (68–86°F). The maximum weight is around 16kg (35lb) and the average length 50cm (20in).

Unlike amberjacks, which dive deep, or wahoo, which tear off into the distance, once hooked, queenfish carry out some of the most spectacular aerial acrobatics.

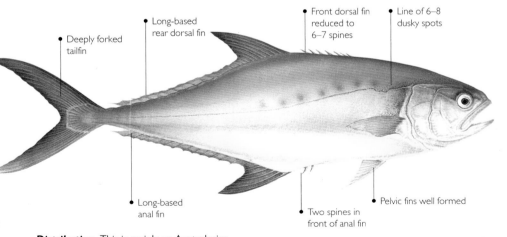

- Deeply forked tailfin
- Long-based rear dorsal fin
- Front dorsal fin reduced to 6–7 spines
- Line of 6–8 dusky spots
- Long-based anal fin
- Two spines in front of anal fin
- Pelvic fins well formed

Distribution This is mainly an Australasian species found to the north of the Tropic of Capricorn, with the highest concentration occurring off the north coast of Australia and its adjacent offshore islands.

The queenfish is often found in shallow water or close to drop-offs, including estuaries, around islands and over reefs, and appears to be especially active around low water.

 Reading Harbors and Jetties 118–19 • Reading Beaches and Bays 120–1 • Reading the Open Sea 124–5

 Mollusks: Clams and Squid 100 • Saltwater Crabs 101 • Saltwater Shrimp and Prawns 102–3 • Saltwater Baitfish 106–7

 Baja 182–3

FOOD AND FLIES

Over 500 years ago, when *The Treatise of Fishing with an Angle* was published – the first book describing food and flies – flies really meant flies. Twelve different artificial flies are described in this ancient work, and it is not difficult to link each of them with a real fly. For example, one recommended for use in May: "The yellow fly, the body of yellow wool, the wings of the red cock hackle and of the drake dyed yellow" matches perfectly the yellow dun, a European species of mayfly with very similar relations in North America.

More than 350 years ago, *El Manuscrito de Astorga* described the essential flies for trout fishing on the rivers of northern Spain. One, recommended during January and February, has a body of dark fawn silk ribbed with white, and *negrisco* and *pardo* hackles from farmyard fowl that were, and still are, bred around Léon for fly-tying. This fly imitates insects in the group of mayflies called march browns.

Fly-fishers' flies representing winged insects dominated fly-fishing into the 19th century. This was partly because the main fly-fishers' fish of the time were trout and grayling that rose readily to eat winged flies on the surface, and partly because they used bait to catch fish that were not rising to take flies. However, some fly-dressers had noticed that fish could be taken with flies that bore no resemblance to insects whatsoever. In his *Northern Memoirs* (1694) Richard Franck described the first, his "glittering fly, the body composed of red twisted silk, intermingled with silver, and eye of gold," and with "a dappled feather of a teal" as the wing. Even today, fly-fishers throughout the world are fishing descendants of Franck's fly: the Teal & Red, Peter Ross, Red Ibis, Hornberg – flies that imitate nothing in nature. But 300 years ago Franck was an exception.

Attitudes began to change through the 19th and early 20th centuries, for perhaps two main reasons. First, fly-fishers wanted to fish the fly even when trout were not rising. So they developed imitations of the underwater stages of insect life-cycles: nymphs, larvae, and pupae. Having made that step, why stop? So they imitated aquatic invertebrates that have no flying stage in their life-cycle, such as freshwater shrimps and hog-lice. And then small fish. Because they were all cast to fish on a fly-rod and line, these artificials were given the honorary title of "fly." Second, there was the influence of North American fly-fishers. They had lots of fish that would not rise to eat tiny insects: in freshwater, northern pike and muskies, pickerel, smallmouth and largemouth bass, shad, and, in the seas off New England, striped bass, bluefish, and weakfish. They wanted to catch these fish on fly-tackle – and suitable "flies" had to be tied.

This section of the book examines the range of fish foods available – from traditional insects to large mollusks, crustaceans, and baitfish – and some of the most modern ways to imitate these foods. However, we still do not know it all, and advances will continue to be made.

INSECT FOOD AND LIFE-CYCLES

OLIVER EDWARDS

Most freshwater fish eat insects, if only when they are fry and too small to devour anything larger. There is one loch in northern Scotland where the only fish is the northern pike; the smaller pike eat insects, and the larger pike the smaller pike. Fly-fishers, however, associate insect food mainly with trout, char, whitefish, and grayling, because these fish species often feed exclusively on insects.

Aquatic and land-bred insects

Fish may eat insects that have developed from eggs laid in the water (mayflies, stoneflies, caddisflies, midges, dragonflies) or from eggs that were laid on dry land (ants, black gnats, crane flies or daddy-long-legs, and grasshoppers).

Adult land-bred insects often fall or are blown onto the water, to be eaten by fish; the immature stages are less commonly encountered because they are hidden away among dense cover or in the soil; exceptions include grasshopper nymphs (p96) and inchworms (p97). You should concentrate on the adult stage when tying flies to imitate land-bred insects. However, fish feed on both the subsurface immature stages and on the winged adults of aquatic insects. So to catch trout or grayling that are feeding on aquatic insects, it is important not only to understand the life-cycles of these insects but also be able to imitate each developmental stage that the fish might eat.

Metamorphosis

All insects undergo a fantastic change of form and structure as they develop from egg to adult, a change known as metamorphosis. Both insect growth and metamorphosis involve molting. Insects have a restricting outer skin, or "shuck," which will allow for only a little expansion. When the shuck is full, the insect cannot grow larger unless it molts from its old skin and produces a new, larger skin. The back of the shuck splits (usually along the rear of the head and thorax) and the creature crawls out through the opening. The new outer skin of the molted insect quickly hardens into a shuck that is slightly bigger than the discarded one. Some insects undergo up to 20 molts in their life-cycles, most of them in the "growing stages" described below.

There are two types of metamorphosis: incomplete and complete.

Incomplete metamorphosis

In incomplete metamorphosis the egg hatches into a nymph. A nymph is a miniature version of the adult insect, although there are differences between the two: adults usually have wings, nymphs do not; nymphs often have gills for breathing underwater, adults do not; nymphs usually have a drab green-olive-brown camouflaged coloration, while many adults are brightly colored. The nymph feeds and grows, molting repeatedly, until it eventually reaches maximum size. It now undergoes a final molt, either at the water surface or after it has crawled to shore, where the adult emerges from the final nymphal shuck.

The life-cycles of mayflies, stoneflies, dragonflies, damselflies, grasshoppers, and land-bugs all follow incomplete metamorphosis. In most species the life cycle takes a full year but in a very few large species two years (about 100 weeks as a nymph). In the aquatic mayflies, stoneflies, dragonflies, and damselflies both nymphs and adults may be eaten by fish, but in the land-bred grasshoppers and land-bugs the adults and nymphs may be eaten only when they fall or are blown onto the water from vegetation.

Complete metamorphosis

In complete metamorphosis the egg hatches into a tiny larva, which feeds and grows until it has reached its full size. In most species the life-cycle takes a full year to complete, though in some very tiny species there may be two or more generations in one year. The larva looks nothing like the adult into which it will metamorphose; it takes the form of a maggot, caterpillar, or even, in the case of midges, a tiny worm. When fully grown, the larva enters a resting stage as the pupa, or chrysalis, during which all bodily tissues are transformed into those of the adult form. The pupa is often enclosed in a cocoon constructed of silk or hard brown chitin and cannot move, although in some aquatic species there is no cocoon and the pupa can swim quite vigorously. When the time comes to hatch the pupa cuts

INCOMPLETE METAMORPHOSIS (STONEFLY)

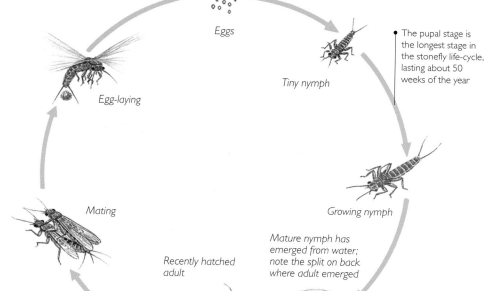

Eggs

Egg-laying

Tiny nymph

The pupal stage is the longest stage in the stonefly life-cycle, lasting about 50 weeks of the year

Mating

Growing nymph

Recently hatched adult

Mature nymph has emerged from water; note the split on back where adult emerged

Adult stage usually lasts for a few days

its way out of the cocoon. Aquatic species then swim to the water surface, where the adult insect emerges from its pupal shuck and flies away.

In all insects, within a given species the timing of the adults' emergence is relatively fixed. For example, the peak emergence of the big mayfly on one Irish lough occurs every afternoon throughout the last two weeks of May. At this time the fish feed keenly on the hatching adults.

Mating follows the hatch, after which the adult females return to the water to lay their eggs. Fish eat large quantities of females that are laying eggs, or that have died on the water after egg-laying.

Caddisflies, midges, and blackflies are aquatic insects, the larvae and pupae of which may be found in the water, with adults hatching from the water surface. In aquatic beetles the larval and adult stages occur in water, but the larvae pupate on dry land. In alderflies, the adults lay eggs on overhanging branches and the larvae drop into the water to develop before crawling out to pupate on dry land, so the fish rarely eat the pupa or the adult. Ants, black gnats, crane flies, and land-bred beetles are examples of those insects that spend their life-cycle on dry land, but as adults they may fall or be blown onto the water.

Crucial stages of insect life-cycles

The following are the stages of insect life-cycles that are exploited by fish, which fly-fishers must be prepared to imitate with flies:

- Growing larvae and nymphs: quite vulnerable, but often hidden away. Fish encounter these when grubbing on the bottom or in weed beds.
- Pupae and nymphs swimming to the shore or water surface to hatch: very vulnerable and many are eaten (one estimate suggests that four of these are taken for every hatched adult). A most important stage to imitate.
- Surface emergers (nymphs or pupae resting at the surface and adults that are in the act of emerging from nymph or pupal shuck at the surface): extremely vulnerable. Huge numbers are eaten by fish during a "hatch." A vital stage for fly-fishers to imitate.
- Adult resting on the surface after hatching: very vulnerable, especially on days when they are not able to fly away quickly (cold or wet weather). A most important stage to imitate.
- Spent females: females that have laid their eggs and died on the water are easy prey. An important stage to imitate.
- Land-bred insects: flies that have fallen or been blown onto the water are usually easy prey when they become waterlogged in the water's surface film. This is an important stage to imitate, especially where the banks are heavily overgrown.

A grayling takes a fly from the surface — it's time for dry fly! Grayling are especially fond of tiny insects, such as midges.

COMPLETE METAMORPHOSIS (CHIRONOMID MIDGE)

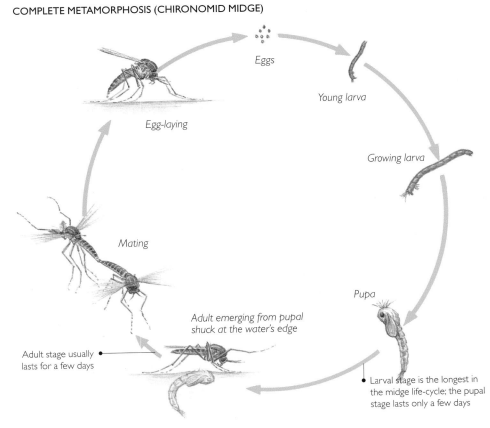

Eggs

Young larva

Egg-laying

Growing larva

Mating

Pupa

Adult emerging from pupal shuck at the water's edge

● Adult stage usually lasts for a few days

● Larval stage is the longest in the midge life-cycle; the pupal stage lasts only a few days

MAYFLIES

OLIVER EDWARDS

Mayflies are among the most important foods for freshwater fly-fishers' fish, particularly throughout the Earth's temperate and sub-Arctic regions. Mayflies belong to the Order Ephemeroptera. They are all short-lived as adults, ranging from a few hours for the tiny adults of some species (such as trichos and curses) to three or four days for most others.

Mayflies have an incomplete metamorphosis that is unique, in that there are two flying stages, not just one as in most insects. The egg hatches into a nymph which, when fully grown, swims to the surface of the water. A drab "dun" emerges from the nymphal shuck and floats on the lake or river surface until it is able to fly off into nearby vegetation. Here there is a final molt: the back of the dun splits and out crawls the sexually mature "spinner." The spinners mate and the female returns to the water to lay her eggs, following which she dies on the water as a "spent spinner."

Mayfly nymphs

Mayfly nymphs can be distinguished from all other nymphs by their three tails and by the gills on the sides of the abdominal segments. Those nymphs that are nearing emergence can be told from younger nymphs by the very dark large wing-buds on the back of the thorax.

Mayfly nymphs can be categorized according to their preferred microhabitat within the lake or river and the way in which they move:

• Burrowers spend their nymphal lives in burrows on the bottom of the river or lake. They emerge only when it is time for them to swim to the surface and hatch into duns.

Unless they are washed from their burrows during a flood, burrowers are not commonly encountered by feeding fish.

• Stone clingers are sturdy nymphs with stout legs that terminate in hooked feet that are adapted for gripping boulders in strong, turbulent currents. They are found in abundance, and are a fairly common fish food in free-stone streams and in rocky lakes.

• Moss Creepers are very poor swimmers that live within the shelter of water-moss, dense weed beds, and leaf-litter. Fish grubbing about on the bottom will often feed on them.

• Silt Crawlers are nymphs of the smaller mayflies. They are camouflaged for crawling through silt or mud on lake- and riverbeds. Fish seem to take them rarely.

• Swimmers are mayfly species that can swim. Some swim slowly ("labored swimmers"); other species can swim quite vigorously ("agile darters").

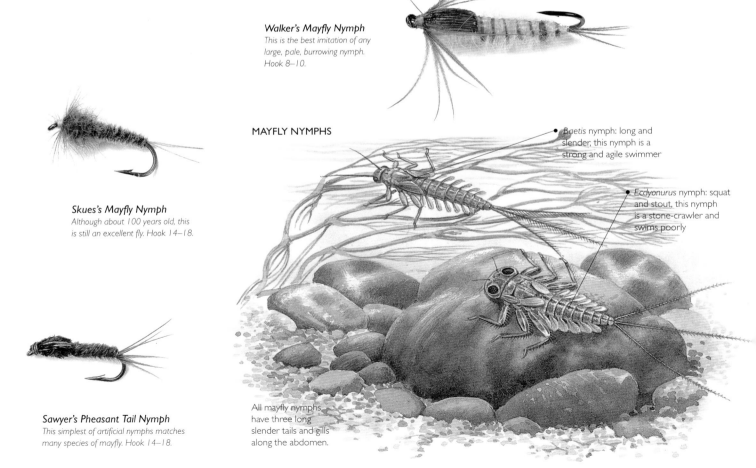

Walker's Mayfly Nymph
This is the best imitation of any large, pale, burrowing nymph. Hook 8–10.

Skues's Mayfly Nymph
Although about 100 years old, this is still an excellent fly. Hook 14–18.

Sawyer's Pheasant Tail Nymph
This simplest of artificial nymphs matches many species of mayfly. Hook 14–18.

MAYFLY NYMPHS

Baetis nymph: long and slender, this nymph is a strong and agile swimmer

Ecdyonurus nymph: squat and stout, this nymph is a stone-crawler and swims poorly

All mayfly nymphs have three long slender tails and gills along the abdomen.

Swimming nymphs are among the most widespread and abundant species. They are readily consumed by fish and are important for the fly-fisher to imitate.

Imitations of mayfly nymphs

Mayfly nymphs have been copied by fly-tyers for many years, although the early artificials were crude. It was not until the Englishman G E M Skues (1858–1949) began investigating nymphs that he found in the stomachs of trout, and matching them on hooks with silk, fur, and feather, that the modern nymph was born. Skues fished the southern chalkstreams of England where the agile darter type of nymph predominates; his series of artificial nymphs remained a standard for many years and is the foundation for many present-day patterns

Frank Sawyer (1906–80) was river keeper on the Wiltshire Avon, a southern English chalkstream, from 1928. He spent much time studying nymphs and discovered that when a mayfly nymph is swimming it holds its six legs tucked in neatly and streamlined on the underside of its thorax. He therefore devised a small selection of nymphs that lacked legs – a complete departure from the Skues style, which had been widely used up to that time.

Sawyer's most famous pattern is his Pheasant Tail Nymph, an artificial that matches many species of darkish "Olive Nymphs." It is world famous and as popular today as it ever was. Vary the size to match the nymph you see in the water. Sawyer's nymphs are unique in that tying thread is not used in their construction. Fine copper wire from small transformers is used instead; this also forms the basic underbody shape and adds the weight that is needed to sink the nymph.

In the years since Skues and Sawyer, most advances in the development of artificial nymphs have been modifications of their techniques. Three more recent nymph imitations are, however, worth describing.

Richard Walker's Mayfly Nymph was one of the first, and is still the most effective, attempting to match the green drake nymph, a large creamy nymph that spends up to two years burrowing in a river- or lake-bed before swimming to the surface to hatch into a dun. This pattern may be used to represent a nymph that has been washed from its burrow or is on its way to the surface. It is a simple fly with a lead underbody, cream angora wool, pheasant-tail fibres, and some black thread.

Modern synthetic materials, particularly fine transparent or colored translucent plastic sheet, have become a popular medium for nymph abdomen construction. They solve the age-old problem of translucence, something that real nymphs have but the older materials lacked somewhat. One of the earliest of these artificial nymphs was devised by John Goddard and called the PVC Nymph.

One group of mayfly nymphs that has escaped the attention of fly-tyers is the "stone clinger" type: those fat, broad-headed, almost crab-like nymphs that scuttle about when you turn over a large rock from the streambed. Having found that these nymphs are abundant in cool, rocky rivers throughout the world, and that trout and grayling love them, I set out to imitate them. Vary the size and color of my Heptagenid Nymph to match the ones you find in your own stream.

Note that flies are sized according to the size of hook on which they are tied. The smaller the fly, the larger the number.

Goddard's PVC Nymph
Translucence is produced by overwinding thin, clear polythene. Hook 14–18.

Edwards' Heptagenid Nymph
Edwards' Heptagenid is an ultra-imitation of a stoneclinger nymph. Hook 14–18.

A clearwater limestone stream where 17 species of mayfly contribute to the trout diet.

Mayfly emergers

When fully grown, the mayfly nymph swims to the surface and rests for a few seconds, without moving, before the dun emerges from the nymph onto the water surface. Once it has emerged, the dun is very vulnerable to predation by surface-feeding fish.

Mayfly emerger imitations

The aim is to have an unweighted nymph pattern floating or "suspending" from the surface film of the water. Many solutions have been produced in Europe and North America, such as small balls of fur, polystyrene balls, or pieces of closed-cell rigid foam fixed to the back of the thorax.

One very successful pattern from Switzerland uses the *cul de canard* feather taken from around the preen gland of the common farmyard duck. This feather is tied in as a loop to hold the nymph in position, and also to suggest the wings of the dun emerging from the nymph's thorax.

Have a selection of Petitjean Mayfly Emergers, and vary them in both size and color in order to match the emergers that the fish are eating.

Mayfly duns

The dun hatches onto the water surface and perches there only long enough to dry its wings and warm its flight muscles. Then it flies away. On warm, dry days the dun might rest on the water for only a few seconds; on dank, cold days it may rest for a minute or more.

Duns can be identified by their two or three tails, long slender abdomen, tiny antennae, long forelegs (in males), and the large forewings that are held together or only slightly apart and upright when the insect is resting. They are fairly drab insects (yellow duns and green drakes are two exceptions) with opaque wings.

Mayfly dun imitations

Mayfly duns are the traditional insects of fly-fishing. Very simple, crude imitations date back to the early 15th century, and it was the copying and fishing of duns that gave rise to that most elegant and graceful form of our sport, dry fly-fishing, in the second half of the 19th century.

While wet (subsurface) dun imitations had been around for centuries, it was Frederick M Halford (1844–1914) who influenced the design of the modern dry fly (on-the-surface) dun. He established new tying styles, materials, and attention to detail that were ground-breaking and last to this day.

Halford's tying style was an attempt at exact imitation which, although producing some of the most beautiful of artificial flies, is unnecessary when it comes to deceiving the fish.

Halford was an English chalkstream angler, but he corresponded with a man on the other side of the Atlantic who was greatly influenced by Halford's work. That man, Theodore Gordon (1854–1915), became known as the father of fly-fishing in the United States.

Gordon fished the Catskill streams, and one early American school of fly-tying developed as the "Catskill style." Halford's influence can be seen in the style of tying, but note how the matching slips of quill feathers are replaced by clumps of lemon wood-duck fibers, which are tied in an upright V configuration.

Both Halford and Catskill dry flies have a wound "collar" hackle. In recent years the

Pettijean Mayfly Emerger
Essential when fish are taking emergers
from below the surface. Hook size 14–18.

Halford Dry Fly
Devised in the 19th century, but the Halford
style will deceive modern trout. Hook 14–16.

Catskill Dry Fly
A traditional North American dun pattern.
Hook 14–18.

EMERGERS, DUNS, AND ADULT MAYFLIES

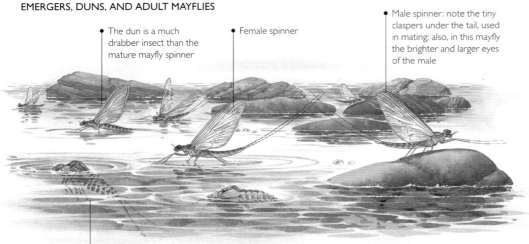

• The dun is a much drabber insect than the mature mayfly spinner

• Female spinner

• Male spinner: note the tiny claspers under the tail, used in mating; also, in this mayfly the brighter and larger eyes of the male

• A mayfly "emerger": the fully grown nymph has swum to the surface and the dun is now emerging through the dorsal side of the nymphal shuck

Parachute Dry Fly
The parachute hackle is now preferred
to the traditional hackle. Hook 14–18.

F-Fly
A simple hackless dry dun pattern.
Hook 14–20.

"parachute hackle" has gained in popularity throughout the world. Instead of being wound around the front of the hookshank, the hackle is wound around a tuft, bristle, or hair-wing so that it radiates out in a circle to support the fly on the surface of the water. This style of dun imitation allows the fly to land more gently on the water; it appears from below – as the fish see it – more like a real dun than many other imitations. It certainly catches difficult trout that have refused the conventional hackle.

So important is the dun, and so many are the innovative fly-tyers from around the world who have sought to imitate it, that there are many other styles of dry dun imitation. They include Marjan Fratnik's *cul de canard* F-Fly, which is simple but effective everywhere. Roman Moser's Screen Printed Synthetic Dun and the Polydun use the most modern synthetic materials in their tying. And the Fan Wing Mayfly, which originated in Ireland, uses a pair of duck breast feathers as wings in a traditional tying that contrasts with the modern Mathews and Juracek Sparkle Dun from the United States.

Mayfly spinners

The molt from dun to spinner is unique to the mayflies. The entire delicate, fine outer skin is shed to reveal a more brightly colored, transparent winged insect with a functioning reproductive system. The sole aim of the spinner is to mate, lay its eggs, and then die.

The swarming display of mayfly spinners takes place in still, warm conditions in the late afternoon, usually away from the water in the lee of trees or bushes, and usually close to some focal point – for example, a post, projecting branch, or large rock. The males fly vertically upward, then swoop or glide down before flying upward once more in a dance that is meant to attract a partner. Mating takes place quickly on the wing. When the female's eggs have been fertilized, she heads back to the water to lay them.

In some species the spinner lays her eggs by crawling underwater, but in many others the female lays them by flying over the water and dipping the tip of her abdomen into it. Her life's work over, she is now a worn-out, almost empty skin, used up and spent. She collapses on the

water, wings outstretched, legs crumpled, her empty abdomen glinting in the evening sunlight.

In a big spinner fall the water surface may be carpeted with literally millions of dead and dying corpses. These are easy meat for the fish, which feast greedily on them. And because the spinner fall usually takes place in the evening, the rise of trout to a fall of spinners has famously become called the "evening rise."

Mayfly spinner imitations

The spent spinner with her outstretched wings has received her share of attention over the years from fly-tyers. Some highly effective patterns were developed by William J Lunn (1862–1936), river keeper on the famed Houghton Club water on England's premier chalkstream, the River Test. For wings Lunn used the tips or points of glassy bright cock hackles, tied flat on either side. Today, a modern, low-density, high-glint synthetic is available. For tails, he used a bunch of bright hackle fibers, and for the body, a wound hackle stalk, which many British and American spent spinner patterns still use for bodies. So might you, almost a century later.

Polydun
One of the most modern dun patterns which can be modified to match a wide range of species. Hook 14–18.

Lunn's Particular
A pattern that will succeed when any small spinner is on the water. Hook 14–18.

Houghton Ruby
A very old, yet still effective spinner pattern. Hook 14–18.

Sparkle Dun
A new North American dun pattern. Hook 14–18.

Fan-wing Mayfly
An ancient Irish imitation of the large mayflies. Hook 8–12.

Sherry Spinner
A superb spinner pattern on all rivers. Hook 14–18.

STONEFLIES

OLIVER EDWARDS

Overall, stoneflies are of less importance to fish and fly-fishers than mayflies and caddisflies. This is because they live only in the coolest, cleanest rivers and lakes and cannot survive even the slightest pollution with which mayflies, caddisflies, trout, and grayling can cope. To find big populations of stoneflies you must look to upland regions or the Arctic and sub-Arctic where human influences on water quality are slight. Here stoneflies are extremely important to fish and to fly-fishers.

Stoneflies belong to the Order *Plecoptera*. In some larger species the adults may have greatly reduced wings and appear wingless, but in most there are four pairs of long wings. These are held flat over the body when at rest; in some smaller species (called needle-flies because of their shape) they are folded tightly around the body. When the insect is airborne the two pairs of wings are unsynchronized, giving the stonefly a characteristically weak flight.

Stonefly nymphs

Stonefly nymphs have slender cylindrical bodies, which in some species are slightly flattened. They have two distinct tails, which may be as long as the abdomen. A very diagnostic feature of stoneflies is that the tails are always well separated at the point where they join the body. They also have two long antennae. The thorax has three pairs of stout legs and, in older nymphs, two pairs of distinctive dark wing-buds. There are no gills on the abdomen. Gills at the base of the legs can be seen with the naked eye only in the larger stonefly nymphs. Most stonefly nymphs are some shade of brown, often with delicate yellow or orange scribbled markings on the upper surface (the nymphs of the yellow sally group of stoneflies are olive-yellow, and those of the black stonefly group are black).

Stonefly nymphs have a life-span of one to three years: the larger the species the longer the time spent as a nymph, and at very high altitudes or in Arctic waters the life-span is longer than in lowland or temperate waters. Smaller nymphs are vegetarian, larger ones carnivorous and often cannibalistic. (Be aware of this if you are collecting nymphs to examine later.)

Since stonefly nymphs spend most of their lives hidden among boulders on the river- or lake-bed they are well protected from the eyes of watchful fish. Some may occasionally be rooted out by fish, others washed out of their niche when the river is in spate. It is, however, when fully-grown stonefly nymphs migrate to the shore to hatch into adults that they feature greatly in the fish's diet.

LIFE-CYCLE OF STONEFLY *PERLA MAXIMA*

Egg-laying female

Dead, "spent" female

Troth's Terrible Stonefly Nymph
The late Al Troth moved stonefly nymph imitation farther by striving to copy the legs of the nymphs that he created. Hook 1–4.

Jorgensen's Stonefly Nymph
Paul Jorgensen went farther with realism with a stonefly nymph imitation that is accurate in size, silhouette, and color. Hook 4–10.

Kauffmann Stone
Another highly regarded pattern of the suggestive type, the Kauffmann Stone, devised by Randal Kauffmann. Hook 2–10.

Whitlock's Stonefly
One of the most realistic, fish-fooling stonefly nymph patterns comes from the vise of Dave Whitlock. Hook 2–12.

Brookes' Stonefly Nymph
A fairly early and highly successful pattern of the suggestive type devised by Montana's Joe Brookes. Hook 4.

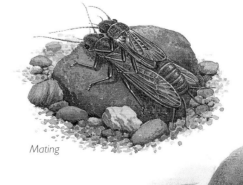

Mating

Adult male

In larger stoneflies, a large proportion of males have vestigial wings and are flightless.

The hatches of the largest species, such as the giant *Pteronarcys* stoneflies that emerge from rivers draining the Rockies and the large *Perla* found in some of the great Alpine streams, are famous and draw fly-fishers from far afield. When these large stonefly nymphs are "on," large catches of trout are made and some big specimen trout landed.

Stonefly nymph imitations

Stonefly patterns can be traced back for at least 200 years, but precise nymph imitations are a recent development originating in the United States. Imitating stonefly nymphs has always been a problem for the fly-tyer: how much of the detail of the natural insect should be copied on the hook? There are two alternative solutions: first, to give a general impression of a stonefly; and second, to tie something more convincing, which really looks like the real thing.

One of the most realistic, fish-fooling stonefly nymph patterns is that of Dave Whitlock, one of today's leading American fly-dressers. You will notice that Whitlock tied this fly "upside-down." This is because he had noticed that weighted flies tied on a down-eyed hook tended to fish the

wrong way up. So he ties his fly upside-down and it fishes the right way up!

Adult stoneflies

Adult stoneflies look just like nymphs with two pairs of wings, although they may be a little brighter in color than mature nymphs, and they may have shorter tails. They demonstrate the simplest of molt progressions through an incomplete metamorphosis. Males are often much smaller than females (in large species only two-

thirds of the female size), and in large species the males are often flightless.

Mating occurs on the ground, on a rock, or on a branch and never far from water, where the female will lay her eggs. In most small species the female lays her eggs in flight: as she flies over the water, she dips the tip of her abdomen into the surface to release eggs. In larger species the female runs or scuttles across the surface as she lays her eggs. It is during egg-laying that the adult stonefly is most important, both as a food for fish and as a fly for fly-fishers to imitate. On some of the great stonefly rivers of the western United States the "ripe" females can literally festoon bankside willows to such a degree that the thin branches bend under their weight. And as egg-laying gets underway these large fluttering females advertise their presence in such a crazy manner that the trout find them an easy target and a big mouthful.

Imitations of adult stoneflies

Most of the best-known adult stonefly patterns originate in the United States, including the Giant Salmon Fly, imitating the huge giant black stonefly or "salmon fly" of rivers in the Rocky Mountains.

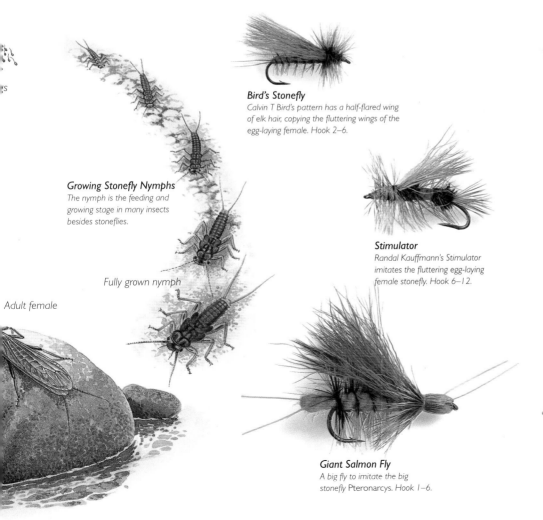

Bird's Stonefly
Calvin T Bird's pattern has a half-flared wing of elk hair, copying the fluttering wings of the egg-laying female. Hook 2–6.

Growing Stonefly Nymphs
The nymph is the feeding and growing stage in many insects besides stoneflies.

Fully grown nymph

Adult female

Stimulator
Randal Kauffmann's Stimulator imitates the fluttering egg-laying female stonefly. Hook 6–12.

Giant Salmon Fly
A big fly to imitate the big stonefly Pteronarcys. Hook 1–6.

February Red
The February red is a stonefly that hatches out in vast numbers on some Finnish streams shortly after ice melt. This imitation mimics the fluttering egg-laying female. Hook 12–14.

Hair-wing Trude
A popular stonefly pattern, this will bring up trout before or just after egg laying, when there are no real stoneflies on the water. Hook 6–12.

Petitjean's Stonefly
A tying that can be used to match all smaller stoneflies. Hook 10–16.

CADDISFLIES

OLIVER EDWARDS

In some parts of the world, for instance Scandinavia and the Alpine regions, caddisflies are more abundant and therefore more important to freshwater fish and fly-fishers than mayflies and stoneflies. No matter where you fish, there will be caddisflies – you might know them by their alternative name of "sedges" – and imitating them should be a major aspect of freshwater fly-fishing.

Caddisflies belong to the Order *Trichoptera*. The wings of adult caddisflies are covered by minute hairs, in contrast to the superficially similar moths that have wings covered in tiny scales. To tell moths and caddisflies apart look at the way they hold their wings over the body when at rest: in moths the wings are held flat, whereas in caddisflies the wings are arranged in ridge-tent fashion.

Caddis larvae

Caddis larvae are grub-like creatures with a soft white, cream, gray, or green segmented abdomen, a thorax with three pairs of strong legs, and a large head that bears powerful jaws. Caddis larvae are divided into two groups.

The first group contains the "cased caddis larvae," those that spend their entire larval life in a hollow portable tube or case. They make the cases themselves by binding bits of twig, leaf, sand, or pebbles together using a fine silk that is secreted from silk glands. As they grow they enlarge their case. Some species of caddis larvae can be identified from the way their cases are constructed. Cased caddis larvae are abundant in both rivers and lakes.

The second group contains the "free-living caddis larvae," those that do not make a case. This category of caddis larvae can be subdivided into three smaller groups:
• Those species that live in tunnels or galleries made from silk.
• Those that construct tiny net-like shelters.
• Those that have no shelter at all and roam freely on the riverbed.
The free-living caddisflies living in tunnels and nets use these as traps for food carried by the current, whereas the roaming caddis larvae are hunters and can catch animals almost as large as themselves such as fish eggs and fry, and large mayfly nymphs. Caseless, free-living caddis larvae are found only in rivers or lakes where a river flows into or out of them.

While most caddis larvae are fairly small, some lake species of cased caddis are 3cm (1¼in) and some roaming free-living larvae 2.5cm (1in). Fish are very fond of caddis larvae. If you catch one that has been feeding on cased caddis you may be able to feel the caddis cases crunching if you gently massage the belly of the fish between thumb and forefinger.

Imitations of caddis larvae

Imitations of caddis larvae are fairly new in the history of fly-fishing, mainly because the natural

Czech Nymph
The Czech Nymph and the Polish Woven Nymph come from eastern Europe. They are very effective at catching trout and grayling. Hook 8–12.

Polish Woven Nymph
Like the Czech Nymph, this suggests free-living caddis larvae. Hook 8–12.

Hydropsyche Larva
Real Hydropsyche larvae are net-weaving caseless larvae. Many get washed from their nets in a spate. Trundle this pattern along the river bed and a trout or grayling will grab it with gusto! Hook 8–12.

Rhyacophila Larva
Real Rhyacophila larvae are those roaming larvae that seek large prey. They are especially abundant around the world in fast-flowing rivers where the boulders are covered in water-moss. Countless trout and grayling throughout Europe and the United States have fallen to this imitation. Hook 8–12.

CADDIS LARVAE

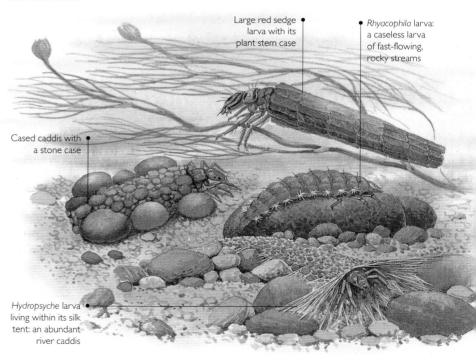

Large red sedge larva with its plant stem case

Rhyacophila larva: a caseless larva of fast-flowing, rocky streams

Cased caddis with a stone case

Hydropsyche larva living within its silk tent: an abundant river caddis

Edwards' Ascending Pupa
The legs and black wing-buds of the adult can be seen. This pattern imitates a pupa swimming to hatch at the surface. Hook 10–14.

Peeping Caddis
Another modern pattern to match any cased caddis larva. The (lead-free) shot gives the fly an upside-down bias and helps prevent the hook point snagging on the river- or lake-bed. Hook 6–10.

Moser's Goldhead Sedge
The gold head helps sink the fly and adds "flash." Hook 8–14.

Lafontaine's Emergent Sparkle Pupa
The Antron used in this pattern simulates air bubbles beneath the skin of the pupa. Hook 8–16.

Huitila's Floating Caddis Pupa
This pattern floats and imitates a pupa at the surface before the adult hatches. Hook 10–16.

CADDIS PUPAE

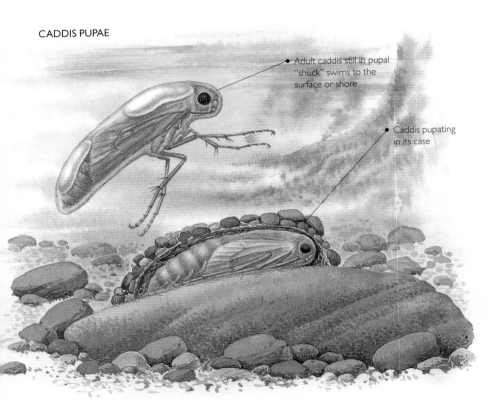

Adult caddis still in pupal "shuck" swims to the surface or shore

Caddis pupating in its case

insects are found on the river- or lake-bed, so effective artificials must be weighted to reach exactly the same position. Early fly-fishers' flies were unweighted and fished on or just under the surface – so it must have been a brave step when the first fly-tyer wound lead wire around a hookshank and began to imitate a cased caddis larva.

However, since the 1980s great strides have been made in producing some effective imitations of caddisfly larvae, especially in European countries such as Finland, the Czech Republic, and Poland, where caddisflies dominate the diets of trout and grayling.

Caddis pupae

When the larva has grown to full size (this takes almost a year in most species, but can take up to two years in some of the larger species) it enters the pupal stage of its development. Cased caddis larvae belay their cases to rocks, block up the entrances, and then retreat into a cocoon, which they spin within their shelter.

Free-living larvae build a small domed shelter of sand or pebbles that is held together by silk, before spinning a cocoon and entering their pupal stage. Few of these caddis pupae are taken by fish.

After about two or three weeks, when the adult form has developed within the cocoon, the pupa uses its sharp mandibles to cut through the cocoon and case. Then it either swims to the surface or to the shore, where the adult hatches from the pupal shuck. Most caddisfly hatches occur in the summer and the early months of fall, and usually in the evening or in complete darkness. At the appropriate time, huge numbers of pupae will simultaneously be swimming to hatch, and the fish will quickly key on to them. You must act quickly, for this movement may last for only an hour or so. Tie on the right fly and you will catch fish after fish throughout. Get it wrong and you might miss the event.

Imitations of swimming caddis pupae

Probably the best-known and most widely used caddis pupa pattern is Gary Lafontaine's Emergent Sparkle Pupa. This utilizes synthetic trilobal fibers (Antron) as a loose sheath or bubble around the abdomen of the imitative fly.

This design resulted from Gary spending hundreds of hours observing caddis pupae swimming to the surface to hatch. He noticed that, on nearing the surface, the pupae appear to be shimmering in a gas-filled sheath. The Antron sheath mimics this effect.

G & H Sedge
*Because it is constructed
mainly of hollow deer hair, the
G & H Sedge will float forever.
Hook 8–16.*

C D C Sedge
*Cul de canard is being increasingly
used for all manner of dry flies.
This one is by Finland's Veli Autti.
Hook 10–16.*

Skues' Little Red Sedge
*A traditional caddisfly imitation by G E M
Skues that is hard to beat.. However,
after being chomped by a fish or two the
feather-fiber wing is apt to disintegrate.
The Slovenian fly-fisher Bozidar Voljc solved
this problem by gluing whole feathers onto
the material used in ladies' panty hose
as a reinforcement. The wing is then cut
to shape. Highly effective!
Hook 12–16.*

Moser's Balloon Caddis
*Roman Moser's Balloon Caddis
with its head of rigid close-cell
foam will float forever.
Hook 10–14.*

Troth's Elk Hair Caddis
*Al Troth's Elk Hair Caddis is probably
the most famous and easily tied of all
dry caddisflies. An American pattern, it
will take trout and grayling from any
river or lake in the world. Hook 10–20.*

ADULT CADDISFLIES

Adult caddisflies: wings
are held tent-like over
body; in most, antennae
are extremely long

Trout surfacing to catch
adult caddisflies: the fly-fisher
can exploit this habit with
a good dry fly

Klinkhammer Special
*An unusual-looking caddis imitation,
but an extremely effective one from
Holland's Hans van Klinken. The
abdomen dips beneath the water
surface, perhaps imitating a female
in the act of laying her eggs. Your
fly-box should always contain several
Klinkhammer Specials in a range
of sizes and colors. Hook 10–16.*

Adult caddisflies

The freshly hatched adult caddisfly wastes no time in leaving the water surface, because it is in mortal danger if it hangs about there. As soon as it is free from its pupal shuck it zooms off toward the nearest fixed object and rests. Therefore, during a hatch of caddisflies, you will see few if any adults on the surface, and a dry caddisfly imitation may be useless because the fish will be concentrating on the thousands of ascending pupae underneath the water surface. That is why many fly-fishers consider caddisfly hatches something of an anticlimax – they fish dry imitations of the adult when they should be fishing subsurface pupal imitations. The adult imitations come into their own when the fish are feeding on female caddisflies that have returned to the water to lay their eggs.

Adult caddisflies can survive for several weeks. Therefore, during periods of cool, wet weather they rest and wait. Then on a warm summer evening the males form huge mating swarms, often under trees overhanging the water. Females are attracted to the swarms by pheromones, which are released by the males, and they quickly mate. Now the females are ready to lay their eggs.

Imitations of adult caddisflies

We are spoiled for choice when it comes to selecting an effective adult caddisfly pattern, because there are so many from which to choose. They are always fished dry, on the surface. You may sometimes fish them passively, letting them drift naturally with the current. But sometimes it is better to fish them actively, tweaking them across the surface rather like a scuttling adult. Plan to experiment every time you go fishing to see which is the best approach.

If you watch carefully on a warm summer's evening you may notice that egg-laying can occur in one of three ways:
● The female flies over the water and dips the tip of her abdomen into the surface. In some species all the eggs are shed at the same time; in others the female may have to dip many times in order to release them all.
● The female swims down to fix her eggs onto the river- or lake-bed. She might dive straight in or crawl in from a boulder or reed stem.
● She scuttles across the surface, depositing eggs as she goes.
● Rarely, some females lay their eggs inside a jelly casing on overhanging vegetation. When the tiny larvae hatch they fall into the water.

After egg-laying is over most females are still capable of flight and of running around. Many of them finish up on the water, hopping and scuttling to and fro, where they make a gourmet meal for a hungry trout.

Evening falls over a trout lake and, as if by magic, huge clouds of caddisflies drift over the water. Such conditions promise exciting sport.

MIDGES, DAMSELS, AND DRAGONFLIES

GARY BORGER

Midges are found in all types of fresh water throughout the world, and are highly important in the diet of many fish. There are thousands of species, spead across at least nine families, and many of them occur in millions in suitable lakes or rivers. By contrast, dragonflies and damselflies occur commonly, though in much smaller numbers, in weedy lakes, canals, and the slower reaches of rivers. A trout devouring one fully grown dragonfly nymph will have to devour hundreds of midges to get the same nourishment.

Midge larvae

Midge larvae are worm-like in appearance. The segmentation is clearly visible in the semi-transparent body. Jointed legs are absent, but short fleshy "prolegs" may occur at the end of the body. Most are a dirty cream, olive-brown, or blood red. They are usually small (3–10mm (⅛–½in) in length), but some lake species can be up to 25mm (1in) in length.

Imitating midge larvae

A host of imitations have been developed to ape these insects, but all show the natural creature's segmentation and imitate the narrow body. The South Platte Brassie is excellent, as are the Fur Midge Larvae and Larval Lace Midge. Midge larvae are present all year, and imitations should be fished dead-drift near the bottom in weedy areas of streams and in the littoral areas of lakes. A strike indicator helps detect the often delicate take of the trout or grayling, and can serve as a suspender device to help hold the imitation just over weeds.

Midge pupae

Chironomidae pupae are mobile, swimming about in the weeds or along the bottom where they can quickly find shelter. This life-cycle stage often sports clumps of gills on the thorax and abdomen. The segmented abdomen is topped off with a robust thorax bearing a pair of wing pads. The pupa is generally 20 per cent shorter than the larva and often very different in color; medium-gray, bright green, medium-yellow, red, tan, black, and olive are most usual.

At maturity, the pupa wiggles to the surface from which the adult emerges. The pupa may hang motionless at the surface for many seconds before the adult can work its way free of the pupal shuck.

Imitating midge pupae

This stage is highly important to the fly-fisher because the fish will feed heavily on the pupae that are concentrated at the surface preparing to hatch. Fish eating pupae will make a classic "smutting" rise: look out for a delicate bulging of the water

South Platte Brassie
A simple red (bloodworm) larva imitation.
Hook 12–18.

Fur Midge Larva
This pattern matches the cream-gray midge larva.
Hook 12–18.

Sparkle Midge Pupa
Vary the color and size to match the hatching midge.
Hook 12–18.

Griffiths Gnat
It may not look to us like a midge – but it does to a fish.
Hook 14–22.

MIDGE LARVAE

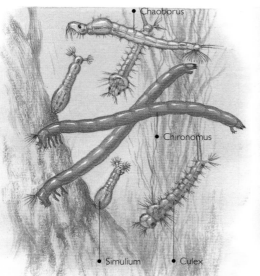

Chaoborus
Chironomus
Simulium
Culex

MIDGE PUPAE

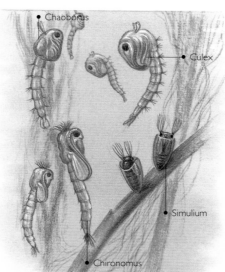

Chaoborus
Culex
Simulium
Chironomus

ADULT MIDGES

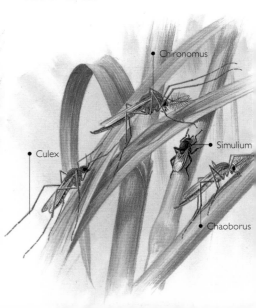

Chironomus
Simulium
Culex
Chaoborus

that pushes low, delicate rings slowly outward on the surface. Sparkle Midge Pupae or Suspender Midge Pupae are excellent choices. These patterns are fished just under the film with a greased leader in lakes and quiet stream areas, or hung several inches below a yarn indicator for fishing in broken-water areas of streams. Because the imitations are usually small, the terminal tackle must be fine; great care is needed to land the sometimes very large fish that are encountered feeding on midge pupae.

Adult midges

Chironomid adults look like mosquitoes but they don't bite. Other midge families are more robust-looking, and some, like the *Simulidae* (reed-smuts or buffalo flies), have a nasty bite. The wide range of colors includes black, gray, olive, and red. Only two wings is a diagnostic characteristic of the scientific Order *Diptera*. Male *Chironomidae* midges also have easily visible, feathery antennae. Long legs hold the body well above the water as a newly hatched insect sits on the surface.

Imitating adult midges

Fish-eating adults also produce a delicate rise form, but look for the fish's snout poking above the surface as it sips in the hapless morsels. Since midges are present year-round, this stage is highly important to the fly-fisher fishing the fall, winter, and early spring months. This is when hatching normally occurs in the midday hours. In summer, hatching is most usual at dawn and at dusk.

The Griffith's Gnat is the best all-around imitation for the adult midge. In its original design (peacock herl body, palmered grizzly hackle) it mimics many species, even those with a different

Chaoborus, the phantom-fly midge, is common in lakes; Culex, the mosquito, is more abundant in small pools. Simulium, the reed-smut or buffalo-gnat, is found only in rivers. Chironomus midges occur commonly in both lakes and rivers. All four insects are favorite food. of fish, in larval, pupal, and adult form.

body color. For picky fish that demand the correct color, use a body of sparkle yarn well picked out before the hackle is wound. When fish seem particularly picky, they may well be eating emerging adults. If this seems to be the case, trim the Griffith's Gnat on the bottom and fish the fly right down in the surface film. This fly also nicely mimics the "clump fly" stage of the adult. During mating, several males will surround a single female as she sits on the water's film. Fish will eat the whole bunch at one time, so a fly several sizes larger than the body of the natural can be just as effective, if not more so, than one that closely matches the natural size.

Damsel and dragon nymphs

Every fly-fisher will know the large, often gaudy adult damselflies and dragonflies that hover on warm summer days over lakes and rivers. Brightly colored adults are imitated with a Braided Butt Damsel, which matches the Common Blue Damsels found throughout the Northern Hemisphere. Nymphs of the damsel- and dragonfly that occupy the weedy areas of lakes and

slow-water reaches of streams are important and effective imitations. Most are 2–3cm (¾–1¼in) long and feed on other insects, crustaceans, and small fish. They vary from pale to dark olive or brown, and can change color to suit their background.

Imitating damsel and dragon nymphs

Damsel nymphs are great swimmers and imitations should therefore show a good deal of motion. The Marabou Damsel Nymph is a particularly fine suggestion of the swimming natural. Dressed in medium olive-brown it will work everywhere. Fish it with plenty of action but not plenty of speed. Strip the fly back slowly – about 30cm (12in) in three seconds – and simultaneously vibrate the rod tip. This will cause the moving fly to jiggle most enticingly.

Dragonfly nymphs are nicely suggested by bulky-bodied flies such as the Fur Chenille Dragon, Fur Strip Dragon, or Feather Bodied Dragon. In lakes, fish the imitation deep over sunken weed beds, working it along with 15cm (6in) pulls. In streams, fish the fly with a dead-drift, bottom-bouncing tactic.

Marabou Damsel Fly
The marabou tail flickers in the water like the abdomen of a real nymph. Hook 10–12.

DAMSELFLIES

Adult Damsel Fly
A super imitation of an adult damselfly. Hook 10–12.

COMMON DAMSELFLY

• Dragonflies and damselflies are among the most colorful of insects

• Nymphs have three leaf-like tails and prominent wing-buds

Terrestrials

GARY BORGER

Landbred insects, or "terrestrials", can be a very important component of a fish's diet. In studies of the feeding habits of meadow trout, for example, some researchers found these insects comprised at least 50 per cent of the fish's diet. Although any terrestrial that falls into the water can become fish food, the most significant are the grasshoppers, ants, beetles, jassids, and inchworms. One or the other of these is on a fish's menu throughout warm months.

Grasshoppers

Most important in the fly-fisher's late summer, these large insects, 18–50mm (¾–2in) long, vary widely in color, but most are green, yellow, or tan. Their jumping habit can get them into trouble with fish. As these insects cavort about recklessly in the meadows and open woodlands along rivers they occasionally end up on the water. Once there, they begin kicking for shore. This activity is a sure lure for any nearby fish.

Grasshoppers are also excellent fliers, and will sometimes migrate in large numbers, ending up quite far from shore in large rivers and lakes. They have been seen in Lake Superior 19km (12 miles) from land, where lake trout were feasting on them.

Fish take grasshoppers in a very positive manner, often slashing them off the surface with a good deal of splash and noise. They will take fly in the same way.

Imitating grasshoppers

Because of their large size and weight, grasshoppers ride very low in the water. Any imitation should do likewise. Delicate flies dressed with plenty of hackle are not as effective as more chunky versions dressed with compact bodies of deer-hair or closed-cell foam. Flies such as the Letort Hopper, Dave's Hopper, and the Bowlegged Hopper are excellent fish-getters because they so nicely mimic the profile of the natural in the surface film. Hopper imitations should be fished dead-drift, or dead-drift with an occasional twitch. But it is easy to overdo the twitching and give the game away.

Ants

These insects are present in every terrestrial ecosystem except the Antarctic. Most are small – 5–7mm (¼–⅜in) – but some are 14mm (⅝in) or more. Colored to match the soil, they are shades of black, brown, rusty red, and tan. In warm months they fall into the water from streamside vegetation. Ants will also swarm: new queens are produced and they leave the parent nest with a host of males (drones) to found new colonies. They often congregate in the thermals above lakes and streams and then drop to the water in untold millions. This is a time of gluttony for the fish and a time of great sport for the fly-fisher.

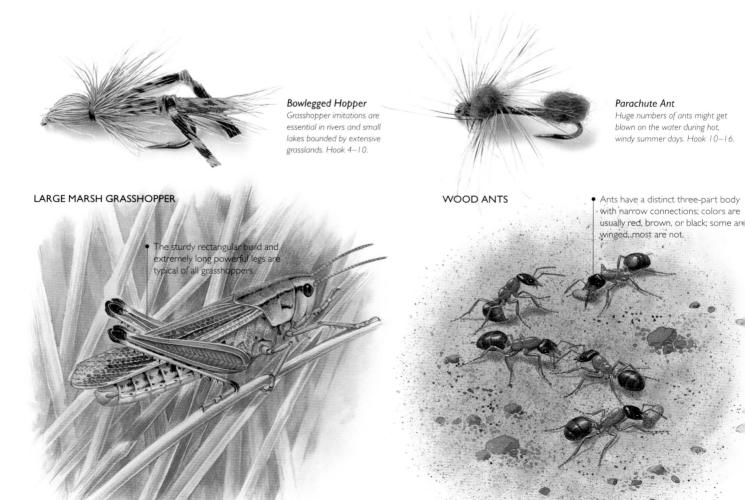

Bowlegged Hopper
Grasshopper imitations are essential in rivers and small lakes bounded by extensive grasslands. Hook 4–10.

Parachute Ant
Huge numbers of ants might get blown on the water during hot, windy summer days. Hook 10–16.

LARGE MARSH GRASSHOPPER

The sturdy rectangular build and extremely long powerful legs are typical of all grasshoppers

WOOD ANTS

Ants have a distinct three-part body with narrow connections; colors are usually red, brown, or black; some are winged, most are not.

Imitating ants

Ant patterns should express the lumpy nature of the natural's body and its widespread legs. Ants lying on the water become mired in the rubbery surface film, riding low and moving very little, if at all. An imitation should be designed and fished to do likewise. The Parachute Ant is a most realistic imitation in this regard.

Ants are often swept underwater in streams, and a wet ant pattern can be effective in streams everywhere. Although separate patterns could be dressed to imitate the drowned insects, I simply fish the Parachute Ant wet instead of dry.

Beetles

Like ants, beetles crawl around in vegetation and frequently fall onto the water. Beetles seem to be especially prevalent in water that runs through wooded areas. Also, like ants, they ride along mired in the film, moving little, their short legs poking out to the side like outriggers or hanging down into the water. They come in a truly vast array of colors, sizes, and shapes, but for the fly-fisher, black, peacock green, and brown are the only colors needed. Imitations should be dressed in sizes from 14mm down to 5mm (⅝in down to ⅛in).

Imitating beetles

Imitations should be compact and designed to sit low in the water. Thompson's Foam Beetle is the best imitation that I have ever used. This artificial fly is fished dead-drift. As with ants, beetles can get swept under. In addition, there are aquatic beetles that live among underwater plants, so fishing a beetle imitation wet can be remarkably effective. I prefer to fish the Foam Beetle with split lead-free shot 15–20cm (6–8in) ahead of it. The foam body makes the fly buoyant and it dances and jigs behind the shot. In fisheries where shot is not permitted, a sinking Latex Beetle imitation is useful.

Jassids

These insects are also called leaf hoppers. They vary from 7mm to as little as 3mm (⅜–⅛in) and come in a variety of greens and tans. During summer months, they jump about in streamside plants and frequently end up on the water. Because they look like tiny beetles on the water, a small Foam Beetle imitation will serve to take fish feeding on these insects.

Inchworms

Inchworms, or measuring worms, are usually a once-a-season phenomenon, normally in late spring

TOP TIP

Since terrestrials are always present, an imitation of one of these insects makes a good searching pattern in meadow and woodland streams. Fish the imitations near overhanging vegetation, casting to place the fly where fish would lie in wait for surface food (usually shallow water near cover).

or early summer. They are the leaf-eating larvae, or caterpillars of a number of tree-dwelling moths. Most are 10–25mm (½–1in) long and green and tan in color. When fully grown they spin a silken line and descend to the earth, where they pupate. Many of them end up dropping onto woodland streams, where they are readily taken by the fish.

Imitating inchworms

A simple fly of correct color and linear shape is all that you need. An inchworm imitation with a deer-hair or closed-cell foam body is most effective. Like other terrestrials, inchworms can drown, and a wet imitation of correct color (dressed with a simple chenille body) can be quite useful when the inchworms are falling.

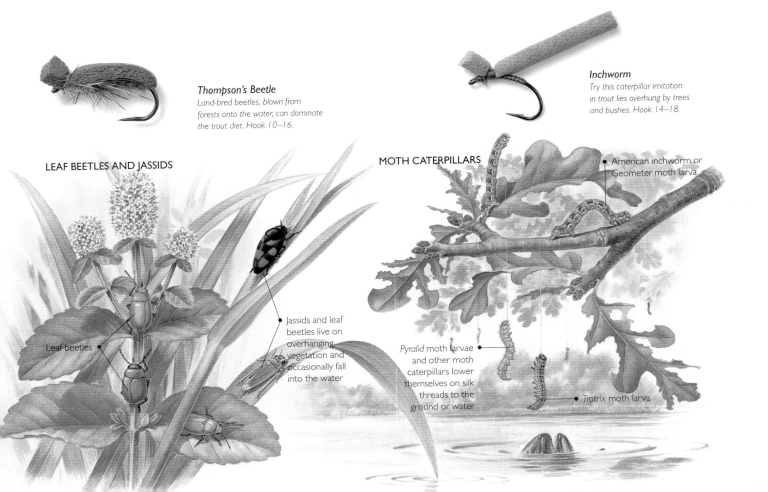

Thompson's Beetle
Land-bred beetles, blown from forests onto the water, can dominate the trout diet. Hook 10–16.

Inchworm
Try this caterpillar imitation in trout lies overhung by trees and bushes. Hook 14–18.

LEAF BEETLES AND JASSIDS

MOTH CATERPILLARS

American inchworm or Geometer moth larva

Leaf beetles

Jassids and leaf beetles live on overhanging vegetation and occasionally fall into the water

Pyralid moth larvae and other moth caterpillars lower themselves on silk threads to the ground or water

Trotrix moth larva

FRESHWATER CRUSTACEANS

GARY BORGER

Crustaceans have a worldwide distribution, inhabiting both freshwaters and saltwaters, and they vary in size from microscopic to as much as 1m (3ft) in length. They are, therefore, an important food source for fish throughout the world. In freshwater, fly-fishers will most frequently encounter scuds, cressbugs, crayfish, and crabs. These organisms live in the clean waters of rivers and lakes and in both warm and cold environments.

Scud

Also called amphipods and freshwater shrimp, these 5–20mm (¼–¾in) long creatures are the most widespread and abundant freshwater crustacean. The body is flattened at the sides and hinged like a suit of armor at each of its 15 segments. The legs project downward along the full length of the body. Scud vary in color from gray through olives to tans. They are denizens of shallow water, most living in areas less than 2m (6ft) deep. Like trout, scud require high oxygen levels. They are most abundant in weedy areas and in other areas where cover is plentiful.

Imitating scud

Scuds are strong swimmers, propelling themselves about rapidly with their bodies held quite straight and their abundant legs whirring in a flurry of activity. Therefore, scud-shaped imitations with built-in action perform the best. Specific imitations such as the Hair Leg Scud and Marabou Scud, and general imitations such as the Muskrat Nymph are excellent fish-taking flies. They should be fished with action. In streams, present the fly down and across and allow it to swing, or bounce and swing on the Leisenring Lift or "induced take." In lakes, retrieve scud patterns by giving a series of 2.5cm (1in) pulls, interrupted with an occasional rest period.

Cressbugs

Much more localized than scuds, these crustaceans are nevertheless an important item in the fish's diet where they do occur. Also known as sowbugs and water hoglice, they are flattened top to bottom and jointed like scuds, but they have lateral legs. These drab crustaceans, in shades of grays, olives, and tans, crawl about slowly in aquatic vegetation of both streams and lakes. If dislodged, they swim poorly, if at all.

Imitating cressbugs

Patterns such as the Hair Leg Cressbug, Fur Chenille Cressbug, Marabou Cressbug, or Muskrat Nymph should be fished dead-drift in streams, bouncing the fly along the bottom. In lakes, fish the imitation with a slow hand-twist retrieve just above submerged weed beds. It is also a good pattern to cast to cruising fish that you have spotted in shallow water.

Crayfish

Also known as "crawdads", these are perhaps the best-known freshwater crustaceans. The long, segmented body resembles that of a small lobster. Crayfish vary widely in size and occupy a host of watery environments, from springs to large rivers, from lakes to moist meadow lands. Typically, they excavate a burrow in which to hide. In rocky streams this may be nothing more than a cave scooped out under a handy stone, but in muddy-bottomed streams and lakes, or in wet meadows the burrow can be an extended tunnel. Because

Hairleg Scud
Another excellent general pattern that will match cressbug and scud. Hook 12–16.

GRAMMARUS – FRESHWATER SHRIMP OR SCUD

CRESSBUG

Muskrat Nymph
A buggy artificial that matches many creatures, including the scud and cressbug. Hook size 14–18.

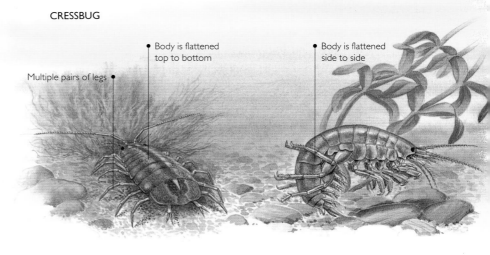

Multiple pairs of legs

Body is flattened top to bottom

Body is flattened side to side

of their often large size and close relationship to lobsters, crayfish are also eaten by humans.

These crustaceans are mostly shades of browns and occasionally olives. They have 10 walking legs, with the foremost pair modified into strong pincers, which are used to capture food and for defense (anyone who carelessly tries to catch one quickly discovers the value of the pincers as defensive weapons). Crayfish can reach lengths of 20cm (8in), but most are under 10cm (4in). Like other creatures with an exoskeleton, they must occasionally molt in order to grow. A newly molted crayfish is referred to as a "softshell," and is a highly prized morsel to fish – the pincers are soft, too, and the crustacean is defenseless. Although crayfish can walk about quite quickly, they flee backward when frightened, using their powerful abdomen to flip the broad telson, or tail, down and under the body, which propels them rapidly away from danger.

Imitating crayfish

Research has shown that fish prefer small crayfish to larger ones and will take females of any size before eating males. Fish also scoop up a fleeing crayfish faster than one that stands its ground with pincers open and widespread. This feeding behavior is directly tied to pincer size and aggressive prey behavior. The bigger the pincer, the greater the threat to the predator. When dressing crayfish imitations, I keep the pincers small and as non-threatening as possible.

I have also tied a fleeing crayfish design. The Fleeing Crayfish is by far the most successful imitation of these freshwater crustaceans. Dressed upside down on a weighted hook, and with a soft body in light rusty brown (to suggest a softshell), and in lengths of 2.5–5cm (1–2in) to suggest the female, the fly can be bounced over a rocky bottom or stripped quickly over gravel or silt areas without fear of it becoming entangled in debris. To suggest a crayfish in retreat, move the fly rapidly, using 30–60cm (1–2ft) strips on the line. An occasional pause often causes a following fish to grab the imitation quickly. More realistic-looking designs showing the creature in full dimension with pincers clearly displayed should be fished slowly to suggest a crayfish that is crawling about the bottom, unaware of impending danger.

Crabs

Freshwater crabs are a most interesting lot. They are not to be confused with crayfish; these are true crabs. The body is shortened and oval

in shape, not long like the crayfish. They occur in streams and lakes at the southern ends of the African and South American continents and in the lower reaches of some European rivers. Here, the 2.5–5cm (1–2in) wide crabs are highly important fish food. Even the largest freshwater fish will find one of these animals an often overwhelming, mouthful. Like crayfish, crabs can be feisty when threatened. They are a dark brownish-black in color and "crab" surprisingly fast when in danger.

Fly-fishers visiting the windswept "bocos" of South America, or those fishing the rocky streams of South Africa's rugged mountains, will find a Fur Chenille Crab or Strip Crab a valuable asset. Fish the imitations with action, bouncing and jigging them in streams, stripping it back with 30cm (1ft) long pulls on a sinking line in lakes.

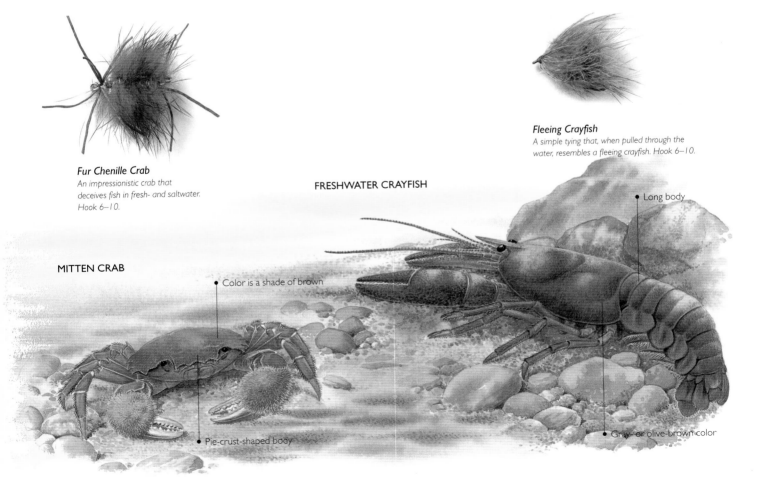

Fur Chenille Crab
An impressionistic crab that deceives fish in fresh- and saltwater. Hook 6–10.

Fleeing Crayfish
A simple tying that, when pulled through the water, resembles a fleeing crayfish. Hook 6–10.

FRESHWATER CRAYFISH

MITTEN CRAB

Color is a shade of brown

Long body

Pie-crust-shaped body

Gray- or olive-brown color

MOLLUSKS: CLAMS AND SQUID

TERRY JENNER

Although they have been relatively neglected by the fly-fisher, mollusks are an important food resource for both inshore and offshore saltwater fish. Inshore fish eat enormous quantities of marine snails and clams that live on the bottom of sandy bays, muddy estuaries, gravel flats, and rocky shores, while offshore species hunt and devour large quantities of squid.

Clams

Clams have two hard shells that can be tightly closed to protect the animal inside from predators, and prevent it from drying out when the tide has receded. Mussels and some other clam species live by attaching themselves to hard structures such as piers and rocks, but the majority of species bury themselves in soft mud and sand. Most of these burying clams remain under the surface even when they are feeding. They extend a long tube, called a siphon, up through the sand, which they use to vacuum the surface of the seabed or suck in seawater. The seawater is filtered for fragments of food, usually bacteria and tiny bits of detritus. The siphon is a trigger for feeding fish. They may grab it or use it as a marker so that they can grub down with their snouts to take the whole clam.

Imitating clams

The artificial Clam-Before-the-Storm matches the shell and long siphon of the real clam. It is a very effective fly for flatfish such as flounders and for bonefish that are rooting clams out of muddy sand. Let the fly drift about in the current close to the seabed, so that it suggests a clam that has been washed out when gale-swept high seas are pounding down on the beach.

Squid

Squid are the most mobile of mollusks; a squid can swim quickly by forcing a jet of water out of the back of its body, although it swims forward at a slower pace when it is not alarmed. In some regions squid often occur in schools large enough to support human fisheries and to attract schools of predatory fish.

Squid have torpedo-shaped bodies, a pair of triangular lateral fins, and 10 suckered tentacles. Two of the tentacles are longer than the others and are used to grasp prey. Most squid have a maximum length of 25cm (10in) – half of which is tentacle – but some grow much larger than this.

Imitating squid

Use the Inshore Squid as a pattern for beach and inshore fishing for species such as bonito, albacore, and, above all, for bluefish and striped bass. This can be cast and fished in the conventional manner: retrieve it by using long, explosive pulls that will closely imitate the squid's pulsating jet-engine.

The Offshore Squid is a different matter, because it is used to entice the huge blue-water species such as tuna, sailfish, and marlin. This is a big fly, 40–50cm (16–20in) in length, and is difficult to cast any significant distance. Instead the fish are "chummed" to the boat, and the Offshore Squid is dropped in front of their noses. When the fly is taken, set the hook and then hang on for dear life.

Clam-Before-the-Storm
Body ("shell") length up to 5cm (2in). Hook 2–8.

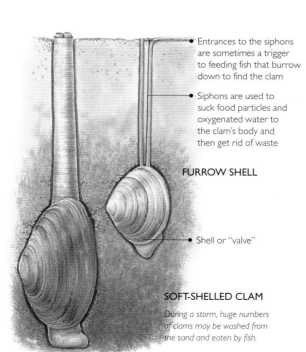

Entrances to the siphons are sometimes a trigger to feeding fish that burrow down to find the clam

Siphons are used to suck food particles and oxygenated water to the clam's body and then get rid of waste

FURROW SHELL

Shell or "valve"

SOFT-SHELLED CLAM

During a storm, huge numbers of clams may be washed from the sand and eaten by fish.

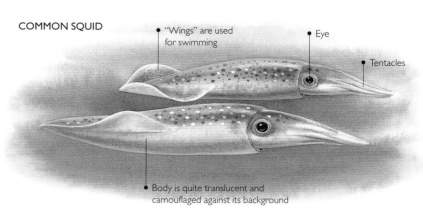

Squid
Most species occur in the size range 10–30cm (4–12in). Hook 4/0–4.

COMMON SQUID

"Wings" are used for swimming

Eye

Tentacles

Body is quite translucent and camouflaged against its background

SALTWATER CRABS

TERRY JENNER

You might imagine that the armor-plated crabs would be quite low on the fish's menu. Yet fish love them. A well-presented blue crab was a widely bait for catching bonefish and permit until fly-fishing became popular. And on the eastern side of the Atlantic, sea anglers have sought freshly molted or "peeler" crabs in their quest for bass, flounder, cod, smooth-hound, and many other species.

Crab eggs hatch into larvae that drift around in the ocean currents as part of the plankton. (Crab larvae look nothing like adult crabs: for one thing, they have long tails.) When the larvae have grown large enough to metamorphose into their adult form they swim down to the seabed, flip their tails under the head and thorax, and look for somewhere suitable to live. (If you look underneath a crab you can see its tail, which is tightly folded under the thorax.)

Rock and reef crabs look for cracks and crannies in which to hide when they are not out feeding. Others look for a soft sand or silty

bottom in which they can bury themselves, often with just their stalked eyes showing. Fiddler crabs dig burrows in mud: when the tide is out you can spot the entrances to their burrows and balls of excavated mud.

Crabs have a round or oval shell and five pairs of legs. The front pair is usually greatly enlarged to form pincers, which the crab uses to grab and cut its food. In male fiddler crabs one of the pincers is enormous. It is used to attract females and to warn off rival males. Although most crabs move by walking sideways with the other four pairs of legs, in many species the rear one or two pairs are flattened and used as paddles for swimming.

Shape varies tremendously from species to species. Some have long spidery legs, others short squat ones. Some have a smooth body, which looks like pie-crust, some spiny bodies, and others hairy bodies. Color also varies, but in most crabs it is a version of camouflaged olive, brown, or deep

blue-gray to match the background. Like insects, crabs can only grow by regularly molting their carapace; you will often find molted carapaces washed up on the strand-line of a beach. Crabs are at their most vulnerable when they are molting, because until their new carapace has hardened and colored it is soft, succulent, and quite pale. Molting crabs (soft-backs) try to hide from predators, but fish will seek them out.

Imitating crabs

Only recently have fly-dressers attempted to make realistic imitations of saltwater crabs. The McCrab has a body formed from deer hair, a buoyant material that is ideal for producing swimming crabs. Del Brown's Merkin Crab, in contrast, has a body made of strands of wool which, when waterlogged, help the fly to sink. More recently, realistic crabs have appeared, such as Epoxy Crabs, which have clear epoxy-resin bodies.

Del Brown's Merkin Crab
Permit love crabs. This artificial is specially designed to sink quickly to the bottom of the seabed when cast to a permit. Hook 4–10.

McCrab
This is one of the best general crab imitators. It is constructed mainly from deer hair. Hook 4–10.

Epoxy Crab
Clear epoxy resin is an ideal medium with which to construct saltwater flies, including crab imitations. Hook 4–10.

VELVET SWIMMING CRAB

Wide, hairy legs used as paddles for swimming

FIDDLER CRAB

One, much larger pincer used for signaling to other crabs

SHORE CRAB

SALTWATER SHRIMP AND PRAWNS

TERRY JENNER

Shrimp and prawns belong to the Order of crustaceans known as the Decapoda, or "10-legs." This is because they have five pairs of long walking legs attached to their thorax. They also have a pair of much shorter paddle-shaped limbs known as "swimmerets" on the underside of each abdominal segment. These are especially noticeable when the creature is swimming, because they beat violently. There is a pair of very long antennae on the head, as well as a second, very short pair. The eyes are on short stalks and very conspicuous. Shrimp and prawns are very similar. The main difference is that prawns have a toothed, pointed snout, or rostrum, extending from the front of the head; shrimp do not. Apart from the limbs the body appears armor plated.

The way that shrimp and prawns move is very important when it comes to presenting imitative flies (see Top Tips). When feeding, they will walk slowly across the sea floor or on rocks or seaweed fronds. When moving about their own little world, shrimp and prawns swim slowly, using their swimmerets, or allow the current to carry them, steering with their swimmerets. Then, if disturbed they can zoom away backward with a powerful downward flick of their abdomen.

Shrimp and prawns are highly camouflaged. It is only when they are boiled that they turn a solid orange-pink. Generally they take on the color of their background, but they also have a distinct translucence. For example, over pink shell-sand or coral their basic hue will be pinkish, over yellow sand a light gray-brown, among beds of seaweed or turtle grass brown or olive-brown, and in turbid estuaries and bays a translucent gray-brown or olive-gray. For this reason it is essential to carry artificial shrimp and prawns in a wide range of

colors, to match the shade prevalent wherever you happen to be fishing. But do make sure – whether you tie your own or buy them – that the colors are subtle and not garish.

It will also be essential to have artificials that match the range of size of the naturals. Shrimp tend to be smaller than prawns: body length in most shrimp is 3-8cm (1¼–3in), in most prawns 3–12cm (1¼–5in), exceptionally 20cm (8in).

Shrimp and prawns are creatures of shallow inshore waters. Bass seek them in estuaries, bluefish in sandy bays, sea trout in rocky inlets, bonefish over tropical flats, and snook among the roots of mangroves.

Although most species of shrimp and prawns are very similar, there are four distinct categories to look out for.

Snapping shrimp

This is a large shrimp that resembles a miniature lobster, with the claw on one of the front legs

Popovics Ultra Shrimp
A great bonefish pattern. Vary the shade to match the real shrimp. Hook 2–12.

Coxon Shrimp
A shrimp devised to catch European bass, but it works worldwide. Hook 2–12.

BANDED SNAPPING SHRIMP

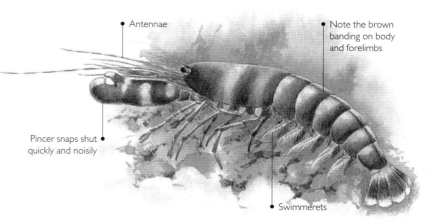

Antennae

Note the brown banding on body and forelimbs

Pincer snaps shut quickly and noisily

Swimmerets

Lureflash Epoxy Shrimp
A great all-round shrimp imitation for flats fishing. Hook 2–12.

much larger than the other. It gets its name from the sound it makes when it snaps the claw closed. If you get close enough you will hear this.

Mantis shrimp

The mantis is a very aggressive little shrimp. Its body is flattened side to side and the front feeding legs are large, strongly double-jointed, and similar to the arms of the praying mantis. The power in these legs can be gathered from two other common names given to this shrimp: thumb-buster and thumb-splitter. Bonefish love them!

Common prawn

This is a species that occurs in cool, clean waters on North Atlantic rocky coasts. It also haunts old wrecks and reefs. It has the rostrum that all shrimp lack. It is sought by bass, pollack, and wrasse.

Brown, white, and pink swimming shrimp

There are lots of species of swimming shrimp, and these are the three main colors.

Imitating shrimp and prawns

The Coxon Shrimp or Prawn includes the long antennae and legs, pronounced eyes and segmented back (made from a section of flexible drinking straw!) of the real thing.

Popovics' Ultra Shrimp is a similarly realistic imitation, with a body foundation of clear epoxy-resin that adds a translucent effect to the fly.

In the Lureflash Epoxy Shrimp this translucence is enhanced by adding pearlescent dust to the clear epoxy.

Of the general shrimp patterns, Carl Richard's Shrimp is one of the best.

Jimmy Nix invented his Snook Shrimp to catch snook on flats at the edge of mangroves, but it will take fish anywhere when they are feeding on shrimp or prawns.

Most artificial shrimp are general patterns in that they can be used to match the entire range of natural species: just vary the color and size. The Mantis Shrimp is an exception: it is a great bonefish fly.

TOP TIPS

• When you don't know the color of shrimp being taken by the fish, choose an artificial from your fly-box that you think the fish will find most difficult to see. For example, in gray-brown estuary water choose a gray-brown one.

• To eliminate the guesswork, you can get a sample of shrimp using a fine mesh landing-net.

• In turbid waters where you cannot see what is going on below the surface, fish the shrimp slowly, letting it drift around on the current if there is one. Occasionally, tweak it back. Remember that most shrimp move very slowly most of the time.

• The many species of shrimp vary in size and color and the fish you are trying to catch may be feeding selectively on only one. Your fly-box must include a range of sizes and colors to match the shrimp the fish are eating.

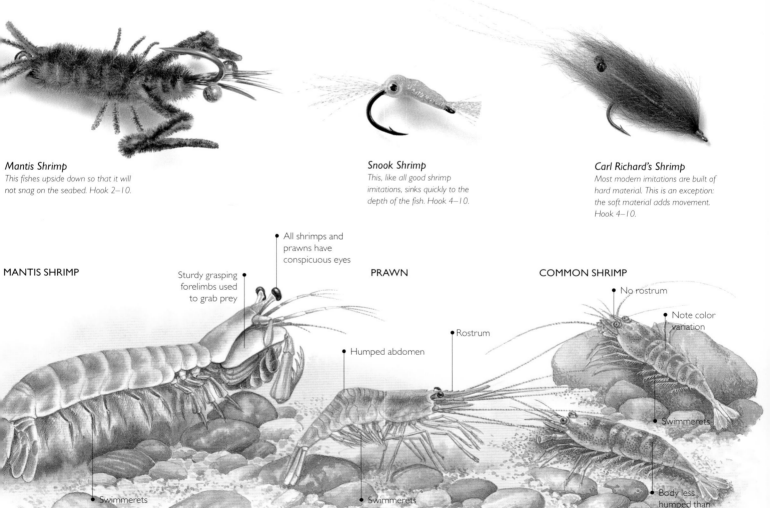

Mantis Shrimp
This fishes upside down so that it will not snag on the seabed. Hook 2–10.

Snook Shrimp
This, like all good shrimp imitations, sinks quickly to the depth of the fish. Hook 4–10.

Carl Richard's Shrimp
Most modern imitations are built of hard material. This is an exception: the soft material adds movement. Hook 4–10.

MANTIS SHRIMP

Sturdy grasping forelimbs used to grab prey

All shrimps and prawns have conspicuous eyes

PRAWN

Humped abdomen

Rostrum

COMMON SHRIMP

No rostrum

Note color variation

Swimmerets

Swimmerets

Swimmerets

Swimmerets

Body less humped than in prawn

FRESHWATER BAITFISH

TERRY JENNER

The preferred prey of predatory fish is fish, and if baitfish are plentiful predators will ignore other food. When they are small they may devour invertebrates, but as soon as they can they move on to fish. Some are cannibalistic: the fry of northern pike will devour their brothers and sisters. When they get larger, pike remain cannibals and will take others little smaller than themselves.

Most fly-fishers associate brown trout with insect food, but given the chance a brownie will turn away from mayflies to chase minnows or trout fry if they are available. The biggest lake brown trout prefer a diet of Arctic char and, given a choice, prefer chars that are about one-fifth their own body length. Of course freshwater fish become accustomed to the baitfish that live in their own rivers or lakes. Therefore, while a general streamer pattern will often take predatory fish, for the larger, older fish or the more selective feeders you may require an artificial fly that more closely resembles the food on which the fish are feeding.

Roach, bream, and miscellaneous fry

A host of cyprinid species is scattered in freshwaters throughout the world; these are important in the diet of predators. The roach is a typical example: a fish with slate-blue back, silvery sides, and white belly, its reddish fins are a trigger for pike; or the bream, a deeper-bodied fish, with gray-brown back, drab sides, and gray fins. Big pike eat big fish, and there are records of 14kg (30lb) pike taking 1.5kg (3lb) bream. But the majority of baitfish taken by predators are fry or juveniles in the 5–15cm (2–6in) range.

Imitating small roach, bream, and fry

A Roach Deceiver with red tied in at throat and tail (to mimic the red fins of natural fish) is a fine roach imitation. Carry two or three sizes, ranging from 7cm (3in) – for when the fish are taking fry – to 20cm (9in) for big pike. Tie some without the red to imitate drabber species like bream.

When feeding on fry, predators will often charge through a school, battering and stunning (sometimes killing) several fry at once as they go. They then turn and take the dead and dying at their leisure. When you are aware that predatory fish are behaving in this way, you will find that a Floating Fry is most effective.

Perch and small panfish

With its spiny fins, olive-green coloring and broad, sooty, vertical stripes, the perch is well known to all freshwater fishers in Europe and temperate North America. Also in North American lakes and slower rivers there are a number of small fish that, with perch, go under the general heading of panfish. These are eaten by northern pike and muskellunge, and the smaller ones by trout, large-mouth and small-mouth bass, and walleye.

Imitating perch and small panfish

A heavily-dressed, deep-bodied Deceiver can be colored so that it matches the natural perch or the panfish.

Smelt

The smelt is an important baitfish in some larger, cooler lakes for fish such as lake trout, big char, and ouananiche salmon. It is a slimly-built fish with a watery olive-green back, silvery sides, and white belly. It reaches an average size of 25cm (10in).

Imitating smelt

Length, slimness, and silvery sides are triggers for your imitations. Fish these fast, speeding up your retrieve for the last few yards.

Roach Deceiver
A version of Lefty's Deceiver, this fly can be tied in a range of sizes from 5cm (2in) to 20cm (8in) to imitate silvery baitfish. Hook 4–10.

Smelt
Dressed on 10–16cm (4–6in) flexible mounts, this is a perfect smelt imitator. Hook tandem mount 7.5–15cm (3–6in) long.

Woolhead Sculpin
Used to imitate sculpin, this fly is 5-9cm (2–3½in) in length. Hook 2–8.

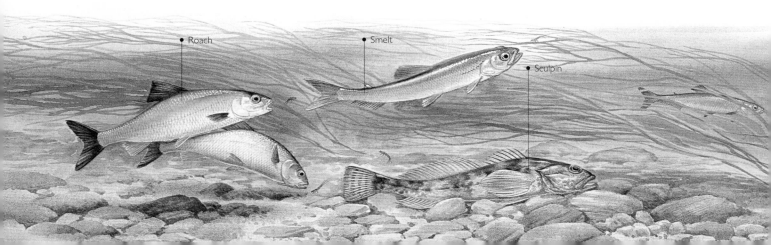

Roach

Smelt

Sculpin

Sculpins

Also known as Miller's Thumb and Bullhead, sculpins are often abundant in cool, rocky, fast-flowing rivers. The large, flattened, wedge-shaped head, tapering body, and proportionally huge fins (especially pectorals) make them instantly recognizable. They spend their entire lives on the bottom, hiding away under boulders and darting out to feed. For this reason they lack the silver coloration of mid-water species and instead are camouflaged to blend in with the riverbed; they are often a dark mottled olive-brown on the back and sides and cream on the belly.

Imitating sculpins

Don Gapen's original Muddler Minnow is still outstanding, but there have been many more recent imitations. The Woolhead Sculpin is one: it avoids the use of buoyant deer hair used in many sculpin patterns. It is important to get the fly close to the bottom, and you might have to wrap wire around the hookshank as extra ballast. You can fish this by working the fly back, but often it is more effective to fish it like a nymph. Cast upstream and let it dead-drift down with the current. I suspect that predators take it for a sculpin that has recently died and is therefore easy meat.

Minnows and darters

These, too, are fish of clean rivers, although they also occur in the shallow margins of cold lakes.

TOP TIPS

- The most effective baitfish imitations have big eyes: choose or tie flies with big eyes.
- Often the best times to use fish imitations are between dusk and dawn, and when the river is colored after a flood.
- If you are starting to tie your own flies, the reversed hair-wing Thunder Creek Minnow and Bucktail Minnow are good flies to begin with: they are fairly easy, and by varying the colors you can imitate other fresh- and saltwater baitfish species.

They are slender, silvery fish that dart around the shallows, often in vast schools. Sometimes you will see a school tightly packed and lying in a few inches of water over the gravel tail of a flat pool. Watch carefully: a big trout may suddenly put in an appearance, scattering the school as it takes a catch. The trout will then return upstream into deeper water. Stay where you are. Slowly the school, minus one member, regathers. Ten minutes later the performance will be repeated. For imitation, my favorites are the reversed hair-wing Thunder Creek Minnow and the Bucktail Minnow.

Eggs and alevins

The eggs of salmon and trout are very large. They hatch in their nest, deep in the gravel, into alevins which have big eyes, a simple body, and a yolk sac. Both eggs and alevins sometimes get washed from their nests and are eagerly devoured by hungry trout, char, and grayling. An orange wool ball or chenille tied on a hook matches the egg. Alevin imitators have the yolk sac and eyes as triggers.

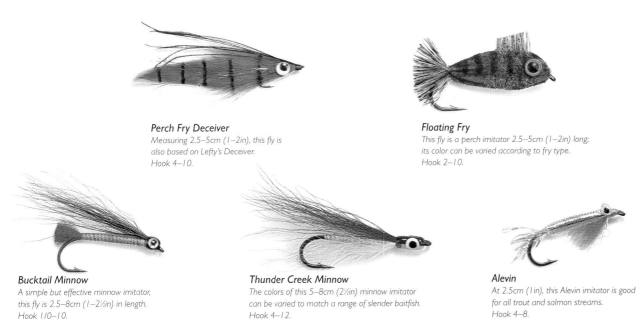

Perch Fry Deceiver
*Measuring 2.5–5cm (1–2in), this fly is also based on Lefty's Deceiver.
Hook 4–10.*

Floating Fry
*This fly is a perch imitator 2.5–5cm (1–2in) long; its color can be varied according to fry type.
Hook 2–10.*

Bucktail Minnow
*A simple but effective minnow imitator, this fly is 2.5–8cm (1–2½in) in length.
Hook 1/0–10.*

Thunder Creek Minnow
*The colors of this 5–8cm (2½in) minnow imitator can be varied to match a range of slender baitfish.
Hook 4–12.*

Alevin
*At 2.5cm (1in), this Alevin imitator is good for all trout and salmon streams.
Hook 4–8.*

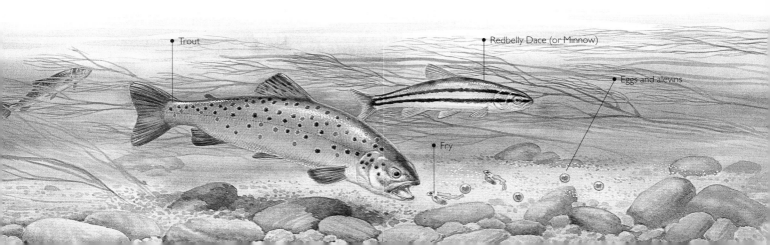

Trout

Redbelly Dace (or Minnow)

Eggs and alevins

Fry

SALTWATER BAITFISH

TERRY JENNER

Although there are vast numbers of saltwater baitfish that are food for fly-fishers' fish, it is not necessary to carry an equally vast number of imitations in order to fish effectively. The main species belong to only a few groups, within which the individual species, such as those in the herring and sandeel families, are very similar. One imitation of each is usually sufficient. The important matter is size: carry a range of fly lengths so that you can match the size of prey being taken by the fish that you are trying to catch.

Herrings and their relations

The herring family includes many species that humans eat: sardine, sprat, anchovy, and the herring itself. Predatory fish love them too, but they also enjoy many other members of the family, such as shads and menhaden, which we avoid because of their many tiny, sharp bones.

Most members of this family are fairly slender. Shads and menhaden are exceptions, as they are somewhat deeper in the body. They all have dark backs (blue through blue-green to brown-green) with silvery or silver-gray sides and white bellies, sometimes with a brassy hue. Some, such as the shads and menhaden, have blackish spots on the sides; some, such as the anchovy, have a dark line along the sides of the body; others have no dark markings at all.

The size varies, from 10–12cm (4–5in) in sprat and Atlantic sardines to 25–30cm (10–12in) in Pacific sardines, and to 37.5cm (15in) – exceptionally as much as 50cm (20in) – in menhaden and herring.

Imitating herring

Lefty's Deceiver tied in a wide range of sizes from 10–40 cm (4–15in) is the ideal imitation. Have some dressed sparsely to match the more slender species, and some dressed heavier to match the deeper bodied menhaden and shads. A few 5–8cm (2–3in) long and very sparsely dressed will match small herring fry. A good alternative is the Surf Candy. The Clouser Minnow is among the most effective small fish imitations, and the simplest to tie. Its lead eyes make it sink quickly to fishing depths.

Sar-Mul-Mac Mackerel
A Sar-Mul-Mac dressed to match small mackerel. Hook 2–8.

Sar-Mul-Mac Mullet
A Sar-Mul-Mac dressed to match mullet fry. Hook 2–8.

Surf Candy
Great sandeel and slender fry imitation. Hook 4–10.

Clouser Minnow
A superb small fish or fry imitation for salt- or freshwater. Hook 2–8.

Lefty's Deceiver
One of the greatest, all-round saltwater flies. Hook 2/0–8

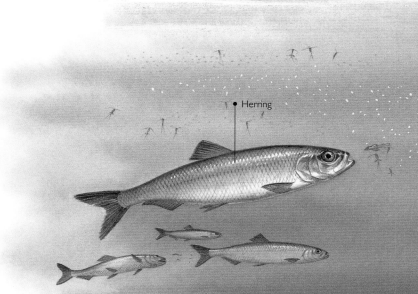

Herring

Sandeels

Sandeels, also called sand launce or sandlance, grow to 15–30cm (6-12in), depending on the species. They are very slender with dark backs (from blue through olive to brown) and silvery sides and belly. Sandeels live mainly in very shallow water over sand, and on the ebb will often bury themselves in the lower, wetter parts of the beach, where they are stranded until covered by the sea on the next flood tide. As the tide floods these lower reaches and the sandeels emerge, so predators such as bass and bluefish move in.

Several other baitfish, including needlefish and small garfish, also have elongated bodies and can be imitated with sandeel patterns. They can be distinguished from sandeels by their elongated jaws.

Imitating sandeels

The very realistic Sandeel looks good, but the Bucktail Sandeel has more action in the water and is a better fish-catcher. An alternative is the Silversides.

Mackerel and mullet

Besides being excellent light-tackle quarry for fly-fishers in their own right, mackerel and mullet are also a major source of food for the larger predatory fish.

Imitating mackerel and mullet

Deceivers are extremely effective, but if you need a more precise imitation, the Sar-Mul-Mac Mackerel and Sar-Mul-Mac Mullet are ideal.

Bottom baitfish

Most marine baitfish live in the open water, although some – such as toad-fish, gobies, dragonets, and saltwater sculpins – live on the bottom, where they seek cover in beds of kelp or bladderwrack, or among boulders.

These baitfish are small fish, with large heads and tapering bodies, that are well camouflaged. They tend to be more numerous on rocky coasts where they are readily devoured by pollack, bass, and sea trout.

TOP TIPS

- Saltwater corrodes ordinary hooks, so tie or buy all saltwater flies on stainless steel hooks.
- Only a very sharp hook will penetrate the bony jaw of most big saltwater fish. So before you start fishing, take a sharpening stone or fine-toothed file and make sure the hook is as sharp as you can make it.
- Keep your eyes open for feeding seabirds. They will lead you to the schools of baitfish and the large predators you are trying to catch.

Imitating bottom baitfish

The Woolhead Sculpin (see illustration p104) imitates bottom baitfish. Tie or buy them on stainless steel hooks. Because of the snaggy nature of a rocky seabed or seaweed beds, make sure you weight them so that the hooks swim upside down, and attach a nylon weed-guard across the hook gap.

Silversides
A great silver fry or sandeel suggestive pattern. Hook 4–8.

Sandeel
An ultra realistic sandeel imitation. Hook 4–8.

Bucktail Sandeel
A simple sandeel imitation where bucktail adds movement. Hook 4–8.

Menhaden

Sandeel

Halfbeak

SALMON FLIES

TERRY JENNER

Up to about 200 years ago, when the scientific study of fish was in its infancy, people thought that salmon, like resident trout, ate flies when they returned to the river. The difference was that they ate larger flies. And several wet-fly imitations were made of the dragonflies and butterflies that salmon were supposed to eat. It is now known that, with few exceptions, migratory salmonids — Atlantic and Pacific salmon, steelhead, and sea-run brown trout and char — do not feed on their return to freshwater. Nevertheless, although the sole purpose of their return is to breed, they can be caught with artificial flies.

Careful observation and experimentation have indicated that salmon were not hungry and searching for food, and that the simplest of flies, copying nothing from nature, were the most effective when it came to catching them. Among the earliest of the simple sombre fly era was a hair-wing salmon fly from Newfoundland dating from 1795, which was constructed from the red hairs of a Hereford cow. This type of fly reached its peak with William Scrope's book, *Days and Nights of Salmon Fishing in the Tweed* (1843), which described just six flies, including Kinmont Willie, a simple sombre fly.

The second half of the 19th century and first two decades of the 20th saw an incredible revolution in salmon fly design and dressing. It started in Ireland, swiftly spread to Britain, and from Britain crossed the Atlantic. The trigger was the sudden availability, from far-flung corners of the world, of the feathers of brightly colored, exotic tropical birds such as cock-of-the-rock, Indian crow, toucan, bird-of-paradise, bustard, and jungle cock. These were imported to adorn the hats of fashionable ladies, but fly-dressers picked them up, made salmon flies of them, and brought fly-fishers into the complex, gaudy fly era.

Complex? Perhaps the most famous of all salmon flies illustrates this: the Jock Scott has 28 different materials in its construction compared with just six in Kinmont Willie. Literally hundreds of patterns were invented in the gaudy fly era. The Silver Doctor, one of the most popular for catching fish, has 23 different materials in it. These flies are beautiful objects, more works of art than flies to cast into the river.

Revolutionary measures

Through the turn of the 19th and 20th centuries the Orvis Company imported into the United States, or had tied there, huge quantities of complex gaudy flies to sell to American fly-fishers. They were used in the rivers draining the western states, in British Columbia for Pacific salmon and steelhead, and in rivers draining east to Canada's Atlantic coast for Atlantic salmon. But then a revolution began in North America that spread across the Atlantic to oust the complex gaudy fly. It gave rise to the modern, simple, fly era.

The basic modern, simple salmon fly is nothing more than a hair-wing streamer pattern. The Silver Rat, one of the North American rat series dating from about 1911, is still one of the best for any migratory fish occurring anywhere in a clear river.

Although most European fly-fishers were still using the complex, gaudy fly early in the 1900s, one great hair-wing, the Yellow Dog, was invented in Scotland. This is still an outstanding fly on any salmon river. Use it when the water is still a little on the high side and has a touch of color during a falling flood.

Silver Doctor
A typical Victorian fully-dressed salmon fly — a work of art. Hook 2–12.

Kinmont Willie
One of the earliest European salmon flies. Hook 2–12.

Red Cow
One of the earliest North American salmon flies. Hook 2–12.

Silver Rat
Hair-wings are highly mobile in the water and are very effective salmon flies for rivers and lakes. Hook 2–12.

Yellow Dog
A very effective hair-wing patterns for rivers and lakes. Hook 2–12.

Silver Doctor Hair-wing
A hair-wing that is extremely effective for lakes and rivers. Hook 2–12.

Red Butt Black Bear
An excellent hair-wing pattern, highly mobile in the water. Hook 2–12.

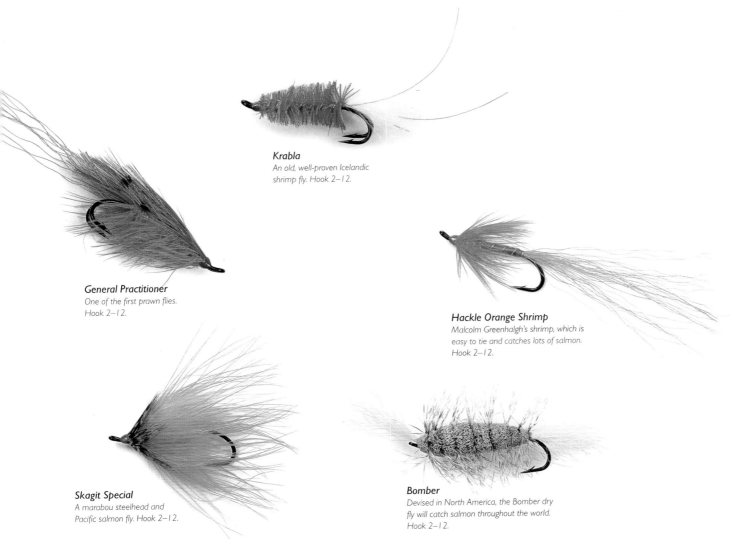

Krabla
An old, well-proven Icelandic shrimp fly. Hook 2–12.

General Practitioner
One of the first prawn flies. Hook 2–12.

Hackle Orange Shrimp
Malcolm Greenhalgh's shrimp, which is easy to tie and catches lots of salmon. Hook 2–12.

Skagit Special
A marabou steelhead and Pacific salmon fly. Hook 2–12.

Bomber
Devised in North America, the Bomber dry fly will catch salmon throughout the world. Hook 2–12.

After about 1950, complex gaudy flies were increasingly abandoned in favor of the simple. But in many flies that are used today, the influence of the gaudy fly can still be seen. This is because many of the more famous gaudy flies were transformed into the simple. The complex bodies were replaced by plain silk and tinsel, and the intricate feather wings by a simple bunch of hair. Therefore, you may now see in fishing catalogues descriptions such as Jock Scott (hair-wing), Silver Doctor (hair-wing), and so on.

New hair-wings

At the same time there has been a proliferation of new hair-wing patterns. One of the best is the Red Butt Black Bear: this wonderful fly will catch steelhead in British Columbia, sea trout in Patagonia, salmon in Russia, and any migratory salmonid anywhere in between. Other materials that pulsate in the water have been introduced to the range of modern simple salmon flies. One of these is marabou, a soft downy feather taken from the thighs of white farmyard turkeys and dyed in a range of colors. If you are going after steelhead, try one of Bob Aid's Marabou Spiders. The Skagit Special is a most effective one and demonstrates vividly that these flies do not imitate fish food.

Yet some salmon flies have been designed to copy baits used to catch salmon. The most notable are shrimp and prawn flies. Shrimp and prawns, in natural boiled pink, or dyed purple or deep ruby-red, have long been known as a killing salmon bait. In recent years they have been prohibited on an increasing number of rivers. To get around the ban, new flies were invented. Among the first, and still one of the best, was the General Practitioner or GP. A second, which really does look like a pink shrimp, is the Icelandic Krabla. However, there is evidence that it is not their resemblance to crustaceans that makes these flies so effective, but their size and color. Pinks, oranges, and reds are highly visible in murky water compared with other colors, and it is probably this that makes them so effective.

> **TOP TIPS**
> ● When choosing salmon, steelhead, and sea trout flies look first to water color: lots of orange, red, or yellow in colored water, silver and blue in crystal clear water. If in doubt go for black.
> ● Timed trials suggest that a little extra flash in a fly (such as crystal hair in the wing) and a small point of fluorescence (such as a red fluorescent floss butt at the end of the body) enhance the attraction of the fly to the fish.

GP and Krabla are not the easiest flies to tie: the Hackle Orange Shrimp is as easy as you can get, and its catch rate matches that of the other two.

Dry flies are being increasingly used to catch salmon. Some have a crude resemblance to insects, but the Bombers, which began life in New Brunswick's salmon rivers and have since spread to salmon and steelhead rivers around the world, have no link whatever with food.

THE CHALLENGE

The book that tells you how to catch each and every fish you come across does not exist, because it is impossible to produce. There are too many variables when it comes to catching a particular fish on fly – and thank goodness for that. If there were a formula that guaranteed success, fly-fishing would no longer be a challenge and would quickly lose its appeal.

Here is a common situation that illustrates the challenge of fly-fishing: you know that several very large trout live in a certain river pool and you set out to catch one. Now work out where the big trout are likely to be lying – read the water. If you just start casting you may hook a smaller fish and, as you are playing that, frighten the larger ones that you are really after.

Get close to the fish so you can see your quarry and make a delicate short cast instead of a splashy long one.

What to cast? You need to fool the trout with an imitation of what it is eating. But what is it eating? And where and when? This takes some detective work. Then you have to choose a fly that looks like the trout's real food.

Next, cast that fly to the feeding trout. The biggest fish always lie in the trickiest of places, so it is not simply a matter of tying the fly to the end of the leader and casting it straight in the general direction of the fish. If the trout is feeding on the riverbed, you must get the fly down through the turbulent current. If the trout is feeding at the surface, you must prevent the fly dragging because of vagaries in the flow. If there is a strong wind blowing, or the trout is in a very overgrown lie, how will you cope? The biggest fish naturally always lie in the trickiest of places.

When you have put the fly in front of the trout's nose and the trout has fallen for the deception, you need to know when to strike to set the hook. This is particularly difficult when the fish are feeding deep and you are unable to see them. A trout can take your artificial nymph into its mouth, realize that it is too hard to be a real nymph, and spit it out in a second. But do it right, and you will hook a fish even as it realizes its mistake.

There are other challenges when fishing for trout in other waters, and still more when you are trying to catch other species, or fishing in a sea or lake. Quite featureless compared with rivers, seas and lakes require new skills in reading the water, in locating fish, and in choosing an effective fly. Some fish have sharp teeth; you must prevent them from slicing through the line, or through you, when you hook them and land them. Some fish are huge and powerful. How will you play one? It's no good trying to work that out the first time you hook one. And then there are the tides, and weather, and ... the list goes on and on.

You can learn the basics of fly-fishing quickly and easily. But the real challenge remains – you versus the fish. That particular challenge is what this section is all about.

READING RIVERS

MALCOLM GREENHALGH

Fish are rarely uniformly spread in a river. Some areas will have large concentrations: other places will be devoid of fish. The reason is quite clear. Fish need a good food supply and shelter from potential danger, and some parts of a river provide these better than others.

When you visit a stretch of river for the first time examine it carefully to look for the best lies. If you spend an hour simply looking at the river you will be rewarded with a better catch than you would if you were to start fishing as soon as you reach the water. I notice this often when I invite guests to fish my home rivers in northern England. Some are so keen to start that they immediately wade out and begin casting as soon as they arrive. With very few exceptions they catch less in their day's visit than those who walk a couple of kilometers of river before setting up their rods, or those who spend some time questioning me closely about the locations of the best pools and lies.

Where fish lie

Look first for lies close to the bank and, particularly on wide rivers, lies close to the bank on which you are standing. Many fish choose to lie close to the bank, especially on the outside of bends, where there is deep water in boulder-strewn riffles, or where overhanging branches, flood-rafts, and beds of tall rushes or reeds provide shelter.

Look for creases in deep river pools: distinct lines on the water surface that indicate boundaries between slacker water or back-eddies and the main flow. Fish often lie near creases, choosing the side that they find most comfortable for resting, and make feeding forays into the crease. No matter where you are in a river, it is always worth looking for creases: in weir pools, below groins or waterfalls, where tree stumps have fallen into the river below, and to either side of islands in the river. Associate creases with good, and often the best, river fish lies.

Weed beds are always worth checking. Many rivers have weed beds broken up by patches of bare gravel or sand. These are ideal lies: the fish have shelter under the swaying fronds, the food-bearing current funnels around the edge of weed beds, and the weeds house massive numbers of invertebrates and smaller fish. Some fishery owners, concerned that weed beds were getting out of hand, completely cleared them , and the fish immediately departed!

Large boulders often make great lies. Fish rarely lie immediately downstream of boulders; they usually lie at the sides or upstream, or if there is a fair depth of water over a large boulder, they may lie on top of it. The boulder provides shelter and the current around it carries concentrations of food. When you are looking for boulder lies look for the tell-tale "bulge" at the water surface immediately downstream of any boulder.

Weir pools and pools below waterfalls are invariably good lies, as are bridge pools. These give cover in the form of rocks, stones, and deep water. Most fish, and the bigger fish, will be lying in creases between the main flow and slacker water.

After heavy rain or snow melt, many rivers flood: the water level rises quickly, sometimes by 2m (6ft) in a couple of hours, and then slowly falls. Most rivers are unfishable when they are in full flood because of all the rubbish being swept downstream. Fish tend to take cover among flooded grass or bushes, or in quieter areas – high-water lies – well away from the main flow. These can be flooded hollows in farmland, where the fish may feed on drowned earthworms and slugs, or normally dry ditches into which the main river has backed up, or roads that, when the river is low, ford the river. Find some high-water lies and you will catch fish during the most violent floods.

In many European trout and grayling streams there is a distinct distribution of trout and grayling. Grayling are schoolfish and they like to lie side by side on bare gravel. Fish in bare weedless areas and you will catch grayling but no trout. Brown trout are far more independent and they like thick cover. So, by fishing the edges of weed beds, creases in

If you want to catch trout in a pool like this one you must concentrate on the neck of the pool, off the gravel bank, and in the shade of the overhanging trees, for that is where the fish lie.

TOP TIPS

These points may seem obvious, but in my experience overlooking them is a major cause of the catch being less than it should be!

- When visiting a length of river you have not fished before, leave your rod and walk the length, looking carefully for lies.
- Fish the lies close to your own bank before wading in the river to fish lies close to the opposite bank.
- If you can, avoid casting blindly or "fishing the water." Instead concentrate on fish that you can see or lies that you know hold fish.
- With the exception of non-feeding species such as salmon, your flies should be imitating what the fish are eating. While examining potential lies, look out for what the fish might be eating to help you make the best choice of fly.
- Wade deep only when you must. Remember that most river lies are shallower than body- wader depth.

SAFETY IN RIVERS

Wear a buoyancy aid to fish deep, big rivers. Use a weighted wading-staff to fish deep, boulder-strewn, turbulent rivers.

deep lies close to the bank, below bridges, or in "hatch pools," you will catch trout but few grayling. The problem for most fly-fishers is that they can see grayling but not trout, so they catch grayling and say that there are no trout in the river.

Rainbow trout have been introduced to many brown trout rivers and, as they are more aggressive, they often take over the best brown trout lies. One such lie, under a small willow bush on the tiny Yorkshire Aire, produced two 1.4kg (3lb) brownies for me, but I did not see any fish there by June the following year. Then I spotted and caught the culprit: a rainbow of about 2kg (4lb) that must have escaped from a fish-farm during a winter flood. Within a week of my taking out that rainbow trout, four brown trout had taken up residence in the lie.

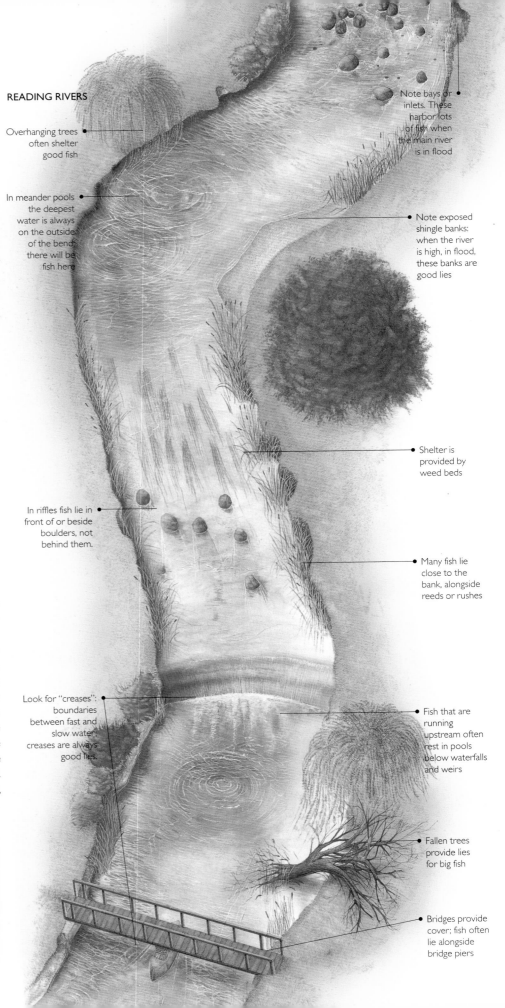

Overhanging trees often shelter good fish

In meander pools the deepest water is always on the outside of the bend; there will be fish here

In riffles fish lie in front of or beside boulders, not behind them.

Look for "creases": boundaries between fast and slow water; creases are always good lies.

Note bays or inlets. These harbor lots of fish when the main river is in flood

Note exposed shingle banks: when the river is high, in flood, these banks are good lies

Shelter is provided by weed beds

Many fish lie close to the bank, alongside reeds or rushes

Fish that are running upstream often rest in pools below waterfalls and weirs

Fallen trees provide lies for big fish

Bridges provide cover; fish often lie alongside bridge piers

READING LAKES

MALCOLM GREENHALGH

There is something mysterious about big, wild lakes. At a cursory glance they often appear to be featureless expanses of water, causing you to imagine that the fish will be evenly distributed throughout, and that wherever you cast your flies there will be a chance of catching one. This could not be farther from the truth. On my first visit to Ireland's Lough Arrow I started with high hopes, but after two fishless days I felt utterly despondent. I sought help from a local fly-fisher, who sketched a map of a tiny part of the lake – a straight length of shore, two bays, and an island. Then he put several Xs on the map, and advised, "Fish hard there!" I did as I was told and, in the following four days, caught 14 trout, including a 2.5kg (5lb 8oz) specimen.

Even in the most productive lakes, some areas will be fishless and some will be hot-spots – caused almost entirely by the way that fish foods are distributed. The more food, the more fish, and some areas produce more fish foods than others.

Productive shallows

Predatory fish such as pike, largemouth bass, and carnivorous trout feed on lesser fish; lesser fish, such as char, whitefish, and smaller trout feed on aquatic invertebrates, which in turn feed on aquatic weeds – and aquatic weeds need sunlight in order to grow. The more sunlight, the more weeds, the more invertebrates, the more fish. Because sunlight is rapidly absorbed as it passes through water, the bottom will only receive light in shallow areas, and this is where you will find weeds and fish foods. Get to know precisely the locations and extents of all productive shallows.

Some years ago I was sitting by a lake, watching trout rising to take lake olives that were hatching in the shallow margin. Two fly-fishers were fishing the lake by casting their flies as the breeze drifted their boat from deeper water in to the shore. However, just before they reached the shallow margin, they reeled in their lines, laid aside their rods, and rowed out once more to the middle of the lake, just before reaching the productive shallows. They caught nothing, simply because they did not fish the shallows where the fish were feeding.

Inflowing and outflowing streams

Inflowing streams will often carry food into a lake, and outflowing streams will draw water out of a lake, often carrying a concentration of food away. Fish will often lie close to these inflows and outflows so that they can intercept this food. These are hot-spots.

Ambush lies

Predatory fish often take up lies from which to ambush lesser fish. It is well worth the effort to look out for such ambush lies. Once they are found they can usually be relied on to yield good-quality fish. Ambush lies typically include the following features: underneath or alongside jetties, under fallen trees or trailing branches, and alongside rock ledges or reed beds.

Underneath or alongside jetties On Ontario's Rice Lake there are seven old wooden jetties standing along one 200m (600ft) length of shore. Some of

LAKE IN CROSS SECTION

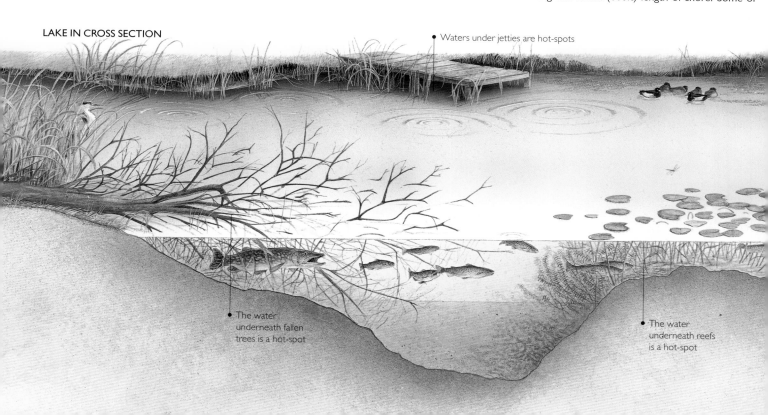

Waters under jetties are hot-spots

The water underneath fallen trees is a hot-spot

The water underneath reefs is a hot-spot

TOP TIPS

- Always keep an eye open for fish moving at the surface. The quicker you can get your fly to a fish the better your chance of catching it.
- If fishing a lake you have never fished before, seek help from other fly-fishers or hire a guide.
- Obtain a map of the lake that shows underwater contours. Look for productive shallow water up to 5m (16ft) in depth.
- Use a fish-finder, but concentrate on water depth as much as fish echoes.
- If you are after predatory fish, concentrate your efforts on potential ambush lies.

this great lake's biggest smallmouth bass live here, lying in wait for schools of small baitfish. They will readily take a bass-bug fished around these rotting jetties.

Under fallen trees or trailing branches About six winters ago a huge pine fell into a small Canadian forest lake, and now a specimen largemouth bass lives under the rotting log. No frog, small mammal, or baitfish that swims past its gape is safe. One day we caught him and released him 800m (½ mile) away. We caught him again the next day, back under his log!

Alongside rock ledges or reed beds There is a superb ambush lie used by pike in a lake at Aykoski, Finland. Close to the outflowing river, where there

are always lots of small baitfish, there is a reed bed extending into the lake as well as some protruding rocks. Pike lie alongside the reed bed and rocks. If you anchor a boat off the rocks and cast a fly so that it fishes 2–3m (6–10ft) off the reed bed and rocks, you are certain to catch a pike. One morning I caught three, and a big rainbow trout.

Deep-water lies

While the best lake fishing is usually found in shallow water, some very special fish can be found feeding in much deeper water. In many deep Arctic and sub-Arctic lakes, huge quantities of plankton are produced in the surface layer of water where light penetrates. Arctic char and several species of whitefish feed by filtering this plankton. Although it is not possible to imitate microscopic plankton,

A small hot-spot on a huge lake, where shallow water holds large salmon schools.

brightly colored flies will catch these plankton-feeders. Flies such as Dunkeld and Whisky-fly with lots of orange and gold are particularly effective.

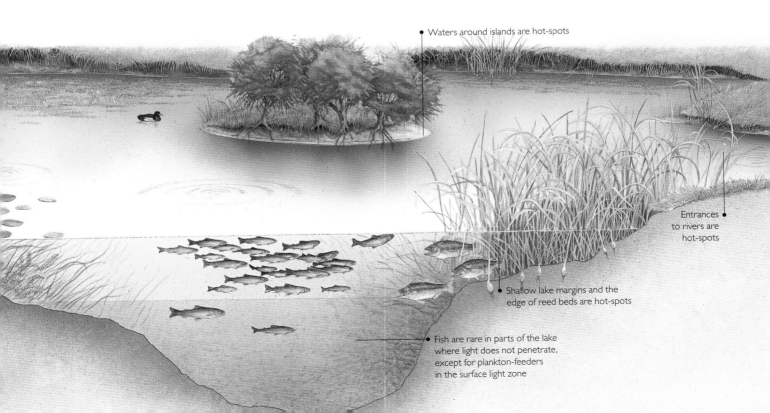

Waters around islands are hot-spots

Entrances to rivers are hot-spots

Shallow lake margins and the edge of reed beds are hot-spots

Fish are rare in parts of the lake where light does not penetrate, except for plankton-feeders in the surface light zone

READING ESTUARIES AND TIDAL CREEKS

MALCOLM GREENHALGH

The best way to work out where fish are in an estuary or a tidal creek is to take the most detailed map you can find and visit at low tide, for now you have an open book. This is particularly the case with larger estuaries in regions where tidal range is great. On two of the estuaries that I fish regularly for sea trout, bass, and mullet, the tidal range is 9.5m (31ft) on a spring tide, and the intertidal zone (distance between low-water and high-water marks) can be as much as 7km (4 miles) wide. In such a vast area of mud- and sandflats there is much fishless water. Knowing such an area is important to safety, too; if you are far out by the low-water channel as the tide floods (at walking speed) it is possible to be stranded and have to swim to the shore.

Low-water channels

Even when the tide is out low-water channels will often hold fish. At that time most or all the water flowing seaward will be fresh, brought into the estuary by the river, and the freshwater influence is greater at the head of an estuary than close to the open sea. Therefore, the fish species throughout most of the low-water channel will be species that can tolerate a wide range of salinities, from full-strength seawater to freshwater. These may include bass (striped and European), mullet, sea

trout, shad, and flatfish such as flounder. Although most fly-fishers would not consider this last to be a fly-fisher's species, it is one of the best low-water quarry. Flounder is one of the few species that does not stop feeding at slack low water, taking a weighted shrimp pattern worked back through the sand of the channel bed.

At low water, look carefully at your estuary and at the tidal creeks that drain into it. Imagine that the tide is rushing in, filling first the hollows that split up the sandflats before covering the banks

themselves. Walk up the shore, noting other hollows and banks as you go. The fish will feed in the deeper hollows before the banks are completely covered, or alongside a bank that has recently been covered. Many estuaries are backed by extensive saltmarshes drained by a network of creeks that dry out at low tide; others may link up with creeks that come from inland and carry freshwater into the main estuary channel at low water. Spend some time at low tide investigating them – and then take a careful look at your map for vantage points: is there a jetty jutting into the estuary, a shingle or rocky point, an old sewage pipe, or some broken sea defenses?

Estuary hot-spots

Many species move into and through the estuary with the flood and back down the estuary again with the ebb, waiting out low water at or outside the estuary's outer limits. Estuaries are highly varied, so it is impossible to describe one pattern that would cover them all. Look for hot-spots where food supplies are concentrated and fish may feed through the flood and ebb of the tide.

Banks Banks that have recently flooded or that will soon be exposed by the falling tide are good spots. The moving water often "rips" around the edges of

ESTUARIES AND TIDAL CREEKS

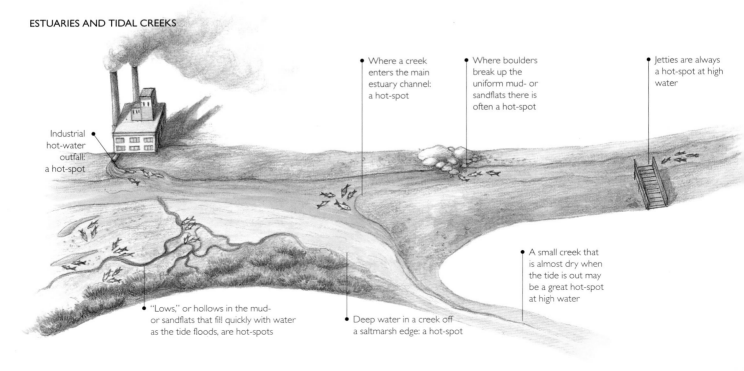

Industrial hot-water outfall: a hot-spot

Where a creek enters the main estuary channel: a hot-spot

Where boulders break up the uniform mud- or sandflats there is often a hot-spot

Jetties are always a hot-spot at high water

A small creek that is almost dry when the tide is out may be a great hot-spot at high water

"Lows," or hollows in the mud- or sandflats that fill quickly with water as the tide floods, are hot-spots

Deep water in a creek off a saltmarsh edge: a hot-spot

sandbanks (causing a steep drop-off from bank to hollow) until they are deeply covered, and this surge of current attracts fish foods and the fish. The problem is that, in most medium-to-large estuaries, the tide will be "just right" for one bank. The feeding fish will arrive, then move on quickly, visiting more than a dozen banks in the course of the flood and ebb. This means that you must follow the fish. A boat is essential.

Start in the outer estuary as the tide begins to move, and anchor up as you watch the first and lowest sandbank being flooded. As soon as the bank is covered move close to it, so that your flies fish along the edge of the bank. In most of the estuaries that I have fished, the speed of the tide ripping around the bank demands a sinking line, although, as the water becomes deeper, the speed of the current diminishes.

If you were fortunate enough to find a school of fish, you might now notice that you are not getting offers as the current slackens. Up-anchor and head up the estuary, looking for another bank that is almost flooded. Continue in this manner, moving from bank to bank. At high water there will be a slack period when you can rest, after which you

TOP TIPS
● Estuaries are dangerous places until you have learned them. Walk or sail them before you fish them, and if possible get a guide.
● On a fast-flowing estuary you will catch more with a sinking fly-line than with a floater.

can fish down the estuary from bank to bank as each becomes exposed by the falling tide.

Junctions Where a large channel joins a main estuary there are invariably many fish feeding on lesser fish, shrimp, and crabs, which are concentrated at the confluence. The predators that you are after will usually take cover just off the main flow, and so I find it best to cast the fly into the faster water, let it swing around to where I think the predator is waiting and, as it reaches the lie, work the fly back. Perhaps the predators see the fish or shrimp imitation coming, expect an easy mouthful, and then respond quickly as the little creature appears to flee. Strikes are usually good pulls.

Promontories and jetties Where a rocky promontory, jetty, or other structure juts out into the estuary the flowing tide will rip around it. Small baitfish and shrimp will tend to congregate on the lee side. So will predatory fish. Cast out into the ripping tide, then, as the fly swings around into slacker water, work the fly back.

Hot water outflows and saltmarsh creeks
Many estuaries have industries based on their shores that need enormous quantities of water for cooling purposes, and they pump the warmed water back into the estuary. If the estuary you fish has a warm-water discharge, then investigate it thoroughly. I know one that flows from a nuclear power station; its warm water holds feeding bass in the fall a month after they have left neighboring parts of the coast.

Dawn, and in this estuary the rising tide is flooding a creek mouth to the left of the fly-fisher. Bass and sea trout will be chasing sandeels and fry — every cast might hook a fish! This is exciting fishing, and well worth the effort of rising early!

Saltmarsh creeks are generally flooded for no more than two or three hours either side of high tide. Your low-water investigations will reveal that their seaward banks are steep: you can stand on the bank top and, in one stride, be in at least 2–3m (6–10ft) of swirling water. Your investigation will also show places where the bank is undercut (don't stand there or it will collapse), and places where two or more big creeks join together. Fish might occur throughout the creek system, but look especially at the entrances to creeks, particularly early in the flood and late in the ebb. At this time predatory fish will be hunting fodderfish and shrimp moving in and out with the tide. Look also at places where two creeks join together, and at the undercut banks that you found earlier, where big fish may lie in wait to ambush lesser fish.

 Saltwater Fish 42–79

 Spotting Fish 126–7 • Night and Day 128–9 • Rain and Sun 130–1 • Tides 132–3

READING HARBORS AND JETTIES

ED MITCHELL

Harbors are home to a fly-fisher's paradox: although they may know their harbors well, and pass through frequently, most fly-fishers never dream of wetting a line so close to port. Too bad, since the fishing may be fine right here at home.

Harbors are often rich in baitfish that attract a wide range of gamefish. Furthermore, these protected waters provide excellent access for shore fishermen as well as for those fly-fishers working from small boats.

Occasionally you find the fish simply by studying the surface of the water. Swirls in the water and gamefish leaping clear are sure signs, but so are subtler clues such as scattering baitfish, flocks of busy seabirds hovering over the water, and slicks created as baitfish are chopped up by their predators. Nevertheless, many times the fish you seek will not show any visible sign of their presence. Then it is up to you to find them.

As in any location, the best fishing and the biggest fish are likely to be found where there is a strong current and rapid changes in contour. In my experience, the tidal rips near the harbor mouth are very productive locations, as are the edges of the main channel. In both situations the fish may be quite deep, requiring a fast-sinking fly-line.

Understanding baitfish behavior is another important key to fly-fishing success. Schools of forage fish frequently migrate with the tide, going to the head of the harbor on the flood and then dropping toward the mouth on the ebb. Gamefish and fly-fishers must follow. Other baitfish will take up a semi-permanent residence near artificial

In busy harbors, the waters can hold large schools of fish in a variety of species. Yet many fly-fishers disregard them as suitable locations in which to fish.

structures such as bridge abutments and dock pilings, making these spots well worth exploring. Where these places have night lights, the illumination will concentrate both prey and predator. I like to cast a fly so it swings from the lit area into the darkness or tracks just outside the shadow line. Given the barnacles and other sharp surfaces that abound in these locations, I use a heavy leader and a fairly tight drag to lessen the risk of the line getting cut.

When fishing a busy harbor, avoid hours when boat traffic is heaviest and, if you are fishing from a boat, be sure not to anchor in a position where you will block the channel.

Fishing from jetties

Slick, stony, and sometimes washed by surf, jetties deserve your respect. Yet for all the risks they are often highly productive destinations — so much so that some of them attract a faithful following of fly-

fishers, the most devoted of whom are called "jetty jockeys."

Jetties provide shore fly-fishers with a firm casting platform that also allows them to move out from the beach in order to reach a variety of water. Still, not all jetties are equal. The most productive jetties, I believe, are invariably those at the entrance to a tidal river, salt pond, or harbor. Here you will find swift-moving water and large quantities of forage fish.

For example, along the southwest coast of Rhode Island there is a series of salt ponds, each with a pair of jetties at the inlet. In season I have caught bluefish, striped bass, Atlantic bonito, and little tuna from these rocky walls.

The tip of a jetty is often the most sought-after spot since it puts you adjacent to the deepest water and, sometimes, the best current, especially on an ebbing tide. Nevertheless, fine fishing can be had all along a jetty wall, particularly where the current approaches. An offset or bend in a jetty wall always deserves your attention for that reason, because you can expect it to cause a change in the current that will attract fish. And do not overlook the start of a jetty where it joins the beach. I have caught fish in this location many times, especially when the wind is blowing straight into the pocket.

Where two jetties are paired, as is common at inlets, very often one is closer to the more productive bottom structure and current, and therefore it fishes far better than the other. So it pays to do some investigating. Be sure to cover

SAFETY
Jetty fishing has special safety requirements. Jetties are often wave-washed and extremely slippery, so take great care. Felt soles are a help, but cleats are better, along with a good measure of common sense. Move deliberately and use caution. Plan a safe route down to the water, before you actually need one to land a fish. And never turn your back on waves breaking over the jetty wall.

the water from top to bottom using intermediate fly-lines as well as rapid-sinking lines. Almost universally, fly-fishers working a jetty cast straight out in the water, but this is not always the right method. Some fish, such as striped bass, hang very close, feeding within a few feet of the jetty's waterline, so a fly traveling more or less parallel to the jetty wall can be deadly.

Plan your fishing to coincide with times of moving water. Remember, however, that the time of tide and the time when the current changes in an inlet do not always coincide. Very often the current runs for a considerable time after the tide has ended. I have fished inlets where the current flows in for at least two hours after the time of high tide. And the ebbing current begins to flow three hours after high tide. Light level should be a factor in your plans as well. Many gamefish are most active during periods of low light, so a prime time for fishing occurs when the current is moving strongly at dusk or dawn.

The tide is falling and a strong current is swirling by this jetty. Baitfish will be sheltering close to the jetty; larger fish will be lying in ambush for them. Cast out, let the current pull the fly around toward the jetty and then start retrieving line. Takes will be savage!

Saltwater Fish 42–79

Spotting Fish 126–7 • Night and Day 128–9 • Rain and Sun 130–1 • Tides 132–3

Cape Cod 160–1

READING BEACHES AND BAYS

ED MITCHELL

Everywhere, the central challenge of the coastal fly-fisher is to find fish, and nowhere is that challenge greater than it is along a vast beach that stretches into the distance. True, diving birds, swirls, slicks, and schools of erupting bait may instantly pinpoint the best action that a beach has to offer. Still, in the long term, when these obvious signs are lacking a fly-fisher's success must depend on the fly-fisher's ability to identify the best-looking water.

When fishing any beach for the first time, assume that it has a hierarchy: some spots that rarely hold fish, some spots that regularly give up a fish or two, and one or more hot-spots that can usually be relied on to provide the finest fishing. One way to discover that hierarchy, of course, is to use a process of elimination – simply to wade in somewhere and begin to fish. Yet this is a slow method and, on the larger beaches, it is totally impractical. It is far better to spend a few moments studying the beach's features in an effort to locate the best-looking water.

Some areas of bottom structure and current may be obvious. Waves breaking over a sandbar, or rocky reefs that protrude through the surface are good examples. In clear water rapid changes in bottom depth are accompanied by noticeable changes in the water color. Often underwater structures have tongues of current associated with

them, and it is here the finest fishing is apt to be found. Dark rip lines, areas of turbulence, and lanes of foam and floating debris will help you to identify the moving water.

After studying the surface turn your attention to the shape of the shoreline: it is an important clue to the shape of the adjoining bottom. The general rule is that the more a part of the beach meanders, the more bottom structure it has connected to it, and so the more likely it is that fish will hold there. Conversely, the straightest portions of a beach have little in the way of bottom structure and rather than hold here, the fish tend to travel through.

It is best, therefore, to focus your efforts on those sections of the beach where the shoreline winds in and out, forming points, cusps, and bowls. Go to the most prominent ones in the area; even if these features are small they deserve your attention. Cover them methodically. Straighter sections should come second: when you fish them, cast and move constantly so that you maximize the territory that you are covering. In both cases, when you are searching the water for fish, remember that large attractor-type flies are better than smaller subtle patterns; intermediate fly-lines often make perfect general purpose lines, but where the surf is strong or the beach deep, sinking lines are preferable.

The physical composition of a beach, whether sand, cobble, or rock, has an effect on the fishing as well. As a rule, the coarser the bottom material the more forage it holds and the more likely you are to locate feeding fish. In addition, places where dissimilar materials meet are apt to be fishing hot-spots. For example, I give special fishing attention to the area where a cobble beach becomes boulders or a sandy beach switches to rock.

Besides the shape and composition of a beach, you should also look at its slope as it nears the water. The steeper the slope, the greater the water depth near shore. Deep water not only holds fish longer into the ebbing tide, but also attracts larger fish by providing them with a suitable habitat even in the brightest daylight. In short, deep water offers consistent fishing. The opportunities on a shallow stretch of beach are usually far more dependent on the level of light and tide. Expect low-light conditions such as dusk and dawn or an overcast day to be best, especially when these are combined with a rising tide.

Fishing in bays

Bays are enclosed bodies of water, frequently bowl-shaped, with wide mouths open to the sea. In fishing terms, I find it helpful to divide them into three different sections: the head, the mid-section, and the mouth of the bay.

BEACHES

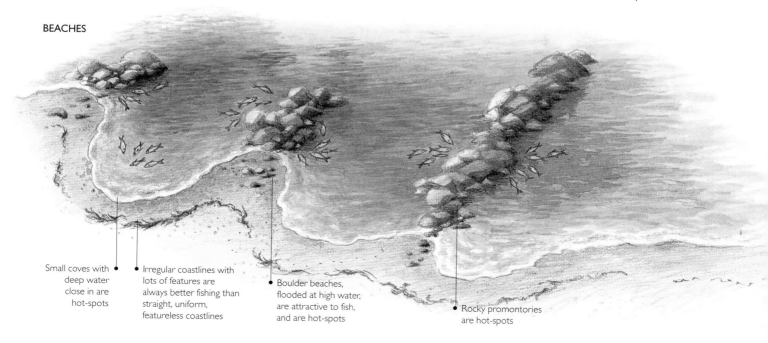

Small coves with deep water close in are hot-spots

Irregular coastlines with lots of features are always better fishing than straight, uniform, featureless coastlines

Boulder beaches, flooded at high water, are attractive to fish, and are hot-spots

Rocky promontories are hot-spots

The head of the bay is often a shallow, sheltered area with modest tidal currents and excellent public access. As a result it may provide fine fishing, allowing fly-fishers to use small boats or even to wade. Given the bottom and current conditions, however, the head of the bay is rarely the right place in which to look for large fish. Instead you should expect to find good fishing for small- to medium-sized quarry. Nevertheless, one important exception must be noted. When a river or stream enters the head of a bay, large fish are likely to be found, either as part of a spawning run or in pursuit of migrating baitfish. You should therefore pay special attention to any rip that forms near the opening of an estuary, no matter how small it is.

Although the mid-section is the largest part of the bay it is apt to have the weakest currents and the least varied bottom structure. As a result, the fishing is not as dependable and the fish you locate are probably passing through. If, however, the middle of the bay contains an island, a reef, or a defined channel, these areas will attract fish, and it is here you should focus your fishing.

The mouth of the bay has the most wind and waves, and the fastest currents, and is closest to deeper water. While these conditions may limit your opportunity to wade or force you to use larger boats, they also draw bigger fish. Even if the mouth of the bay is highly symmetrical, do not assume that fishing is equal everywhere. The tidal currents are probably much stronger on one side of the mouth, and this is where the best action will take place. Be sure to cover carefully any reef or bar lying near the mouth, particularly those over or around which strong rips form.

BAYS

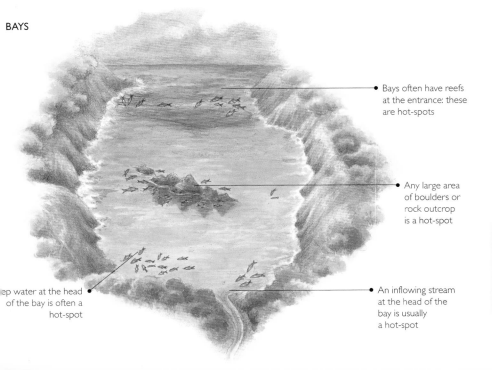

Bays often have reefs at the entrance: these are hot-spots

Any large area of boulders or rock outcrop is a hot-spot

...ep water at the head of the bay is often a hot-spot

An inflowing stream at the head of the bay is usually a hot-spot

When fishing beaches, it is advisable to wear chest-high waders so that you can wade out beyond the nearest breakers. You can then fish your fly more effectively. But beware: on some coasts "under-tow" may drag you seaward, so check that the beach is safe for deep wading before you start.

 Saltwater Fish 42–79

 Spotting Fish 126–7 • Night and Day 128–9 • Rain and Sun 130–1 • Tides 132–3

READING FLATS

LEFTY KREH

Saltwater fly-fishers call the shallows lying close to the shore the flats. Water on the flats ranges from a few centimeters or inches to about 2.5m (8ft) in depth, and some may be exposed and dry at low tide. Although the best-known flats are in subtropical and tropical areas, such as those that nestle against the Florida Keys, some flats are not tropical, such as the extensive shallows along the northeast coast of the United States, where big striped bass often prowl waters that are less than 1.5m (5ft) deep.

Flats are among the richest areas of the sea. Some are fed almost constantly by nutrient-rich river water; others are backed by extensive saltmarshes and mangrove swamps that provide shelter for fish and add nutrients to the water. These nutrients support immense populations of tiny invertebrates that feed a huge variety of fodder-fish and larger invertebrates, including crabs, shrimp, squid, snails, clams, and worms, all of which are the food of the fly-fishers' fish.

The best flats for fishing are covered with clear water and this is what makes fishing them so enjoyable. You will actually see most fish before you cast – it is a form of hunting and fishing combined. It is very tempting, when you first visit a flat, to start casting. Don't do it! You will scare – not catch – species such as bonefish, permit, and tarpon. Find the fish first.

Searching for fish on flats

If you have never flats-fished before, hire a guide who will pole you through the shallow waters in a flats boat, point out the main fish-holding features, and demonstrate how to spot the fish. Your guide will bring you within casting distance of the fish, and you will perhaps then see how easy it is to spook the fish with a clumsy cast, let alone by bad wading or splashy boat handling.

After that introduction you may decide to wade a shallow flat, or take a boat out on a slightly deeper flat with a friend (taking turns to pole the boat and fish). Move very, very slowly, with the sun behind or to one side of you, as you slowly search the water. As you go, look out for the different features of a flat that attract fish and that help you to locate them.

The flat's bottom may be pure sand, over which fish may cruise in search of crabs, marine worms, and clams. Many flats are carpeted in

dense aquatic grasses. In the tropics, turtle grass is the most prevalent and it harbors a great variety of food. Other flats may be solid coral, and you might think that they wouldn't hold anything for the fish to eat, but you would be wrong. Coral has millions of small depressions and holes in the limestone rock where creatures live.

Other flats are of soft mud (don't try to wade these!). Mud flats house shrimp, crabs, clams, and worms. On tropical mud flats you will often see up-thrusting cones of mud with a hole in the top, indicating a large worm lives within. Although the worms emerge to feed only at night, bonefish, snappers, and many other fish eagerly seek them, and some will delve into the conical burrow to catch them.

Channels and ridges

Flats are often bordered by channels, and sometimes channels cross flats (beware if you are wading). These provide avenues for fish to traverse the flats and escape routes when being pursued. If the flat is very shallow the predatory fish that you are seeking will either be close to or in the channels at low tide. If you spot fish there, present a fly on a fast-sinking line to produce good catches. When the tide is rising, the predatory fish will leave the channels and move onto the flats. Look for them at the channel edges or try to intercept them as they move up the channels and onto the flats. Remember that very large bonefish, permit, and many other predatory species rarely move far away from deeper channels.

Many flats will have underwater ridges, which predatory fish will cruise, attempting to trap their prey against the uprising. The shallow ledges separating a bed of turtle grass from the slightly lower bare sand of the flats are a good example. Barracuda will often lie against a ledge and wait for some lesser fry to swim by.

When fishing flats from a boat (above), a guide will help you to spot the fish. If you want to wade a shallow flat (right), move slowly, and spot your fish before making a cast.

Keep your eyes open on sand or mud flats for disturbed, cloudy water. Some schools of fish (bonefish and sea trout are two good examples) will gather together and tear at the bottom searching for food. This causes the cloudiness. A shrimp or crab imitation carefully fished in cloudy water will often be rewarded.

Mangroves

In warmer seas, the flats are almost always edged by mangroves. Two types of mangrove are most prevalent: red mangrove, with spider-like legs for roots, and black mangrove, which has a tree-like trunk and air roots near the base that resemble asparagus. These mangroves furnish a perfect habitat for fish and the creatures on which they prey. A rising tide is often not the best time to fish close to mangroves, for the fish's foods will swim

well back in the mangroves and the fish will follow them. But as the tide falls the fish will move out after their food and will be easy to catch. One hot-spot is where there is deeper water close to mangroves: approach carefully, and cast a long line delicately if you want to catch any fish that are lying there.

Always watch for feeding seabirds, especially when the tide begins to drain from the flats on the ebb, or begins to spread out from channels on the flood. The seabirds will locate the largest concentrations of baitfish, crabs, shrimp, and other food, and the big fish that you are after will also be found there.

Seasons also have a major effect on how you find fish on flats. Water temperature often governs when baitfish and the fly-fishers' fish appear and disappear. Take temperature readings and record your observations. Over the years, you will gather information as to when the fish visit your flats to feed, and you will be able to forecast good fishing.

Saltwater Fish 42–79

Saltwater Baitfish 106–7

The Florida Keys 164–5 •
The Bahamas 162–3

READING THE OPEN SEA

PHILL WILLIAMS

The open sea can seem a bewildering expanse of featureless water. Yet to the experienced fly-fisher it is marked by signs that point to where fish are feeding. Some signs are easy to read, others so subtle that deciphering them seems like witchcraft. Nevertheless, a practiced eye can spot some tiny scrap of evidence, one that makes one piece of the apparently uniform ocean "fishy."

Submerged obstacles interrupting the flow of the tide, particularly in shallow open water, invariably reveal themselves with obvious changes in ambient wave patterns. Sudden boils or surface swirls indicate abrupt seabed changes; their position and identity can be fine-tuned by reference to a navigation chart and echo sounder. However, such places can be treacherous in severe gales, or when the wind is blowing directly against the current of a fast-flowing tide.

Wrecks offer the best available cover for fish along their edges or where they are broken up. Find where the baitfish are lying in or around the wreck and you will find their predators. Because of their sheer bulk, wrecks also serve to deflect the tide, creating mid-water pressure waves. Some schooling bait species such as mackerel thrive along these pressure waves, so this is where predatory species are most likely to be found.

Large, natural subsurface features can have a similar effect. The Hump off Islamorada, Florida, is a prime example. Like the wrecks off Key West, it attracts large numbers of huge, hungry amberjacks during the spring. Hard-fighting blackfin tuna also gather high above the Hump and these, along with the amberjacks, attract some very big sharks.

Banks and reefs are usually best fished along their uptide edge where the tide roars up the shallowing slope. If the water is shallow enough this will show as a disturbed line on the surface. Water color can also rapidly change at this point. In tropical waters, dorado, small tuna, sharks, and barracuda love these drop-off edges and, in the cooler seas around Europe, they attract pollack or bass. In very deep water you will need an echo sounder to locate the reef edge.

Predatory fish often follow established, unvarying routes as they patrol their home range. These often include the deeper channels cut between inshore flats and offshore banks. Many species use them to travel from one shallow-water feeding area to another. Sharks, barracuda, and jacks spend a lot of time both feeding in and traveling along these deeper channels.

Transient hot-spots

Not all holding areas occupy fixed positions. For example, offshore tidal currents may change position through the tidal regime and attract fish to one small area of the open sea for only a few minutes. The question is, how do you find these transient hot-spots? And how do you find

A patch of boiling water in the open sea indicates a large school of feeding fish. A well-cast fly will almost certainly be taken immediately.

A certain hot-spot. The gulls are feeding on baitfish that have been forced to the surface by predatory fish — the ones we are trying to catch.

otherwise featureless but fish-holding hot-spots where blue water dominates, and where the depths are too great for fixed physical features to "show" themselves through surface signs?

One answer lies in watching the behavior of seabirds. Flocks of terns feeding on tiny baitfish or fry at the surface are a sure sign that large predatory fish are below, taking the lesser fish and forcing them to the surface. Sometimes the baitfish themselves might even show as a foaming mass or as a darker patch of water as the big predatory fish herd them together at the surface.

The predator's identity will depend on the location and the underlying depth. Off Mexico's Cabo San Lucas we used to look for birds circling high in the sky. As we followed them, they would suddenly drop to the water's surface. This was our cue to look for the sickle-shaped tail of a striped marlin. Off the coast of Gambia the sign was baitfish being compressed and then driven into a boiling mass, with common terns feeding in huge numbers from above and a school of crevalle jack from below. The crevalle jacks appeared to be driving the bait in a fixed direction. It was then simply a case of positioning the boat to intercept the mayhem and putting a fly through the boiling water.

Flotsam and jetsam

Look out for debris on the water. This may be natural clumps of weed, or flotsam such as a floating fish-box. I have spent hours searching out small clumps of weed off the Florida coast, under which I can cast shrimp patterns to tripletails hovering a few feet down.

Out in deeper water, cut fish pieces chummed into the water around floating objects invariably draw up scores of dorado that will then fall to a Deceiver. On more than one occasion the commotion that was caused by the dorado has attracted the larger predators, most notably sharks, within fly range.

Wind-blown lanes or big rafts of tangled weed, particularly Sargassum weed, are not uncommon many miles from shore. Small baitfish use these lanes as natural cover. The numbers of fish present are often proportionate to the size of the lane or raft and this frequently means very large numbers of fish indeed. All the open-water predators are going to be on the cards. Far offshore these are prime areas for marlin, and closer to the deep water drop-offs for sailfish, a wide range of tuna species, and wahoo.

 Saltwater Fish 42–79

TOP TIP

Invest in a local navigation chart and echo sounder. By studying the chart at home you will be able to pick out many likely hot-spots. When you are at sea the echo sounder will confirm or reject your homework, and show you precisely where the hot-spots are. It will show the exact location of wrecks, reefs, and deeper channels, whether the bottom is rock, sand, or mud, and the precise depth, so you can mark them on your chart. The echo sounder will also show you the positions of schools of fish, some indication of how big the fish are, and the depth that they are swimming. All you have to do is get the fly down to them!

SPOTTING FISH

LEFTY KREH

When fly-fishing in saltwater there are many situations in which seeing fish is essential to catching them. This is especially true on saltwater flats. Most fly-fishers know that bonefish or tarpon have to be seen before a cast is made. If you cast randomly without first spotting the fish you will be lucky if you catch either of these very sensitive species. Any time that you throw a fly to a fish that you have spotted beforehand in freshwater or saltwater, you will greatly improve your chances of catching it.

The art of fish-spotting

In the water, fish don't look like they do out of the water. Each species has its own special underwater appearance. Fish with silvery, mirror-like sides, such as bonefish, tarpon, and permit, reflect the bottom over which they are swimming. Other fish use camouflage. A smallmouth bass, with its mottled coloring, is very difficult to see. A brown trout, even a big one, lying on a gravel bar is almost invisible until it moves. A flounder covered with sand is one of the most difficult to locate. Steelhead in a fast, clear river pool are sometimes tough to spot.

On bright days, you may spot some fish only when you see the shadow that the sun casts underneath them. This is especially true of bonefish and larger trout. And often, the best way to spot a tarpon that is swimming over green grass is by its large dark eye.

Some fish that are camouflaged, such as trout, are easy to spot when they are feeding – the inside of the mouth is white. Spot the white mouth of a feeding trout, cast your nymph to it, and you will see the white mouth open again as the trout takes your fly.

One of the most important factors in seeing fish is to recognize how the sun's angle can help or hinder you. Sun produces glare, and any time that the sun is in front of you, glare becomes a problem. Whenever possible, keep the sun behind you, or at least to the side. In this way, glare will be reduced to a minimum.

Background may have a great deal to do with how much glare is on the surface, too. White clouds may make it impossible to see through the surface of the water, whereas a dark green shoreline of trees or a high cliff may enable you to see every tiny feature of the bottom.

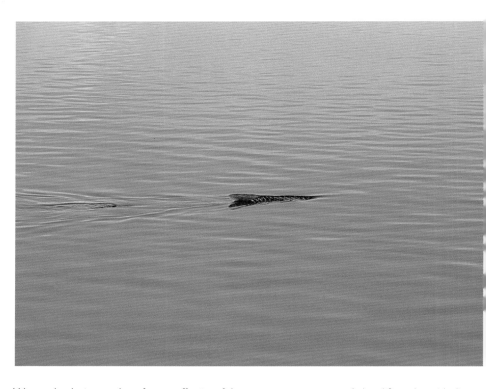

A dorsal fin and a quick glimpse of a broad back. This fish is moving right. Don't cast to the fin but several yards in front.

Water depth is another factor affecting fish-spotting. In very shallow water, fish may be easy to spot provided you haven't scared them, but in deep water you may have to look hard. Move your head up and down and from side to side: you will sometimes spot some movement from the corner of your eyes, even if looking directly at the water picks out nothing.

If fish are moving about in shallow water (less than a foot), they will create wakes that indicate the direction in which they are swimming. However, the telltale "V" will be behind the fish. Many fly-fishers make the mistake of casting to the "V" when the cast should be made several feet in front of it.

Even at night, saltwater fish can be spotted in the lights of bridges, piers, and docks. Look carefully and you can often see fish that are lying close to the surface of the water. They are waiting for the tide to carry minnows, shrimp, or other food toward them.

These fish will always be lying on the up-current side of a structure and they will appear as gray forms at the edge of the shadow cast by a bridge, pier, or dock on the illuminated water. Spot these fish and cast your offering well up-current of them. This can lead to some terrific fishing.

Wear polarizing glasses

While they cannot remove all glare, polarizing glasses do a remarkable job and are essential for sighting fish. I recommend that you purchase those that are either scratch resistant or those that have the polarized film shielded by glass. You can obtain several tints or colors of polarized lenses, and you should consider having more than one pair. Most people agree that the best all-round glasses are those with a brownish-yellow tint – they improve

TOP TIPS
- When fishing in the daytime, always wear a hat with a dark brim and polarizing glasses.
- When trying to spot fish, don't expect them to look like they do in photographs or paintings

Fish survive because predators find them difficult to spot. If you want to catch them, you must spot the fish before they spot you!

contrast and help you locate fish easily and quickly. For offshore fishing, I prefer gray-green tints.

I also own a pair of prescription-ground polarized glasses with a very light yellow tint. On overcast days or when fishing in wooded trout streams, they help me to see better than glasses with darker tints would.

You can assist your polarizing glasses under some light conditions. When you are looking into the water at some angles to the sun, your polaroids may not appear to be doing their job of removing the glare efficiently. If you feel you should be spotting fish better than you are, try tilting your head to one side or the other to remove the glare.

Wear a hat

It is essential to wear a hat when fishing. A brim will shade the eyes, but if it is light in color on the underside, glare will be reflected from the water

Silvery, almost translucent forms are lying in shallow water over turtle grass.

into your eyes. If the underside is dark, the glare will be reduced and your vision greatly improved.

Use field glasses

One tool that has helped me catch many fish is a pair of field glasses. For trout fishing, I have a pair small enough to fit into my fly-fishing vest. Field glasses let you locate trout before approaching the stream, and they allow you to identify the insects that the trout are eating. They also allow you to watch what other fly-fishers are using to catch fish.

When offshore fishing, I prefer a pair of 8 x 30 or more powerful waterproof glasses. They help locate feeding birds or fish breaking the surface that you might otherwise miss.

 The Fly-fishers' Fish 14–79

 Reading Rivers 112–13 • Reading Lakes 114–15 • Reading Estuaries and Tidal Creeks 116–17 • Reading the Open Sea 124–5

Night and day

MALCOLM GREENHALGH

One particularly hot August day, many years ago, I went trout fishing on the north of England's River Lune. The river was running low and was crystal clear. The sky was cloudless. Slowly, I worked my way up 3km (2 miles) of river, peering into every tiny pool. The river was fishless. I sat back in the shade of a waterside alder and fell asleep. I woke up as the sun was dipping behind the high hills, which were casting a lengthening shadow over the valley. Sitting up, I looked at the river and then rubbed my eyes in disbelief. As I gazed downstream, every pool seemed alive with rising trout. That evening I caught 16 trout from the "fishless" river.

Trout feed throughout the afternoon in spring. But in clear, low water, and bright, sunny summer weather they become crepuscular, even nocturnal. This is logical, for in such conditions they are visible and vulnerable to predators, and their survival depends on hiding throughout the day among boulders, bushes, and tree branches that trail in the water and under overhanging banks. Like the quarry, a summer trout fly-fisher ought also to be crepuscular, even nocturnal. Although trout fishing on lakes, like rivers, is best in spring and fall between late morning and dusk, in summer the trout start feeding at dusk and continue to feed through the night until dawn. To go afloat on a trout lake on a bright, hot summer's day is usually a tiring waste of good time.

Sea trout (sea-run brown trout) feed most keenly on tides that flood and ebb between dusk and dawn, so the best time to catch them in the sea is at night. However, when they return to freshwater on their spawning runs, sea trout usually stop feeding. They will ignore lesser fish and invertebrates that live in the river pools, so the vast majority of sea trout that you catch in the river have empty stomachs. However, for some unknown reason some sea trout will suddenly, for a moment or two, give up their fast and take a fly. This is one of the mysteries of fly-fishing. And although sea trout that have just returned to the river may be caught on fly by day, mainly when the river is high after heavy rain, they are more likely to take a fly between dusk and dawn, as they are when they are in the sea.

Dusk, when the sun is setting, is always a good time to fish, whether you are fishing rivers, lakes, or the sea, because fish feed keenly in half-light.

There is hectic activity under Lapland's midnight sun, and an Arctic char comes to the net.

Many other saltwater species, such as striped bass, weakfish, sea-run brown trout, and European bass feed more keenly through night tides than they do through day tides. If you want to catch a trophy fish it must be caught at night. The same is true of bluefish, which can be caught during the day and night in quiet waters but feed only at night in busy harbors and bays, and snook, which seem to take the fly better in the half light of dawn than they do at any other time of the day.

Most pike fly-fishers go out in the morning and return home in the evening. Yet, especially in heavily fished water or where there is a lot of disturbance by boats, pike feed most keenly after dusk. Even in the depths of winter, when water and air temperatures are close to freezing, on a

SAFETY

Safety aspects are of paramount importance:
- Wade very slowly at night.
- If night fishing on the coast, take especial care on cliffs and jetties, and when fishing in a maze of creeks and mudflats where the advancing tide may cut off your retreat.
- Before you go night fishing somewhere that you don't know well, always make an earlier visit in the day to note possible hazards.

lake close to my home in Lancashire, England, the best times to catch a pike on fly are around dawn (7:30–8:30am) and from dusk (3pm) until well into the night.

Coping with nocturnal fly-fishing
These few examples clearly demonstrate that, often, the best fly-fishing is to be had under cover of darkness. And there are other advantages. On the coast the fish come closer inshore. In lakes and rivers you can get closer to the fish at night, so there is less need for extra-long casts. But night fishing causes problems for many fly-fishers. Not least of which is fitting it in with the demands of family and work.

At night, no matter how well you cast, wind knots appear in the leader as if by magic. Check the leader regularly and, should a knot appear, immediately change the leader. A wind knot greatly weakens nylon leader strength. Don't try to cast out of sight and, to reduce the chances of tangles and wind knots, have only one fly on the leader, and make no more than one or two false casts. Incidentally, at night fish seem to fight much harder than they do during the day, so check that your tackle is strong and has no flaws.

To change your fly or leader you may need to use a flashlight. Some fish will flee a lamp flashing on the water, so use a small light and keep its beam

off the water. A red filter is useful to prevent the light ruining night vision.

Some fly-fishers do not like being out alone in the pitch dark. The near-human cough of a deer, the hoot of an owl, or the rattle of a rabbit running across the shingle may well send them scurrying homeward with their hearts racing.

Time and experience of night fishing is the only cure. Persevere, for there is something atavistically satisfying about being alone in the darkness beside a wild river or by a roaring sea. Your senses are heightened and you feel you have become part of nature. And when a great bass takes your fly from the surf or a big sea trout strikes in a pitch dark river pool – well, these are magic moments in the life of any fly-fisher.

The Fly-fishers' Fish 14–79

Rain and Sun 130–1 • Tides 132–3 • Coping with the Wind 134–5 • Getting the Fly Down 136–7 • Inducing a Take 142–3

RAIN AND SUN

MALCOLM GREENHALGH

Weather and its consequences rule the pattern of a fish's life – and they must inevitably rule the fly-fisher's life, as well.

Fish and temperature

Fish, being cold-blooded creatures, are greatly affected by water temperature, which is influenced by water depth, air temperature, and sunlight.

Tropical saltwater flats are shallow and their water responds more quickly to air temperature changes than deeper water. Therefore timing is important when fishing for bonefish, as the prime water temperature range is 21–25°C (70–77°F). Bonefish come to the flats when seawater temperatures over the flats reach 20°C (68°F), and as the temperature rises so bonefish feeding intensity grows until it hits a peak at about 23°C (73°F). However, as the temperature continues to rise bonefish feeding intensity declines and, should the seawater over the flats reach 27°C (81°F), the bonefish will quit the flats for deeper, slightly cooler water. Other major species on flats, including tarpon and permit, show similar sensitivity to temperature.

For striped bass fishing off the shores of North America and for European bass and mullet the critical minimum water temperature appears to be about 10°C (50°F). During the fall, at 8°C (46°F), these species either become dormant or migrate to warmer waters to the south where they may continue feeding. As the shallow seas washing the coastlines warm up in spring and reach that magic 10°C (50°F), the fish return to the shallower coastal waters and begin feeding. In bass, feeding activity appears to peak in the 13–18°C (55–64°F) range, and in mullets in the 13–20°C (55–68°F) range. If temperatures continue to rise, so feeding activity declines, making fly-fishing more difficult.

Many freshwater fish will feed and take artificial flies in extremely low water temperatures. Some species, such as Arctic char, grayling, and pike, can provide excellent sport in the winter months and can even be caught on flies fished through holes cut in the ice of frozen lakes, where the temperature is only 1 or 2°C (34 or 36°F).

Migratory salmon will run from the sea when the river temperature reaches about 4°C (39°F), and they are capable of leaping waterfalls when the water temperature exceeds 8°C (46°F). Once there are salmon in a river, the size of flies and methods that you might use to catch them will be influenced by water temperature. In general, the colder the water, the larger the effective fly and the deeper you must fish it. There is no month in the British Isles when you cannot fish for sea-silver Atlantic salmon. From January to March, and from late October to December, water temperatures are usually very low, with pools ice-rimmed and the surrounding hills blanketed with snow. You can catch fresh-run salmon in these conditions, but you must fish a big fly, very slowly, on a fast-sinking fly-line. In midsummer, on the same rivers, with water temperatures between 12 and 20°C (53 and 68°F), the salmon are more alert and therefore will respond well to a tiny fly fished on a floating line close to the water surface.

Fish and rain

Heavy rain has a great effect on freshwater fish and fishing. However, in my experience, even closely related species may respond to rain quite differently. Salmon will take a fly during all but the heaviest of rainstorms, whereas sea trout will refuse a fly in anything heavier than light drizzle. Once, in a week of sweltering hot weather and thunderstorms in Ontario, it seemed to me that smallmouth bass were prepared to grab a fly in heavy rain, whereas largemouth bass were not.

A long spell of heavy rain will cause many rivers to rise rapidly in flood. Floods usually begin with a "clear water rise" of only a few inches. This is followed by a "dirty water rise" that continues to the peak of the flood – the "filthy flood." At this stage the river can be quite violent, bursting its banks, felling trees, washing big boulders downstream, and carrying seawards all kinds of flotsam, from leaves and weeds to dead livestock. The height of a flood and the speed of the rise depend on the size of the river and the amount of rainfall. Some smaller European rivers can rise over 1.5m (4ft) in three hours, and I once witnessed Norway's Namsen River rise by almost 2m (6ft) overnight. As a flood begins to subside, flotsam disappears as the "dirty water fall" is reached, soil settles out of the falling water, and the final stage of the flood, the "clear water fall" is reached.

Fly-fishing potential varies greatly throughout a flood. During the clear water rise, which may last anything from a few minutes to an hour or so, fishing can be outstanding. This is, perhaps, because the initial rise alerts fish and makes them more responsive to natural foods and artificial flies.

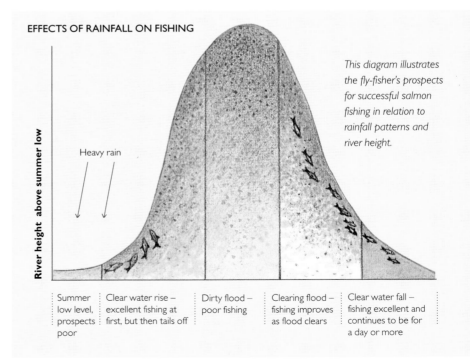

EFFECTS OF RAINFALL ON FISHING

River height above summer low

Heavy rain

| Summer low level, prospects poor | Clear water rise – excellent fishing at first, but then tails off | Dirty flood – poor fishing | Clearing flood – fishing improves as flood clears | Clear water fall – fishing excellent and continues to be for a day or more |

This diagram illustrates the fly-fisher's prospects for successful salmon fishing in relation to rainfall patterns and river height.

On one occasion, after two months of drought, when fish had been almost impossible to catch, I caught four sea trout and lost five other fish in the 22 minutes of a clear water rise. They simply hurled themselves at the fly as soon as it hit the water. But then it was over, for during the dirty water rise and filthy flood, fish usually take cover. However, in fly-fishing there are exceptions to most rules. I once caught eight trout and three chub that were feeding on drowned earthworms in a flooded field about 40m (120ft) from the main river channel.

Fly-fishing prospects continue to improve during a dirty water fall. Resident species seek a wide range of food, from earthworms, slugs, and insect larvae washed into the river, to minnows, sculpins, and other small fish that predators can ambush in the murky water. This is the time to catch that big trout on a sculpin or minnow imitation.

Migratory fish begin to head upstream in earnest during the dirty water fall, but often they will be so intent on running that it can be almost impossible to get one to take a fly. However, during the dirty water fall there will be a short period (perhaps just as the fish decide it is time to move) when fish after fish can be taken. Hugh Falkus, the English author, film-maker, and world-renowned fly-fisher, coined the term "magic moment" for this brief unpredictable period, a period that may last only a few minutes, but during which a fly-fisher whose fly is in the water may catch six good fish.

The prospects for fishing, particularly in rivers, depend very much on the amount of rainfall and the available sunlight.

The last stage of a flood – the clear water fall – is usually the best part. Resident fish will continue to feed keenly throughout the day, and migratory fish will continue to run upstream but, instead of ignoring our flies as they did in the dirty water fall, they now stop at regular intervals, providing us with a great chance to catch them.

TOP TIPS

- Buy a fly-fisher's thermometer and take the water and air temperatures every time you go fishing.
- Keep a fishing diary and record these temperatures, your catch, effective flies, and any other points of interest from each day. Over the years you will build up a bank of information about places that you fish regularly, and will begin to notice patterns that may prove helpful in increasing your future success.

 The Fly-fishers' Fish 14–79

 Food and Flies 80–109

 Spotting Fish 126–7 • Tides 132–3 • Coping with the Wind 134–5

TIDES

MALCOLM GREENHALGH

For the saltwater fly-fisher, tides are of the utmost importance. A knowledge of them is essential for understanding the movements of fish and their food. Even more important, an understanding of tides can save lives.

At most places on the coast there are two tides every day, in which the tide floods to "high water" and then ebbs to "low water." The time between consecutive high waters varies from approximately 12 hours 18 minutes to 12 hours 50 minutes, with an average of approximately 12 hours 25 minutes. Therefore, anyone fishing a tide that attains high water at 1pm will probably sleep through the next high water, which peaks at about 1.25am, and may be out fishing the next one, which will peak at approximately 1.55pm.

Official tide tables are available that provide the predicted timing of every high water and low water for all the world's major ports and harbors, for every day in the forthcoming year.

Because tides are largely controlled by the position of the moon and sun relative to the Earth, the state of the moon – whether full, half, or new – is also given in tide tables, as are the times of sunrise and sunset. By using these tables the fly-fisher can choose to fish night tides that coincide with full moons, or tides where high water coincides with dusk or dawn. These are always good times for inshore fly-fishing. The tide tables will also give the height and range of tides.

In coastal sites the tidal range may vary from one location to another. In some areas there is virtually no tidal movement whatsoever, for example in the Mediterranean and the Baltic Seas. In others there is a tremendous tidal range. In my own estuaries of northwest England, the maximum range between the low- and the high-water marks is 10.6m (33ft), whereas on the opposite side of the Irish Sea at Dublin, the range is a mere 1m (39in). Similarly, close to the mouth of

Canada's Bay of Fundy, the tidal range is 2.5m (8ft 3in), while at the head of the bay the range is a massive 27m (88ft 6in).

Where there is no tidal movement, the fish either feed all the time or, far more commonly, they tend to feed more keenly around dusk and dawn, or through the night (see p128.) Where there are tidal movements, fish tend to feed as the tide floods, covering the shore or carrying baitfish, shrimp, and prawns up channels, and from channels into the shallower waters of flats. At high water, when tidal movements may completely cease for anything up to half an hour or so – high water slack – fish often stop feeding or reduce their feeding intensity, perhaps because baitfish and other foods disperse in slack water. But then, as the tide ebbs and carries foods off the flats, down creeks and estuaries, and out of bays, so the predatory fish start feeding once more and follow these concentrations of food.

The reading of inshore waters such as estuaries and bays is to a large extent a matter of working out when and where the fish you want to catch will be feeding at particular stages of the tide. These places will often be where there is a strong current. The current may be strong enough to concentrate food and attract predators for only a few minutes of flood and ebb. For example, there is a sandbank in Ireland's Moy estuary where, as the tide floods around it, sandeels are concentrated, and sea trout feed like pigs for about 8–10 minutes. When the bank is completely covered by the tide, the current dissipates, the sandeels spread out, and the sea trout move on to the next sandbank.

Even when tidal range is very slight, its flow is important. On the Fisher Creek flats on the Leeward Island of Barbuda, the tidal range is only about 30cm (12in). But as water floods up the deeper channels and onto the flats, and later ebbs back from the flats, species such as bonefish and barracuda feed more keenly as they intercept shrimp and baitfish moved by the tide.

Spring, neap, and ebb tides

Tidal range also varies according to the stages of the four-week lunar cycle. At the new moon and, two weeks later, at full moon, when the sun and

When and where fish feed in inshore waters often depend on the tide cycle. Here, for example, fish move from bank to bank as the tide floods, following a quite precise route. You must know this if you want to fish estuaries and bays successfully.

moon are aligned, there are spring tides when high water floods high up the beach and low water ebbs far down the beach. Between these two periods of spring tides are the neap tides, when at the half moon, with the gravitational forces of the sun and moon working against each other, the tide floods less far up the beach and ebbs less far down the beach.

If you fish the last of the ebb, through low water and into the beginning of the next flood of a spring tide, you will be covering ground that is never exposed to the air. Shrimp and baitfish that feed over the shore when it is covered by the tide retreat here when the tide is out. A wide range of invertebrates live here that cannot withstand exposure to the air, and the predatory fish you want to catch will be here too.

Where there is a large tidal range, this sub-littoral zone is well worth visiting at low water of spring tides. However, safety can be a problem if you are walking and wading. One outer estuary channel that I used to fish at low water of spring tides involved a 4km (2½-mile) walk across undulating sandflats. I would follow the spring tide ebb down to the channel and then have four hours fishing before it was time to leave. Had I waited another hour, I would have had to swim across some of the "lows" in the sand flats that had flooded behind me. And I would have had to walk quickly, for on spring tides the flood advances at up to 3kmph (1½mph) here. By contrast, on neap tides I could fish six hours and still have plenty of time to get back to high ground.

Spring tides usually produce a higher catch rate than neap tides because of their stronger currents, which concentrate the fish's food. However, if you

can find places with a good current, even neap tides can be very productive. The problem is that good spring tide marks may be different from the good neap tide marks. For example, in one complex of channels and islands the best spring tide marks for bass are along one particular deep channel, and the best mullet fishing over a mudflat covered by 1m (3ft) at high water. By contrast, during neap tides both of these are useless, because the mud flat is not even covered at high water neaps. However, excellent fishing can be had from the southern tips of two islands that jut out into the sea, where the current is quite strong, even on a neap tide.

Wind can greatly affect tidal range and currents. A tide with a strong to gale force wind behind it may rise 10–20 per cent higher than that predicted in tide tables, or fail to reach the predicted height if the wind is against it. As long as there is not an associated change in water temperature that puts the fish off feeding, an increase in current speeds with a gale-backed tide often enhances sport. But notice also that, in a gale, the big breakers thundering down on a beach as the tide floods will often wash out food items such as crustaceans, and also encourage the fish to feed more keenly.

Tides and migratory fish

Tides will also affect the runs of migratory fish through an estuary from saltwater to freshwater. Therefore they will also affect fly-fishing for these species in lower stretches of the river.

Species such as salmon move up the estuary on the flood tide, but move back on the ebb, often for many days or even weeks until water conditions in the river are right for them to run upstream. The river flowing down into the estuary must be carrying enough water to enable the fish to swim into it. In small shallow streams this usually means following heavy rain when the river is in spate. The temperature of the freshwater flowing into the estuary must be within a range suitable for them to run (usually higher than 4°C [40°F] but less than 20°C [68°F]). When conditions are right, the fish move up on the flood and then, instead of retreating on the ebb, they continue on, upstream.

Spring tides reach higher up estuaries than neap tides, and it appears that fish prefer to run from salt into freshwater on these bigger tides.

 Saltwater Fish 42–79

 Reading Harbors and Jetties 118–19 • Reading Beaches and Bays 120–1 • Reading Flats 122–3 • Reading the Open Sea 124–5

COPING WITH THE WIND

ED JAWOROWSKI

Most fly-fishers, after they have learned the fundamentals of casting, are probably concerned with increasing distance more than anything else. Although distance is not all-important or always called for, the ability to cast farther will enable you to meet a greater variety of situations. For example, if you are fishing a large body of water from the shore, the farther you can cast, the more fish your fly is likely to encounter. There are times when extra distance alone spells the difference between success and failure.

At other times, distance may not be what is needed, but rather an efficient cast, powerful enough to cover a distance or overcome wind, yet smooth and – above all – not tiring. Wind, rather

By keeping the rod and line low, you can "cut" under the wind and improve the casting distance into the wind. Note how the left hand is being used to speed up the line as the forward cast is begun.

than great distance, may be the fly-fisher's greatest challenge. Consider these two scenarios:

• In a strong wind the best fishing in a small lake will often be from the shore onto which the wind is blowing. So, you must cast straight into the wind. However, many beginners will walk to the other end of the lake – the worst place – so that they can cast easily with the wind at their backs. Or, if brave enough to face the wind, they will attempt to cast into it by increasing effort. It is even worse for saltwater fly-fishers casting out from the beach, for here the prevailing wind is almost always onshore, into your face. Here, you must cast into the wind.

• When fishing a big river for steelhead or salmon the best casting angle is usually down and across the stream. Imagine yourself, a right-handed fly-fisher, on the left bank, in a gale blowing downstream from your right. You make a conventional forward cast and realize that the wind is blowing the extending line and fly straight toward you.

As these examples show, casting distance is entirely relative. Casting a heavy fly 15m (50ft) into

a breeze may readily equate with casting a fly of negligible weight 25m (80ft) or more. What is needed in every case is not simply more or less force on the part of the fly-fisher, but efficiency. Efficient casting means maximum return for the minimum effort.

The efficient cast

The casting stroke varies, and is determined by the results the fly-fisher wants. Don't think of a fly-casting stroke as a constant, based on pre-determined arm direction and distance movement. Starting and stopping positions and stroke length are variables, and any instruction that ignores this is poor instruction. An efficient cast is based on invariable physical principles, but not on fixed rules of arm and hand motion. Arm and hand movements must be varied as situations demand.

A cast works like this: the hand moves the butt of the rod while the weight of the line delays the tip, which forms the bend in the rod. When the hand stops abruptly, the rod straightens, thereby

launching the line. The first step to efficient casting, therefore, is to practice moving your hand faster and faster, especially over the last few inches of the casting stroke, to a sudden stop. More acceleration produces more bend (it "loads" the rod). hence more distance, and the quick stop assures that the rod imparts maximum launching speed. Of course, from the start the line must be taut against the rod tip, otherwise the rod will not bend as the hand moves and shock waves will result when the moving rod, after getting rid of the slack, comes hard against the line's weight and generates vibrations.

The next step is to employ your line hand (left hand for a right-handed caster). When your rod hand makes its final fast acceleration just prior to stopping, you can enhance the rod load that this motion generates by simultaneously pulling down quickly on the line with your line hand and then releasing it at the moment that your casting hand stops. I emphasize that the speed of the pull-down, or "haul," not the length, is paramount.

This haul requires some practice to co-ordinate the hand motions, but in the end increases the efficiency of any cast and can be applied to back as well as forward casts. When hauls are made on both back and forward casts they are known as the "double haul." Extending line on the back cast will also help in gaining distance, since the additional line weight translates into more load on the rod during the forward cast. Two additional principles come into play. First, the line can only travel in the direction the tip was traveling when the rod launched the line. Physics and common sense dictate that if the tip of the rod is higher at the start of the stroke than at the finish, the line is thrown downward. Conversely, if the tip is lower, then the direction of the cast is up and away, like elevating a gun or arrow or throwing a ball. It isn't, therefore, where the rod stops but rather the direction from which it was coming that is more important.

If you want to cast farther, all other conditions being equal, start with the rod back farther, even nearly to the water, so that it finishes by throwing the line up and away. Understanding this point is vital to dealing with demands of distance or wind.

TOP TIP

One solution that will help you casting into a wind or across a strong wind is to stand with your back to where you want the fly to go eventually. Your back cast now becomes the presentation cast. It seems crazy, but it works. This is commonly done in windy saltwater situations by fly-fishers already accustomed to making long back cast strokes.

Second, the longer the casting stroke (that is, the total distance the arm and rod travel), the easier it is to make a long cast. It makes no more sense to move your arm within a predetermined, limited range for every cast, any more than it does to move your arm the same distance when throwing a ball 7m or 20m (22ft or 22yd). The longest cast calls for the longest arm/rod movement, with the rod and line in as close to a straight line as conditions permit at the start of the cast.

These principles work in harmony. The key to making longer casts is simply turning your stance a bit more to the side and getting your arm back farther and lower when making the back cast. Coming back to the side, rather than overhead, makes this longer back cast much easier and is a more natural motion. The forward cast will now consist of a longer stroke, at a higher trajectory, with faster hand acceleration (matched with a quick, short line haul) just prior to a quick stop. Practice these techniques and you will make longer casts with far less effort.

Wind effects

Now consider the effects of the wind. If the wind blows from behind your back cast should be low and to the rear, ending with rod and line in a straight line so that your forward cast will finish going up and away. Casting with a high back cast generally results in the fly hitting you on the forward cast.

When casting into the wind, make sure that your forward cast ends going straight into the wind, and keep your cast low, close to the water. If you cast high, after the line straightens and begins falling, the wind will push it back, costing distance, accuracy, and line control.

In windless conditions, very long casts can be made by aiming high. Keep the cast low in high winds. Alternatively, if you can, wade closer to the fish and make shorter casts.

If the wind is blowing from your casting arm side (that is, from your right if you are a right-handed caster) and blowing the fly toward your cranium, as it hurtles out on the forward cast, try one of the following solutions:

- Learn to cast with your other hand.
- Cast with your normal hand but, instead of casting over that shoulder bring the rod across to the other side of your body and cast over the other shoulder. This will keep line and fly safely downwind of your body. It seems strange, at first, casting with the rod held across your body. But with a little practice you will find it quite easy.

Casting the fly over a short distance, so that it goes precisely where you want it to go, is easy in perfectly calm conditions. It is when we need to cast that bit farther in a stiff breeze that problems may arise. When covering a lie close to the far bank of a river, when casting to a fish rising far off a lake shore, when presenting the fly to a spooky snook that is lying at the mangrove edge – all demand a good technique, and lots of practice.

A final important point: practice at home ... not when you are fishing!

Reading Rivers 112–13 • Reading Lakes 114–5 • Night and Day 128–9 • Tides 132–3 • Other Casting Techniques 136–3

GETTING THE FLY DOWN

TOM EARNHARDT

For most fly-fishers the world of fly-fishing is a surface activity. Trout and salmon are caught at the surface with dry flies, or just under the surface with a variety of streamers and nymphs. The situation is similar in saltwater fly-fishing: most fly-fishers catch fish in very shallow water or in the first few feet of the water column. Indeed, shallow water fish such as bonefish, tarpon, and permit are the ones most fly-fishers closely associate with saltwater fly-fishing. Therefore they choose floating and intermediate fly-lines that will fish the full water depth on shallow flats where these species live, or the top few feet in deeper water.

This can be a great mistake, and can hinder many opportunities for sport. When the fish are not feeding at the surface, or in very shallow water with little in the way of a current, the best chance of catching a fish is to get the fly down – deep down, near the bottom where the fish are feeding.

Techniques

You can get the fly down by using several methods, either individually or in combination. First, by using fly-lines of varying density: in deep or very fast flowing water a fast-sinking full fly-line or specially designed shooting head may be essential. Second, by fixing weights, such as split-shot or tungsten impregnated putty, to the leader. These greatly hinder casting, however. Third, by using leaders of varying density (these are usually braided, with the sinking compound incorporated in the braid matrix); because sinking leaders have been specially designed for fly-fishing they are easier to cast than lumpy weights fixed to the leader. Finally, by fixing weight to the fly; this may be lead or lead substitute wire wound around the hookshank, or weighted eyes (lead or bead-chain), or a weighted head (gold- and silver-heads). Note that if the weight is added to the top of the hookshank the fly will tend to swim upside down, and is less likely to snag weeds or rocks on the bottom.

Sinking lines

Sinking lines, especially sinking shooting heads, have a variety of applications in freshwater and saltwater that can help to catch fish that ordinarily cannot be caught with a floating line. For example, on the east coast of the United States striped bass often hang at least 1.8m (6ft) deep in the water column near bridge pilings. Floating lines, even with

the most heavily weighted fly, will not get down to fish holding at that depth, but a fast sinking shooting head will easily do so. Then there are times, for example on the Florida Keys, when tarpon move off the flats into deep channels. Although it is not as exciting as "sight fishing", experienced fly-fishers will visit these deep channels with their sinking outfits and fish their flies effectively in 2.4–4.5m (8–15ft) of water. Similarly, offshore fly-fishers can use fast-sinking shooting heads to get the fly down quickly around wrecks, and catch king mackerel, amberjack, and other wreck-loving fish that are unapproachable with floating fly-line. Finally, for fly-fishers who are working heavy surf or working in strong currents (whether in freshwater or saltwater) no lines work better than sinking lines or sinking shooting heads.

It must be understood that, when using a fast sinking line, standard leaders of 2.1m (7ft) or more should not be used, because they tend to defeat the object of using the sinking fly-line. You must use leaders of less than 1m (3ft) in length when using a fast sinking line. The reason for this is that the long leader tends to "plane-up" and tends to sink far more slowly than the fly-line, so that, while the belly of the fly-line may be at the fish's depth, the fly is being held high above them by the leader. This defeats the purpose of the sinking fly-line.

Some fly-fishers are reluctant to use such short leaders because they feel that the fish may be scared from the fly by the close proximity of the fly-line. This is not the case in water of the depth that we would choose to fish a fast sinking fly-line, because at such depths there is less light and the fish would not see the fly-line.

The roll cast

If you have never fished a fast sinking fly-line before, it is important to remember that these lines do not cast like regular floating or intermediate lines. If you try to lift one of these off the water (as you can with your floater or intermediate) to make the next cast, the sunk line will either overload the rod to breaking point or come shooting back and, often, hit you full in the face. Instead of trying to lift off, you must first execute a roll cast.

While retrieving the sinking line the rod-tip should be held low, pointing at the water. When you are ready to make the next cast (all running line should have been retrieved if fishing a shooting

head), raise the tip of the fly-rod slowly to a point just past vertical, pointing slightly behind your shoulder. From this position (often referred to as one o'clock) drive the rod forward sharply, stopping the cast abruptly. This will cause the line to roll out of the water and extend in a straight line on the surface in front of you. As soon as the sinking line has unrolled and hit the surface, and before it has even a split second in which to sink, pick the line up in a conventional back cast, using the friction of the line on the water to help load the rod. This is known as a "water haul."

With the water haul helping you load the rod on the back cast, the forward cast should be made at an angle of approximately 45° above the horizon. This release, at a higher than normal angle, will then allow a long, smooth delivery at considerable distances.

Master the roll cast and you will find sinking lines easy to use. But one more important point. We hear a lot today about casting with tight loops and high line speeds. When you are using sinking lines, it is better to slow down the back cast and use a more open loop to present the fly.

It is a beautiful thing to watch a caster using a floating line and making tight loops with high line speeds. It is also a joy to behold a complete fly-fisher who can effectively use a quick-sinking fly-line, and who can use both surface and sinking lines to catch fish wherever they are found.

Many fish – such as the grayling pictured here – will not move up through the water to take flies when they are feeding deep. So the flies must be fished at their level.

 Freshwater Fish 16–41

 Reading Rivers 112–13 • Coping with the Wind 134–5 • Rivers and the Problem of Drag 138–9 • Inducing a Take 142–3

RIVERS AND THE PROBLEM OF DRAG

SIMON GAWESWORTH

Perhaps the biggest problem a fly-fisher fishing a river has to overcome is how to fish the fly as naturally as possible, without the allowing the fly to drag in or on the current.

The dry fly is most effective when it is fished dead-drift and not dragging across the current. Fish get used to items drifting freely on the current – if the current swirls or accelerates, then the leaf or bug floating down will also swirl or accelerate. Anything drifting past the fish in an unusual way, not following the current, is suspicious and usually left well alone. The key to success, therefore, is to ensure that your fly follows the current accurately. This is easily done if the water you fish has an even flow through it with no change of speed or direction, and no submerged rocks creating awkward swirls. But you are unlikely to come across many that are as "user friendly" as this. In most pools the changing speeds, directions, and eddies of the current can kill your fly's natural drift, arousing the suspicion of the fish. You really need to stop the drag before it happens, so there is no danger of the fish being alerted.

Suppose a fish is lying in slack water in the lee of a boulder or bridge abutment. If your fly is to behave naturally, it will have to sit still where the fish is lying, as the water will have no, or little, flow. The difficulty is that by casting your line across the faster moving current between you and the lie, the current acts on the line where it is lying on the surface and drags your fly, in an unnatural way, out of the area where the fish is lying. Somehow you must get your fly to stay in the slack water long enough to enable the fish to take it before the drag sets in.

The easiest way to do this is to put a "mend" into the line over the faster water. However, if you are fishing a dry fly, you cannot mend the line once the fly has landed, as this will move the fly out of the lie, or perhaps even drown it. What is required is an "aerial mend," one that you cast into the line before the fly lands, so giving the fly those precious few seconds to sit still where it has landed.

As with any cast, this is difficult to visualize from a description, but try this. Start false casting your fly toward where you want it to land and, on your delivery cast, shoot about 2m (6ft) of slack line. As the line is shooting out, move your rod-tip to the left and then back to the right about 1m (3ft) if you want the mend to land with a curve on

TOP TIPS
● You are more likely to hook and less likely to spook fish using the downstream dry fly.
● Tying your leader too long and too fine will result in a cast that doesn't turn over – ideal for a few seconds of drag free drift in a back eddy.
● Avoid giving too much slack with the slack line cast, otherwise you will not be able to strike quickly enough.

the left-hand side, or right then left if you want a right-hand curve. After some practice you will be able to put the right-sized mend where you want.

Another way to ensure your dry fly sits without drag for a few seconds is to set up your rod with a leader that is too long and too fine. When you cast this the fly-line turns over and the leader doesn't, resulting in 1.5–2m (5–6ft) of slack around the fly. As the current acts on the fly-line it drags the slack leader, and eventually the fly, straight, but at least this allows you a few seconds in which the fish could take your fly.

Downstream

Most fly-fishers fish the dry fly upstream because the current helps with the drift of the fly. With the dry fly cast downstream, the current moves away from you, the fly doesn't, and drag sets in immediately. You can avoid this by giving the fly some slack. It will drift with the current until the slack runs out and then start to drag, but you will manage to get a drag-free drift for a few feet; enough, hopefully, for the fly to reach the trout and be taken before the slack runs out.

Other ways to produce slack

The parachute cast is a simple way to control how much slack you give to the fly. The technique involves casting your fly beyond the fish you are aiming at, and before it lands, gently lifting your rod back to about 11 o'clock. This pulls the fly back and makes the line slack. Once the fly has landed, lower the rod at the speed the current flows. This allows the fly to drift naturally and yet retain enough tension to set the hook. It takes a little practice to be able to judge how much lift of the rod you need, but there is no better way of fishing the dry fly downstream.

Another way to produce a downstream, drag-free drift, is the slack line cast. This involves shooting slack line on the forward cast and instantly wiggling the rod from left to right, sending two or three sideways waves down the fly-line that land on the water. Again, allow the fly to drift while the current pulls out the curves. Once the line is straight the fly will start to drag again.

Fly-fishers develop many methods to enable them to fish the downstream dry fly successfully. The way you do it matters little as long as the fly has enough free drift not to spook the fish. I consider the downstream dry fly the most effective way of catching a rising fish, but do check on the fishery rules as many waters only allow the dry fly to be fished upstream.

WEIGHTING FLIES AND LEADERS

It is often essential to use extra weight to get the fly down to deep-feeding fish, especially in rivers and estuaries where the current slows the fly sink rate. Use sinking fly-lines; drilled brass beads, often gold- or silver-plated, may be fixed at the front of the fly, or a ball of tungsten putty molded around the leader. A common way of weighting leader or fly is to use lead, but unfortunately metallic lead is harmful to creatures that might pick up and eat bits that have been lost. Fine lead wire or foil are often wound around the hookshank and the fly dressed over the lead. This is harmless but in some regions even this use of lead is prohibited. Lead shot or lead wire are often fixed to the leader. This is effective, but results in the loss of some lead particles. Do not use lead; instead use lead-free shot. Throughout this book, when the term "shot" is used, we assume you will use lead-free shot.

Avoiding the curse of drag may involve your standing position, the direction of cast, and special casting techniques.

Freshwater fish 16–41

Reading Rivers 112–13 •
Coping with the Wind 134–5 •
Coping with an Obstacle Course 140–1

COPING WITH AN OBSTACLE COURSE

SIMON GAWESWORTH

The biggest difference between a very good fly-fisher and others is undoubtedly the ability to get the fly to the fish in almost any situation. We all start off by learning the good old overhead cast, which seems to work in enough places to keep beginners happy. As your skill level increases, you may move on to the roll cast (to cope with a bunch of trees right behind) or even the side cast (used to keep the fly-line and fly low, level with the water and just right for getting underneath an overhanging branch). But then what?

There are at least 16 different casts to learn, each of which has a particular use to cope with certain problems (usually an obstacle that hinders the fly from getting to the fish). Most of them can be joined together to create new and more useful casts.

The roll and side cast hybrid

Most fly-fishers know that if you have some trees close behind the easiest cast to use is the roll cast. It has no back cast and, therefore, there is little danger of your fly getting caught behind you. For overhanging trees in front, there is the side cast: an ordinary overhead cast but executed with the rod traveling back and forth some 60cm (2ft) above the water, sideways. The problem comes when you have obstacles behind and overhanging trees in front. The roll cast is no good as the forward stroke would roll the fly neatly onto the overhanging branches. The side cast is no good as it has a back cast and the fly would get snagged, or lost, behind. The answer is to combine the two: begin a roll cast, drawn back slowly, then just before starting the forward cast, turn the rod onto

its side and then finish with a sideways power stroke. The result is a perfect cast that avoids the snags behind and gently unrolls under the branches of trees and shrubs in front.

Shepherd's crook cast

A major problem that faces the upstream fly-fisher is how to get the fly slightly upstream of a fish without casting the fly-line directly over its head. This is solved with the shepherd's crook cast. Start casting with your rod horizontal, some 30–60cm (12–24in) above the water, back and forth with

Little streams will often hold some very big fish. But you must be able to get your fly to them!

To the left and slightly upriver of the big boulder there is a good trout lie. The question is, how do you get the fly there without scaring the fish?

enough speed to keep the line in the air, holding the line tight in your non-casting hand. On your last cast, just as the line is unrolling, give a short, sharp tug of the line with your non-casting hand. This will accelerate the turnover of the fly, and it will travel so quickly that the last bit of fly-line and leader kicks into the shepherd's crook shape. The hard part of this cast is being able to judge how much to bend the line and when to tug. As this cast relies on a lot of line speed to make it kick round, it is essential that your leader is short, and very steeply tapered.

Combining casts

With a little practice you can link together two, three, or even four types of cast (see Principal Casts and Their Uses, below) to overcome a problem.

I remember one day on the Wharfe in Yorkshire when the trout were proving difficult. I had yet to make a catch. I came across a pool with a number of good fish rising under an overhanging tree, some 25–30m (75–90ft) upstream. There was a wall of trees behind me and water much too deep in front, with no other visible way of getting nearer to the fish. After some thought I started casting using a switch cast, but this did not have enough speed to reach the fish. So I started to double haul the switch cast and on the final cast turned the loop onto its side with a side cast. I don't think the fish had ever seen an artificial fly, because in four casts I caught four trout, all a good size, which I know I would not have got near without linking several casts together.

WILDLIFE AND MONOFILAMENT FISHING LINE

Monofilament fishing line is an environmental disaster in the countryside. It tangles around the legs of small animals, and the legs and wings of birds. It lacerates skin and muscle, and prevents these animals from moving about freely.
Each year hundreds of creatures die a slow and painful death from this one needless cause.
Take all waste line home with you and burn it.

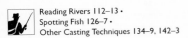

Reading Rivers 112–13 •
Spotting Fish 126–7 •
Other Casting Techniques 134–9, 142–3

PRINCIPAL CASTS AND THEIR USES

Cast	Use
Overhead cast	Accuracy, working out a line with back space.
Roll cast	Obstacles behind, short line, no change of direction.
Double haul	Increased line speed.
Side cast	To put a fly underneath an overhanging branch.
Switch cast	Obstacles behind, no change of direction, reasonable distance.
Single Spey	Obstacles behind, change of direction, reasonable distance.
Double Spey	Obstacles behind, change of direction, reasonable distance.
Snake roll	Obstacles behind, fast change of direction, reasonable distance.
Aerial mend	Control of fly's drag in the water.
Shepherd's crook cast	To bend fly around an object, or to avoid "lining" a fish.
Reach cast	Move the whole line, in mid-air, to avoid an obstruction in front.
Tuck mend	To create slack to get a drag free drift of fly.
Nymph pitch cast	To make the fly hit the water hard and sink.
Parachute cast	To create controlled slack to get a drag-free drift of fly.
Steeple cast	To keep the back cast high, or the forward cast low.
Slack line cast	To create slack to get a drag free drift of fly.

INDUCING A TAKE

SIMON GAWESWORTH

There are generally three reasons why a fish may take an artificial fly: hunger, aggression, and curiosity. Usually, the motive for a strike will be some combination of the three, and you can often help a fish find a reason to take your fly.

A trout, largemouth bass, or huge pike watching an artificial fly drifting along in the current finds it very difficult to resist snapping at the fly if it makes a sudden movement. The fish behaves much like a kitten playing with a piece of string twitched along a floor. It is the movement of the fly, seemingly trying to escape, that arouses the fish's attention. The direction of the "escape" hardly matters. Vertical movement (towards the surface) or sideways movement will excite the fish, although a vertical escape or "lift" is often most effective. If you know where a fish is lying you can persuade it to take your fly by "inducing the take" (the term used in Europe) or employing the "Leisenring Lift" (the North American term), whether the fish is feeding or not.

Techniques

If you are fishing in gin-clear water and can see the fish, cast your fly upstream of where the fish is lying (because of the refraction of light through water, the fish is always closer to you than it looks). Allow the current to wash the fly toward the fish, retrieving line at the same speed as the current, to keep in contact with the fly. As the fly approaches your quarry, steadily and quickly raise your rod-tip about 125cm (48in). This movement makes the fly accelerate past the fish and toward the surface. The first time you do this you will be surprised how quickly the fish reacts and grabs your fly. If the water is not clear enough for you to see the fish, try this method in known, or likely, lies.

You could also try a series of random induced takes, a technique known as "sink and draw." Cast upstream and retrieve the line as it drifts back, although this time raise the rod, then drop it quickly back to the surface, pull in a little more line and repeat (raise rod, lower rod, pull in line), perhaps twice more in the drift. Takes will come both on the lift and the drop, particularly if you use a fly with some weight. Be alert, watching the tip of your line for the slightest twitch that will indicate a fish has grabbed the fly. I advise heavily greasing the first 60cm (24in) of fly-line and 30cm (12in) of leader butt to ensure that they float high on the

water and are easily visible. You can also buy strike indicators in a number of different designs, which you attach to the tip of your line and watch, hawk-like, for any sign of an offer.

A few days before I sat down to write this I took one of my students up to a small pool to show him the induced take. The water was not clear enough to see the trout lying in the pools, so I had to show him how to use the second method, sink and draw, when you cannot see the fish. Success was immediate, with over 20 takes in the pool in the next 15 minutes or so.

If you want to induce a take to a fly cast downstream, your first task is getting the fly to sink to the depth at which the fish are lying, using a weighted fly or sinking leader. Alternatively, in shallow water, you can often get enough depth by paying out slack line. Once the fly is close to the fish, hold the line tight and the current will bring the fly to life and induce the fish to grab it. The hard part is judging where your fly is in the water as it drifts along, and knowing when you should stop paying out line. You can enhance the lift of the fly with a slight lift of the rod as you see your line tightening in the current.

One technique I use to great effect for salmon, trout, and sea trout is "controlled drag." For best results you need to know where a fish is lying. Stand upstream of your quarry and cast your fly slightly beyond the fish and about 3m (10ft) upstream. As soon as the fly lands, start paying out slack, quicker than the current, until your fly is within a foot or so of the fish. Then hold the line tight. The slack will wash out of the line and, as the line tightens and drag sets in, the fly will lift toward the surface and swing across the fish's nose. To achieve the best results the fly must lift rapidly and very close to the fish, so you need a relatively

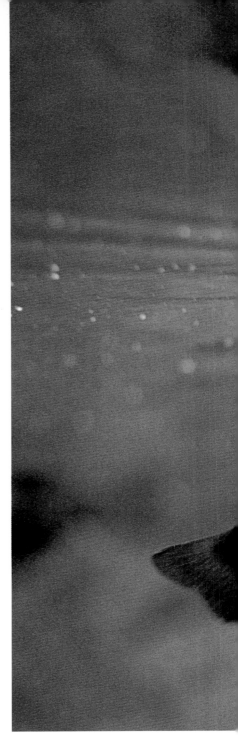

A brown trout takes a fly from the surface. It is just as important to make sure the way the fly behaves is correct, as well as the way it looks.

short, 1.2–1.5m (4–5ft) leader. Success is usually instantaneous, and because your line is taut in the current you get a great hooking rate.

There is no doubt that the sudden movement of your fly through the water induces the fish to take. I use the induced take, in one way or another, every day I am out on the river, and I teach all of my students this deadly technique.

This trout refused a passively drifting nymph, but took when the nymph was "lifted" through the water. It is attempting to splash free from the fly.

 Freshwater Fish 16–41

 Food and Flies 80–109

 Coping with the Wind 134–5

HANDLING FISH

PHILL WILLIAMS

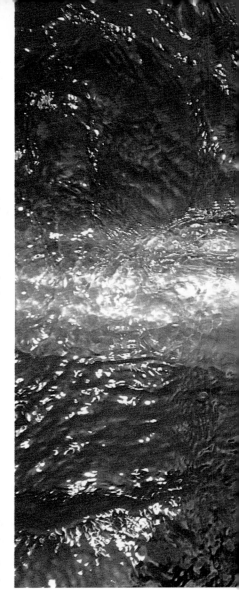

For some fly-fishers, simply getting a hook to go into a fish's mouth is problem enough. But, getting it out afterward, particularly if the fish has teeth or other sharp features, can prove little short of a nightmare. It is important to learn to handle difficult fish that have sharp teeth, needle spines, razor-edged scales, and powerful, unpredictable muscles if you want to avoid injury to yourself and to the fish you want to release.

The best rule to follow is "When in doubt, keep fingers out." There is nothing wrong with releasing a fish without the use of life-threatening surgery; provided hooks are made of lightly coated, non-stainless steel, they will corrode and free themselves, usually within days. This is one of the strongest arguments against dressing flies on stainless steel hooks. Although stainless steel is durable, particularly in saltwater, the reality is that it has a poor track record when it comes to holding a sharp point, and is most definitely not suited to releasing a fish with the hook still in place. If you do use stainless steel hooks, always remove them from a live fish that you are releasing.

With smaller fish, which can be easily handled, you need a firm grip and possibly someone to help you. When taking hold of any toothy or spiny fish, always work your hand backward along its body, gently increasing the grip pressure from the head, so you flatten down sharp spines in fins and gill covers by working "with the grain."

Tools for removing hooks

For medium-sized or large spiny or toothy fish you usually need some specialist equipment.

The effectiveness of each tool depends on the size of the hook you use, the size of the fish's mouth, skin texture (for example, sharks have very tough skin that is loath to release barbed hooks), and whether the fish is to be kept or released. Obviously when you wish to release the fish, you need to take greater care, and this invariably involves using some type of hook-gripping disgorger and fish-holding device.

Heavy duty leather or rubber gloves are needed to protect your hands and enable you to hold onto fish firmly without damaging the skin. Long-jawed, snipe-nosed pliers are very effective for removing large hooks from large, toothy jaws. Artery forceps (hemostats) are ideal for removing smaller hooks from smaller toothy jaws.

The Hookout is a de-hooking tool with a tiny jaw several inches from the handle. This allows you to disgorge deep hooks at a comfortable and safe working distance. Pressure applied to the trigger is multiplied tenfold at the jaws. However, large, deeply embedded hooks in awkward corners – those you would most like the tool to cope with – can deform its jaws at the hinge, greatly reducing their ability to grip.

A de-hooking mat is something you can make at home from a large piece of plastic cloth and Velcro straps. Medium-sized fish, up to about 23kg (50lb) can be held firmly with only their mouth exposed, enabling you to remove the hooks. Any spines on the fins and gills are covered.

The Boga-grip holds onto the fish without damaging it while you remove the hook with artery forceps or pliers. It also includes an accurate scale so that you can weigh the fish without bringing it on board.

Other equipment

Small or moderately sized fish are often landed in a landing net. You can remove the hook from such fish while they are wrapped up in the netting itself. Put the disgorger through the mesh. A couple of layers of mesh between your fingers and the fish's teeth or spines usually make a safe cushion.

The salmon-tailer is ideal for holding toothy or spiny, small- to medium-sized fish. This is a snare-like wire noose at the end of a long handle. When the fish is played out, slip the noose over the fish's tail and tighten it to take a firm hold by sharply lifting the handle. A small fish can be held high, a

larger one held against the side of the boat while the hook is removed. And the fish swims away unharmed, when the wire noose is slackened.

It is much easier to remove barbless hooks, and in many freshwater fisheries around the world the rules insist on these. From my own experience, could genuinely not attribute any losses to the hook having no barb. Most fly-fishers buy hooks with barbs, which they must flatten down later.

Leader tippets for toothy fish

Fish teeth can cut lines just as easily as they can cut flesh. Where fish have short abrasive teeth, you need a 30–45cm (12–18in) length of much thicker mono at the end of the leader to which the fly is tied. But where the teeth of the fish are likely to slice through mono (as in pike, barracuda, and shark), there must be a short length of wire between mono leader and fly.

Tippet wire comes in three forms: braided plastic coated, and plain solid. The best is plain solid wire, and it can be attached easily to fly and mono leader by small Haywire loops.

TOP TIPS
- Fish to be kept for eating should be killed swiftly before the hook is removed.
- Don't hold a fish you want to release with warm, dry hands. The heat and dryness will tear the protective slime on the fish's skin and allow pathogenic bacteria and fungi to get in. Wet and cool your hands first in the water.
- Never allow any potentially dangerous large or very large fish into a boat. Instead, assuming you wish to release the fish alive, have one person hold the fish alongside while a second person removes the hook.

Gloves are very useful aids to have available when dealing with large or spiny fish. But use them with care, making sure that their coarseness does not dislodge scales.

The Boga-grip holds the fish, weighs it, and then releases it. This is one of many commercially produced tools specially designed for handling big fish safely without harming them.

 The Fly-fishers' Fish 14–79

 Sheer Power 148–9 •
Catch and Release 150–1

CATCHING SALMON IN FRESHWATER

MALCOLM GREENHALGH

When a salmon returns to freshwater from the sea it usually stops feeding. This change in behavior is caused by nervous and hormonal changes, which switch off the desire to feed and in turn cause the salmon's digestive system to atrophy. This is a quite remarkable evolutionary trait for the survival of salmon species. At sea, they gorge and grow quickly on a diet of lesser fish. If salmon returning to freshwater retained their voracious appetites they would wipe out future generations of their own species, since the rivers and lakes to which adults return are full of tiny fry and parr that have yet to go to sea.

This non-feeding behavior creates problems for fly-fishers, whose artificial flies usually imitate what fish they are eating. What to do if the fish are not feeding? Exploit their innate aggression. Instead of imitating some sort of food, your fly must infuriate the salmon into grabbing it and trying to destroy it.

Of course, the practice is not quite that easy. Following its return to the river, a salmon runs upstream until it finds a suitable lie where it will remain until spawning time. When it is running, the

A Norwegian salmon that is almost ready for landing. The fly that caught it did not look like anything edible, but annoyed the fish into grabbing it.

salmon is at its most alert and it will react strongly to any lesser creature that gets too close. Therefore, when a salmon pulls in for a brief rest during its upstream journey, a salmon fly-fished in front of it may be seized, savagely.

There are some places in a river (often a tiny area of water next to a big boulder) where fish after fish after fish will pull in for only a few moments before continuing their upstream journey, and where a fly-fisher might catch as many as 12 salmon in one day. I remember one such lie that measured barely 16 sq m (144 sq ft) in extent, where I caught seven fish in nine casts.

Arousing a sleeping salmon

Eventually a salmon comes to rest in the lie where it will remain until spawning time. In some Atlantic salmon rivers, such as the Tweed and Tay in England, salmon may remain there for a year, doing nothing but breathing and waiting. The longer a salmon is in its lie, the more its aggression diminishes. After a week or so a salmon may be virtually uncatchable. There may be hundreds of salmon in a pool but, sadly, they all ignore the fly. But there are a few tricks that may arouse a salmon: pestering it by making cast after cast after cast is one. Of course, you may make 427 casts before a fish suddenly "cracks" and grabs hold.

The great American salmon fly-fisher Joseph D Bates Jr provided an excellent piece of advice on arousing a sleeping salmon with a dry fly. You must know precisely where the salmon is lying, then cast your fly upstream of the salmon and let it float down to a point where the fish will be able to

see it. Just then, quickly lift the fly from the water. Repeat this for 20 or 30 casts. Slowly the salmon's brain becomes accustomed to this pesky little thing that, every few seconds, drifts down the flow and then flies away. Now you repeat the cast, but this time let the fly continue down over the salmon's nose. And then up the salmon comes – in a foul mood – to grab the impudent fly!

The salmon fly

If the salmon fly does not have to imitate food and is simply something that goads the salmon into grabbing it, what fly is the best to use?

The warmer the water, the smaller the fly should be. So, in January and February on a Scottish river, or after ice melts in May and June in a Russian, Norwegian, or Icelandic river, the most effective fly could be dressed on a 7.5cm (3in) tube or Waddington Shank, or on a size 1/0–2 salmon hook.

To catch salmon in July and August, when the water is very warm, a small fly tied on a 20mm (¾in) tube or shank, or a size 12–14 salmon hook may be the most effective. In very cold water fish the fly just above the salmon's nose. In warm water fish a fly just below the water surface or use a dry fly on the surface.

You can use any pattern of wet fly provided you take into account these points. I know one fly-fisher who uses only Munroe's Killer, another Ally's

Sockeye, like all salmon, eat virtually nothing on their return from the ocean. To catch one you must exploit its aggression with your fly and fly-fishing technique.

Shrimp, another Willie Gunn, and another Thunder & Lightning. Black salmon flies are always good, simply because they are visible in all water conditions. Visibility can be improved by a bit of "flash": a few strands of crystal hair or flashibou certainly seem to enhance a salmon's response to the fly. In peat-stained water, flies with orange or red in the dressing seem to have a certain magic; in very clear Icelandic rivers, flies with a lot of blue in the dressing are often considered essential. For a dry-fly, use any special salmon dry-fly such as the Bomber, or a dry Caddisfly or Daddy-long-legs that a trout might take as food but that a salmon will seize through aggression.

Salmon 18–25

Salmon Flies 108–9

Reading Rivers 112–13

TOP TIPS
- When you go salmon fishing, don't worry about fly pattern. Size of fly and depth of fly are far more important: in cold water fish a big wet fly deep and slow; in warm water fish a small wet fly more quickly close to the surface, or a dry fly on the surface.
- Remember that you are trying to irritate the salmon into grabbing your fly and that you may need to pester it for a considerable time before it grabs hold.
- Persevere: if there are salmon in the river, keep on fishing.

SHEER POWER: PLAYING HUGE FISH

LEFTY KREH

A "huge" fish can mean a large brown trout on a fragile 5x tippet, or a 45kg (100lb) sailfish or a tarpon on a 20kg (50lb) line. In either case, the encounter often ends when the fish escapes. There are two reasons for this. First, most fly-fishers only occasionally encounter a fish that is capable of breaking their leader or straining their tackle, so they do not equip themselves properly for the battle. Second, most fly-fishers don't know what to do when they do hook a very big fish on relatively light tackle. This is a shame, because of all the catches most fly-fishers make, it is that huge trophy that is most fondly remembered. Even worse, of all the fish hooked, the ones best remembered are the huge ones that got away.

Tackling up for big fish

Landing a huge fish begins with proper preparation of your tackle. This may sound obvious, but if your tackle fails you will not land that big fish. First, select a good reel. Some fly-fishers will tell you that, in fly-fishing, the reel is simply a spool that stores line. Nothing could be farther from the truth when a big fish is on the line. The reel should have very light drag that starts easily and has just enough resistance so that it won't overrun and tangle the line if the fish surges away quickly. It should also have a good drag-adjuster that allows you to easily increase or decrease drag while you are playing your fish. The reel should have adequate capacity for the fly-line and the backing line that may be

When a huge fish leaps, your heart beats that bit faster. Will the tackle hold? Will the hook break free? Will the fish be lost? Probably not — but do accept that you will not leave with all the fish you hook!

(And if you are practicing catch and release, remember that the quicker you play out a fish and remove the hook the quicker the fish will recover so always get a fish in as quickly as you can.)

First, let the fish run, and as soon as it has completed its first run, pull hard two or three times to make sure that the hook is well in. It takes a lot of force to sink a big hook firmly into the jaw of a fish. If the hook-hold fails now, tell yourself that it was so weak that it would have failed later anyway.

Throughout, never let the fish have a moment's rest. You must keep it on the move. If it is swimming away from you, let it work for every yard of line by increasing the reel-drag or holding your finger against the reel spool. When it stops running, work hard to retrieve line. Or, as someone once put it, "When it pulls, let it; when it doesn't pull, you pull!"

Side pressure

Use side pressure whenever you can; it will beat any fish, from trout to sailfish. When the fish swims in one direction, lay the rod low to the water in the other direction. This will exert a force on the head of the fish that will pull the fish off balance. As soon as the fish has adjusted to the side pressure, swing the rod over and exert side pressure from another direction.

Side pressure causes the fish to use up more energy and tire quickly. For example, I once used a lot of side pressure on a huge Atlantic salmon on the River Alta in Norway. As the fish moved left, I lowered the rod to the right to apply side pressure. As the fish was pulled to the right, I was able to recover some line. Once the fish was to my right, the rod was moved low to the left, and as the fish again was moved, I managed to reel in yet more line. By doing this constantly, I was able to swim my salmon right up on the gravel bar without it taking any control in the fight. And I landed that fish in a few minutes instead of many.

Provided your tackle is sound and knots all well tied, it is – for the beginner – surprising how much pressure can be put on when playing a big fish.

needed to land your fish. For big trout 69m (225ft) of 9kg (20lb) Dacron backing may be fine, but you will need a bigger reel that takes 183m (600ft) of 14kg (30lb) Dacron if you hope to land a big salmon or inshore saltwater species such as a striped bass.

If you are after billfish, wahoo, or some of the tuna that make incredibly long runs, you will need at least 320m (1050ft), sometimes 500m (1500ft), of backing. Massive amounts of backing mean lots of bulk on the reel, but you can reduce this bulk and select a smaller and lighter reel if you use some of the newer, finer backing lines.

What is vital when placing backing on any fly reel is that it is reeled on under tension. If not, when your big fish makes a long run and you reel to recover line, the backing that you retrieve tightly may dig down into soft turns below. Then, when the fish runs again, the tight turns will be trapped in the backing, everything will jam up, and the leader tippet

will break. This is a major reason why many people fail to catch large fish on the ocean.

It is also vitally important that the knots holding your backing to line, leader to line, fly to tippet, and all other connections are well chosen and perfectly tied. Practice tying knots at home so you can tie them properly when you are out fishing.

Playing a big fish

Playing huge fish is the most exciting part of fly-fishing, provided your tackle is sound and you know how to go about it. It is an art in which you use your own muscles and agility, rod and line, current, and the power of the fish itself to subdue the fish. Playing a big fish requires thoughtfulness and skill – not brute force and ignorance.

Remember, the longer the fish is played, the greater is the chance that the hook-hold will fail. You need to land the fish quickly, but not so roughly that the tippet will fail or the hook pull out.

 The Fly-fishers' Fish 14–79

 Handling Fish 144–5 • Catch and Release 150–1

CATCH AND RELEASE

MARTIN JAMES

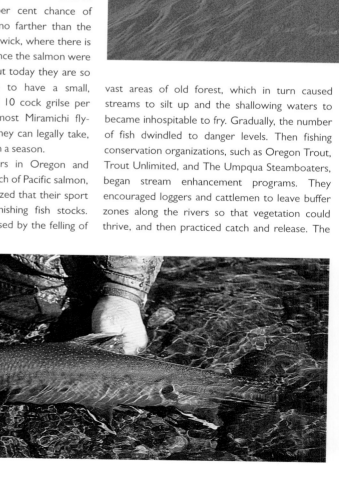

Catch and release is an emotive phrase in fishing circles simply because some fly-fishers want to kill every fish they catch, while others demand that every fish caught should be returned to the water alive. This argument is not really necessary. On the one hand, it is a fact that, unless there is some control over the number of fish killed, most sportfish stocks will collapse; catch and release is one way to control the number of sportfish. On the other hand, there is nothing immoral in killing a fish for the table. What we need to ensure is that any harvest taken by fly-fishers should not endanger future stocks, especially today, when there are more and more people wanting to cast a fly.

Throughout the world, freshwater and saltwater fisheries are under pressure – not just from overfishing but also from pollution, diversion for industry and agriculture, intensive grazing, forestry, and the dumping of rubbish by industry, agriculture, and the general public. Countries in both the Northern and Southern Hemispheres continue to treat the world's rivers, lakes, and oceans as waste disposal units. Through our actions, the world's sports fisheries are no longer the rich resource they once were. Even the most prolific fisheries, such as the Canadian salmon and oceanic tuna fisheries, are showing signs that not all is well. It is time to consider seriously whether those wild fish that swim in our inland and coastal waters are far too valuable to be killed.

Each fish killed is one less to be caught in the future. And each fish killed is one less fish to spawn, which means that by killing fish we are perhaps putting at risk the long-term future of our sport. Should a fish be a large one for its species, not only are a lot more eggs or sperm lost, but the gene pool suffers by the loss of important genes for fast growth and perhaps great longevity.

Each year on my local river, the Ribble, I witness the sickening sight of gravid hen salmon being killed and displayed to all and sundry in

Ideally, when practicing catch and release, don't remove the fish from the water. Hold the fish gently but firmly, remove the hook, and then hold the fish upright, with the current, and wait for it to swim away.

macho fashion by their captors. Alas the salmon cannot hit back. Later that salmon is gutted and the eggs – the potential stock for future generations – are thrown into the trash can. Yet the fly-fisher who caught and killed that fish will join with scores of others, many of whom have done exactly the same, to bemoan the fact that salmon runs in the Ribble are not what they should be. They will blame high-seas or estuary netting, or the government agency responsible for not raising enough salmon fry in the hatchery. They do not think of their contribution to the dire state of the river's salmon stocks.

Survival rates

Many of those opposed to catch and release will tell you that released fish won't survive. But released fish do survive. It is a fish that is killed and not released that has no chance of survival. In North America it has been proven that released fish have at least an 85 per cent chance of spawning successfully. Look no farther than the Miramichi River in New Brunswick, where there is a catch and release regime. Once the salmon were threatened with extinction, but today they are so abundant that it is possible to have a small, carefully regulated harvest of 10 cock grilse per season, per fly-fisher. And most Miramichi fly-fishers return much of what they can legally take, rarely killing more than one fish a season.

Some years ago, fly-fishers in Oregon and Washington, who were in search of Pacific salmon, steelhead, and wild trout, realized that their sport was in danger through diminishing fish stocks. Much of the problem was caused by the felling of vast areas of old forest, which in turn caused streams to silt up and the shallowing waters to became inhospitable to fry. Gradually, the number of fish dwindled to danger levels. Then fishing conservation organizations, such as Oregon Trout, Trout Unlimited, and The Umpqua Steamboaters, began stream enhancement programs. They encouraged loggers and cattlemen to leave buffer zones along the rivers so that vegetation could thrive, and then practiced catch and release. The

United States Fish and Wildlife Service also became involved, and it became law that all wild fish must be returned alive, and that only stocked fish may be killed. To aid identification, all stocked fish have their adipose fins cut off so the lucky fly-fisher can see at a glance whether the fish that has just been landed is wild or stocked. From being on the verge of extinction, steelhead and trout stocks are now superb and the fishing is excellent.

Another enforced catch and release system occurs in the Slovenian Soca River. Here, trout and grayling will already have spawned at least twice before they can be killed – a harvest is taken that does not damage future stocks. Similarly on Iceland's Hafralonsa River, managers encourage fly-fishers to return the larger two-sea winter salmon, and also encourage them to take the less valuable small cock grilse.

Practicing catch and release

To practice catch and release you must follow some very simple rules, the first of which is to use barbless hooks. There is no justification for fishing with anything else. I don't believe I have ever lost a fish because my hook was barbless. I do lose fish,

but invariably because I do something silly, such as giving slack line or letting the fish get into a snag, not because I use barbless hooks.

• With small fish of about 2–3kg (4–6lb) there is often no need to use a landing aid. Some 95 per cent of the small fish I catch are released without being handled. Just bring the fish close to hand, slide your fingers down the leader, and remove the barbless hook.

• Use a net to land small- or medium-sized fish from a boat. Do not use knotted nets as the abrasive knots will rub off the fish's protective scales. All nets should be made from a soft, knotless material.

• It may be necessary to "beach" very large fish, but choose soft sand or a mud bank. A great alternative is the "salmon tailer" – a wire noose that holds the fish around the base of the tail.

• Be sure that a fish is capable of swimming away strongly. Never simply drop a fish back into the water. Hold it gently just beneath the surface – head upstream in a river, head into the waves or current in the sea – so that refreshing oxygenated water will wash through its gills. Watch the fish carefully: the tail will flicker and the fins flutter slowly as it regains strength. And then, with a few

With big fish, help from other fly-fishers or guides is useful, as they can handle the fish while you hold the rod. This salmon will soon be on its way.

powerful strokes of the tail, your fish will slowly swim away from your grasp.

This may take some time. Big grayling are often slow to recover: it took me more than 30 minutes to release a very large Ribble grayling. But it is not time wasted, for as that fish swims away you will have developed a closer affinity for the fish and gained a feeling that those who seek to kill all the fish they catch can never attain.

The future of our game fisheries depends on fly-fishers and the policy of catch and release.

 The Fly-fishers' Fish 14–79

 Handling Fish 144–5 •
Sheer Power: Playing Huge Fish 148–9

GREAT FLY-FISHING AREAS of the WORLD

Until some 40 years ago, fly-fishers were largely a parochial bunch, usually fishing the waters close to their homes and traveling only relatively short distances each year for a week's holiday. A very small minority had the time and finances to travel farther: among these were the British nobility who, from the mid-1800s, crossed the North Sea to spend the summer fishing for salmon on Norway's great rivers. But they were the exception.

Up until about the 1950s most fly-fishers concentrated on just one or two types of fly-fishing, depending on what was available locally. For example, someone living in Shetland, midway between Scotland and the Faroes, was not likely to become a tropical flats- or pike-fisher. Similarly, a resident of Houston, Texas, would have been unlikely to fish for salmon on a regular basis.

Things have changed since then: now it is possible to fish your local trout stream or bass harbor today, and be 4400km (2700 miles) away tomorrow. Linked to accessibility has been opportunity. Forty years ago people were lucky to have two weeks' annual vacation; today five or more weeks is not unusual. Our parents retired at the age of 60 or 65; now many are free to follow their passions at 55 or even 50.

The boom in communications, including the angling press, books, and television, gives us a tempting view of what is possible. The range of fish species that can be caught on fly is vast; we described many of them earlier in this book, but there are scores more that we were unable to include. The range of fish-holding waters, each with its special challenge, is also vast and, to take the opportunity to fish for even a small proportion of species, you must travel. And just by boarding a plane with multi-piece fly-rod, reel, lines, and flies stowed in your suitcase, you have the opportunity to broaden your fly-fishing experience.

And you will not be alone when you arrive. Today, if you visit a Norwegian salmon-fishing hotel you are quite likely to join guests from Germany, France, Spain, the United Kingdom, Australia, South Africa, Japan, and North America. Go to Canada's Matapedia River, to a fly-fishers' bar at Key West, or to New Zealand's Lake Taupo, or visit the tackle shop in Stockbridge by England's River Test at mayfly-time, and you will hear as wide a collection of accents as you might find anywhere else in the world. The common interest is fly-fishing.

This chapter is for you, the 21st-century travelling fly-fisher. In it we have invited fly-fishers from around the world to describe some of the greatest fly-fishing areas they know best. There are obviously more missing than we can present here. Had we accommodated 100 more, we would still be missing at least twice that number. Yet all are out there, waiting for you to discover their charms and to cast your fly onto their mysterious waters.

THE MINIPI WATERSHED

JOAN SALVATO WULFF

The name "Minipi" conjures up images of giant brook trout. Is this a vision of the past? Yes, not only of the past, but of the present and, we hope, the future. It's a success story!

Minipi lies 90–100km (50–60 miles) southwest of Goose Bay, Labrador, in eastern Canada. It was 1957 when Lee Wulff first saw the uncharted Minipi watershed, while exploring this wilderness for the province of Newfoundland and Labrador in his Piper Super Cub.

"The sun shone on unbroken forests of spruce and fir, divided by a chain of lakes at a 1300-ft elevation. They lay like mirrors in a breathless calm, insect-rich, broken only by the dimples of trout," he later wrote. "Fast flows tumbled between the shallow lakes, where, from the air, the underwater grass beds showed up in wide areas like submerged golden carpets. I pictured the grass as being heavy with nymphs. In June the green drakes would burst their imprisoning underwater cases and rise in clouds to the freedom of the air." Wulff landed his float plane on one of the lakes.

Lee's "flight suit" included waders and he carried a fully rigged 2m- (6ft-) fly-rod in his float plane. After taxiing to shore and taking a dozen steps into the water, his second cast connected him to a brook trout of over 3kg (6lb). None of the four others he caught that first afternoon were smaller than 2kg (4lb). He had found something truly extraordinary.

Wulff kept the Minipi fishery a secret from the public while he tried to convince the provincial government that it should be set aside as a no-fishing sanctuary and, perhaps, as a source of supply for stocking other areas, so that biologists could study the results of nature's management. He failed in these efforts. However, Lee thought up another plan that would safeguard the future of this wild-fish gene pool. He looked for and found the right men to set up a fly-in camp and prevent fly-fishers from taking out coolers full of trout (as had happened earlier throughout Newfoundland wherever a prolific fishery had been discovered). This was the mid-1960s.

Bob Albee financed it and Ray Cooper was the manager. Minipi was decreed "catch-and-release, fly-fishing only." with each fly-fisher allowed to take only one trophy fish for his time there. The concept proved successful and today the only outfitter licensed to bring fly-fishers to this watershed, Jack Cooper, of Goose Bay, continues the tradition. As one of a select handful of fly-fishers, you can still catch dream-fulfilling wild brook trout – and on dry flies.

Many records have been set in these waters, including a 3.9kg (8lb 8oz) brookie on a 1kg (2lb) test leader. The largest trout taken has been one of 4.5kg (10lb) – in June 1987 – but every year at least one trout of 4kg (9lb) is landed. Trout of 1.5kg (3lb) and over are designated "book fish." and it is common for a party of six fly-fishers to land 75 of these fish in a week, perhaps hooking and losing as many more. Records for the past few years indicate weekly totals of up to 118 fish, and a heart-stopping entry for two fly-fishers in a day: 54 brook trout of over "book fish" size. Between the years 1993 and 1996, the season low of "book fish" was 853, and the high was 998.

Lee believed the secret of these superb trout lay in the water, organically and chemically rich enough to support great quantities of insect life: "The lakes are shallow enough to let sunshine reach their beds and warm them into great productivity. Through thousands of years of undisturbed natural selection, the trout have

SEASONS

June 10 to September 15 is the maximum season, with ice-out determining the beginning.

FURTHER DETAILS

Coopers' Minipi Camps, PO Box 340, Station B, Happy Valley, Labrador AOP IEO, Canada
Tel: (709) 896 2891
Fax: (709) 896 3024

learned to fit into and use their environment. These deep, full-bodied squaretails are mayfly-conditioned and dry-fly conscious."

God's River in Manitoba and the Broadback in Quebec have large brookies but never in such abundance; nor are they usually caught on the surface. Good brook trout water is special, chemically and physically, and Minipi is the place on the North American continent to take these fish with dry flies.

Successful dry-fly patterns – sizes 8–12 in the early season – are pretty traditional: the Wulff patterns (Royal, White, Gray, etc), Elk Hair Caddis, Green Drake, Brown Drake, and Humpy. Green drakes are the main hatch and the largest of these come in mid-July through early August. Effective fly sizes diminish in the late season to 12–18. Underwater streamers such as Mickey Finn and Black-nosed Dace are successful and, of course, Woolly Buggers and Leeches, if you must.

The lakes also contain northern pike, up to 12kg (26lb), and Arctic char to 5.5kg (12lb). Char will take dry flies in the early season and then respond to fluorescent colored streamers, the brighter the better. Muddlers and Matukas work well. Streamers, tarpon flies, Mickey Finns, and Deer-hair Mice are choice for pike. These are wilderness fish; there is no need to come up with any of the exotic patterns.

A 3m (9ft), number-6 rod is all that you need, unless you want to back yourself up with a number-8 weight in order to handle the occasional strong winds. Delicate presentation is often essential, but Coopers' excellent guides position your canoe within easy casting distances on the lakes; by wading it is easy to approach the fish closely in the run-outs.

Your trip begins with a flight from Montreal or Halifax to Goose Bay, Labrador. Another 25–40-minute flight by helicopter, fixed wing, or a combination of both completes the journey to camp. Coopers' Minipi Camps are at four locations, all south of Goose Bay: Anne Marie Lake Lodge, the original site; Minonipi Lodge on the headwaters of the Minipi; Minipi Wilderness Resort, also on big Minipi Lake where the lake converges to the mighty Minipi River; and Three Rivers, which supports overnight trips from the base at Minipi Wilderness Lodge. All camps have hot showers and flush toilets, and you will enjoy delicious home-cooked meals. One guide is assigned to two fly-fishers.

Charming names describe fishing areas: Lover Boy, Woody Char Hole, Halfway and Beyond, the Old Tree, Bathtub Rock, Big Hairy, Rose's Brook.

The weather is cool to hot (several layers of thin clothing are better than one lot of thick). Take polarizing glasses, sunblock, insect repellent, etc.

My last trip to this wonderful wilderness was too long ago – in 1991. My largest trout was 3.5kg (7lb 12oz), on my favorite fly pattern, the Royal Wulff.

I, a Wulff, must go back!

Labrador's Minipi Lake is one of the world's quietest and most remote places – a land of big forests and lakes, and big brook trout.

QUEBEC'S MATAPEDIA RIVER

RICHARD FIRTH

Canada is known for its huge forests, lovely lakes, and free-flowing, crystal-clear rivers. The Matapedia River is located on the beautiful Gaspé Peninsula, on Canada's eastern coast, in the province of Quebec.

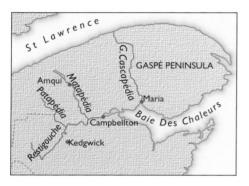

The Matapedia is part of the Matapedia-and-Patapedia Crown Reserve, which is managed by the Corporation de Gestion des Rivières Matapédia et Patapédia (CGRMP). The CGRMP is a non-profit organization that has a mandate to conserve and enhance the salmon stocks of the Matapedia watershed.

The river flows through the Matapedia valley, some 80km (49 miles) downstream to its confluence with the Restigouche. It draws the majority of its water from Matapedia Lake, which is some 20km (12 miles) long and averages a width of 1.6km (1 mile). Five tributaries flow into the Matapedia at different places along the valley.

The Matapedia is a world-famous salmon river, along with other Quebec rivers such as the Grand Cascapedia, the Restigouche, and the Moisie.

What makes the river so great for salmon fishing is the length of the season, and the numbers and size of the fish. Early runs of fish arrive in the last week of May, and the last runs do not end until September. On average some 4000 salmon, ranging from 1.5–18kg (3–40lb) or more, migrate up the river each year. The Matapedia is also very accessible by road via route 132 east from the cities of Montreal and Quebec, and it is only a 45-minute drive from major airports and railway stations.

The Matapedia flows through the town of Amqui and some 20km (12 miles) farther downstream, passes through the center of the small city of Causapscal, where it is joined by its main tributary, the Causapscal, at the famous Forks Pool. From there on, it flows through a beautiful valley for another 60km (37 miles), downstream to the village of Matapedia, where it joins the Restigouche.

The four sectors

The river is divided into four sectors for fly-fishing purposes. Sectors 1 and 3, which are situated between Causapscal and Routhierville and some pools in Matapedia, offer fantastic fishing with unlimited rod access to as many as 37 pools. This portion of the river is fishable by boat and by wading. The pools are fished by rotation on a first-come-first-served basis. Fly-fishers wishing to hire a guide may do so by calling the CGRMP's office. However, a guide is not mandatory in order to fish sectors 1 and 3.

Some of the better-known pools are the Forks, Heppel, Adams, and Salmon Hole, to name but a few. No reservations are needed to fish this section. Prime time here runs between the fourth week in June until the first week in August, but there's some great dry-fly fishing to be done in August and September. September fishing is done on a catch-and-release basis, with the possibility of keeping two grilse per day.

The most sought-after stretch of water on the Matapedia is sector 2, commonly named the Glen Emma; it has 27 pools. This is fished by a maximum of 10 rods per day, with guide and canoe required. Here the river produces some of the best salmon fishing you'll find anywhere in the world. Some of the pools – such as Milnikek, Kennedy, Richard's, Angus, Glovers, and Jim's Rock – may hold as many as 300 fish by the middle of August. Spring fishing (June) on the Glen Emma section offers the fly-fisher the possibility of hooking onto fish that may weigh in excess of 18kg (40lb); fish in the 15kg (30lb) range

SEASON
June 1 until August 31.

PERMITS AND FURTHER DETAILS
You must purchase a seasonal salmon license and a daily permit from one of CGRMP's two offices in Causapscal and Matapedia (open 7am–9pm daily through the season). CGRMP, 53b St-Jacques Sud, Causapscal, Quebec G0J 1J0
Tel: 1 888 730 6174 Fax: 1 418 756 6067

are fairly common. If dry-fly fishing is what you are interested in, then you must fish this sector of the river during August.

Finally there is sector 4, which offers unlimited access at very low cost. This stretch of water has an educational function. People who are learning to cast a line usually spend some time on this sector. There is always a chance of tackling a salmon but, most of the time, the daily catch is sea-run trout. Sector 4 is a great place for all members of the family to learn how to fish, and to have some fun at the same time.

As with all salmon rivers that still contain a fair amount of fish, there is, unfortunately, always some poaching. The CGRMP is well aware of this. With the aid of the Richard Adams Foundation it is educating the children of families that have regarded poaching as their birthright through many generations. Small incubators, which nest some 300 salmon eggs, are installed in elementary schools of the Matapedia valley. Children in the fifth grade learn the life-cycle of salmon. They nurture the young throughout the winter and in

the spring they deposit the young fry in the Matapedia or in one of its tributaries. By this action, the Corporation considers that the awareness program will help to change the mentality of the future generations regarding the conservation of salmon and the river.

If you are planning your first visit, I would suggest that you arrive in the middle of June. At this time the Matapedia produces lots of big, bright silver salmon, and they can be quite a challenge to the fly-fisher wading in the relatively deep water. Although most of the pools are accessible by wading, when you hook onto a huge spring salmon of 11–18kg (25–40lb) and it decides to head downriver you had better have several hundred feet of good backing on your reel. If not, you'll be running downriver bobbing in and out of the water along the shore trying to save your fish.

The other solution is to hire a guide and canoe so that you can get afloat and follow the fish easily. Spring fishing translates into sinking lines, heavy leaders, and big flies, so come well equipped. The best times of the day to fish are usually between

7am and noon, and again between 4 and 9pm. The choice of fishing equipment for the Matapedia is fairly straightforward. Most fly-fishers use 2.7 or 3m (9 or 9ft 6in) rods. A very important piece of equipment is the reel. You must have one that has a good drag system, because those big spring salmon will play havoc with a reel that doesn't have one. We use tapered leaders with a tippet varying from 3.5–9kg (8–20lb), depending on the season – heavier in late spring, lighter in the summer. Fly sizes vary between number 2/0 to number 12, depending on the water level.

If you are a novice, when planning a salmon fishing trip on the Matapedia call the CGRMP's office in Causapscal and get the most up-to-date information and advice possible.

Quebec's Matapedia River, which meanders through magnificent northern forests of pine, is one of the great Atlantic salmon rivers on the North American continent.

THE CATSKILLS

ERNEST SCHWIEBERT

The beautiful Delaware River rises on the western slopes of the Catskill Mountains. On the eastern slopes are the Schoharie and other famous tributaries of the Hudson – the Catskill, Rondout, and Esopus. Together these waters provide the roots of fly-fishing in North America.

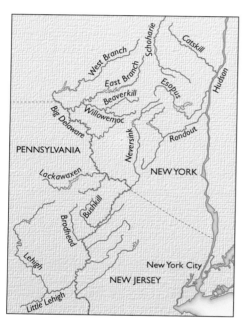

The Catskill River was named "Kaaterskill" by Dutch settlers, since cougars were plentiful there at that time. Later, the name was also given to the mountains. Somewhat south there is the Esopus, another lodestone of American fly-fishing, which rises north of Doubletop Mountain before circling back through Phoenicia and Mount Temper into Ashokan Reservoir. The Esopus remains justifiably popular, and the Rondout is mentioned often in the writings of Ray Bergman, whose *Trout* was the most popular American fishing book of the 20th century. Theodore Roosevelt loved his Rondout holidays under Peekamoose Mountain.

The Delaware and Beaverkill

The big Delaware remains a beautiful river that mirrors its thickly wooded mountainsides. It was once famous for its smallmouth bass; they feature in the writing of the novelist Zane Grey, who is buried in the churchyard at Lackawaxen. The Delaware holds big brown trout, is celebrated for its wild rainbows, and has abundant fly hatches. It was not a trout fishery until large reservoirs were built on its headwaters. Their tailwaters have transformed both the west and east branches of the Delaware into superb trout habitats.

More has been written about the remarkable Beaverkill than about any other North American trout stream. It has witnessed a steady parade of famous fly-fishers since the Ontario and Western Railroad reached its railhead in 1872, providing

SEASONS

Generally, from April 1 to September 30 (for example in the Catskills in New York State, although in some areas the season lasts all year round). In Pennsylvania the season opens on April 15.

PERMITS

Permits are widely available at fly shops and other stores throughout the Catskills.

M ost fly-fishers think that the name Delaware is of tribal origin, but the river was named in honor of Baron de la Ware, a British colonial governor. Although the first fly-fishers in the Americas were British officers, several Americans were writing about their sport as early as 1825, such writings owing much to books by British writers such as Richard Bowkler, Alfred Ronalds, and G P R Pulman. Yet it was to be another 50 years before the literature of angling in the United States began to find its own discrete voice. These stirrings took place in the Delaware region, with the publication of a book by one Thaddeus Norris. Norris was a successful tackle-maker from Philadelphia. At the threshold of the Civil War, he published *The American Angler's Book*, which became the bible of American fishing. It explored the entire Delaware region, and remained in print for half a century.

The Schoharie has a heritage of great fly-fishers, including Arthur Flick, who ran the inn at West Killin, and in 1947 published *Streamside Guide to Naturals and Their Imitations.*

fly-fishers with a service from Boston, Philadelphia, and New York. Ogden Pleissner's watercolor of the bridge at Beaverkill – *Covered Bridge Pool* – is perhaps the most famous landscape painting in American fly-fishing.

In recent years the Beaverkill and its fishing hotels have experienced a remarkable renaissance. Most fly-fishers agree that it now offers the finest public fishing in the eastern United States. Yet it is impossible for a contemplative fly-fisher to fish its storied pools without thinking of our heritage – of echoes of a sweet alchemy that are missing from most other rivers. Such reveries become particularly intense at twilight, on historic pools such as Cairns and Hendrickson and Painter's Bend.

There are still old-timers on the river who remember many of the Catskill giants such as the Dean of the Beaverkill, Richard Robbins, who loved to fish at night because his failing eyesight mattered less after dark. The spirits of these men seem almost palpable at twilight, and there are times when it is not difficult to picture Robbins hailing another fly-fisher to replace a fly in the falling light of age and evening.

The Willowemoc River is one of the trout streams that forms the roots of American fly-fishing. To fly-fish such rivers is more than simply trout fishing … it is meeting with history, and fishing where the fathers of American fly-fishing once fished.

now fine fly-fishing available on the lower Neversink, in a valley of grouse, wild turkeys, and bears. There is still private water at Big Bend, on what remains of the Hewitt tract, but its world has irrevocably changed. Hewitt and his famed fishing camp are gone, and his acolytes are dead. But the clapboard church at Claryville remains faithful to the fishing past, with a cherrywood trout as its weathervane.

South of the Catskills

Although the Catskills are considered the wellspring of American fly-fishing, this perception is not entirely correct. There are other rivers farther south that were popular well before the Catskills became accessible to venturesome fly-fishers, and they share a venerable history.

The American gunsmith Samuel Phillippe, who is credited with making the first six-strip rods from Calcutta, came in 1845, and lived at Easton, where the Lehigh River joins the Delaware. His artistry evolved on both rivers, as well as on fertile New Jersey trout streams such as the Pequest, Paulinskill, and Musconetcong.

The Lackawaxen was a well-known trout stream before the Civil War, and its Blooming Grove and Shohola tributaries became private waters after wealthy sportsmen formed a summer colony at Blooming Grove Park. Wallenpaupack Reservoir now lies on the Lackawaxen at Hawley, and its tailwaters still surrender trophy browns.

The gentle Brodhead was famous for its brook trout when the clergyman George Washington Bethune published the first American edition of *The Compleat Angler* in 1848. Henryville House sheltered every important American fly-fishing writer between the time of Bethune and Ray Bergman, author of the classics *Just Fishing* and *Trout* in the 1930s. The Brodhead's colorful Pied Piper was James Leisenring, who fished the river at Analomink. Leisenring's portrait hung for years in the hotel at Analomink, along with a set of the flies he described in his work *The Art of Tying the Wet Fly*. Many years ago the simple hotel was destroyed by fire, and Leisenring and his faithful flies, the 12 Apostles, are gone. Henryville House is abandoned. Yet the Brodhead still fishes well, and its rich history is older than the heritage of the Catskills.

The Willowemoc and Neversink

The Willowemoc is a remarkable trout stream and, except for the Beaverkill itself, is perhaps the most fertile river in the Catskills. The Willowemoc meets the Neversink at Roscoe in the famous Junction Pool. George M L LaBranche became a regular pilgrim at DeBruce before World War I, and in his book *The Dry Fly and Fast Water* he tells us that he took his first trout on dry fly from the Willowemoc.

Although the most famous mileage of the Neversink now lies entombed under the reservoir at Bradley, this beautiful Catskill river retains a place of honor in the pantheon of American fly-fishers. The fly-fishing history of the Neversink began with the arrival of Theodore Gordon in 1893. His fly-fishing observations appeared regularly in print in both Britain and the United States. Today he is considered the father of American fly-fishing.

Gordon died in 1915. Alas the Catskill spring proved too wintry for the gravediggers of Claryville, so Gordon was not buried by his beloved river. Instead the great angler lies in New York's Marble Cemetery, trapped in a sooty cul-de-sac in the cacophony of Manhattan.

Shortly after Gordon's death, Edward Ringwood Hewitt became enthralled with the Neversink. Hewitt controlled several miles of the river at Big Bend, where he later completed books such as the classic *Telling on the Trout.* Hewitt's money came from old Gramercy Park wealth in Manhattan, but his fortune was decimated in the Depression, and Hewitt was then forced to share his Neversink water. His circle included other famous fly-fishing writers of the time, such as John Alden Knight, Dana Storrs Lamb, John Atherton, and "Sparse Gray Hackle." However, their cloistered little world was destroyed when the New York Water Supply Board took the property. Since then most of the Hewitt mileage has been drowned by the Neversink Reservoir.

The vigilance of groups such as the Theodore Gordon Flyfishers of New York has secured optimal discharges below the reservoir dam. Considerable access for public fishing has been purchased by the State of New York, and there is

CAPE COD

ED JAWOROWSKI

Cape Cod, and the islands of Martha's Vineyard and Nantucket immediately off its southern shores, comprise a saltwater fly-fisher's Mecca. This is one of the finest venues in North America, and probably the best on the east coast.

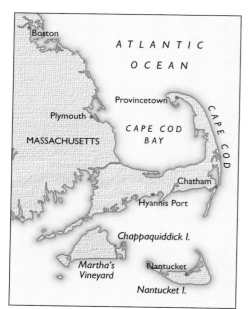

From the time the Pilgrims landed at Plymouth in 1620 until the present day, this spit of land, hardly more than 97km (60 miles) in length and far less in width at any point, has had a major role in American history. When it comes to beauty, color, charm, romance, and fishing excitement you can travel a lot farther but generally won't find better. The long, crooked finger, jutting into the Atlantic Ocean from southeastern Massachusetts and intersecting the migratory routes of so many game species, seems to be beckoning fly-fishers to test its waters. From the Cape Cod Canal, itself a remarkable fishery that today separates the peninsula from the rest of Massachusetts, to Provincetown, lying on the very tip and about 80km (50 miles) southeast of Boston, Cape Cod is the fly-fishers' heaven.

A variety of habitats

Cape Cod boasts a wide variety of inshore habitats, appealing to local game species and fly-fishers alike. The estuaries are popular sites, particularly on the south shore and on Martha's Vineyard. Sand beaches dominate the 48km

(30 miles) from Chatham, on the southeast corner, to Provincetown, as well as Nantucket Island and little Chappaquiddick Island, the easternmost appendage of Martha's Vineyard. Harbors, marshes, and bays large and small (locally called ponds) support baitfish and serve as sheltered feeding locations for striped bass and bluefish. Tidal flushings from numerous pond openings and inlets often provide explosive fishing. The Monomoy National Wildlife Refuge south of Chatham features yet another brand of fly-fishing little developed until recently – flats fishing not unlike that long practiced for bonefish in more tropical waters. Plenty of jetties, groins, and shoreline rock structures are also available for the shore-bound fly-fisher.

In a sea kayak, flats skiff, or more seaworthy vessel you can explore the nearby underwater lumps and rips. The largely irregular shorelines and the general layout of the Cape and its islands ensure that you can find fishable windward and leeward locations as the conditions dictate. You will not be "blown off" in a gale here, as it is very easy to find a sheltered spot.

The big four

Of the dominant local species – the "big four"– striped bass are unquestionably the most sought after. Late spring fishing is notable inside Cape

Cod Bay and around Martha's Vineyard. When summer arrives, nearly all shores reveal school-sized stripers of 1.5–5kg (3–10lb) in abundance, with larger fish showing on the eastern Cape around Chatham Inlet, Pleasant Bay, and Nauset Inlet. The Cape boasts a number of fly-caught fish in excess of 18kg (40lb). Shore-based fly-fishers especially prefer night-fishing for bass. Bluefish, despite greatly diminished numbers in recent years, still provide excellent sport, from May onward around Martha's Vineyard. Race Point at Provincetown is legendary for June blitzes, though these too are less than they were in the 1970s and 1980s. Peak bluefish activity occurs off Nantucket in July and August, but blues frequent most local waters until fall storms and lowering temperatures drive them off, generally by mid-October.

The other members of the "big four" are little tuna (false albacore) and Atlantic bonito. From August into October, more and more fly-fishers make the trek to Cape Cod for these speedy junior members of the tuna family. Since the waters to the north of the Cape maintain

In a Cape Cod pond – one of many inshore habitats – pike, perch, and trout are available for the fly-fisher.

unusually cold temperatures, they limit the range of these fish and others such as weakfish. The south shore, especially the waters surrounding Martha's Vineyard, are the most popular albacore and bonito spots.

Chasing and sight casting to intermittently surfacing schools of the 3–6kg (7–15lb) little tuna and slightly smaller bonito rate high on the saltwater fly-fishers' list of preferred sport. The watery swirls and showers of tiny baits, followed by fish erupting on the surface or leaping clear of the surface, are among the most exciting images in saltwater fly-fishing.

Tackle concerns needn't fluster visiting fly-fishers. Numbers 8- through 10-weight rods, fitted with intermediate or floating lines are *de rigueur*. Cape Cod fly-fishers also widely employ fast-sinking "shooting heads." Reels call for good corrosion resistance and the ability to withstand the relentless charge of huge cow stripers and blistering runs by the albacore. Standard fly patterns will put you in good stead.

SEASONS
No official season; the fishing is best between May and October.

PERMITS
None needed.

Clouser Deep Minnows, largely with chartreuse, alone or in combination, take more bass than any other fly. When fished slowly, particularly in shallow waters, Lefty's Deceivers in a variety of sizes favorably imitate most baitfish — spearing, menhaden, herring — and abundant squid. Epoxy minnow imitations, notably Bob Popovics' Surf Candies in green/white and blue/white, are the preferred albacore and bonito offerings. In addition, good tiny sandeel patterns are indispensable. Many popular patterns are available locally to replicate these prolific baitfish. Finally, you can meet the spring "worm hatch" in salt ponds and estuaries with any of several 5cm (2in) red or orange worm patterns.

Accessing the fishing
For a good sampling of the Cape's marvelous fishing, focus on the key centers. You enter the Cape over the Bourne bridge, at the town of Buzzard's Bay or via the Sagamore bridge farther to the north. From the former bridge you can easily access the towns along the Cape's western and southern flanks, or catch the ferry from Wood's Hole to Martha's Vineyard. Cuttyhunk Island, famous for more than a century for its productive striper fishing, is the last island of the Elizabeth Islands chain, but access and accommodation are severely restricted. These areas must be fished by boat. Route 6 runs the length of the peninsula from Sagamore Bridge to

The best saltwater fly-fishing in the northeastern United States is to be found in and around historic and legendary Cape Cod.

Provincetown. The ferry for Nantucket sails from Hyannis Port. First-time fly-fishers would do well to consider the following areas: Martha's Vineyard, using Edgartown as a base; Chatham, one of the most charming communities in New England, located at the knuckle of the Cape Cod finger and offering access to Chatham Inlet, Pleasant Bay, and the Monomoy Islands; the Orleans-Eastham area, which gives access to the Nauset Inlet, Nauset Beach, and the 11,000ha (27,000 acres) Cape Cod National Sea Shore, which occupies much of the north–south tip of the finger. Excellent fly-fishing guides, tackle stores, and accommodation are plentiful.

Finally, if you can spare the time, take your light freshwater rods. There are no freshwater river systems on the Cape but several dozen ponds, variously holding trout, bass, pickerel, and white and yellow perch, afford intimate and uncrowded sport for fly-fishers. Since Henry David Thoreau sang its glories, Cape Cod has been a focal point for fishers and vacationers alike and the subject of history, song, and legend. The only difference is that the fishing may be better now than it ever has been.

THE BAHAMAS

CHARLES JARDINE

*When nature decided to mix her own Caribbean cocktail – a dash of Gulf Stream,
a tincture of shiny white coral sand, and a good measure of sapphire blue deep water,
garnished with sunshine and wavering palm trees – she unwittingly (we might imagine)
created what must be the fly-fishers' paradise.*

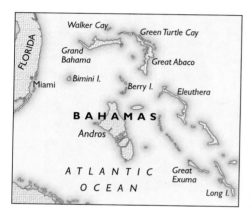

From the millionaire playgrounds of Bimini and Grand Bahama, with their explosive, bluewater sport, aggressive billfish, and sleek rigged vessels, to the stealth and cunning of the bonefish flats on the far-flung islands and crazy paved atolls. If it's saltwater excitement you crave, you will find it here. In fact, everything your fly-fishing heart could desire – maybe more – is among these islands in the Gulf Stream.

The biggest problem in describing Bahamian fly-fishing is where to start. But I suppose it should be with what you know best, and I have come to know Bahamian bones, not intimately you understand, but sufficiently to ensure I break out in sweat at the prospect of tangling with them. There are, I am confidently told, better places with more fish, destinations that contain bigger fish, locations with a better chance at permit and so on. But where could you find quite so much variety in such a comparatively small area, with the degree of infrastructure – lodges, guides, boats, and all the other paraphernalia that goes to make a near-perfect saltwater destination? Just as soon as my feet slide through that shimmering white sand and I feel the warm pearly waters play around my legs, I know I am experiencing some kind of piscatorial Nirvana.

But what is it that makes these islands so special? There is, certainly, the variety, both in terms of species and location, and in the sheer numerical possibilities. Tactically, there is a kaleidoscope of opportunity. Yet for many fly-fishers the holy grail is a bonefish.

Bonefish have achieved near legendary status throughout most of the islands, almost to the exclusion of other wonderful sporting species – such as barracuda, permit, African pompano, the occasional tarpon, and the bluewater giants: marlin, sailfish, tuna, wahoo, dorado – all feasible on the fly-rod. But the bonefish Eldorado is Andros, which has its share of legendary Leviathans – a double-figure fish is always on the cards on an Andros flat. Then there are the sheer numbers of fish haunting Exuma's attenuated flats, a patchwork of marl and secret mangroves. On any day there is a likelihood of catching a dozen or more fish, and they are not small. All are schoolies in the 1.3–1.8kg (3–4lb) class, many will be around 3–3.5kg (7–8lb), and the occasional few over 6kg (13lb). But I digress.

The best islands for fishing

In any "destination" fishing some detective work is vital; you may only have a few days, a week, or two at best, in order to fulfill an ambition, a dream. Selecting an appropriate place is as critical as the tackle you take. A quick run-through of the best fishing islands in the Bahamian chain would go a little like this. Walker's Cay, famous for Flip Pallot's *Chronicles*, offers more in the way of offshore and reef fishing, with a chance of wahoo, grouper, snapper, yellowfin tuna, and marlin. The smaller neighboring islands have flats ideal for bonefishing. Grand Bahama is set for fishing of an entirely different kind, but even here good offshore opportunities exist, with the "millionaire" species, marlin and sailfish, to the fore. On this island too is Deepwater Cay Club, one of the most popular bonefish lodges in the world, and rightly renowned around the world for the quality of its flats fishing. Great Abaco and the island of Treasure Cay, geared to billfish, is popular, and it also harbors bonefish flats. Green Turtle Cay is also more geared to the offshore species, but bonefish are there too.

Chub Cay has gained an enviable reputation for bluewater fishing, especially in the ocean tongue and the pocket area, which are haunted by billfish. Yet even among this group, the Berry Island chain, there is bonefishing – exceptional, so I am told, on the flats around Amergris Cay. There is even fishing to be found in the tourist-laden, duty-free infused island of New Providence.

As I mentioned, there is Bimini, with its sophisticated casualness. Eluthera is legendary for all manner of species, especially bonefish, as is Long Island, with its 24km (15 mile) flat. There is more and, when you tire of those, I have heard of unexploited cays seething with bonefish. But I confess my favorites are in that maze of flats that surrounds Exuma and Andros. They are favorites for entirely different – and personal – reasons: Andros, because as well as breathtaking and adrenaline-charged bonefishing, there is the chance of tarpon, that silver king of the salt, in the jungle-like ponds and lakes on the eastern side of the mangrove – Cargill Creek Lodge is the place. With Exuma it's different. You have the angst and dry-mouthed tension of stalking flats of a hundred permutations – marl, sand, turtle grass, and mangrove-dappled mud. They're all here, and then, conversely, there is the sheer majesty of a deep blue encounter just a few miles away.

Tackle and flies

So how exactly should you go about this phantasmagoria of fly-fishing? I travel, out of necessity, in a general way, ready for a variety of

---

SEASONS

Bonefish: All year, peaking February–May.

Tarpon: Localized, as for bonefish.

Permit: All year, peaking March–July.

Barracuda: All year, peaking in midsummer.

Marlin, sailfish: March–June.

Dorado: Late March–May.

species, and, travel being what it is, minimalism is the order of the day. I have just about restricted things (well, as much as any fly-fisher could) to three outfits: a number 6 light stalking outfit for really nervous tailers on the flats and for maximum fun; an all-rounder, dependable number 8, which seems to cope with the vagaries of wind and unexpected tarpon, permit, and almost anything else that comes along; and a number 10, which copes manfully with big blue inhabitants.

Now I am well aware this may not be a perfect choice. Indeed in some ways it is idiosyncratic, but it does the job. What else could you wish for? All you then do is match them up with a suitable reel, loaded with a minimum of 200m (650ft) of appropriate backing and a floating line. Rather like the reels, a line does need to be somewhat specialized. Do get the proper lines. For deep-water use, a "slime" line and a fast sinker would be welcome traveling companions as well. Of course leaders, shock tippet, and the now mandatory fluoro-carbon tippet for bonefish in 3.5, 4.5, 5.5 and 6.5kg (8, 10, 12 and 14lb) are vital to tactics. It is just worth mentioning that it does pay to use as long a leader as you can handle.

For flies, I am guided locally, and you should be, too. But I always carry a couple of personal favorites for the sake of my own confidence. The rule as far as bonefish are concerned is to match the bottom coloration. And certainly one fly that reigns supreme throughout the Bahamas is a Mcvay Gothcha – in sizes 8, 6, and 4. Charlies, in similar sizes, and the old standby, Chico's Bonefish Special, have a permanent place in my box. Clouser Minnows in various shades work well for deeper-water fish, as does the Slider in larger sizes, 6 and 4 (a great favorite on Andros). There are also the odd crab pattern for bonefish and a fleeting "pop" at a permit, Cockroaches for the tarpon and a few chartreuse attenuated barracuda patterns, Bangers, Anchovies, and Chartreuse Mullet and Candys for big deep blue.

The last and possibly the most important part of the tackle is your guide. Yes, it's possible to fish alone; I have had some glorious days pottering about with only a rod for company. But a good guide equals fish. Guides are the best eyes and the most learned book you could ever have. They are also great fun.

A unique experience

But what is the place like? You have the tackle and the information: what are you getting yourself into? Basically, paradise. Of course each island is different, displaying a unique charm. However, there is something Utopian about the gentle symmetrical curve of white sand, echoed by the

The crystal clear blue waters of the Bahamas are a fly-fisher's paradise. The flats offer magnificent fly-fishing for tarpon, 'cuda, and permit. A short trip by boat to offshore waters brings you to sails and marlin.

wind-ruffled palm fronds, which are held aloft on graceful trunks, and the stark white of an egret seen against the deep green of a mass of mangrove leaves.

Then there is the water: layer upon layer of white into turquoise, into azure, then ultramarine and indigo. There you are, feet and senses taut as a violin string, as toes drift noiselessly through puffs of sand. Suddenly it's there – what looks like smoke blowing across mother of pearl. The smoke splits and dawdles, and first one fin slices the surface, cutting water and shimmering with a sliver of light, then another, and another. They're working closer now, good fish that are 2 or 3kg (5 or 6lb). Your mouth is as dry as a mistral, your muscles twitch and tighten, you lower yourself, crouch, and shake the fly from beneath your white knuckles. The line is free of the tip, the rod arcs and the line cuts the Bahamian air towards the puffs of sand and the fins …
Welcome to paradise.

THE FLORIDA KEYS

CAPTAIN BEN TAYLOR

The Florida Keys provide endless fishing opportunities, and their boundless shallows offer some of the world's best sight fishing for giant tarpon, large bonefish, and huge permit. However, the 6436 sq km (4000 sq miles) of water surrounding the Keys also hold other delights for those willing to take advantage of the day's best offerings.

The Florida Keys are a chain of tiny islands extending some 196km (122 miles) between the Atlantic Ocean and the Gulf of Mexico. The area is easily divided into three regions, each with its own unique fishing opportunities and ambience.

The Upper Keys – Key Largo to Long Key – border the Gulf's Florida Bay. The myriad bay shallows provide year-round fishing for redfish, snook, and bonefish, and are a focal point of tarpon activity. Ashore, amenities abound, with solitude and good fishing a short boat ride away. Fly-fishers are well cared for and well positioned to catch a wide variety of fish.

Marathon marks the boundary between the Middle and Lower Keys. Here the Gulf is relatively broad and deep, although it is interrupted by enough flats to provide good shallow-water fishing. Permit fishing is better here and tarpon are easily found in season. Ashore, Marathon resembles the Upper Keys, but other islands are less crowded.

Again in the Lower Keys, the Gulf side is punctuated by myriad flats and islands. Permit fishing here is excellent. Outside of Key West, much of the region retains a wild charm. Key West, although awash with the activity of a small city, is a fly-fisher's delight.

The length of the Keys is flooded by migrating tarpon. It is easy to find a string migrating along a shoreline, as fish move from Miami, Florida, to the Lower Keys in the late spring, beginning in late April or early May. The procession of schools heading toward Key West lasts for six or seven weeks, and fly-fishers guarding oceanside migration spots may make over a hundred casts during a tide to these moving schools.

Some schools take up short-term residency in Gulf-side "lakes" – basins separating the endless flats. Laid-up tarpon, those sunning themselves or just resting, take flies with often reckless abandon. However, migrating fish that are pushing along the shoreline are usually reluctant to take a fly, especially when conditions are bright and calm. The best guides quickly seek those hungry backcountry targets, laid up in the "lakes." It is often mid-July before the majority of tarpon abandon the Keys, as rising summer water temperatures drive them away.

Bonefish and permit

The majority of world records for bonefish are fish caught in waters of the Upper Keys, including Miami's Biscayne Bay. The bonefishing in the backcountry of Islamorada in the summer and fall is likely the best that the world has to offer. But big bonefish equal popularity, and the place can be busy. By contrast, the Lower Keys backcountry offers similarly excellent fishing, but the fish here are often smaller so there is less activity, which means you may be able to fish in delightful solitude. Permit are considered the ultimate prize of the flats. They are tough to approach and tough to take with a fly, but discoveries in the past decade make them a reachable goal. Permit are crab-eaters. Crab-imitating flies that are tied so that they sink to the bottom and hide in the grass, as a real crab might do when it is attacked, are the preferred attractor for permit. The most recognized fly pattern for permit today is

Del Brown's Permit Crab, which features a set of lead dumbbell eyes that quickly puts it on the bottom. The fly is tossed in a permit's sight window, stripped hard to arouse the fish's attention, then allowed to sink, hoping the fish will follow it to the bottom and dig it out. They do this just often enough, and any permit captured on a fly-rod earns instant bragging rights! While available throughout the Keys, fishing for permit is best in the Middle and Lower Keys.

There are many other things to do in the Keys with a fly-rod. During cooler months, one of the simplest activities leading to captures of big fish is hunting barracuda. They're aggressive and quite active on the end of a skinny rod. A sliver of a fly represents their favorite food. A 15cm (6in) length of fish hair about half the diameter of your little finger, consolidated by glue or braiding, and tied in chartreuse, white, or flame orange, will elicit strikes when stripped across their path at post haste speeds. Barracuda put on a nice aerial show and drag off backing at an alarming rate.

Offshore, the many charter operators who cater for fly-fishers are masters at chumming blackfin tuna, mackerel, bonitos, and dorado within range. While you can find mudding bonefish throughout much of the Keys in the winter and chase sea trout or redfish in the Upper Keys backcountry, the experience pales when compared with fishing a school of blackfin tuna foraging through a chum line of herring.

You will catch tuna and their smaller cousins, the bonitos, on small white bucktail streamers with reckless abandon when foraging in a bait chum line. The bonitos, which seldom scale as much as 4.5kg (10lb), are worthy adversaries on a 9-weight rod. The blackfins sometimes scale more than 13kg (30lb) and exhaust fly-fishers armed with a number 12 weight outfit that is considered appropriate for tarpon.

A couple of handfuls of Key West guides have mastered another challenge for the windiest of winter days. They drift the larger Gulf side channels while dragging a partially filleted barracuda carcass as chum. The scent trail arouses a great many sharks, from blacktips in the 50kg (100lb) category, and lemons of over 115kg (250lb), to bulls of almost 270kg (600lb), as well as the odd hammerhead and tiger shark. An accurately cast orange streamer fly disappears within great maws at astounding speed, and leads to battles seldom won but never forgotten. The best bait for a truly large bull or hammerhead shark is a 50kg (100lb) blacktip shark or tarpon, but the sea monsters readily eat a fly dangled in a scent trail. It is an experience you should not miss if visiting the Keys during the winter months.

For a memorable experience a visiting fly-fisher needs only to explore wisely the Keys' possibilities and choose a specialist guide or charterboat captain who caters for fly-fishers. Specialists can provide tackle, rigging, and flies by arrangement. Ask about tackle availability, particularly if you reel with your left hand. You can fish here about 330 days of the year. Plan several days' fishing so you get a variety of weather conditions and fish.

CHUMMING

Chumming is a method of bringing a fish – usually a big saltwater species – within fly-casting distance. It also encourages fish that are not feeding to seek food, the "chum" being an hors d'oeuvre that whets the predator's appetite. There are two main ways of chumming. In the first, using whole food items, a few shrimp or small herring fry are scattered into a tidal channel to attract such species as bonefish, snook, or bass. In the second, which uses mashed food items, fish, especially fish waste from fish docks, are macerated into "chum" or "rubby-dubby." To enhance the perfume of the chum, extra fish oils, such as cod or halibut, may be added. Once the boat is in position the chum is put into a net bag and suspended overboard. This lays out a scent trail that may attract predators over a wide area.

The flats and mangrove swamps of the Florida Keys provide one of the most accessible opportunities for you to catch a wide range of tropical saltwater fish.

YUCATAN AND BELIZE

DICK BROWN

Of all the flats fishing destinations in the world, the eastern coastline of Central America — from Mexico's Yucatan Peninsula down along Belize's coastal and atoll fisheries — will give you the best chance to hook and land a permit on a fly rod that you will ever have in your lifetime.

As the pink rays of the early morning sun kiss the edges of the flat waters of Ascension Bay, you squint hard, searching for the subtle movements of a school of bonefish. It is then that you see the big-chested, silver shadow for the first time. It moves left to right at 23m (75ft), then turns and angles toward you. Each of the fish's two pencil-thick fins slices the surface, lazily waltzing across the watery dance floor as they trace the rhythmic path of the big permit feeding 60cm (24in) below. This rarest of gamefish is one of the most incredible sights you will ever see in a lifetime of fishing and, in your heart, you know you must connect with it. This is a moment you will take to your grave.

Permit do that to you. And I can think of no better reason why you must fish the east coast of Central America at least once in your lifetime.

This fantastic fishery offers tremendous variety of permit and other tropical saltwater fish and terrain. You can stalk on foot after fat bonefish in 75mm (3in) of skinny water on Turneffe Islands' bountiful atoll. You can chase schools of tarpon from the bow of a skiff at Ambergris Caye. Or you can wang poppers into mangroves at Boca

Paila, where big-mouthed snook will engulf them in watery explosions. But of all the attractions of this shallow, turquoise-jeweled necklace that stretches along the emerald jungles and Mayan ruins of Central America's eastern shore, some stand out above all the others. This is the Grand Slam capital of the world and the permit epicenter of the universe.

The Yucatan coast

The northernmost stretch of this Central American fly-fishing bounty is the coastline of Mexico's Yucatan Peninsula, ranging from Cancun at its north border to Belize at its southern edge. The most productive fishing you will find here is at Boca Paila/Pez Maya and Ascension Bay. These two areas of Yucatan and Belize hold large schools of small to medium-sized permit, tarpon, and bonefish. They also offer one of the best chances in the world for a Grand Slam.

This tropical fly-fishing paradise holds some of the most bountiful flats fishing — especially for bonefish and permit — in the world. You can take 10–20 bonefish a day and see permit every time you go out. Flats here produce large numbers of smaller fish, and it is not unusual to log in a 100-fish week. Other fish seen include small tarpon, snook, barracuda, jack crevalle, and cubera snapper. Extensive flats, lagoons, and mangrove islands give fly-fishers a variety of fishing environments, allowing them to find shelter from winds. Most fishing is done from skiffs, but wading is possible on some hard-bottomed flats. While the fish are not as big on average as other locations, Boca is an ideal place for fly-fishers to take their first bonefish and permit trip, in order to get the experience of stalking and playing these dynamic quarry.

The Ascension Bay area

Ascension Bay is a remote, wild place of giant fisheries and giant fish. The Ascension Bay flats lie inside an enormous bay located halfway down the coast of Mexico's Quintana Roo on the

Yucatan Peninsula, and the entire area is inside the Sian Ka'an Biosphere Reserve, a 500,000 sq. m- (1.3 million-acre-) nature reserve operated by the Mexican government.

Inside the bay, you encounter hundreds of big schools of 1–2kg (2–4lb) bonefish and plenty of barracuda and jack crevalle. But the quarry that will spike your daily heartrate is the permit. Ascension Bay — and in particular the Casa Blanca camp on its southern rim — is the place to go if you want to stalk really big permit. These hulking 9–14kg (20–30lb) silver monsters are seen cruising every day, and many are hooked every season. A 17kg (38lb) world record was recently established here by a first-time permit fisher.

The many hard-bottomed flats of Ascension Bay support both wading and poled-skiff fishing. Flats such as Laguna, Santa Rosa, Esperanza, and Tres Mares can be reached in a relatively short time by skiff, and here the pressure from other fly-fishers is extremely low.

Belize

Lying just south of Mexico's Yucatan Peninsula, Belize harbors several major flats fisheries, including some of the best on-foot flats fly-fishing for big bonefish in the Atlantic. With neon-green rainforest jungles growing along its coastline, Belize offers a more tropical environment for

SEASONS
The best times to go are April–June and October–November.

PERMITS
None needed.

TRAVEL AND ACCOMMODATION
Your first visit is best arranged through a specialist fly-fishing/travel agency, which will book flights, accommodation at one of the many specialist lodges, boats, and guides.

hunting bonefish than do northerly locations. It contains three main fishing areas: the flats around Ambergris Caye at the northern end of its coastline, the Turneffe flats area that lies inside an offshore atoll, and the mainland coastal flats. Each of these fisheries is different. Some have mainly large schools of smaller fish, while others hold large fish. Places such as Ambergris Caye offer only poled-skiff fishing, while others can be both waded and boat-fished. Belize contains one of the most varied fisheries of any of the bonefish destinations, with abundant permit, tarpon, snook, and barracuda.

Ambergris Caye flats

Ambergris Caye is inside Belize's barrier reef area, which forms the geological end of the Yucatan Peninsula and is located 24km (15 miles) offshore from Belize's northernmost coast. You fish this area from poled skiffs for schools of 1–2kg (2–4lb) bonefish. Some fish run larger. Sight fishing for permit and tarpon also attracts fly-fishers to Ambergris Caye. Permit run larger than in the Yucatan but smaller than they do in Ascension Bay, the Bahamas, and the Florida Keys. Tarpon run at 9–45kg (20–100lb). Some bigger fish are found in crystal-clear, 1–1.5m (3–5ft) deep waters. The area contains an abundance of shallow flats, but their soft bottoms do not support wading.

Turneffe area

Turneffe Islands, Belize's large, northern atoll, lies 48km (30 miles) off the coast. Typical of most atolls, the Turneffe Islands area consists of a ring of reefs that rises abruptly from the ocean floor, surrounding a circular lagoon full of sandflats, cayes, mud, and mangrove stands. This is Belize at its best. Turneffe offers you the excitement and intimacy of on-foot atoll fishing – both flats and reefy edges – for bonefish, permit, barracuda, snapper, and even grouper. You can wade/stalk some very big bonefish, averaging 2–2.5kg (4–5lb). You will find wading and visibility excellent on bottoms of hard sand and coral with scattered grass. But this can be very technical fishing too. Large fish often feed selectively here. They can become extremely nervous in the thin water of the atolls. You sometimes stalk fish in water so shallow you can see the fish's eyes and backs bulge from the water. This is really a very special place.

Mainland flats

Numerous flats and cayes lie off the mainland and are easily accessible by boat. People who fish these flats, inland of the great barrier reefs, will find them somewhat silty, soft-bottomed and not

suitable for wading. Constant wind and wave action, together with active feeding fish, turn these waters muddy. This limits most sight fishing to hunting for easily spotted tailing fish. Fish average 1–2kg (2–4lb). Schools of 25–50 or more fish are common.

The unspoiled coastline of Yucatan and Belize offers some wonderful fly-fishing for a host of saltwater fish. Here you will catch some of the most keenly sought species, such as permit, barracuda, and tarpon.

PATAGONIA AND TIERRA DEL FUEGO

ERNEST SCHWIEBERT

The southern extremities of South America are a remote, windswept world, with lakes and rivers that harbor thriving populations of trout and land-locked salmon. They include the diverse areas of northern and southern Patagonia as well as Tierra del Fuego. These are wonderful places to be, and magnificent places to fly-fish.

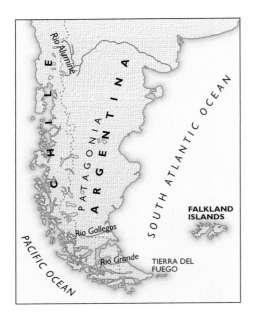

We will start in northern Patagonia – an area containing 30 Andean lakes – with one of the region's 50 rivers, the Rio Alumine. The Alumine is a large river with a number of fine tributaries. From its source in two mountain lakes it winds south through wind-polished foothills and great forests of monkey-puzzle trees.

The Alumine offers big rainbows in its swift reaches, with formidable browns lurking in its canyon pools. Native mapuche live in the waters of the lower canyons, and fly-fishers who float the Alumine between Pilolol and Malleo report excellent fishing. All the Alumine tributaries are productive, especially in spring, when they teem with big rainbows.

The Alumine tributaries

One Alumine tributary, the Malleo, is the finest dry-fly river in Argentina, where success depends on matching the hatch to highly selective trout. The Malleo rises in Lago Tromen, which has brook trout weighing up to 5.4kg (12lb), but the finest fly-fishing is at Tres Picos, where the river meanders like an English chalkstream through extensive water meadows. Another Alumine tributary, the Chimehuin, is the most famous trout river in South America. Rising under the Lanin volcano at Lago Huechulafquen, the river has many productive *bocas* (pools), including the Boca Chimehuin where Jose de Anchorena caught a 10.8kg (24lb) brown trout. The tributaries of the Chimehuin, such as the Currhue and Quilquihue, are also well worth visiting. They offer numerous rainbows in the spring, and April floods help big browns ascend in the austral fall.

Below its confluence with the Chimehuin, the Alumine is known as the Collon Cura. Here it is an intimidating maze of large channels in thickets of mimbre and poplar trees, with gargantuan pools of Stygian depth. These are guarded by cliffs that shimmer in the February heat like the Valley of the Nile. The main tributary of the Collon Cura is the Caleufu, a river that rises in a number of large Andean lakes. The Lago Meliquina is one. It was celebrated by Roderick Haig-Brown in his classic *Fisherman's Winter*, and still surrenders the silver land-locked salmon that Haig-Brown sought from its cool waters.

The River Limay rises in Lago Nahuel Huapi and flows north to three great reservoirs (Alicura, Piedra del Aguila, and Chocon), which have drowned the river's former desert canyons. The tailwaters below these impoundments have begun to surrender trout of crocodile proportion.

Although a relatively small tributary of the Limay, the Rio Traful has a remarkable sporting reputation. It drops steeply between its source at Lago Traful and Confluencia, with water so transparent that its fish are clearly visible: trophy rainbows in the spring, and monster browns and land-locked salmon dropping back from the lake between late February and April. Salmon, which were introduced from Maine a century ago, are this river's unique treasure. It was here, in 1992, that I caught and released the largest fly-caught land-locked salmon ever recorded, a cock fish weighing over 9kg (20lb). Its lifesize portrait hangs over the fireplace at Arroyo Verde.

Feeder-streams flowing into Lago Nahuel Huapi can offer great fishing. Boca Correntoso once surrendered a 18kg (39lb) brown trout on a big spoon, while Totoral and Pireco have produced brook trout of 4.5kg (10lb).

Southern Patagonia

Many fly-fishers believe that the fishing in southern Patagonia, south of San Carlos de Bariloche, improves the farther south you go, but such perceptions are flawed. There is good fishing, but winters are more severe and the little pancora, a freshwater crayfish found above Bariloche in astonishing numbers, becomes increasingly scarce to the south. This crustacean is the secret of most Patagonian fisheries, feeding trout and salmon to large size. Another problem is that there are great glaciers to the south of Bariloche, and some rivers are discolored with their milky runoff.

The Manso drains the icefields of Tronador and its headwaters are opaque with chalky discharges. It is joined by a tributary, the Foyle, loops north into Chile, and is finally joined there by the Rio Puelo. The Rio Puelo flows almost entirely in Chile and contains a good population of salmon and trout.

The Rio Futaleufu drains another formidable watershed that rises in a region of great mountain lakes. Its northernmost tributary is the Rio del

SEASONS

Usually from the middle of November (the austral spring) to the middle of April (the austral fall).

PERMITS

Permits are necessary in all areas. They can be obtained from local biological officers/wardens in the national parks, for example Parque Lerces, from the national parks' headquarters, most campsite owners, and in most cities.

Tigre, which feeds Lago Chollila. There are salmon and trout at Chollila, and fly-fishers can float the river to explore its beats down to Lago Rivadavia, which is situated at the threshold of Los Rierces National Park.

Tierra del Fuego

Tierra del Fuego is a treeless world of rolling grasslands, with the Cordillero de Darwin (Darwin mountain range) on the horizon and interminable winds that moan across kelp-stained beaches to the sea. Scottish settlers grew so homesick that they introduced both gorse and thistles. They also brought sea trout to Tierra del Fuego.

Rio Gallegos, which flows north of the Strait of Magellan and enters the Atlantic close to the mouth of the Rio Chico, was first planted with sea trout in 1922. Fly-fishers stay at Hosteria Truchalke, close to the tideway, and can fish both rivers. It is agreed that beats on the Gallegos near Estancia Bella Vista consistently offer the best fly-fishing. Late summer migrations of sea trout

ascend the entire watershed to spawn in Chile, and in the austral fall there is good February sport on the main tributaries, the Rubens, and Penitente. However, the principal fishery of Tierra del Fuego is the Rio Grande, a large pampas river that has its source in Chile.

The lower reaches of the Rio Grande offer the best fly-fishing, when big sea trout arrive in midsummer, as bright as freshly minted coins. Later in the year the upper reaches and tributaries fish well into the fall, although most of the sea trout have lost their sea-polished magic by late March. Sea trout here average 3.5–4.3kg (8–10lb) in weight, and the river system produces some remarkable trophies in the 9–13kg (20–30lb) class.

Certainly the Rio Grande is among the best trout fisheries in the world. But fly-fishers with adventurous spirits cannot be blamed for exploring other rivers in the Land of Fire.

The Rio Fuego can become murky near Estancia Viamonte. However, its upper beats on

This is one of the world's last wildernesses – where the fly-fishing for trout and land-locked salmon is superb, and certainly undisturbed.

Estancia Buenos Aires, where it meanders through empty meadows, provide good fly-fishing. Farther south there is the Rio Ewan, and beyond that you reach the Rio San Pablo, which offers utter solitude at the misty threshold of the Darwin mountain range.

Lago Fagnano, situated between the Sierra de Beauvoir and the Cordillero de Darwin, resembles a great Norwegian fjord. The Rio Claro rises in the Sierra Beauvoir and receives the discharge of Lago Yehuen before flowing into Lago Fagnano. Stories of land-locked salmon, immense brook trout, and the ubiquitous huge sea trout, as well as both the sport and the utter solitude in these stormy latitudes, provide the alchemy of Tierra del Fuego.

WHITE RIVER, ARKANSAS

DAVE WHITLOCK

Born and nourished by 100–125cm (40–50in) of annual rainfall, hundreds of turquoise tinted, limestone spring creeks, and the mineral-rich forested Ozark Mountains, the White River provides some of the most fascinating freshwater fly-fishing opportunities in the world, with as wide a variety of fish as can be imagined.

The White River begins its journey near Fort Smith, in northwestern Arkansas. It first flows north into southwestern Missouri, and then loops south back into the northcentral part of Arkansas after which it continues its southward journey until it meets the Mississippi River.

Before the 1940s, the White River was a cool- and warm-water bass, panfish, and catfish fishery. However, that changed as a series of huge hydroelectric and flood control dams was constructed between 1940 and 1965, converting the system into a complex and unique cold, cool- and warm-water river with large, deep, cool-water lakes. More than 160km (100 miles) of premium, cold, tailwater rivers stretch below the four artificial dams. The White, with its main tributaries the James River, Norfolk River, Crooked Creek, and Buffalo River, and the four lakes formed by the dams, are a year-round, four-season paradise for fly-fishers, and there are no closed periods of the year.

The fisheries contain rainbow trout, brown trout, cutthroat trout, and brook trout that were introduced into the river once the cold tailwaters were created. Also inhabiting these waters are largemouth, smallmouth, and spotted bass, striped bass, 12 varieties of sunfish, walleye, pickerel, white bass, and about 60 other lesser species of fish.

Most fly-fishers who travel to the White River do so for its trout and smallmouth-bass fishing. The nutrient-rich tailwaters only vary about 9–18°C (45–65°F) annually, thus stimulating trout to grow to 20mm (¾in) in length per month. Because the rivers are so dynamic, rich, and clear, they grow strong, heavy, full-bodied trout and smallmouth bass with beautifully dense coloration and vivid markings. Rainbows grow to 8kg (18lb), browns to 18kg (40lb). (The current world record of 18.2kg (40lb 5oz) is from a tributary tailwater of the White.) These huge browns, unlike those elsewhere in the world, reach this size within river habitats only, spending no part of their lives in oceans or large lakes. Brook trout will grow to 1.8kg (4lb) and cutthroat to 3.5kg (8lb), while smallmouth bass occasionally exceed 2.3kg (5lb).

Although some natural reproduction of trout occurs, especially brown trout, the river system is stocked with approximately three million trout per year – mostly 15–30cm (6–12in) rainbows. Although the entire river is superb for fly-fishing, there are now catch-and-release areas on the White that are producing good populations of larger trout. The section of the White River below Bull Shoals Dam and its tributary, the 6.4km- (4 mile-) long Norfolk River below Norfolk Lake Dam, are truly amazing tailwaters.

SAFETY

Hydroelectric generators at dams can cause the White and Norfolk Rivers to fluctuate between 30cm and 3m (1–10ft) daily. This fast rise is not predictable or announced, so you must keep a very cautious eye on the river. I would advise you, on your first visit, to hire a guide or to fish with a local, experienced fisher. These rises are much like strong ocean tides and can be extremely dangerous for any inexperienced wading or boating fly-fisher. Almost 200 fly-fishers have drowned below these dams since they were constructed, so please be aware.

The waters are practically silt free and seldom become discolored. You can often see the bottom in 6m (20ft) of water. Their cold, nutrient-rich waters support an amazing amount of diverse plant and animal life, which serves to create one of the world's richest trout habitats. The trout feed constantly all year long on aquatic and terrestrial insects, minnows, scuds, crayfish, sowbugs, leeches, and aquatic worms, and eagerly take a variety of flies. The water levels of these tailwaters fluctuate daily as the dams release flood waters or generate hydroelectric power. This creates one of the most complicated fisheries in the world. The daily water change provides the fishery with a water flow that is like a huge, shallow spring creek during low tide (minimum flow level) changing to a roaring, fast river at high tide similar to large West coast steelhead and salmon rivers. During low-water times, small flies (18 and 24), long leaders, and 1–5-weight floating lines are ideal. As generators are turned on, the current rapidly speeds up and the river rises, making larger flies, and heavier floating and sinking lines more practical.

The best areas

The best areas to fly-fish are currently three, 1600m (1 mile) long, catch-and-release, trophy trout areas on the White, and one on the Norfolk River. These areas are restricted to barbless single hook rules and have trout that average 40–60cm

Dave Whitlock landing a fine trout from a White River tailwater. This is one of the world's great trout rivers and offers fishing the year round.

(16–24in). You might catch all four trout species on the same stretch on any day, truly any trout fly-fisher's Grand Slam! But do not neglect several other excellent areas that lie along these rivers.

When water is at minimum flow, use very small imitations of scuds and sowbugs, and match the hatches of midges, mayflies, and caddis. During moderate generation, these areas fish well with San Juan worms, egg patterns, sculpin streamers, crayfish, and shad streamers that are fished next to the bottom.

The areas on White River are downstream from Beaver Dam, downstream from Bull Shoals Dam, and in the Rim Shoals area halfway between Cotter and Buffalo City.

On the Norfolk River there is a special area for children up to 16 years old and for the disabled (there are ramps at streamside platforms) between Otter Creek mouth and the handicapped access at Dry Run Creek just below Norfolk Dam.

When to go

In spring, the conditions are excellent and the weather mild, with frequent rain showers and temperatures of 7–24°C (40–75°F). Hatches are good from March to June.

In summer, expect hot weather and higher water levels, but fish feed well in water at the ideal temperature of 11–18°C (52–65°F) all season. Air temperatures range from 18–38°C (65–100°F). You can try some mayfly and midge fishing, but the best results are usually achieved with some terrestrials, streamers, sowbugs, scuds, and crayfish.

Fall has mild, cool, and excellent weather with a temperature range of 2–27°C (35–80°F).

Rainbow and brown trout spawn from late October to January. Nymphs, terrestrials, caddis, streamers, and egg patterns have proven to be the most productive.

In winter, the weather ranges from 1–13°C (30–55°F) and the river fishes well all winter. River-water temperatures range from 9–11°C (48–52°F). Streamers, nymphs, eggs, and midges work well.

Fishing the tributaries and lakes

From October until mid-June, trout move up cool-water tributaries of the White River. These are excellent alternatives if the White is too high to find good wading. The best of these tributaries are Bruce Creek, Crooked Creek, Buffalo River, Piney Creek, and Sylamore Creek. From March until October these same streams are excellent wade- or float-streams for smallmouth bass. If you prefer lake fly-fishing, Lakes Tannycomo and Bull Shoals have excellent trout fishing from October to May, when surface temperatures are usually ideal. Trout focus on scuds in Tannycomo and threadfin shad in Bull Shoals.

Fly-fishing along the shorelines of all the lakes of the White River Valley from April until November is excellent for largemouth, smallmouth, spotted, striped, and white bass, and for several species of sunfish. Threadfin shad, emerald shiners, and crayfish imitations are most effective – especially from first light to one hour after sunup and from sundown until dark.

PERMITS

Arkansas and Missouri: Non-resident Fishing License and Trout Stamps are available at fly shops, local sporting goods stores, and trout docks. Public and private accesses are plentiful along the rivers. Some private accesses charge a small daily fee for each wade or bank fly-fisher. John boats and outboard-motors are available at the trout docks.

FURTHER DETAILS

For the upper White, make your base at Fayetteville or Eureka Springs, Arkansas. The middle portion is best accessed from Branson, Missouri and the lower 129km (80 miles) on the White and Norfolk rivers are best accessed from Mountain Home, Arkansas. There are camping and lodging sites, fly shops, and guides in these areas. For specific information, contact the Chamber of Commerce in these cities, or Dave and Emily Whitlock's Fly Fishing School, PO Box 319, Midway, AR 72651.

YELLOWSTONE NATIONAL PARK

CRAIG MATHEWS

Nowhere else in the world but in Yellowstone National Park can the fly-fisher fish for wild trout, grayling, and mountain whitefish while nearby, geysers erupt and mud volcanoes belch, bubble, and spurt. In the park bison, elk, moose, deer, bear, and wolves wander unmolested as fly-fishers cast to rising trout.

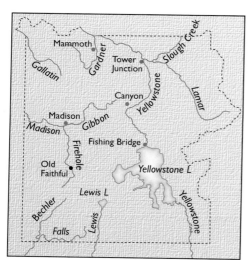

Yellowstone National Park comprises approximately 900,000 ha (2,221,000 acres) spread across the spine of the Rocky Mountains, where the western states of Wyoming, Montana, and Idaho come together. With over 1600km (1000 miles) of river and 100 lakes within its boundaries, Yellowstone National Park has more wild trout water than anywhere else of comparable size in the world.

Seven species of gamefish live in Yellowstone. Cutthroat, Arctic grayling, and mountain whitefish are native to the park, and rainbow, brown, brook, and lake trout have been introduced.

From fall to spring the park is completely snowed in and there is no fishing. The Firehole river is the first body of water to clear of snow and ice, and often the only one fishable on opening day, in late May. All other rivers and lakes thaw during June, so that, by the end of the first week of July the fishing season is underway everywhere with peak hatches.

For those who wish to fish lakes, August is a great time to visit the many back-country lakes of the park. Most rivers also fish well during August because, as aquatic insect hatches wane, terrestrials such as ants, beetles, and grasshoppers play an increasingly important role in the trout's diet.

In the late season – September and October – only a few hatches occur. October is the best month to come if you want to catch huge, migrating brown trout in the several rivers. As spawning time nears and the weather becomes more like winter, these large trout become aggressive and territorial, attacking baitfish imitations and other large streamer patterns.

The northwest section

This section contains four of Yellowstone's most popular rivers: the Madison, Gallatin, Gardner, and Gibbon. The Madison has been called the world's largest chalkstream, where massive hatches of caddisflies, mayflies, and stoneflies bring on huge rises of trout. Brown and rainbow trout along with mountain whitefish average 38cm (15in) in length and fish weighing nearly 2kg (4lb) are not uncommon. The best times to fish are June, September, and October. A spawning run of browns and rainbows begins in late September, the optimal time to take bigger trout on this river.

The Gallatin is a pleasant mix of mountain freestone and meadow water. It has a fine population of rainbows, along with browns, cutthroats, grayling, and whitefish. Trout average 30cm (12in), but browns can be twice that size.

The Gardner is a small boulder-strewn river where, because the only important hatches are salmonflies and golden stoneflies, the most productive artificial flies are often attractor dries, nymphs, and streamers. Look out for terrestrials in late summer, when grasshopper, beetle, and cricket imitations work well. The average trout (cutthroat, brook, brown, rainbow, and mountain whitefish all inhabit the Gardner) is 30cm (12in), but an occasional lunker brown will make you wish you'd put fresh backing on this season. The Gardner also receives a fall spawning run of browns from the Yellowstone River in September and October.

The Gibbon has it all. Big brown trout inhabit the meandering meadow stretches, rainbows thrive in the riffles, brook trout hold in the pockets, and the secluded pools are occupied by the elusive Montana grayling. In the meadows the river is like a spring creek – slow-moving with undercut banks. The hatches resemble those of a spring creek, with several mayflies and caddis species. The rest of the river is mostly canyon water, best fished with high-floating attractor patterns such as Wulffs and Trudes. In late October there is a spawning run of browns and rainbows. They move upstream from Montana's Hebgen Lake, attracting fly-fishers from around the world.

The northeast section

The Lamar is usually the last river in the park to clear of snowmelt. In late July fishing with grasshopper and other terrestrial flies can be fast and furious. Rainbow and cutthroat trout averaging 38cm (15in) inhabit these waters.

The Yellowstone is both the showcase of American trout streams and the world's finest trout stream. It has the most prolific insect hatches and is the park's most popular river for fly-fishing. Cutthroats are more numerous and larger than they were 30 years ago, averaging 43cm (17in) in length.

SEASONS

From late May (the Saturday of Memorial Day weekend) to the first Sunday of November. There are some exceptions, so always check the park's booklet.

PERMITS

Anyone aged 12 or over must have a valid Yellowstone National Park permit. Children aged 11 or younger may fish without a permit, but must always be accompanied by an adult. Permits are available at main entrance gates, ranger stations, and fishing stores in gate communities.

FURTHER DETAILS

There are camping areas and facilities inside the park and in surrounding towns.

Slough Creek is a park favorite. Nestled at the foot of the Beartooths, where the mountains snag the clouds, Slough purls its way through meadows and some of the most spectacular scenery in the area. Its slow, clear flow breeds selective trout. Rainbow and cutthroat trout in the lower stretches, and cutthroats in the upper meadows average 40cm (16in). They are some of the most challenging trout to fool on a fly.

The southeast section

The southeast section of the national park is one of the most remote areas in the United States and contains the largest concentration of grizzly bears found anywhere in the lower 48 states, as well as elk, moose, bison, wolves, and wolverines. The Lewis River and Yellowstone Lake are its most important waters.

The Lewis River leaves Lewis Lake and offers good fishing for brown and lake trout that move in and out of the lake. These fish average 43cm (17in). Below the Lewis River Falls, the river is like a large spring creek, with slow-moving meadow water and large, wary brown trout. There are good hatches of small mayflies, which, along with several caddisfly species, can bring these big trout to the surface.

Yellowstone Lake is the largest wild cutthroat trout fishery in the world. The resident cutthroats, which can be found in the shallow water along the shoreline of the lake, average 38cm (15in).

The southwest section

This section of Yellowstone is characterized by spectacular geysers, lakes, and waterfalls. Its rivers are inhabited by prolific caddisfly and mayfly hatches, producing the most consistent dry-fly angling in the entire park.

The Bechler and Falls Rivers offer great fly-fishing and spectacular scenery, having more than 20 of Yellowstone Park's waterfalls. Both rivers get brown, gray, and green drakes that bring up big trout, as do the abundant terrestrials: ants, beetles, crickets, and grasshoppers. The higher upstream you hike, the larger the resident rainbow and cutthroat trout become. Lower down, 25cm (10in) is the average; hike farther upstream and the trout average 40cm (16in).

The Firehole has been called the "strangest trout stream on earth." Geysers, fumeroles, and bubbling mud pots make this one of the most interesting rivers to fish. From the Old Faithful geyser down to the cascades lie 20km (12 miles) of river, most of it meadow water. This is prime dry-fly water, with fine hatches of caddisflies and mayflies. Firehole's browns and rainbows average 30cm (12in) in length; with fish measuring 40cm (16in) not uncommon.

The essence of Yellowstone National Park: mountains, forests, and rivers — beautiful rivers, full of hard-working trout.

THE BIGHORN RIVER

GARY LAFONTAINE

Flowing through the prairies in eastern Montana, the cold and enriched water spouting from the bottom of Yellowtail Dam feeds the Bighorn River, one of North America's most prolific brown and rainbow trout rivers. Magnificent hatches of many fly species help make the Bighorn dry-fly perfection.

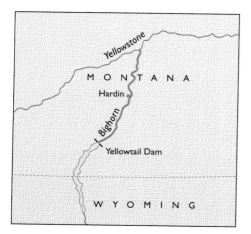

The Bighorn River flows through the Crow Indian Reservation, an area that has its own kind of beauty, although its vast grassland expanse does not fit the general idea of what trout country should look like. Yet there is something magical about this place, despite the fact that the river is an artificial one, formed by the dam. When I am standing in a riffle, casting a small fly to a huge rising trout, the fact that the river is there as a result of human intervention is irrelevant. It is down to me and a fussy trout that is staring hard at every wisp and turn of my imitation.

The trout portion of the Bighorn is divided into the Upper Water and the Lower Water. Most fly-fishers head for the upper 21km (13 miles), from the Afterbay below Yellowtail Dam to the Bighorn Access. This Upper Water is by far the most productive in terms of number and average size of trout. There are trout below this upper section, all the way down through the Lower Water to Two-Leggins, but the number of fish drop as the river becomes siltier and warmer. The charm of the lower water is that there are fewer fly-fishers and some very large trout.

Floating the river

There are two ways of fishing the Bighorn: wading and fishing by yourself, and floating the river in a boat with a guide. Access along the banks is good

and the wading is easy, so an experienced fly-fisher will have no trouble wandering alone and catching lots of trout. But a few days floating the river with a guide will give the fly-fisher new to the Bighorn a look at the entire river. It will also provide information about the best flies and the tactics to use. Also, floating the river is great fun.

Drift boats are a feature of the upper river. They move in lock-step, each boat with its two fisherman stopping at a particular riffle for 15 or 20 minutes. Standard practice is for the fly-fishers to cast out a rig with a bright strike-indicator, set at roughly one-and-a-half times the depth of the water, a 2.7m (9ft) leader tapered to 5X or 6X draped with lead split shot or lead wraps, and one or two nymphs. The rods are typically 2.7m (9ft) or longer. As soon as the strike-indicator bobs below the surface the line is tightened and the trout played. This is a fairly simple and effective technique because, with the design of drift boats, the fly-fisher is positioned high above the water, standing in the kneelocks of the boat, and it is easy to fish a fly repeatedly through a good run. Patterns imitating scuds or aquatic worms are most effective. It is such an easy method to teach that guides can guarantee the freshest beginner a day of steady action on large fish.

For many, especially the first-timers, this bottom-hopping with a nymph is good enough. But for me the charm of the Bighorn is all in the hatches. I carry three rods in the boat, and if you want to enjoy all the fly-fishing possibilities that the Bighorn can offer I recommend that you do the same: a 2.7m (9ft) number 6–7-weight rod rigged with a streamer, a 2.8m (9ft 6in) number 5–6-weight rod set up with a strike-indicator and a nymph, and the main outfit, a 2.4–2.7m (8–9ft) number 3–5-weight rod with an emerger or a dry fly tied to the leader point.

For really exciting sport, use the main outfit whenever there is a hatch. The wonder of the Bighorn is that on most days, even during the winter, trout feed on emergers or hatched insects at the surface. Only when bad weather (when it is

too hot, too cold, or too windy) depresses the hatches, when the high runoff of spring sends warmer water from the surface of the reservoir over the top of the dam, or when Yellowtail Reservoir "turns over" in the spring and fall will the trout not rise. My guess, based on records of fishermen who are on the Bighorn constantly, is that a fly-fisher can find trout feeding at the surface on over 300 days of the year.

Midges and stoneflies

Constant-flow tailwaters (in other words, rivers such as the Bighorn, formed by the outflow of big dams) usually have insect populations that may be incredibly large but that are not particularly diverse. It is a simple equation that means only one thing – there may be only a handful of hatches but they will be really heavy. They put enough food into and onto the current to make big fish rise freely.

Midges hatch continually on the Bighorn – in spring, summer, fall, and winter. And these are not always small insects; size 16 and 18 black midges, emerging in the spring, bring pods of nice trout to the top. Even during the summer, when larger mayflies, caddisflies, and stoneflies are popping, there are important midge hatches filling in the gaps at all hours of the day. One of the secrets on the Bighorn, when trout are refusing all other imitations, is a good midge pupa imitation.

The Bighorn is a smooth-flowing, low gradient prairie river. It does not have the rushing, pure water running over a gravel bottom that most species of stoneflies need to become abundant. The one stonefly, however, that does produce good populations in the river is the ubiquitous yellow sally. The adults fly from mid-July right through early September and trout feed on the egg-laying females. A good size 16 dry-fly imitation makes a good afternoon and early evening searching pattern.

Caddisflies and mayflies

Every great river has its famous hatches. The Bighorn has the black caddis that starts in mid-August and lasts until mid-October. Fly-fishers plan their trips around this insect. Both the emerging pupae and the egg-laying females trigger afternoon and early evening feeding sprees. Trout roll and slash, taking one or the other, and the fish can get selective. What do the smart fly-fishers do? They use a two-fly rig, dangling a number 16 or number 18 black pupa imitation 23cm (9in) behind a number 16 or number 18 adult imitation.

SEASONS AND PERMITS

Regulations are often subject to alteration. For current information on seasons, regulations, permits, and so on for fishing the Bighorn River, it is best to contact one of the organizations listed below.

FURTHER DETAILS

Bighorn Canyon Natural Recreation Area, Dept FS Box 458, Fort Smith MT 59035

The Bighorn Trout Shop, PO Box 477, Fort Smith MT 59035 Tel: (406) 666 2375

There are other important caddisfly hatches. The spotted sedge starts in mid-August, just like the black caddis, but it emerges late in the evening. This is a big insect, which is matched with a number 12 brown-winged and yellow-bodied fly, and it gets the attention of big trout. The summer flyer, a number 10 speckled cinnamon sedge, becomes important in September.

Any one of four important mayfly species can blanket the Bighorn River with insects, and bring trout up to feed in lazy, sipping pods. The blue-winged olive is important from April through to May, and again from mid-September through to the beginning of November.

Pale Morning Duns hatch from mid-July through early September, a long spread of time that gives the trout the chance to lock into very selective feeding. The mating clouds of tricos start at around 9am every morning from mid-August until October. The females land on the water and the trout feast on the spent insects. The fly-fishing problem is too many mayfly spinners – the artificial fly is competing with so many naturals. The canny fly-fisher picks one trout, times its feeding rhythm, and presents the fly to coincide with the rise of the trout.

The tiny blue-winged olives are small, equal to a number 26 hook, but they hatch in such great numbers that they overwhelm any other insects on the water.

The duns ride the water a long time and trout concentrate on them. A Comparadun or No-Hackle hooks the fish, but it is always a problem landing them with such a tiny fly and a fine tippet.

Evening on Montana's Bighorn River – a great fly-fishing experience. As the light falls, caddis- and mayflies swarm over the water and the trout rise.

SNAKE RIVER, IDAHO

DENNIS G BITTON

*Rising in southeastern Idaho, the upper stretches of the Snake River feature some
fantastic trout fishing. The Snake is formed by the confluence of two streams:
the famous Henry's Fork and the lesser-known South Fork. Both run clear and
cool all summer long and have myriad insect hatches.*

Sometimes the only problem in fishing Henry's
Fork and South Fork is choosing which of the
several hatches on the water to match. It is a
constant, wonderful challenge. July, August, and
September are the best fishing months, although
October on the South Fork can provide some
excellent brown trout weighing up to 5kg (10lb).

Henry's Fork

The upper stretches of Henry's Fork sit at 2000m
(6000ft) elevation at the base of still-higher
mountains that form the Continental Divide of
North America. The source of the river is Henry's
Lake, which is a great fishery in its own right.
However, most fly-fishers prefer fishing Harriman
State Park, several miles downstream from the
lake. This is an area of placid waters, with lush
aquatic plants providing cover for rainbow trout.
It is also the home of the 20/20 club. To qualify
for membership you must catch a trout 50cm
(20in) or longer on a fly pattern size 20 or smaller.

Much has been written about this stretch, to
the point that some visitors think these few miles
of the Henry's Fork at Harriman are the most
productive, and also the most demanding test a
fly-fisher can face. It certainly is demanding fishing.
There are upper and lower parts to Henry's Fork,
with the lower sitting at an altitude of about
1700m (5000ft) and running through farm
country, with crops and storage sheds often
coming right up to the edge of the river. Virtually
every one of the 110km (70 miles) or more of the

entire Henry's Fork system supports an abundance
of trout: the most productive stretches hold more
than 1200 trout per kilometer (2000 per mile),
others at least 500 trout per kilometer (about
1000 per mile).

Delicate dry-fly patterns, rods, and lines rated
at 6-weight or lower are all you'll need to fish
Henry's Fork. The 4.5kg (10lb) fish is rare, those
of 25cm (10in) more common. But the possibility
of hooking a fish of 4.5kg (10lb) while you're
fishing trout of indeterminate length and weight is
what brings international fly-fishers back to
Henry's Fork year after year. It is worth the trip.
And if one length is not fishing well when you get
there, move somewhere else. Often, if one
portion of the river is quiet, another portion may
very well be lively indeed.

South Fork

The South Fork of the Snake River is much larger
than Henry's Fork, often running at 10 times the
flow of its more famous sister stream. The volume
determines the type of fishing. The South Fork is a
drift-boat fishery. What amounts to a slightly
redesigned dory carries two fly-fishers and an
oarsman. Fishing from a drift boat is different, so if
you have never fished from one before you should
practice short and cross-body casts (you must not
cast overhead and risk hooking anyone else in the
boat) before you come here.

The South Fork can be demanding in terms of
making accurate casts and learning to read the
local water. Most trout are not in the deepest
water of this big river. They are in "seams" or
"creases" at the edge of big water, or completely
out of the main channel in numerous side
channels. Every day on the South Fork is
an adventure.

The upper stretch of the South Fork runs from
the base of a dam – named Palisades – about
20km (12 miles) south to a little town called Swan
Valley. Eating, lodging, and the all-important
shuttling (a vehicle with boat-trailer attached)
services are available there. The canyon float is

32km (20 miles) of roadless isolation – and i
nothing short of magnificent. You should allow a
long day for this float. The lower South Fork run
through farmland.

Native cutthroat trout still dominate the South
Fork, and they are lots of fun when sipping
mayflies, caddisflies, pale morning duns, blue
winged olives, or grasshoppers. A drift boa
provides fly-fishers on the South Fork with eas
access to shallow riffles in the middle of the bi
river, riffles that wading fishermen can't reach
That's when the lightweight rods (numbers 2–4
come out, and quiet fly-fishers "look for heads.'
However, fly-fishers should be aware that bi
brown trout and rainbows also reside in this bi
river, and that it is possible to take a 50cm (20in
specimen of each species in a single day. It is also

possible to catch and release 40 fish a day. Fish counts on this river run up to 3600 trout per kilometer (6000 per mile). Allocate at least four days to fishing the headwater streams of the Snake, although a week would be better. Allow a minimum of two days per river so that on the second day you can make up for any mistakes you made on the first.

Flies for the Snake River system
The following are some consistent fish producers for the Snake River system. Late May and most of June is the best time to fish stonefly imitations, and many dark patterns work well; size 10 is a good all-round size. Sofa Pillow and Elk Hair style dry flies, numbers 6–10, are effective in broken water. The Western Green Drakes, numbers 10–12, typically

The Snake is one of the world's greatest trout rivers, but it is a challenging one for the fly-fisher.

hatch during the second half of the month into the first week of July. Carry an assortment of caddis dries, too, such as Troth's Elk Hair Caddis and Kaufman's Stimulators, numbers 10–16. The Pale Morning Dun is perhaps the most popular midday hatch, so count on these and Rusty Spinner imitations, numbers 14–20, and try No-Hackle and Comparadun. In July and August, add hoppers, ants, and tricos. For September and October, try small Blue-Winged Olives. Most popular western flies will give results along South Fork. Local favorites include the Girdle Bug.

BRISTOL BAY, ALASKA

JIM TEENY

Anyone who likes to fly-fish should experience Alaska at least once in their lifetime, and Bristol Bay is a great place to start. Millions of salmon, including sockeye, king, and silver, as well as fish such as Arctic grayling, northern pike, rainbow trout, Arctic char, and dolly varden, provide some of the best opportunities for fly-fishing in the world.

My first trip to Alaska was to the Bristol Bay area in 1975. This was to be my once-in-a-lifetime trip to the state. I have been back every year since, and some years I have been back two or three times. When you are thinking of truly great fly-fishing for wild fish, in sometimes unbelievable numbers, Alaska should be first in your thoughts. Take your best fishing dream ever and multiply it by 10. You just might be close to imagining what Alaska is really like.

The Bristol Bay area is about an hour's flight from Anchorage, which makes it remote, yet fairly close to civilization. Even in Alaska, if you want to fish uncrowded great rivers a float plane is a must. For example, great rivers like the Kenai or Russian Rivers are excellent fishing, but when the fish really are running they can be crowded with fly-fishers. So if you can, organize a fly-out trip to get away from the crowds and enjoy a true Alaskan experience. And go to the Bristol Bay region.

Of all the wonderful places you can fish in Alaska, Bristol Bay is probably at or near the top of the list. Every season 15–40 million or more sockeye salmon come into Bristol Bay: the average is probably close to 20–30 million. King salmon, the largest of the world's salmon, come in by the thousands, chum salmon by the hundreds of thousands, and pink salmon by the millions.

Silver salmon, which are fresh from the Pacific and have not yet acquired their spawning colors, are most sought by fly-fishers because they are extremely fast and powerful fighters. Probably my two favorites are sockeye and king salmon. Kings possess great size, strength, and beauty when fresh from the sea. They display energy and power that rival any other freshwater gamefish. They will wear you out during the fight – although, once you have landed and released the fish you will miraculously regain your strength and go back out for more action. When the fish are "on," fly-fishers possess the ability of finding hidden energy reserves from somewhere.

My other favorite fish is the sockeye, simply because, on my first trip to Alaska, the guide and game warden told us the sockeyes were in, but that they wouldn't take the fly. They did, and we were never disappointed. Sockeye salmon have a beauty, speed, power, and jumping ability possessed by no other salmon.

A wealth of fly-fishers' fish

In the Bristol Bay area you will find Arctic grayling, northern pike, rainbow trout, Arctic char, dolly varden, and the five North American species of Pacific salmon. Unlike Atlantic salmon, all Pacific

SEASONS

Generally, June 30– September 15 for salmon. Specific information can be obtained from the Division of Sport Fish, A D F & G 33, Raspberry Road, Anchorage AK 99518-1599. Telephone (907) 267 2220.

PERMITS

Licenses and King Salmon Stamps can be obtained from Dept. of Fish and Game, Licensing Section, PO Box 25525, Juneau, Alaska 99802-5525. Residents or nonresidents under the age of 16 years are exempt. Allow at least two weeks if applying by mail.

salmon will die after spawning. It's part of the life-cycle of the fish, and ensures their offspring can feed on the carcasses of their parents after they have hatched from their eggs the following spring. The mass deaths of salmon are also vitally important for many other animals that scavenge on their dead and dying bodies – the bears, eagles, and other omnivores and carnivorous animals that help make the Alaskan wilderness what it is, and a great and very special place to visit.

As for the timing of the salmon runs, I have found some windows that are quite important if you're planning a trip for certain fish. For example, kings, chums, and sockeyes may start running in from the sea around mid-June (some kings run earlier) and run through the end of July. Peak time seems to be the last week in June through to the third week of July. Remember that good fishing can also be had at either end of the window, depending on the area you may choose to fish. Pink salmon only show up in serious numbers in even-numbered years. There are many times you

might consider these salmon annoying, for example if you are targeting other fish. On average pink salmon run much smaller than other salmon; 1–2kg (2–4lb) for the most part, making the use of a 4-weight outfit lots of fun. The pink-salmon run usually starts in the latter part of July and continues all through August. Coho start up about the beginning of August and begin to peak from mid-August through to mid-September.

Record catches

For size range, kings are truly the largest. A 57kg (126lb) fish was taken many years ago in a commercial net and the rod-caught record (not on fly) is a 44.2kg (97lb 4oz) fish taken from the Kenai River. In almost all areas a fish of more than 23kg (50lb) is the trophy of a lifetime. I've been very fortunate in that three fish over 27kg (60lb) and 14 over 23kg (50lb) have hit the shore on my fly-rod. My biggest in length and girth was a 130 by 82cm (52 by 33in) girth fish: this would have weighed about 31kg (69lb). Chum salmon

average 4–6kg (8–12lb), with anything over 7kg (15lb) considered a big fish. I have landed large chum salmon in the 11kg (25lb) class. Coho salmon average 3–4.5kg (6–10lb) with 6–7kg (12–15lb) a very nice size – you may catch bigger.

The rivers of Bristol Bay

In my travels to Alaska I have found the southeast and Bristol Bay areas to be the most beautiful. Mountains, lakes, rivers, and wildlife all add to the excitement. If you are lucky you will see moose, bear, caribou, and wolf. The premier rivers in the area include the Alagnak. Every year several million fish swim into this river system. Another is the Nushagak River, a big watershed that is truly loaded with big fish. In talking about Bristol Bay it would be improper to ignore the large Illiamna River rainbows. Every year many people travel to Alaska mainly to fish for rainbow trout, for the Illiamna system produces silvery rainbows scaling well over the 4.5kg (10lb) mark. These have grown up in lakes; the rainbows that are resident

If you want to catch wild fish in wild places, Bristol Bay, Alaska, will be just right for you. Salmon, trout, pike, and char all abound.

in the rivers have many more spots and often deep purple-red sides. Northern pike can be found throughout most of the system with quiet back sloughs the most productive areas to fish. There are grayling, rainbow, and northern pike, along with dolly varden and year-round fish in the river systems. Some char and dollies are migratory, like the salmon.

I have wonderful memories from my Alaskan trips, and you should have too. It is well worth taking a good camera and lots of film, because you will be going to one of the most incredible of the world's fly-fishing areas. Bristol Bay has never disappointed me, and it will not disappoint you. Big wild fish, and lots of them, should make this the trip of a lifetime.

STEELHEAD IN BRITISH COLUMBIA

EHOR BOYANOWSKY

Eons ago, the steelhead, a descendant of an ancient polar salmonid, colonized the rivers of the geologically restless land that is British Columbia. Today, wild steelhead — the most beautiful of the migratory species — enter the crystal-clear streams of this, the most westerly Canadian province, in every month of the year.

Discovering this phenomenon as a young migrant fly-fisher from the east, I vowed that I would fish steelhead rivers nowhere else until I had fished all the major streams of British Columbia. Almost a quarter of a century later I must admit delicious defeat. There are just too many waters for one lifetime.

Living in Vancouver, I fished the delightful small mountain streams such as the Seymour, which remains in a wilderness state and has steelhead entering it all year round. There I found solitude and abundant wildlife, with bears, cougars, and mountain goats only 15 minutes from my house. They are still there.

If I wanted to encounter fish — and fly-fishers — in great numbers during the mild Pacific winter, I ventured into the Fraser Valley 80km (50 miles) distant and fished the Chehalis River and the Chilliwack-Vedder, a tumbling rocky stream that meanders after entering lowland farmland. A special joy is the "fly-fishing only" season that begins on May 1 on the Vedder, when there are many fish but few fishers.

However, I am always torn at that time of year, because it is the height of the season on the mighty Squamish, a system of five rivers an hour's drive north of Vancouver. From February to the peak in May when spring freshets engulf the riffles, first a trickle and then sometimes schools of diamond-bright steelhead, each of them weighing 5–14kg (10–30lb), ascend the river to slash at the fly-fishers' flies. On weekdays this can be a wonderfully lonely place, with its chorus of spring avalanches — and logging trucks. Logging has devastated the east bank. However, the Steelhead Society of BC, the province's premier river conservation organization, is working hard (through its Habitat Restoration Corporation) to restore spawning tributaries damaged by logging, and to protect the yet-untouched 32km (20 miles) of the precipitous west bank from the same fate.

Vancouver Island is synonymous with BC steelhead. It is a tragedy that, among the fabled streams flowing east into the Strait of Georgia — Campbell, Salmon, Nanaimo, Nimpkish, Oyster, the Qualicums, Puntledge, Adam, Eve, Tsitika, and Englishman — only the Cowichan retains a reasonable vestige of its original glory. Savage logging practices and, more recently, forces more mysterious at sea have rendered virtually extinct those runs that were already teetering on the brink.

Fortunately, the west coast rivers on the island continue to harbor strong returns with the substantial winter and summer runs of the magnificent Gold River leading the way. The legendary Stamp also has good returns of steelhead; sadly, however, most are hatchery fish chased by crowds of guide boats baitfishing cheek to jowl — not my idea of a good time.

The steelhead odyssey

In summer there is a dream odyssey that fly-fishing members of steelheading's Thirteenth Tribe undertake. It begins with a week on the Dean River, a mainland, mid-coast river that, flowing out of a large lake, starts in its headwaters as a chalkstream and becomes a mighty salmon stream from the impassable falls to its estuary in the fjord, Dean Channel. Beginning in June and peaking in August, mighty steelhead averaging 5.5kg (12 lb) and ranging to 14kg (30lb) or more, make their way like so many thousands of shards of leaping silver, snarling and snapping at flies as they burst over bars and glide through runs, pausing briefly in

Fishing for steelhead in the depths of winter: steelhead run from the Pacific into the rivers of British Columbia throughout much of the year.

the historic pools — historic only in BC terms, as the river was first fished in the 1960s. Because of the Dean's recent rise in popularity, a lottery is used for nonresidents of the province to control the numbers of fly-fishers.

In September, the steelhead odyssey moves north to Skeena River country — a system of rivers flowing into the sea at Prince Rupert. This is perhaps unlike any other river on Earth for beauty, variety of terrain, and fish. Early in the season in low-water years the fly-fisher can fish the mainstem Skeena below the town of Terrace, then follow the steelhead upriver into tributaries such as the Copper, a lovely wild stream, and the Kispiox, a small river in a setting of unsurpassed beauty. The Kispiox boasts the world's largest steelhead — there are reports of specimens of 18kg (40lb), but since the imposition of catch and release, only photographs are available for proof.

The most popular tributary is the Bulkley, a gentle, broad trout stream that wanders through a pastoral valley, which is more evocative of Wordsworth's poetry than grizzly bears — except

for the occasional set of rapids and a 2300m (7000ft) mountain in the background. And the steelhead are very trouty, rising freely to the dry fly. Devotees claim that only a cad would fish for them here with a sinking line.

The most distant and mysterious tributaries are the Babine and Sustut. While the Babine thunders through a steep rift valley patrolled by grizzly bears, with eagles circling overhead, the Sustut, by contrast, is a broad, sweeping stream that is ideal for wading and, until recently, was untouched by the chainsaw. Steelhead to 14kg (30lb) await the fly-fisher.

The mighty Thompson

When the cold winds and frosts descend on the Skeena, faithful fly-fishers head south, below Kamloops where the Thompson River issues forth from the lake to wander among the desiccated cliffs and sagebrush. It is shirtsleeve weather again, and the Thompson steelhead are relentlessly surface-oriented. This is one place in the world where dry flies can beat wet flies and equal bait

when the river is low. The river is massive, with huge, terrifyingly slippery rocks. It is bounded by the Trans-Canada Highway on one bank and by rail lines on both. Publicity has made this a busy river and many lament the crowding. But the Thompson's greatest enemy is the gillnet fishery. By the time the mighty fish leave the Fraser to enter the river at Lytton, gillnets have reduced a run of 20,000 giants to a few thousand.

For all that, when the air is pungent with sagebrush, the bighorn sheep have come down from the mountains to Spence's Bridge, and great fish are pitching and rolling in the Graveyard Pool, there is no place on earth I would rather be.

PERMITS AND FURTHER DETAILS
Permits, and information about fishing sites, can be obtained from the Fisheries Branch, Ministry of Fisheries, 780 Blanshard Street, Victoria, British Columbia V8V 1X4.

BAJA

NICK CURCIONE

In my early teens, when my family moved to Southern California, I thought I had found the fly-fishers' paradise. All that changed, however, when later I discovered the true fly-fishers' paradise – the Baja. Here I found seabirds, marine mammals and fish in abundance.

About 20 million years ago, the region we now know as the Baja California peninsula was part of the Mexican mainland. Gradually, through a series of enormous movements in the Earth, a strip of Mexico's west coast broke free, and the Pacific Ocean flooded in to fill the 1100km (700 mile) trench that lies at the southern end of the San Andreas fault.

Naturalists have referred to Baja as a sea of life surrounded by desert; the variety and abundance of flora, fauna, and marine life make it a veritable biological horn of plenty. In the gulf region alone, there are more than 50 islands and, despite the arid environment, scientists have identified more than 570 plant species. The nutrient-rich waters give rise to an ecosystem teeming with seabirds, marine mammals, and fish in concentrations found nowhere else in the world. Black petrels, Heermann's gulls, and California brown pelicans have established major colonies throughout the region. The largest variety of whales – bluefins, humpbacks, Bryde's, and sperm – regularly

traverse these waters. Of course, of major interest to fly-fishers are the finned creatures that cruise the peninsula. Marine scientists have documented as many as 132 different families of fish, which are represented by more than 800 species. Practically every major species of saltwater gamefish is present here.

My first trip to Baja was in 1959. A pair of my high-school chums had recently fished off Ensenada, a major port city approximately 121km (75 miles) south of the border. After listening to their excited accounts of the fabulous fishing they had enjoyed, I finally made the trip myself.

Down Ensenada way

The Transpeninsular Highway did not exist then and, for all practical purposes, Ensenada was about as far as you could travel without really roughing it. Four-wheel drives were a rarity and no one I knew had access to one. Fortunately it wasn't necessary to venture farther south because the quality of fishing at Ensenada was far beyond most people's expectations. The city was dubbed the yellowtail capital of the world, and for very good reason. At times, yellowtail fishing can be excellent at Mexico's Coronado islands, a relatively short ride for San Diego-based sport fishing boats. But down Ensenada way, especially at Todos Santos Island, you can still find some phenomenal fishing, not only for yellowtails, but also for barracuda, bonito, calico bass, white sea bass, yellowfin tuna, and dorado.

With the completion of the Mexico Highway 1 in 1973, areas were opened up that previously had been fished only by those who had access to private aircraft. As a result of calmer coastal conditions and a more tropical climate, the initial wave of resort development took place primarily at the tip (Cabo San Lucas) and on the Gulf of California side of the peninsula. Today, however, increasing numbers of hotels and marinas are beginning to dot Baja's Pacific coast. It is now possible to reach virtually every region in Baja traveling by boat, plane, or car.

If you choose to drive, do so with caution and common sense. Contrary to some ill-founded reports, there aren't hordes of *banditos* waiting to ambush you when you cross the border. However, Baja can pose some challenging driving conditions and you should be thoroughly prepared before making the trip. Farm animals crisscross the road and, for this reason alone, it is best to avoid driving at night.

Baja is a land of dramatic contrasts, a fact mirrored in its incredibly diverse fishery. Along most of Baja's Pacific coast, from the border all the way south to Guerro Negro, the most readily accessible inshore species for fly-fishers are barred perch, yellowfin croaker, corbina, halibut, and calico bass. Working from a skiff (called a panga), you can augment this line-up with barracuda, bonito, yellowtail, and white sea bass.

The primary dietary items for perch, croaker, and corbina are sandcrabs. Therefore, small 2.5–5cm (1–2in) bonefish type patterns and Clouser Minnows tied on hooks from number

FURTHER DETAILS

A tourist card is necessary. It can be obtained at the border, from Mexican consulates, or from travel agents on production of a valid passport or birth certificate.

● For those 16 years' old or above, a Mexican fishing license is required (obtained from the Mexican Department of Fisheries). When fishing from a commercial passenger-carrying vessel operating in Mexican waters, the license is normally included in the price of the trip.

● If driving from the US, you must secure Mexican insurance for the vehicle (and boat if you are towing one) and a Mexican boat permit. Policies can be purchased at a number of outlets located conveniently near the border crossings.

● Further information is available from the Mexican Department of Fisheries in San Diego. Tel: (619) 233 6956.

4s to 1/0s are a good choice. In addition to simulating sandcrab coloration, which can vary from tan to gray, bright attractor colors such as yellow, orange, and lime green also work well. Depending on surf conditions, 6- to 8-weight outfits with sinking lines are ideal. Stripping baskets are a must when fishing from the shore. Winter months tend to be prime for perch while spring and summer yield the best action on corbina, croaker, halibut, and calicos. A 10-weight outfit is a good choice for most panga fishing, but when targeting yellowtail and white seabass, a 12-weight is more practical. These fish routinely top the 9kg (20lb) mark, inhabit structure-infested water and, particularly in the case of yellows, are exceptionally strong fighters. Deceivers and Clousers from 50–125mm (2–5in) long on 1/0 to 3/0 hooks will cover a variety of skiff fishing conditions. All-white, blue/white, and blue/green are productive color combinations.

With the absence of a turbulent surf and its more estuary-like setting, the Gulf of California side of Baja is more hospitable to shorebound fly-fishers. The variety of gamefish that cruise the coast could fill a marine biology textbook. Some of the more popular species are jacks, ladyfish, sierra, needlefish, pompano, pargo, and the greatest prize of all, roosterfish.

The Gulf of California is productive all year long, but there are some seasonal fluctuations worth noting. Winter months are generally best for sierra, while late spring and summer will see more consistent action on ladyfish and roosters. However, regardless of season, a critical factor is the time of day you choose to fish. Particularly on the Gulf of California side, where tidal surges are not as dramatic as on the Pacific, the best fishing coincides with periods of minimal light intensity. Early morning before the sun hits the horizon is a prime time to present your offerings. Baitfish congregate close to shore during low-light periods and their pursuers are seldom far behind.

Initially, the gamefish that brought Baja the most notoriety were billfish, primarily in the form

If you fish the waters surrounding the Baja peninsula, you can never tell what will take your fly next, so great is the variety of fish inhabiting its waters.

of sails and striped and blue marlin. These species and many others, such as dorado, tuna, and wahoo, are available to bluewater fly-fishers in Baja. From just south of La Paz to the tip of the peninsula at Cabo San Lucas, striped marlin, wahoo, yellowfin tuna, and dorado are present all year. Sailfish and blue and black marlin are more abundant when the temperature soars, typically from late June to early October. Because of its location at the southernmost tip of the peninsula, Cabo San Lucas (the Cape), at the confluence of the Pacific and the Gulf of California, is the most consistently productive spot. One school of fish may be migrating into the gulf while another is making its way out. Either way, there is always some worthy adversary eager to take your fly.

TROUT FISHING IN NEW ZEALAND

JOHN GODDARD

*Since their introduction to New Zealand in the 19th century, trout have established
fast-growing populations that attract fly-fishers from around the world.
If you want to catch that elusive double-figure wild brown trout, you are
more likely to succeed here than you are anywhere else on Earth.*

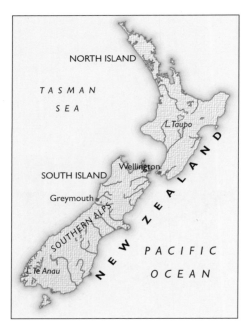

Trout were first introduced to the Antipodes in the last quarter of the 19th century. After much trial and error the first successful batches of brown trout eggs (from Scotland's Loch Leven) were received in a hatchery in Tasmania following a long sea voyage. Later, eggs from the Tasmanian trout stocks were taken to the North Island of New Zealand, and other eggs were imported directly from Britain. Within a year or so, eggs were also received from steelhead stocks from the western rivers of the United States.

The crystal-clear lakes, rivers, and streams flowing out of the many mountainous areas of both North and South Islands provided the perfect sanctuary for both brown and rainbow trout. They thrived and grew to enormous size. By the end of the first quarter of the 20th century the trout fishing in New Zealand had reached its peak, and was absolutely fabulous. In 1926 Zane Grey, the American author and fisherman, made his first extended visit to fish there, and later described his experiences in *The Angler's Eldorado*. In those halcyon days both brown and rainbow trout had to

be well over the 4.5kg (10lb) mark before they were even worth a mention. Apart from the very large average size of the trout at the time, Zane Grey also wrote in his book about the large numbers of trout that they caught nearly every day throughout his visit. As a result of this a myth very quickly became established – that even a tyro could catch numbers of very big trout in a day on any New Zealand river he chose to fish.

This is, of course, very far from the truth, as Zane Grey failed to point out that most of his fishing took place on the Tongariro River during the winter months. At this time of the year vast numbers of both brown and rainbow (steelhead) trout travel up the river from Lake Taupo to spawn in the Tongariro's headwaters. Even today, at that time of the year on the Tongariro a competent fly-fisher can expect to catch upward of a dozen trout a day, which will probably average around the 2kg (4lb) mark.

While fishing in New Zealand during these winter months can be very exciting and very rewarding, it is very restricted because most rivers are closed. Only those rivers (including the Tongariro) that have a winter run of steelhead may be fished. Consequently these rivers become quite crowded, with as many as 10 fly-fishers having to share each pool.

The best fishing

I recommend that the fly-fisher planning to make a first visit to New Zealand consider the summer instead of the traditionally more popular winter months. The season opens in October and, while dry-fly fishing is probably best during this month and November, the weather is often cold and wet. But it does depend on how your luck is running, for I have experienced some lovely warm sunny days during these months. Avoid December and early January, as at Christmas all Kiwis are on holiday; because most of them fish there is a lot of pressure on the rivers. February and March are excellent months for visitors, as the weather is usually more settled, particularly in North Island.

While the fishing is probably better and certainly more varied in South Island, where brown trout predominate, the weather can be more unpredictable, with the chance of often heavy and prolonged rain, especially along the west coast and in the Southern Alps. This is a great pity, as some of the best rivers in the country are in these areas. Many times over the years I have arrived in either Greymouth or Te Annau only to be greeted by torrential rain, with all the rivers in flood. When

this happens it pays to be mobile so that you can retreat back over the Southern Alps to the Central Plateau, where drier conditions can often be found.

The trout fishing in both islands is very similar, with the emphasis on being able to spot trout in the gin-clear waters, then having the ability to choose the correct dry fly or nymph, and then being able to present the fly both accurately and delicately. Don't forget that in New Zealand you are dealing with wild fish, and most of them will allow you but one mistake. It should also be noted that the fishing can be very physically demanding, because the better fishing is always in the less accessible areas. This usually means long tramps over rough, hilly, or mountainous country, often finishing with a tough descent into a gorge. But the rewards are often worth the effort, as a competent fly-fisher should take four or five trout per day averaging 2kg (4lb) or better.

Finding the hot-spots

Lake fishing is physically far less demanding, and as there is a wealth of excellent lakes in both islands it

SEASON

October 1 to April 30, except for certain rivers (e.g,, Tongariro), which are open all year round.

PERMITS

Permits can be obtained from New Zealand Tourist Offices in all major towns and cities. All fishing equipment brought into the country must be sterilized.

will certainly pay the visiting fly-fisher to spend at least some time on these. Again, most lake fishing consists of sight-fishing from the shore and, as most of these lakes are large, the secret of success lies in finding the hot-spots. This is where a guide can make the difference between success and failure on both lakes and rivers. Without one you may find that you waste most of your holiday fishing sterile water. Unfortunately guides are expensive, even in New Zealand, but I would advise visiting fly-fishers to hire a guide for at least

a few days during their visit. Most guides have four-wheel-drive vehicles for getting into the less accessible areas. Also, for a price, they can arrange transport by helicopter to wilderness areas where, if conditions are right, you will have a day's fishing to remember.

If money is no object and you wish to be assured of success, arrange to spend two or three weeks at a New Zealand fishing lodge. Most offer excellent accommodation and food, your own personal fishing guide, and helicopter trips into the many fabulous wilderness rivers.

If you want to catch that elusive double-figure wild brown trout, you are more likely to succeed in New Zealand than in any other country in the world. Give it a try before you are too old to climb down some of those formidable gorges.

The tranquility of a New Zealand
dawn on Lake Moana, and the
fly-fisher awaits with anticipation
the first trout of the day.

THE SALMON RIVERS OF NORWAY

THORBJORN TUFTE

*Alta, Tana, Namsen, Gaula, Orkla, Vosso, Laerdal, Suldal — these are the names
of the mighty salmon rivers of Norway, and there are many more. These rivers
have been places of pilgrimage for salmon fishers for almost 200 years. In
Norway you have the chance of catching a really big salmon on the fly.*

Some might say that when nature created
Norway a salmon fisher was involved in the
planning. From its border with Sweden in the
southeast, then north and west along the coast to
the Arctic Circle, and finally eastward to the
Russian border, the coastline measures 20,000km
(12,500 miles), and is indented by long, sinuous
fjords. Although tourists come to gaze at the
fjords, fly-fishers are more interested in the rivers
that flow into them, for these rivers wash down
from high mountains, where melting snow keeps
them full of cool, clear water throughout the short
summer. It is the cool, clear waters that make
these great salmon rivers. And there are almost
400 of them.

It was early in the 19th century that pioneering
British fly-fishers made the relatively long journey
across the North Sea and discovered the salmon
rivers. They arrived in Norway at a time when the
Norwegians themselves had no idea about rods,
reels, and artificial flies. The salmon that the
Norwegians needed for food were taken by
means of gaffs, or by building fences into the river
to lead the running fish to traps. Yet the
Norwegians learned quickly that the salmon has a
value beyond food. Today salmon fishing is a

thriving industry, centered on fishing hotels,
camps, and lodges. Many Norwegians act as
guides for visiting fly-fishers, and very many more
enjoy fishing their native rivers.

Of the great Norwegian salmon rivers the Tana
is the greatest of all. Each year fish run
250km (150 miles) from the sea at Tanafjord and
300km (190 miles) in wet years when there is
sufficient water for them to leap Suorbmofossen.
The Tana system has 1058km (680 miles) of
salmon water, including tributaries. The run of fish
includes many thousands of grilse as well as lots of

two- and three-sea-winter salmon. In 1928 the
Tana yielded what is still the world record for
Atlantic salmon, a fish of 36kg (80lb). This river
remains one of the very few where a 20kg (44lb)
salmon might still take your fly. One estimate
indicates that at least 20,000 salmon are caught in
the Tana each year.

If the Tana is the mightiest Norwegian salmon
river, then the Alta is the queen, and the greatest
when it comes to fly-fishing. It has long been
known in Norway as the home for big fish. The
average weight is close to 10kg (22lb), and fish of

about 20kg (44lb) are caught most years. Local residents are entitled to 90 per cent of the fishing on Alta's 44km (27 miles) of salmon water, but visitors may apply for one of the very few licenses for fishing during the period July 1 to August 31. It is a lucky man or woman who has a friend in the town of Alta, for that is the key to fishing this wonderful river.

Incidentally, the visitor to Finnmark should note that all other salmon rivers in the region are owned by the state and that the Alta is the exception. In practice this means that Finnmark rivers are open for everyone, and that you may purchase a permit (usually from the local fishing club). So forget the Alta if you cannot get a permit. In this northern part of the country you can travel around and fish salmon rivers of almost equal importance without the need to make any reservations in advance. And there are some super rivers, such as the Borselv, Komagelv, Kongsfjordelva, and Lakselv (which is reputed to have produced a 32kg (70lb) salmon to rod and line). In the other parts of Norway, and certainly on the great rivers in the country, book well in advance of your visit to avoid disappointment.

SEASONS

On most rivers, June 1 to August 31.

PERMITS AND FURTHER DETAILS

Each year Nortrabooks (of Nortra Produksjon AS, Oslo) produces *Angling in Norway: A Comprehensive Guide to Fishing Facilities.* This publication will give you all the information you need to plan your visit.

Of Norway's 400 salmon rivers, about 200 are important and, by most standards, they are great rivers. However, only a few of these can be referred to as mighty. These are scattered the length of the country and, except for a very few including the Alta and Laerdal, all of them are readily available for the visiting fly-fisher.

The Gaula has 95km (60 miles) of salmon fishing between the sea at Trondheim Fjord and the impassable Egga Foss. In recent years fly-fishers have landed between 17,000 and 25,000kg (37,500 and 55,000lb) of salmon from this river, equivalent to about 4000 fish. Salmon run about

70km (40 miles) of the Orkla, and more than 2000 fish are caught each year. The middle beats are the best, and July is the prime month.

On the 50km (30 miles) of river from the impassable Nustadfoss down to the sea, the Stjordal is an excellent salmon and sea trout river. It produces about 2000 salmon and 1000 sea trout per year. Salmon will weigh on average about 3kg (7lb), and some will weigh over 10kg (22lb). While most sea trout will scale up to 2kg (4lb), the record is 14.5kg (32lb).

The Namsen is a huge waterway where, on the wider, lower stretches, fishing is mainly by harling (towing or trailing flies or bait from a boat). But upstream from Grong the river is narrower and more suited to conventional fly-fishing. About 3000 salmon, averaging 5kg (11lb), are taken from 60km (40 miles) of river in the short, three-month season. And each year trophy fish of 20–25kg (44–55lb) are caught. The river record is 31.6kg (69lb). Incidentally, most great rivers have lesser tributaries where the fishing is usually less expensive and easier to arrange. The Namsen is no exception: the Bjora River is only 4.5km (3 miles) long, has an average annual catch of 250 salmon, and produces some very big ones – the record is 31kg (68lb).

The Suldal River is 22km (14 miles) long, and is fed by a large lake, Suldalsvatn. It is also one of Norway's more southerly salmon rivers, and remains open until September 30. While some very big salmon have been caught here – the record being 25kg (55lb) – most of the annual catch of up to 1300 fish average 5kg (11lb).

Unfortunately some of Norway's rivers and two of its mighty rivers, the Vosso and the Laerdal, have suffered in recent years and are no longer open for fly-fishing. Acid rain from industrial Europe has ruined several rivers in the southwest, including the Vosso, and the salmon stocks in rivers such as the Laerdal have been destroyed by a parasite, *Gyrodactylus*. Attempts are being made to rectify the situation, but check the latest information when planning your visit.

For the great and mighty rivers, I recommend a 4.5–4.8m (15–16ft) rod with number 10–12 line (floating, intermediate, or sinking, depending on water conditions). Flies from 7.5cm (3in) tubes and Waddington Shanks, down to size 12 trebles and doubles are required. In August, dry fly and nymph are effective on a double-handed rod for grilse and sea trout.

Norway's mighty rivers have lots of salmon and, among them, some very big fish. This, the Alta River, is one of the best for fly-fishing for salmon.

FINLAND

OLIVER EDWARDS

Finland is a country of vast coniferous forests, spangled with thousands of lakes and clean, clear rivers, which teem with salmon, trout, grayling, and whitefish. This is truly a place for the dedicated fly-fisher who is capable of changing fly and tactics to cope with changing water conditions.

Finland is a long landmass, bordered on its eastern flank by Russia and on its western by the Gulf of Bothnia, Norway, and Sweden. From the air you look down on a landscape of forest and water – an exciting scene for any fly-fisher making a first visit. There is so much water. In fact, Finland boasts an incredible 186,000 lakes of more than 200ha (500 acres). Some, such as Inari, are vast inland seas, and they all have fish, lots of fish, since Finland has little pollution.

Approximately one-quarter of Finland is within the Arctic Circle where, in summer, there is no night. This is Finnish Lapland, the land of the Sami people and their reindeer.

The history of fly-fishing in Finland begins early in the 19th century, when many British sportsmen spent the summer fishing there. But the Finns themselves are mainly spin-fishers, and it is only recently that fly-fishing has become popular. Today about 100,000 people out of a total population of 5.7 million are keen fly-fishers.

Central Finland appears to be half water and half forest. Many of the lakes are huge and not particularly good for fly-fishing. The great fly-fishing is provided by the many beautiful fast-flowing rocky rivers that flow between the lakes. Here there are big predatory brown trout that leave their lairs to pursue the prolific baitfish, bleak, and dace. For these trout you might try a large streamer or baitfish pattern and pull this through the water on a fast-sinking fly-line. Be prepared: these trout will often grow larger than 5kg (11lb) in weight. In the turbulent fast river they are a match for the best tackle.

There are also good fly hatches here, and large populations of shrimp, nymphs, and larvae living among the riverbed boulders. Fish dry fly in the hatch, or a weighted nymph with a sinking leader when the insects are not hatching, and your efforts may well be rewarded with some lovely grayling and fine trout (both brown and, in some rivers, introduced rainbows). The best centers for these are Viitasaari, Saarijarvi, and Rautalampi.

Northeast Finland

This area includes the wonderful rivers of the Kuusamo area. The town of Kuusamo is about 30km (19 miles) from the Russian border. Two truly fabulous rivers, the Kitka and Kuusinki, flow across the border to vast lakes on the Russian side. Big, feisty "Russian" trout run from the lakes to spawn in the rivers around Kuusamo – and they are big. Fish approaching 10kg (22lb) have been landed on fly outfits and some well in excess of that have been lost after a hard scrap. You should catch several fish in at least the 1–5kg (2–11lb) category, but expect to hook into something bigger.

Big streamers and baitfish imitations are most often used, but outsize dry flies and nymphs will also work. These will also take some excellent grayling, but beef up your tippet strength and double-check your knots.

Inside the Arctic Circle

In northern Finland you are fishing in the home of the Lapps. You are now well inside the Arctic Circle and will have noticed how the pine forests have thinned out as you drove north, and that much of the countryside is clothed with silver birch. Occasionally, you might see a reindeer: be careful when you are driving, because reindeer have no road sense and are a major cause of road accidents. Your destination is the Teno River (Tana in Norwegian, since here in the north this river is the border between the two countries.)

For the 80km (50 miles) down to Utsjoki, the Teno is fly-fishers' heaven. This is famed Atlantic salmon territory and, while fly-fishing is practiced, harling (towing or trailing flies from a boat), or trolling a spinner or plug from the back of a long, narrow, shallow-draft boat is the most popular way of fishing this huge river.

However, in the "flats" the river is often 200m (650ft) wide, and the shallow current flows over a fine gravel or pebble bed that offers splendid wading for the fly-fisher. The wide flats heave with grayling. The smooth water surface can be alive with fish rising to take hatching caddisflies or a fall

of midges. If it is your first visit, be warned. You will find the sight of so many grayling making pigs of themselves so exciting that you will fumble about as you tackle up, and you will certainly tie at least one knot badly. Turn away from the spectacle and concentrate on making sure that you set everything up properly, and then feast your eyes on the fish. Even if nothing is rising, try a dry fly on the flats, for the fish are very obliging and you will get quick action. Slowly wade out, casting as you go. Don't make long casts –

SEASONS

Remember that most rivers and lakes are iced over until April (May in the north) and that fishing continues until September. And when planning your visit contact the Finnish Sportfishing Association (FSA), which will direct you to the water most suited to your needs.

PERMITS

Contact the Finnish Sportfishing Association, SUKL, PL12, FIN-00271 Helsinki, Finland.

perhaps 10–15m (30–50ft) – and concentrate on preventing the fly from dragging unduly. Work the water around you before moving on.

After perhaps 500m (1600ft) of shallow flats the river will flow into a stretch of rapids (*koski* in Finnish), or the flow and depth might be increased considerably by a tributary joining the main river. The bottom will then become rocky, with big boulders and, sometimes, outcrops of bedrock. You can still wade, but take care. These *koski* are the main salmon lies and you may cast a fly for them if you wish, but you do not need to rely on the salmon for rod-bending excitement. The grayling fishing in the *koski* is quite outstanding. In fact, it could be described as fabulous, because most fly-fishers fish for salmon, so the grayling will have never seen a fly before!

On my first visit, at Laevvajoki, I had my two most memorable days of grayling fishing. Fishing with heavy nymphs on my first visit, I landed five grayling in five casts, and each grayling was larger than any I had previously caught anywhere in the world. We didn't weigh them, but quickly measured their lengths: 50, 49, 47, 47, and 46cm (20, 19½, 18¾, 18¾, and 18¼in). On the second

Aykoski, in central Finland, is just one of this northern country's great rivers for trout and grayling.

visit, two Scandinavian friends and I landed and released more than 100 grayling, the majority exceeding 40cm (16in), many touching 48–49cm (19–19½in) in length. The fighting quality of grayling in the Teno is quite incredible, and several times I found myself hard pressed to subdue the larger fish in less than 10 minutes. (At home in England a minute would be a long time.) I like to land fish quickly so that they recover quickly when I return them, and my number 5-weight rod was bent like the proverbial hoop all the time. These are phenomenal fish.

Finland offers unspoiled countryside, with vast amounts of beautiful, unexploited waters where tourists do not venture. Go there soon, while it is still like that. Take weight number 4–6 outfits for the trout and grayling, and number 9–11 if you fancy having a shot at the salmon. The Finns are lovely, accommodating, friendly people, and the fishing is reasonably priced and readily available.

SCOTLAND'S WILD TROUT LOCHS

LESLEY CRAWFORD

*Loch trout fly-fishing can be found the length and breadth of Scotland, including
the outlying islands such as Orkney, Shetland, and the Hebrides. The main proliferation
of wild trout waters lies in the Highland Region, and as a very general guide,
the farther north you go the better the gamefishing becomes.*

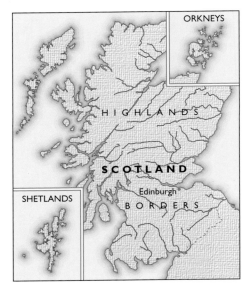

The country of Scotland sits proudly atop the United Kingdom, and although comparatively small in size, it is a land of dramatic contrasts. Traveling north, the rolling hills and the gentle farmlands of the Borders give way to the bustling industrialized central belt. From there modern road systems speed you up to *Braveheart* country, with its beautiful Trossachs, and then on towards the rugged mountains and heathery glens of the Scottish Highlands.

Wild brown trout have been at the center of Scotland's fly-fishing heritage for centuries, and strains of Scottish trout are now found worldwide, having in the past been exported as far away as New Zealand. The indigenous trout are extremely adaptable, growing to a size sustained by the amount of food available in their own loch. So in those lochs where food is sparse they may reach only a few ounces in weight, whereas in more productive lochs they may grow to several pounds. Their fighting qualities are unsurpassed; even a 500g (8oz) fish makes for heart-pounding work on light tackle, and the contrasting markings of this elegant fish are an absolute delight. Depending on where you fish you may meet with

the black asterisk-spotted, silver-flanked "Leven" strain, said to emanate from the world renowned Loch Leven near Edinburgh, or the widespread deeply spotted "fario" strain recognized by the faint blue-green tinge on the gill covers and its sprinkling of black-and-red spots along golden flanks. There is also the chance of catching the "ferox" strain – larger, powerful trout that can attain weights that are well in excess of 4.5kg (10lb). But whatever type you encounter, the beauty of all Scottish trout demands respect. Populations of brownies are found throughout most of our rivers and lochs, but – if you are visiting Scotland for the first time – for great sport in fabulous scenery, head for a few of the many thousands of lochs in the Highlands and Islands.

The lochs

In choosing which lochs to visit, you should bear in mind the differing environmental characteristics of Scotland's numerous freshwaters. Our lochs range from limpid, alkaline shallow waters where the trout grow fat on shrimp and caddisflies, to dark, acidic mountain tarns, where feeding on stonefly and midge is the norm. The surrounding geology of any loch exerts a critical influence on the size of fish caught: lochs lying on limestone or the machair of the Hebrides are the most productive in terms of trout food and growth. But appearances can be deceptive, for even in apparently remote, barren, mountainous Highland areas there are many fertile waters holding some very large trout.

Because of the number of Scottish lochs available for fishing (Sutherland alone has over 2000 lochs) it is important to set your priorities in advance of your trip. Do you want challenging, difficult "big fish" waters, or confidence-building lochs almost bursting at the seams with speckled trout eager to snatch at your fly?

Most fly-fishers like a mixed selection, and whatever fishing region you choose, from the Borders to Caithness, your every need will almost certainly be accommodated.

Scotland is not only home to some spectacular trout, it is also the birthplace of the technique of fishing known as "lochstyle." Obviously if you are fishing Scottish wild waters for the first time you are likely to want to try the traditional local method, and accordingly you should arm yourself with a light 3m (10ft) carbon rod, floating and intermediate lines, 2kg (4lb) nylon, and a selection of bushy size 10/12 flies, including wet flies such as the Soldier Palmer, Zulu, and Invicta variants. These wet patterns do not represent any particular natural insect and are principally "attractors." designed to stimulate curiosity and aggression in the trout.

Fishing tactics

Tactics for using this equipment, either from the bank or in front of a drifting boat, fall into traditional "top of the water" fishing with a floating line. Use teams of wet flies (normally three) around 1.2m (4ft) apart on the leader, cast these out and bring them back with a moderate to fast retrieve until the flies are about 6m (20ft) away. Then raise the rod-tip and dibble the bushy top dropper on the water surface to attract any feeding trout. Given the right conditions this technique can be universally successful throughout Scotland. However, in more difficult circumstances I favor using only one or two flies fished with a moderate to slow "twitched" retrieve on a long

SEASONS

March 15–October 6 for wild brown trout (the best months, which vary according to area, are normally April to mid-September).

PERMITS

Permits (usually inexpensive) are normally required. Ask locally at tackle shops, hotels, tourist office,s and so on. Tourist information centers also provide a selection of area fly-fishing guidebooks.

leader, with around 1.8m (6ft) between flies. I also prefer the variation of using a dry fly such as a dry Wickham's Fancy or Sedge variant on the top dropper and a sunk wet on the point. My two flies then act as if they are unrelated, and work at completely different depths to cover more options, rather than constantly whipping three flies back through the water at about the same depth.

It is vital however, whatever method of lochstyle you choose to use, that you work your flies around where the fish are lying. And you should always try to place your cast just where the shallow water begins to deepen. Any weed beds, promontories, rocky shelves, collections of boulders, old fences, or walls will help to break up the uniformity of the water surface and harbor trout food. So you should concentrate your first efforts near these.

Scotland's wild trout are territorial and do not move around in schools. Each trout will have its own selected lie next to convenient sources of food and shelter, so whether you are boat or bank fishing, in order to be successful you must keep moving and covering new trout lies.

The biggest challenge in Scottish loch fishing for wild trout comes not so much from the fish but from the influences of the prevailing conditions. Scotland's weather is notoriously fickle and can play havoc with the best laid plans, so for best results adopt a flexible approach. In calmer, bright water conditions try fishing an intermediate line with a bright wet fly such as a Dunkeld on the point, and a small dry fly such as a Wickham's (size 14–16) on the top dropper for any surface-feeding fish. When dull, rainy, and/or windy conditions prevail use larger dark patterns such as the Zulu, Bibio, Kate McLaren, Claret

Much pioneering work into lake fly-fishing has taken place on the varied and wild trout lochs of Scotland.

Bumble, or Clan Chief on either floating or intermediate line. Matching the hatch is not always required, as the wild loch trout are opportunistic feeders. Only in the most food-rich lochs (for example the machair lochs of the Hebrides or the limestone lochs of Durness) are the trout selective feeders. Anything from damselflies, mayflies, stoneflies, midge, sedge, or craneflies, to nymphs, sticklebacks, caddisflies, shrimp, or snails is happily taken. Most seasoned fly-fishers favor using first lochstyle wet-fly tactics, but should these fail they will then experiment with imitative dry-fly or nymph fishing.

Go thou and do likewise.

THE ENGLISH CHALKSTREAMS

MAJOR SIDNEY VINES

The countryside of the English chalkstream is not spectacular countryside like that of the Alps. Rather, it is quiet, soft, and gentle. For those who live and work in cities and suffer the "sick hurry and divided aims" of modern life, it is balm for the spirit. It is also part of fly-fishing history, where we rub shoulders with fly-fishers of a bygone age.

As Dermot Wilson stalked a trout, I watched, keeping well back from the river. We were spending a day together (a happy day, as it always was) on the upper Wiltshire Avon below Amesbury – water that we had both known and loved for more than 30 years. We were on a gentle bend, and a fish was rising regularly on the far bank, below a clump of meadowsweet. It was not easy, because of the problem of drag. A fish here, in steadier water beyond the main flow, would never take a dragging fly. Dermot liked such a challenge. Indeed, he would often ignore fish that were in a straightforward position. "Not that one," he would say. "It's too easy." I thought, when I first knew him, that he was shooting me a line, but far from it. He was very gifted, a natural athlete with a good eye.

He approached the fish slowly, crouching low, and then knelt by the bank. He began to cast, slowly extending line. Just before the fly landed, he flicked a "mend" into the line, so that it fell in an upstream loop. This prevented the fly dragging as soon as it landed, which would have scared the fish off. Now, with that little mend, it would float freely for a yard or so before drag took over. The fly landed, soft as thistledown, a foot or so above the fish, which immediately rose and took it.

Dermot did not so much strike as tighten the line, without fuss, and the fish was firmly on. He netted it after a brief fight, keeping the head of the fish above water as he did so to lessen its struggles. It was a lovely golden Avon trout of about 700g (1½lb) – a worthy reward for a perfect piece of chalkstream fishing, elegantly done.

Dermot was one of those, as gifted with the pen as with the rod, whose lives have enriched the chalkstreams. In 1957 he published his classic book *Fishing the Dry Fly.* For while fly-fishing is rich in its literature, the chalkstreams are richest of all.

There are two kinds of writer. In the first group are those who propound new theories, such as F M Halford (1844–1914) the father of the dry fly, sometimes accused (unfairly in my opinion) as the archetypal dry fly snob. Later came G E M Skues (1858–1949) who discovered that fish took hatching nymphs in the surface film, and finally Frank Sawyer (1906–80), who discovered that fish took the nymph below the surface, while it was ascending to hatch. Sawyer's Pheasant Tail nymph, which he designed to imitate the sunk nymph, is used all over the world, wherever fly-fishing is practiced. These three are the great originators.

The second group of writers are those who write to share the joys of fishing the chalkstreams: men such as Arthur Ransome, master of elegant prose, John Waller Hills, whose writing lets us see what the Test was like in its great days, or Harry Plunket Greene, who fished the little Hampshire Bourne with a band of friends in the early days of the 20th century.

Dermot Wilson, who died in 1996, belongs to this illustrious band; his writings enliven our long winter evenings when we all feel, with Brian Clarke, that "the close season lasts so long."

Southern chalkstreams

The southern chalkstreams flow in four counties – Rivers Test and Itchen (Hampshire), Avon (Wiltshire), Frome (Dorset), and Kennet (Berkshire). These are the major rivers, but there are also about 20 tributaries, such as the Wylye, Anton, and Lambourne, which are important fisheries in their own right. There are more than 1600km (1000 miles) of chalkstreams available in the four counties. In addition, the geological quirks have resulted in a fine chalkstream, the Stour, in north Kent, and another, the Driffield Beck, in Yorkshire. They are, as may be imagined, highly prized and carefully preserved by local fly-fishers.

The popularity of chalkstreams

Why are the chalkstreams so popular? First, these rivers flow through some of the loveliest countryside in all England. Second, they have great fly hatches and they are the traditional home of the dry fly, which is the acme of fly-fishing. The thrill never fades – and I speak after doing it for 40 years. The reason, of course, is that fly-fishers can see everything as it happens. They see the fish lying in the crystal clear water, and they see it making little darts to take a real fly. They even see its mouth opening. And if they are wary enough to get close enough, and to cast accurately with a fly

SEASONS

The seasons vary from river to river, but are generally May 1 to September 30 for trout fishing, June 15 to December 31 (some to March 15) for grayling.

PERMITS

Chalkstream fishing is often expensive. Twenty million people live within a couple of hours of the southern chalkstreams. But for those of us who do not have deep pockets, do not despair. Day tickets are available for those who wish to dip a toe in and see what the chalkstreams are like. Check with current UK fly-fishing magazines and local tackle shops. The Salisbury and District Angling Club (29 New Zealand Avenue, Salisbury, Wilts SP2 7JX) has about 16km (10 miles) on the Avon and Wylye.

Dermot Wilson fishing the River Test, a trout stream that every fly-fisher would love to fish at least once. To fly-fisher Oliver Kite the Test was the "Rolls-Royce of trout streams."

that the fish likes, they will have the supreme moment of seeing the fish rise, open its mouth, and take the fly.

Nymph fishing, like dry-fly fishing, has its origins here on the chalkstreams. Upstream nymphing requires more skill than dry-fly because there is a third dimension – depth. The dry fly floats in the one surface plane. The artificial nymph must swim down past the fish at the right depth, where the fish can see it. To achieve this is a matter of fine judgment. When the fish takes, all you see is a slight check on the cast, and you must strike like lightning, for as soon as the fish tastes the nymph it will eject it.

The fish that Dermot Wilson caught, as related in my opening paragraph, was a brown trout, which is the natural denizen of the chalkstreams. It is a magnificent fish, both to look at, and in its fighting qualities. Some rivers are now stocked with rainbow trout from the fish-farm. I do not think rainbows should have any place on chalkstreams. Nature has given us the brown trout. It behoves us to cherish it. The third fish to be found on the chalkstreams is the grayling, also of the salmonid family, which rises freely to the fly. It gives good sport, especially in the fall when the trout are preparing to spawn.

Choosing a dry fly

Which dry fly to use? If you visit a tackle shop, you will see a bewildering and tempting array. The best fly-fishers I have known used only a few flies.

Dermot Wilson used the Beacon Beige. Oliver Kite used his Kite's Imperial. There are times, of course, when the fish can be maddeningly choosy, but generally it is the way that the fly is presented that is all important, and not the pattern of fly. The fly should float high on the water, standing up on its hackles, and swim down naturally, without drag. But even more important – the fish must not have seen you.

GREAT TROUT LOUGHS OF IRELAND

JOHN TODD

Corrib, Conn, Mask, Melvin, and Erne — these are the famous five, the greatest wild trout loughs of Ireland. Their awesome size and the majestic scenery surrounding them make them very special places to fish. So too does their place in the history of fly-fishing, for trout have been taking the fly here for over 300 years.

There are other great loughs in Ireland, such as Carra, Sheelin, Arrow, Ennel, and Owel, but they are not quite as special as the famous five, where finding the trout is a fly-fishing challenge and handling the boat in a high wind and big wave a test of seamanship.

And then the trout: big lusty trout abound in most of the great loughs. Trout with yellow bellies, red spots, and pink flesh that, with a summer salad, are the match of any salmon. On Melvin there are special trout — the gray, black-finned sonaghen that lives in the deeps, and the brilliantly colored red-and-orange, spotted gillaroo that haunts the sun-dappled shallows.

The mayfly season

Mayfly time is possibly the period for which the great loughs are best known. And, to be sure, it can be a wonderful time. To drift a big wave along a rocky tree-lined shore with the fish rising to the green drake is an experience that is hard to beat. Three pounds of trout slash at your Golden Olive Bumble, and you feel its power as you set the hook and it pulls hard on the rod-tip, stripping line from the singing reel. But then, in the evening, the wind drops, the lough calms to the lightest of ripples and the spent gnat begins to fall in vast numbers. Now, in the half-light, the really big fish start to feed in earnest and you sneak the boat into a position from which you can cover them easily. A trout rises to take a natural, and you drop your artificial into the ring-of-the-rise. Up again comes that trout. You must not be too quick on the strike or you will drag the fly from the open mouth of the fish. Get it right and you may well find yourself playing the fish of a lifetime.

But mayfly time is not the only time when it is worth coming across the water to Ireland. Trout will rise the season through on the great loughs, and you will catch them if you have the right flies. The season starts with the duck-fly fishing. Duck-fly are what we call the big midges and these begin hatching at the water surface, bringing up the trout with them, from mid March right through April and into May. Then the lake olives start to hatch and give sport up to the start of the mayfly. The mayfly season lasts well into June (sometimes hatches continue into July, and on Conn trout will take mayflies into August.) Now the weather takes control. Unless there are strong winds and an Atlantic sky, in high summer the best of the fishing is late in the evening when the big sedges — murroughs, green peters, and speckled peters — are running about on the dark lake surface. On warm still nights the sedges might be "on" and the trout rising to beyond midnight. Forget the Guinness, and keep with the trout. With the drop in temperature in September, the trout will be feeding through the day. They may be taking small sedges, or olives, or duck-flies. But if you are lucky they will be taking daddy-long-legs, blown onto the water from the surrounding cow pastures. You can have some great sport with the cork-bodied Rogan's Daddy in September, and have plenty of time left for the Guinness!

There is something traditional about fishing the great Irish loughs. That tradition has a lot to do with the flies we use, many of which were invented more than a century ago. A big old clip fly-box, full of jewels such as the Black Pennell, Connemara Black, Mallard and Claret, Dark Claret, Fiery Brown, Duckfly, Red Arrow, Sooty Olive, Golden Olive, and Claret Bumbles, Kingsmill, and wet mayflies such as the Lough Erne Gosling, Melvin Gosling, French Partridge, Green Mayfly, and Straddlebug, is a joy to behold. You can try new-fangled flies: things like the Gray Wulff — an excellent fly to use at mayfly time— and the Cul de Canard — a great fly to use when the trout are taking duck-flies, olives, or small sedges.

The great loughs are fished from boats: you are wasting your time if you try to fish from the shore. Weather conditions can play a huge part in

the decision about when you can fish and where the trout are likely to be. When it is blowing a gale these places are dangerous. A wave that is perfect for fishing the wet fly can lift the boat by about 1m (3ft) and bring it crashing down by the same distance. In a fair wave the trout will often be found feeding in very shallow boulder-strewn water. If you let the boat drift into these lies and it crashes down on a sharp boulder, you are likely to be shipwrecked. So, unless you know the lough really well, you would be wise to employ a good local boatman who will show you the best drifts and the safe runs between drifts. While the boatman is handling the boat, holding it in safe water but within casting distance of the shallows, you can spend your time concentrating on catching the trout.

The best times to fish

The old maxim of "when the wind is in the west the fishing is best" is often true of these loughs, perhaps because this wind direction often sets up a "soft"' day – a day when there is no bite in the wind and a little moisture (the Irish for persistent light rain!). Westerly winds may also suit some of the drifts better and are associated with a soft light as opposed to the harsh glare that accompanies the east winds. What you do not want are blazing hot days with a flat calm. Then the trout will leave the shallow drifts and head into deeper water where they are almost impossible to tempt out with a fly. They may return to the shallow waters after dark if there is a good fall of spent gnat or a hatch of sedges.

What you also do not want are cold winds from a north through east to southeast quarter, especially in the spring. Flies will hatch in these winds, but although the surface of the lake may be covered with them, not one trout will be seen to rise. As in hot weather, it seems that in a chill wind the trout quit the fly-fishing shallow drifts for deeper water.

Do not be surprised if you catch something other than trout on the great Irish loughs. A pike that has grabbed the fly can get the heart fluttering. If you are fishing close to the mouth of an inflowing stream (such as in Victoria Bay on Conn and Rossinver on Melvin) you are quite likely to find yourself playing a salmon that has taken the fly. And in Lough Erne sea trout are becoming more common every year, and they take the fly well.

SEASONS
February to 15–September 30.

PERMITS
For Lough Erne get a Northern Ireland Dept. of Agriculture permit. You don't need one for great loughs (but check locally).

FURTHER DETAILS
Lough Corrib and Lough Mask: Western Regional Fisheries Board, Weir Lodge, Earl's Island, Galway (Tel: 353 91 65548); Lough Conn: North Western Regional Fisheries Board, Abbey Street, Ballina, Co. Mayo (Tel: 353 96 22623); Lough Melvin, Northern Regional Fisheries Board, Station Road, Ballyshannon, Co. Donegal (Tel: 353 72 51435); Lower Lough Erne: Fisheries Conservancy Board, 1 Mahon Road, Portadown, Co. Armagh (Tel: 01762 334666).

A fish has taken the fly! A typical scene of partnership between fly-fisher and boatman on Lough Melvin.

ICELAND

ROY ARRIS

*Going to Iceland is one of salmon fishing's great experiences, and it compels many
fly-fishers to return again and again to the land of fire and ice. There one finds some
of the most productive and reliable salmon fishing, set in a pristine environment
of crystal clear rivers and pure, light air.*

The marketing slogan used by that small island nation anchored just below the Arctic Circle in the North Atlantic is "Iceland, Jewel of the North." This certainly rings true for the visiting salmon fisher. The pure, crystal clear streams flow through a landscape of stark, rugged beauty. The river valleys harbor rich meadows crammed with grasses, buttercups, clover, and cottongrass. On the horizon are jagged volcanic peaks, from which glaciers make their rasping, creeping journey. Anticipating a return to this paradise each summer will brighten a long winter spent close to the fireside: to be free once more on the banks of a favorite river, with a fresh breeze blowing away the worries of a world left behind, and with the burbling cry of the whimbrel blending perfectly with the sound of running water as you make the first cast of the year.

Salmon conservation

Rod-fishing for salmon was introduced to Iceland by English fly-fishers in the mid-19th century, and all the traditions of the sport have been preserved on most of the rivers. The most important factor in Iceland's development into a top salmon destination is that the government took the enlightened step of banning all ocean fishing for salmon in 1930, and has actively encouraged the development of rod-fishing rather than netting in rivers and estuaries. Today the fish have a clear run to their home rivers. This has greatly benefited the small communities of the river valleys. Only

one or two esturial netting stations remain on the big glacial rivers, where there is no rod-fishing. There is no coastal salmon farming in cages to cause sea-lice problems; moreover, the state-run and private sea-ranching stations folded because they were uneconomic.

Salmon return to their natal rivers between May and September, with the main runs arriving in July. The fishing season runs between May 20 and September 30, and each river is allowed to set its own 100-day season within this period. The season on rivers on the southwest coast usually begins a couple of weeks earlier than those on the north and east coasts. The prime time of July is normally given over to foreign anglers, and is reserved for fly-fishing. The decision about the number of rods that are allowed to fish on a river is made by the Fisheries Directorate; this measure ensures that there is plenty of water for each rod. Water is divided into two-rod beats, where each pair of fly-fishers is looked after by one guide, and the fishing

FURTHER DETAILS
Landssamband Veidifelagá, Bolholt 6, 105 Reykjavik, Iceland. Fax: 354 568 4363.

CLOTHING AND TACKLE

Iceland has a very changeable and usually cool climate. A good selection of woolens or fleeces is advisable. Neoprene waders and a good waterproof wading jacket are a must. Iceland is virtually free of biting insects, but a head-net may be called for to keep the sometimes abundant, non-biting black fly away.

For the larger rivers a 4.5m (15ft) rod, coupled with floating or intermediate lines and tube flies is quite standard. In very windy weather a fast-sinking shooting head can be the only way to combat the conditions. For the medium and small rivers a 2.7–3m (9–10ft) rod for a 6- or 7-weight line is ideal, as flies down to size 14 may be used.

day is split into two six-hour shifts. The shifts are usually from 7am to 1pm and from 4pm to 10pm.

The salmon rivers

Of the 100 or more salmon rivers in Iceland, a number are members of the organization Landssamband Veidifelagá – The Federation of Fishery Owners – and market their fishing through this body. Their brochure covers 11 salmon rivers and includes some of the top ones in the country. It is a must for anyone contemplating a salmon-fishing trip to Iceland.

The rivers offering fishing are: Laxá i Dolum, Flekkudalsá, Fljotaá, Grimsá, Hitará, Laxá i Kjoss, Langá, Midfjardará, Rangá, Vatnsdalsá, and Vididalsá. There is a wide variety of waters, so there is fishing to suit all tastes and styles.

All the rivers are suited to fly-fishing and respond well to a variety of tactics. Most of the fishing is for grilse and many of the locals prefer to use short rods and weight-forward lines. While this is fine for most of the small rivers, the medium-sized and big rivers call for a double-handed rod. The big two-handers are also ideal for coping with the often windy conditions.

Big rivers such as Sogid and Rangá provide fishing in the British style: that is 4.5m (15ft) rods and a long cast in order to cover the wide pools. The medium-sized rivers such as Grimseá, Vatnsdalsá, and Midfjardará, have a wide variety of pool sizes and characters throughout their courses. You will be fishing pots and small runs in the upper reaches, and then covering wide glides in the lower river.

The smaller rivers provide quite a different challenge, as the fish you will be trying to catch are often visible in the pools. They have to be carefully stalked and you must present the fly delicately to them. Under such circumstances the riffle hitch can be a very successful and most entertaining tactic. To see fish coming through the water to the fly – often several times before taking – only to turn away at the last moment, is heart-stopping stuff and is highly recommended.

The water in Icelandic salmon rivers is among the clearest in the world. And, perhaps for this reason, Icelandic salmon have a reputation for preferring flies with lots of blue in the dressing: Silver Blue, Blue Charm, and Silver Stoat with blue hackle are ideal. In recent years, however, the weighted Red Francis has become popular.

Iceland is not renowned for its big fish, but there are many rivers with a good run of two-sea-winter salmon in the 5–8kg (12–18lb) class. Its rivers have earned more of a reputation among fly-fishers for producing good numbers of grilse.

While you might visit Iceland for the salmon fishing, you ought also to take the opportunity, if you are on a beat close to the tide, of catching a sea-run Arctic char. These leave the river after ice melt and feed at sea for a few weeks before returning to the river at the end of July and through August. Most weigh in the range 1–3kg (2–7lb), and they take the fly very well.

The salmon rivers of Iceland are clear, rugged, and set amid stunning scenery. They are also full of silver sea-run salmon. Most salmon will be small grilse, but among them will be the occasional larger specimen.

GREAT FRENCH STREAMS

MARC PETITJEAN

The Jura scenery is dominated by limestone and chalk, by summer meadows that are an eye-catching mass of colorful mountain wildflowers, by verdant oak and beech forests, and by the two rivers, the Doubs and the Loue, that are home to the most beautiful of grayling and wild brown trout.

The River Doubs rises on the French-Swiss border and flows northeastward through the small towns of Pontarlier, Morteau, and Goumois before swinging in a broad loop to a south-west direction to Besançon. By the time it has reached that ancient town the Doubs has already flowed for 160km (100 miles) and it still has another 50km (31 miles) to go before it meets with the Loue. In contrast the Loue is a much shorter river, rising about 10km (6 miles) above the pretty little town of Ornans and meandering for some 80km (50 miles) to its confluence with the Doubs.

The best beats

On the Doubs the premier beats – and these are where you should head when you visit this river – are on the 25km (15 miles) that form the French-Swiss border close to Goumois (the "Franco-Suisse" section). If you want to fish the Loue, then head to the beats around Ornans. Fish here and you are fishing classic water. This is river that was considered by the hotelier and fly-fishing legend Charles Ritz as among the best trout and grayling fishing the world can offer. And Ritz was qualified to offer an opinion, for he somewhat neglected his work as hotelier to fly-fish his way

around the world's greatest rivers. And not only Ritz, for both the Doubs and the Loue have tempted many of the world's greatest fly-fishers. They really are international rivers.

Both rivers have the perfect fly-fishing character, with long gravel-bedded and streamy riffles separating wide, deep, slower pools. Where the river is very wide you will be tempted to wade out to cast your fly to the other side. But beware: on some beats wading is not permitted and on some the wearing of chest-high waders prohibited. Even so, remember that here some of the biggest trout lie close to the bank on which you are kneeling, and wading may disturb them. Approach the bank carefully to avoid scaring the nearer trout, and search the water under your bank before trying to catch those near the opposite bank.

In places where, in favorable light conditions, you can see through the water, you may spot groups of grayling and small trout feeding over bare gravel. Before casting to these, take extra care to examine the margins of weed beds, for the bigger trout – the ones you have traveled here to catch – will be taking advantage of any cover that is available. With the increasing welcome trend to catch and release, these big trout may well associate the falling of a fly-line over their heads with the discomfort of being hooked and played, even though release followed last time, as it will this. They do not know that.

Yet as long ago as 1953 and before fly-fishers took catch and release seriously, Ritz was aware of the nervousness of trout in the Doubs and the Loue, for in his book *Pris sur le Vif* he noted: "On the wide shallows of rivers such as ... the Doubs, and the Loue, it is very difficult to place the fly accurately at the first attempt. If the point of the rise has not been accurately marked, it is better to wait for another."

Malcolm Greenhalgh playing a grayling on the River Loue – one of the world's great grayling rivers.

In other words, cast accurately to where the fish has risen and, if you are not certain precisely where the fish rose, wait for it to rise again before casting to it. All too often fly-fishers terrify trout on these clear streams by casting at random or casting inaccurately.

Both the trout and grayling that live in these fine streams are strikingly beautiful fish. The vermilion-red of the huge dorsal fin of the adult

grayling is incredibly bright, while the fin also has almost luminescent green flecks. In contrast, the brown trout native to both rivers are, as Ritz put it in his book, "big, fat trout with zebra stripes." These vertical, dusky-black stripes on the sides are unique to Doubs and Loue trout. As you peer down into the water from a vantage point, such as the bridge over the Loue in Ornans, you initially wonder if you have spotted some obscure species of perch, and not a trout at all. There can be no doubt that these stripes do help camouflage the trout, because they break up the outline of the fish in the sun-drenched, weedy water and can make the trout difficult to spot. Most grayling you catch here will average 25–30cm (10–12in) in length, with exceptional specimens reaching 40cm (16in). Trout average 30–35cm (12–14in), with fine specimens more than 50cm (20in).

Both rivers are highly productive of lush weed beds that harbor a vast and diverse population of insect larvae and nymphs. In the deeper pools, or more turbulent areas below natural weirs, a weighted nymph pattern is highly effective when there is no hatch. To help get the nymph down try a weighted leader, or do as some of the local experts do: fish your weighted fly on a very long fine leader that sinks quickly. However you do it, you must get the fly deep when trout and grayling are grubbing about on the riverbed.

During spring afternoons, and summer and fall evenings well into nightfall, a wide range of mayflies, stoneflies, and caddisflies hatch, bringing feeding trout and grayling to the surface. Both rivers have the classic mayfly *Ephemera danica*, the duns of which hatch in spring afternoons, while the spinners fall in the evening. When hatches of this mayfly are over for another year, the blue-winged olive appears and may dominate evening rises until the season's end. Both rivers also have that biggest of European stoneflies, *Perla grandis*, which hatches in large numbers from the end of May through to the beginning of July. This is the time for dry-fly, of matching the hatch, of seeking a rising fish and covering it accurately.

SEASONS

March–September for brown trout, May–October for grayling. However, these do vary from year to year, so check first.

PERMITS

You need a national license, federal license, and permit to fish for the day. Currently, there is a visitor's license called *La Carte Vacance*, which acts as combined national and federal license for visitors. Some beats of both rivers are private; for others you may obtain a day-ticket. The beats available change annually, as do rules and regulations. Some allow spinning and fly-fishing: most visitors might wish to avoid these. For up-to-date information, contact: Agence de Développement Economique du Doubs, 7 Avenue de la Gare d'Eau, F 25031, Besancon, France (Tel: 33. 381.65.10.00, Fax: 33.381.82.01.40).

THE RIVERS OF SPAIN

TONY PAWSON

Northern Spain offers a fascinating variety of fly-fishing, especially for trout.
The best locations for fish range from lush meadows around León to the
rugged grandeur of the Pyrenees. Here, fly-fishers have been tying flies
and casting them to trout for over 350 years.

With a climate switching suddenly from winter chill to extreme summer heat, the south of Spain is unsuitable for cold-water fish such as trout. Even on more northern areas some dam-controlled rivers like Castille's Carrión can become unfishable after June as water is drawn off to irrigate parched land. Madrid is at the divide, with fine fishing to the north and virtually none to the south. The river closest to the capital is the Dulce. This stream, which abounds in food for the fat trout, is sweet indeed for those who are lucky enough to fish it.

Spanish fly-fishing traditions are perhaps even older than England's. The publication *Manuscrito de Astorga* (1624) pre-dates Walton's *Compleat Angler* (1653), and contains higher-quality fly-tying instructions. The manuscript includes reference to using hackles from specially bred local farmyard fowl called *coq de León*. Today, more than 375 years later, these fowl are still bred around León and their feathers are sought by keen fly-dressers around the world. The *Manuscrito* was written in León, the centre of Spanish trout fishing, and eventually fell into the hands of that most enthusiastic angler, General Franco. Alas the original manuscript was destroyed by fire, but facsimiles exist. Franco's main passion was to improve the limited salmon and sea-trout fishing, especially on the Sella and Narcea rivers in the Gijon region. These two fine rivers are similar in character to some of Scotland and Iceland's best, but have only moderate runs of salmon.

Appropriately, it is León that stages Spain's annual international Trout Week. There fishermen have six fine rivers from which to choose, including the one flowing past the city. Close by are the Torio, the Curueño, and the rapid, gravel-bottomed Esla, where falcons wheel above the surrounding hills. Even more delightful and prolific is my favorite, the Porma, where many waterside fields blaze with wildflowers, including many varieties of orchid. That is true of the de Condado beat near Cerezales, further enlightened for me by the river keeper riding up on horseback to check permits. In the clear swift river a variety of waterweed ensures food in plenty for trout, while thick clumps of white-flowered *Ranunculus* brighten some bankside runs. Despite the fishing pressure on the Porma, good fly-fishers should expect, on each visit, a dozen or more trout averaging close to 450g (1lb).

The Órbigo

The Órbigo has the highest reputation and deserves it, except where pike have made inroads into the trout stocks. The most interesting of the 80km (50 miles) of controlled beats is the Sardonedo near San Martina. There is the added bonus of Patricio's, a real fly-fishers' pub with a double figure Órbigo trout among the fishing pictures lining the walls. Abundant fly life in the Órbigo ranges from tiny black gnats to huge stoneflies. The pools vary from shallow runs to long flats, the trout from the easy to the challenging. As in most of these rivers dry flies matching the hatch, or a Sedge or Gray Wulff to bring the fish up when there is no hatch, provide the most satisfying method. Scouring the streams with wet flies can work well, particularly if a dropper fly is bobbed on the edge of the runs. For many Spaniards, bubble-float fishing is the preferred method, with a team of four flies above the float, and a single tail-fly below.

A favorite trout stream of mine is Castille's Pisuerga, especially on its upper waters near Cervera. The Quintaluengos beat is outstanding, with permits available at Pallencia's fishery office, where the town is overlooked by a striking 60m (200ft) high effigy of Christ. This is another clear stream with a variety of pools, but the most interesting challenges are in the rapid runs and cascades from the face of the weirs. The plentiful trout run up to 1kg (2lb), with even larger ones usually caught on streamers rather than dry fly.

The Pyrenean streams

Different in character are the snow-fed Pyrenean streams. Rocky banks and beds full of boulders make fishing physically demanding. Once snow melt clears the wary trout are easily spotted in the translucent water. For those wishing to add some high mountain trekking there are the *Ibones*, which are remote little lakes but rarely fished.

Wild browns are predominant in these tumbling streams with a few stocked rainbows

The River Aragón is a typically rugged Spanish trout stream. Here it is not the size of trout that counts: what matters is being there, deep in wild Spain.

added. A daily limit of 20 trout indicates the prospects of good sport with mainly small fish. As the water drops and warms, barbel up to 6kg (13lb) move upstream, sometimes taking flies and breaking the leader of the unwary fly-fisher. In some Pyrenean reservoirs American black bass thrive and can be caught on streamers, poppers, or large bushy flies. Other coarse fish sometimes caught on the fly in Spain include carp and catfish, running to 14kg (30lb) or more.

There is a wealth of options in the five Pyrenean provinces. Huesca offers the greatest opportunity for the energetic since it covers the highest parts of the mountains, and so has fewest fly-fishers. Navarra and Lerida also have delightful streams. Overall the best rivers are Segre, Ara, Gallego, Aragón, Subordan, and Esca.

Different in character again is Salamanca's Tormes. The prime stretch is the 30km (18 miles) from the Santa Teresa dam, which controls the flow, to Alba de Tormes. Prior to the dam's construction the fish stocks were poor, as a result of the summer low water and high temperature. Even though the dam makes this an artificial river, fish thrived here after trout were stocked from the upper reaches above the reservoir and from the Órbigo. The early profusion was not sustained but, apart from the indigenous trout, huchen are stocked and big barbel and other coarse fish abound. However, the quality of the fly-fishing can depend on the level of recent stockings. The river itself is a joy to fish with many different challenges; dry and wet fly are equally successful. The river is about 50m (160ft) wide and chest waders are needed for best results. The trout average 400g (12oz), but a few much larger ones can be caught. While floating or slow-sink lines are preferable, there are some deep eddies where a "Hi-D" line helps get the fly down.

Fly-fishing in Spain is relatively cheap. For example, in the Pyrenees it is less expensive to fish the Spanish side than the French. Accommodation is also inexpensive. Plan your trip carefully and Spain offers a variety of superb fishing even if you go "on the cheap." If you prefer to do it in style there is nothing to beat a week's stay in León's San Marcos Hotel, coupled with dry-fly fishing on the pick of the nearby trout rivers, notably the Órbigo and Porma.

SEASONS

The season varies a little from region to region, but generally it is March 1– July 31 (trout) with the best months being May and June; for other species it is June 1– March 14.

PERMITS

There are two sorts of beat: "free" and "controlled." To fish the free beats you need a cheap general license. To fish controlled beats or *cotos* you must apply well in advance, for there are a limited number of rods available each day. The Spanish tourist office can provide up-to-date advice.

SLOVENIA

MALCOLM GREENHALGH

Despite its small size, the country of Slovenia provides some of the very best river fly-fishing for trout and grayling in Europe. The streams, set amid the grandeur of the Julian Alps, are crystal clear and fast-flowing, and produce immense amounts of insect food, which generate large stocks of rapidly growing fish.

Set among densely forested mountains topped by snowy peaks, the Soca River is a truly breathtaking sight. Edged with wide, brilliant white gravel banks, the translucent ultramarine water is so crystal clear that it seems only a few inches deep. The intense beauty of the setting, together with the constant swirls in the river that indicate fish, make the Soca an exciting and invigorating place to fly-fish.

The Soca rises in the mountains north of Bovec and flows southeast through the towns of Tolmin and Most na Soci before entering Italy (where it is called the Isonzo) and flowing into the Adriatic. Together with its tributaries, the Lepena, Koritnica, Tolminka, and Idrijca, it has large populations of fish.

Brown and rainbow trout were introduced about 100 years ago and have thrived. Both spawn freely and attain weights of 2kg (4lb) or more. During one evening rise in the Idrijca I caught two rainbows in successive casts on dry fly; one scaled 3.5kg (7lb 8oz), and the other 3.7kg (8lb 2oz).

The most abundant native fish in the Soca are grayling. They are not big when compared with the grayling you can catch in Scandinavia, running three fish to the kilogram, but they are beautiful fish: a *café au lait* color and not the steel gray of most grayling. Try a size 14 Orange Partridge, one of the world's oldest wet flies, at dawn or dusk in the river above Tolmin, and fish the open water well away from the bank. You might easily average a grayling for every three or four casts when the fish are "on." But then, if you change your fly for a big black marabou streamer and concentrate on the deep water underneath the trees on the far bank, you will catch rainbow trout one after the other. You also stand a good chance of hooking a marbled trout.

The marbled trout or "marmorata" is of great interest to the fly-fisher. It was once found in most of the rivers draining into the Adriatic, but pollution and hybridization with introduced brown trout exterminated the marmorata from every river except the Soca. If it had not been for careful conservation, including the Tolmin Fishing Society raising and releasing pure marmorata from their hatchery, this exciting fish would be on verge of extinction here too.

Small marmorata eat insects, and you will catch them on dry flies and nymphs. However, marmorata do not grow big on insects; they grow big on a diet of grayling. Today, most weigh up to about 5kg (11lb). However, in 1968 a 20.9kg (46lb) fish was caught on a size 14 Orange Partridge. That fish didn't take the tiny wet fly. It took a grayling that had just taken the fly-fisher's Orange Partridge!

If you want to catch a big marmorata – say one of 3kg (7lb) or more – you must fish a big fly and have a strong leader. The big black marabou streamer is good, but I would recommend a fry imitation on a size 2–6 streamer hook, and a leader tippet of no less than 4kg (9lb) test. The marmorata leave their lairs at dusk and hunt the grayling schools. Watch for them chasing grayling, cast your fly in front of them, and hold tight.

Other rivers of interest

Several other rivers flow eastward through Slovenia, eventually to join the Danube. For the fly-fisher the Iscica, Kolpa, Krka, Radovna, Sava, and Unec are outstanding. Brown and rainbow trout have been introduced to most rivers and breed freely. However, most fly-fishers visit these rivers for their superb grayling fishing.

Close to the town of Planina, the Unec is a cool, crystal clear, weedy chalkstream that meanders through a wide plain of meadow and pasture. Here there are grayling that exceed 1.5kg (3lb). In the heat of a summer's afternoon, the fish will rise to take a grasshopper that has accidentally leapt onto the water, and they will fall for a well-cast artificial.

The fishing starts late here, in June, after the winter floods have receded. Then, through to the end of the season, evening hatches of sedges

SEASONS
March 1–September 30 (October 31 for brook trout, rainbow trout, and grayling).

PERMITS
Available from hotels and tourist agencies.

FURTHER DETAILS
Zavod Za Ribistvo, Zupancieceva 9, 61000 Ljubljana, Slovenia.

encourage the fish to rise freely and provide super sport on dry fly.

It is interesting to note that while most grayling are steel gray fish, and most Soca grayling a *café-au-lait* color, in the Unec the grayling are a lovely creamy color with beautiful apricot fins.

Fishing on the Unec is a challenge, but the river Krka, between the villages of Krka and Zagradec, is far easier, simply because the river is not a clear, slow-flowing chalkstream. The Krka is a series of deep pools interspersed with shallow runs, and it has a great head of brown and rainbow trout and grayling.

Farther north in the Sava river, close to Bohinska Bistrica and downstream from Ljubljana, the number of large grayling is amazing. During an evening hatch of olive duns or sedges it is possible to catch a dozen big grayling without even moving. Using a dry fly, a typical evening might yield more than 50 grayling, as well as a few brown trout.

The Radovna, by contrast, lacks grayling, but the brown trout fishing is excellent, and there are also rainbow trout. However, the fish to look out

for here is the brook trout. This is one of the few European streams where this North American char was introduced and has thrived.

The huchen

The Iscia and Kolpa are superb brown trout and grayling streams, and these rivers also have huchen (as does the Sava). This fast-growing salmonid is, like the Soca's marmorata, a fish-eater, and has become very rare in its native Danube catchment. However, the Slovenian Zavod za Ribistvo has established a hatchery that has ensured the survival of this great fish in these three Danube feeder-streams. To stand by one of these rivers in the early evening and watch grayling scatter as a huchen bow-waves towards them is an incredible experience.

Most huchen are small, somewhere in the 2–4kg (4–9lb) class. However, if the Slovenian fishery team's attempt to propagate this magnificent fish continues to be as successful as it has been in the past, perhaps we will again see the 10kg (22lb) huchen that were once famous throughout the entire Danube Basin.

The Soca River at dusk: this is one of the greatest of great trout and grayling rivers. Marbled trout occur here – and nowhere else in the world.

Big streamer patterns or freshwater baitfish and fry patterns are ideal for huchen. Don't forget to press down the hook barb and release the fish quickly back into the river.

For fishing all Slovenian rivers weight number 5–6 outfits are ideal. Floating lines are fine, but you will need some heavy leaders to take your nymph to the bottom of the fastest pools. Stoneflies and caddisflies are the most abundant water-bred insects, so you should carry a range of suitable imitations. Tippet strength is important: 1.5kg (3lb) test is fine for dry-fly and nymph fishing, but if you are fishing for big rainbow trout, marmorata, or huchen with big streamers of baitfish imitations, 4kg (9lb) test is essential. I carry a second set of tackle for this sort of fishing: a very strong 3m (10ft) number 7 outfit. Only a fool risks getting smashed by these big fish.

GLOSSARY

Anadromous Relating to fish that spawn in freshwater but that, as juveniles, go to sea to feed and grow before returning to spawn.

Backing, backing line Because fly-lines are very short (rarely more than 30m [98ft]) a much longer length (ideally at least 200m [656ft] when fishing for large or powerful fish) of fine but strong backing line is used between fly-line and reel.

Baitfish A small fish that may be eaten by a larger fish and that may be imitated with a fly when trying to catch large fish-eating fish.

Bass bug A floating fly used to catch largemouth and smallmouth bass.

Benthic Relating to the bottom of lakes, rivers, and the sea.

Bomber A type of dry fly that is used to catch salmon and steelhead.

Cast The way the rod is used to cast the fly-line and to fly the fish. There are at least 18 types of cast, each designed for a specific purpose or situation (see also Leader).

Chum/chumming Marine predatory fish can often be attracted ("chummed") to casting range by releasing a mixture of minced fish and fish oil ("chum") into the current.

Crease The boundary between fast and slow flows or flowing and still bands of water in a river pool or riffle. Often clearly visible as crease-like lines on the water surface; large feeding fish often lie in or by creases.

Crystal Hair (also Flashibou) A synthetic sparkling hair that has great fish-attracting attributes and is ideal for use in salmon, streamer, and baitfish flies.

Dead-drift The passive drift of a fly down a river at the same speed as the flow.

Disgorger A term (ancient in origin) that describes any tool used to remove the hook from a fish's mouth. Today artery forceps are used for small- to medium-sized fish, fine snipe-nosed pliers for

larger fish, or specially designed tools are used (eg Boga-grip) in conjunction with barbless hooks.

Dry fly A term originally used to mean an imitation of a insect standing on the water, is now taken to mean any fly that floats on the water (see also Emerger, Wet fly).

Echo sounder see Fish-finder

Emerger A fly that fishes both above and below the water surface (see also Dry fly, Wet fly), and mimics a hatching insect where the emptying nymphal or pupal shuck is just below the surface and the adult hatching onto the surface.

Evening rise The hectic period around dusk on rivers and lakes when huge numbers of aquatic insects hatch and the fish feed keenly at the surface.

False cast Where the line is cast to and fro without line or fly touching the water. False casting is used when lengthening line to make a longer cast, or when drying a sodden dry fly.

Fish-finder An electronic device, used when fishing from a boat, that can detect and display visually, on a screen or paper trace, water depth and bottom contours, and the position and sizes of fish beneath the boat. It is sometimes called an echo sounder because the device works by sending out a pulse and analyzing the returning echo.

Fishing the water Casting the fly where fish are thought to be (see Sight-casting).

Flashibou see Crystal Hair

Flats Large areas of shallows in the sea, usually close to land, that can be fished by wading or from a very shallow draft boat. Flats attract some of the finest saltwater quarry species for the fly-fisher.

Fly Originally used to describe winged insects and the fly-fishers' attempts at imitating these natural flies in their artificial flies. Today artificial flies are tied to match any natural food of fish, from small

insects and crustaceans to small mammals, amphibians, and baitfish. Some "flies" do not match any specific food item (see Lure, Streamer).

Fly-line The specially tapered line that is used to propel the fly. It is the weight of this line that we use in casting, and learning to cast means learning to manipulate this long, fluid weight. Fly-lines come in different tapers and weights (from fully floating or slow sinking "slime-lines" to extremely fast sinkers). Fly-line technology is constantly advancing, so take advice before buying one.

Fresh-run An anadromous fish that has recently returned from the sea to freshwater.

Fry A tiny juvenile fish that has recently hatched from the egg, also sometimes taken to include tiny fish.

Fusiform Spindle- to cigar-shaped body in fish.

Gamefish Originally used to describe members of the trout and salmon family, now the term is used to describe any worthwhile quarry of the fly-fisher.

Grilse A salmon that has spent only one winter at sea; also referred to as 1SW.

Hackle Feathers that are tied into the fly and then wound around the hook so that the "hackle fibers" become separated to simulate legs, fragile wings, or simply to add movement. Body or palmered hackles are wound the length of the hookshank; collar hackles are wound at the front of the fly.

Haul (as in "line haul," "double haul") Where the non-rod hand is used to pull down quickly during casting to prevent slack line developing during the cast to speed up the fly-line and to make crisper, longer casts.

Haywire twist The best method of putting small loops at the end of wire traces.

Hold The purchase of the hook in the jaw of a fish.

Hooks The ultimate link between fish and fly-fisher, and the foundation upon which the fly is tied. Buy the best. Use them barbless (press down the barb) to make removal easier. In saltwater use stainless steel hooks. Hooks are sized by number, generally the larger the size the smaller the number (sizes 2–30), with the bigger hooks used mainly in saltwater fishing being numbered (1/0–10/0).

Hookshank The wire of the hook between the hook eye and the round bend of the hook onto which the fly is tied.

Ichthyology The study of fish: fly-fishing is applied ichthyology.

IGFA International Game Fishing Association

1SW see Grilse

Juvenile A fish that has not reached sexual maturity. The juvenile stage may only last for 1–2 years in small species of fish, but 5 or more years in larger species (see also Parr).

Kelt A fish that has recently spawned and not yet recovered from the ordeal.

Lateral line A usually distinct line running along either side of a fish that is extremely sensitive to vibrations, and that will warn the fish of an approaching heavy-footed fly-fisher.

Leader The first line between fly-line and fly (see also Tippet, Wire trace).

Line a fish In shallow, calm water the splash of a fly-line over a fish will usually scare the fish away. Never "line fish" in this way: cast to one side or let only the fine leader fall over the fish.

Littoral Of or relating to the tidal foreshore.

Lure All flies could be described as lures, for they entice the fish to take hold of them. Some fly-fishers reserve the term for flies that do not match food items closely (eg gaudy streamers and salmon flies).

Milt Sexual product of male fish.

MSW Multi-sea winter fish: anadromous salmon, trout, and char that have spent more than one winter at sea.

Parr Juvenile trout and salmon.

Parr markings Dark oval marks found along the sides of the body of parr.

Pattern (of fly) Most artificial flies have a recipe or pattern of materials and techniques that must be followed when the fly is tied.

Pelagic Refers to fish that live in mid or surface waters of the ocean.

Play (a fish) Hooking a fish on a line is one thing. Fish, especially big and powerful fish, do not then meekly swim in; they must be played until they can be brought close for landing. Playing a fish is an art in itself.

Popper/popping bug A buoyant fly that, when pulled back through the water surface, creates a loud popping or splashing sound and a big wake. Most predatory fish are readily attracted by poppers.

Rays and spines All fins (except adipose fins in members of the salmon family) are supported by soft rays, and sometimes hard spines. Beware of spines, for they can cause you serious injuries if a fish is badly handled. Some fish also have razor-sharp spines on the gill cover.

Retrieve (the line/fly) In most cases, after casting the line and fly out onto the water, line must be retrieved to bring the fly back in an attractive manner. Often the way the retrieve is made (how fast, whether in a straight line or arc, whether smooth or jerky) can mean the difference between abject failure and outstanding success.

Rip/tide rip (in the sea) A particularly fast stretch of water (often a narrow band) where the current is being funnelled or deflected (eg by a submerged reef). Usually outstanding fish holding positions, but beware: rips can be dangerous water.

Salmon tailer A tool for landing small to medium–large fish, where a wire noose is slipped over the tail and pulled tight. The fish is then unhooked, and freed unharmed by releasing the noose.

School A congregation of one species of fish.

Sea-run (fish) A fish that will run to or has returned from the sea.

Sebago A form of silvery, spotted land-locked salmon.

Shuck The empty nymphal or pupal skin left after the adult insect has hatched.

Sight-casting Casting the fly to fish that are visible (see Fishing the water).

Sound When a hooked fish dives deeply, it is said to "sound."

Spines see Rays.

Streamer A usually large and sometimes extremely gaudy fly that, when fished quickly through the water, attracts fish. Certain streamers have some resemblance to baitfish; others look like nothing that ever lived (see also Lures).

Strip in line To pull in line (or make a medium to fast retrieve). Also, to "strip" line from the reel means to "pull" line from the reel.

Tailwater(s) The river flowing from a reservoir dam.

Take When a fish grabs hold of or "takes" the fly.

Tease To excite, with your fly, curiosity, anger, or a feeding response in a fish that does not necessarily want to do anything but rest quietly in the water.

Test (of leader or tippet) The breaking strain of the line, usually expressed in kilograms or in pounds and ounces.

Tippet The front part of the leader immediately behind the fly. It is usually the finest part of the fly-fishing rig, but where the fish has a coarse or toothy mouth a short heavy nylon or wire tippet might be used.

Troll To trail a fly (or bait) from the back of a moving boat.

Wet fly A fly that fishes underneath the water surface.

Wind knot These are simple knots that appear, as by magic, in the leader. They reduce the strength of the leader by at least 50 per cent, so should one appear, tie on a new leader. In truth they are caused by poor casting.

Wire trace A short, fine wire tippet tied at the end of the leader when fishing for toothy predators such as pike and barracuda.

Zoöplankton Animals (usually tiny) that drift in the open water of the ocean and lakes.

PICTURE CREDITS

Endpapers Michel Roggo; 2 Malcolm Greenhalgh; 6–7 Michel Roggo; 8–9 Hedgehog House/Nathan Secker; 11 Malcolm Greenhalgh; 12 R Valentine Atkinson; 13 Lefty Kreh; 14–15 Michel Roggo; 16–17 Sam Talarico; 19 Michel Roggo 21 Trey Combs; 23 Jim Teeny; 28 Michel Roggo; 29 Michel Roggo; 30 John Goddard; 37 Dave Whitlock; 38 Sam Talarico; 42–3 Sam Talarico; 45 Graeme Pullen; 47 Ed Mitchell; 48 Lefty Kreh; 49 Lefty Kreh; 51 Sam Talarico; 52 Trey Combs; 53 Trey Combs; 54 John Goddard; 55 Hedgehog House/Ron and Valerie Taylor; 57 Sam Talarico; 60 Tom Earnhardt; 61 Nick Curcione; 62 John A Kumiski; 64 Ed Mitchell; 65 Robert Harding Picture Library/Jeremy Lightfoot; 66 Trey Combs; 75 John Goddard; 77 Robert Harding Picture Library/Silvestris; 79 Phill Williams; 80–81 Don Muelrath; 83 Michel Roggo; 84 Reed Consumer Books Limited/Jason Smalley; 85 right Malcolm Greenhalgh; 85 top Reed Consumer Books Limited/Jason Smalley; 85 top right Reed Consumer Books Limited/Jason Smalley; 85 bottom Reed Consumer Books Limited /Jason Smalley; 86/92 top left Reed Consumer Books Limited/Jason Smalley; 93 Malcolm Greenhalgh; 94/109 Reed Consumer Books Limited/Jason Smalley; 110–11 Edward Jaworowski; 112 Malcolm Greenhalgh; 115 Malcolm Greenhalgh; 117 Malcolm Greenhalgh; 118–19 Ed Mitchell; 119 Reed Consumer Books Limited/ Jason Smalley; 121 Edward Jaworowski; 122-123 Sam Talarico; 123 Malcolm Greenhalgh; 124 Lefty Kreh; 125 Sam Talarico; 126 Lefty Kreh; 127 Dick Brown and Carol Wright; 128 Malcolm Greenhalgh; 129 Malcolm Greenhalgh; 131 Malcolm Greenhalgh; 132-133 Sam Talarico; 134 Sam Talarico; 135 Sam Talarico; 136–7 Michel Roggo; 139 Edward Jaworowski; 140 Edward Jaworowski; 141 Sam Talarico; 142–3 Michel Roggo; 143 Malcolm Greenhalgh; 144–5 top Trey Combs; 144–5 bottom Edward Jaworowski; 146 Malcolm Greenhalgh; 147 Michel Roggo; 148 Sam Talarico; 149 Lefty Kreh; 150 Trey Combs; 150–1 Trey Combs; 152–3 Hedgehog House/Colin Monteath; 154–5 Don Muelrath; 156–7 Corbis UK Ltd; 158–9 Edward Jaworowski; 160 Edward Jaworowski; 161 Edward Jaworowski; 163 Robert Harding Picture Library/Charles Bowman; 164–5 Don Muelrath; 167 Don Muelrath; 169 Hedgehog House/Colin Monteath; 170–1 Dave Whitlock; 173 Craig Mathews; 174–5 Edward Jaworowski; 176–7 Dennis G Bitton; 178–9 J P H Foto; 180–1 Ehor O Boyanowsky; 183 Edward Jaworowski; 184–5 Hedgehog House/Andris Apse; 186–7 Malcolm Greenhalgh; 188–9 Malcolm Greenhalgh; 191 Lesley Crawford; 193 Renée Wilson; 194–5 Malcolm Greenhalgh; 197 Malcolm Greenhalgh; 198–9 Malcolm Greenhalgh; 200–1 Hutchison Library/Nick Haslam; 202–3 Malcolm Greenhalgh.

INDEX

THE BOOK OF
ANGELS

Illustrations by
Ruth Thompson, L. A. Williams,
and Renae Taylor

Text by Todd Jordan

Sterling Publishing Co., Inc
New York

Published by Sterling Publishing Co., Inc.
387 Park Avenue South, New York, NY 10016

© 2006 by Tarnished Images, L. A. Williams, and Renae Taylor

Distributed in Canada by Sterling Publishing
c/o Canadian Manda Group, 165 Dufferin Street,
Toronto, Ontario, Canada M6K 3H6

Distributed in the United Kingdom by GMC Distribution Services,
Castle Place, 166 High Street, Lewes, East Sussex, England BN7 1XU

Distributed in Australia by Capricorn Link (Australia) Pty. Ltd.
P.O. Box 704, Windsor, NSW 2756, Australia

ISBN-13: 978-1-4027-3837-1
ISBN-10: 1-4027-3837-4

For information about custom editions, special sales, premium and
corporate purchases, please contact Sterling Special Sales
Department at 800-805-5489 or specialsales@sterlingpub.com.

Contents

In the beginning

"Angels transcend every religion, every philosophy, every creed. In fact, angels have no religion as we know it, as their existence precedes every religious system that has ever existed on earth."

—St. Thomas Aquinas

Versions of the word "angel" occur in the languages of many different cultures. The Greek word *angelos* translates to "messenger" and is commonly considered the basis for modern-day literary interpretations. However, many other languages have descriptives that serve the same function. *Angelos* derives from the Hebrew term *mal'akh*, which literally means "the shadow side of God," and there is the Latin word *angelus*, which also refers to a type of messenger. *Angiras*, from the ancient Sanskrit, means "divine spirit," and the Persian term *angaros* translates to "courier." The "official" Latin term that eventually became affixed to any traditional religious view of angels is *Angelus Occidentalis*, which describes any celestial servant of the leader of a monotheistic religion such as Christianity or Judaism.

The concept of angels has been with us since before we began to mark time, and certainly predates the formation of any organized religion. Angels appear in the writings of many different cultures, where they are invariably depicted as winged, powerful beings who bear a close resemblance to humans and mediate between God and man. In Judeo-Christian literature, angels predate the creation of Earth, as the first War in Heaven occurred sometime previous to the seven days God spent creating the world.

THE HIERARCHY OF ANGELS

"And I looked, and behold, a whirl-wind came out of the north, a great cloud, and a fire infolding itself, and a brightness was about it, and out of the midst thereof as the color of amber, out of the midst of the fire. Also out of the midst came the likeness of four living creatures. And this was their appearance; they had the likeness of a man."

—Ezekiel 1:4-5

The angels serve as the Celestial Host, and over the centuries, religious scholars have categorized angels in dozens of differing ways. In writings concerned with Celestial Hierarchy in the *Summa Theologica*, St. Thomas Aquinas states that there are nine orders whose numbering is determined by their proximity to God's grace:

1. Seraphim
2. Cherubim
3. Thrones
4. Dominions (Dominations)
5. Virtues
6. Powers (Potentates)
7. Principalities
8. Archangels
9. Angels

A further delineation separates Aquinas's nine orders into three houses: The Angels of Contemplation, The Angels of the Cosmos, and The Angels of Earth.

THE ANGELS OF CONTEMPLATION

Angels of pure contemplation oversee the entire universe. They are solely concerned with manifestations of divine grace within Creation, and concentrate their energies upon God. They do not interact with humankind in the direct way that Archangels and other angels do.

This order includes the Seraphim, the highest of the nine orders of angels, who serve as caretakers at the foot of God and sing his praises with eternal vigor. They form a circle of grace around the throne of The Lord, communicating His decrees and commands as waves of indescribably beautiful song sound. The celestial light that envelops them as they bask in the Creator's presence is so overpowering that no other being, not even the other angels, can rest their gaze upon them.

In the Book of Isaiah, the Seraphim are described thus: "I saw The Lord sitting upon a throne, high and lifted up; and his train filled the temple. Above him stood the Seraphim; each had six wings: with two they covered their faces, and with two they covered their feet, and with two they flew."

They are also mentioned in the Book of Revelation: "And the four living creatures, each of them with six wings, are full of eyes all around and within, and day and night they never cease to sing…"

The second of the order are the Cherubim. They exist just beyond the throne of God and outside the Seraphic processional. They are the guardians of light and the stars, and the divine light that they radiate covers the universe in warmth and love. They are characterized as being the keepers of all knowledge and secrets, both Divine and Earthly.

The physical form of the Cherubim is described as a melding of typical angelic features; they have two or four wings, similar to those of common animals although presented in an unearthly manner. In Ezekiel, they are described as having four faces: that of a lion, an ox, an eagle, and a man. Later, they are said to have the head of a lion, the hands, arms, and torso of a man with legs, and the hooves of a calf.

Thrones are the last order of the upper echelon. Their primary purpose is to serve as the bearers of the throne of God, but they also serve as the first line of many angelic dominions who concern themselves with celestial law and justice as decided on by The Lord. Thrones have the task of pondering the initial disposition of any Godly decree that is related to divine law and passing sentence upon the guilty. They then relay their decision to those below them, who must either execute the verdict or pass it along to their subordinates. Thrones are known ultimately to be humble creatures, which allows them to maintain their neutrality and objectivity when dispensing justice.

Possessing simple yet overtly bizarre physical characteristics, Thrones are basically large intangible orbs, or wheels, covered in reflective eyes and glowing with a magnificent nimbus of shimmering, iridescent light. This is how they were described when they served as God's chariot, Merkabah, when He came down to Earth in the Book of Isaiah: "The four wheels had rims and they had spokes, and their rims were full of eyes round about." The Thrones are often referred to as "the many-eyed ones" and it is known that no act in Heaven or on Earth can escape their gaze. They exist in a transitional state between the physical and celestial worlds, which is why their countenances seem so odd compared to the rest of the Host.

A Dominion and his scepter

THE ANGELS OF THE COSMOS

The second house of angels is concerned with maintaining an orderly unification between the spiritual and corporeal universes. Because this calling compels them to pass often between the two planes of existence, these three orders are called The Angels of the Cosmos. The triad will sometimes, albeit rarely, come in contact with humankind, which magnifies their risk for compromise by man's flawed nature. These three wings of the Host are focused on a celestial balance, and since there cannot be good without evil, their exposure to that constant, intense duel between the moral poles places them in a precarious position. Those who are purest are the most susceptible to impurity.

Beginning the second choir of the hierarchy are the Dominions. They comprise the top tier of the next three flights of angels, and their primary purpose is to maintain the lines of communication between the spiritual and material worlds so that, when the Word comes down from The Creator, it is clearly and quickly spread through the whole of the universe. Like the Thrones, they exist in a state of flux between the two planes of existence and assist in the integration between the Heavens and the rest of the universe by maintaining order and balance. Secondarily, they serve to regulate the duties of the angels below them in the hierarchy.

The Dominions see across the infinite worlds through an endless array of eyes, and have the ability to shift their physical bodies into whatever aspect they wish. Since they exercise this trait continuously, it is rare to find two Dominions who resemble one another, and thus they are often considered to be the most *outre* of the angelic host. One distinguishing trait of Dominions is that they usually carry a large orb or a massive scepter as a symbol of their authority. These items continually emanate a holy radiance of shimmering greens and golds and create a distinct aura around the angel. They are travelers and often extend themselves out over Creation to commune with the corporeal world.

Next are the Virtues, who act as channelers of vast energies from The Creator and His

closest orders, distributing it throughout the cosmos in myriad forms. Their primary job is to convey the unending supply of spiritual energy from the Heavens to the material worlds, where it can be disseminated into the collective human consciousness. These beings of light and grace are charged with the bestowing of Heavenly Miracles upon the world and Holy Blessings upon those individuals whom God chooses to favor. The Virtues are, in the Earthly sense, most often associated with heroes, and those who strive for good and seek courage in their darkest hour.

These inspirational angels manifest in the physical world as beings of pure light who, as Angels of the Cosmos, communicate with and oversee all the stars, planets, and moons that fill the galaxies. They oversee the nature of things as well, marking the paths of the seasons and the elements.

Also acting as vast generators and beacons, they impart their brilliance to those bodies, celestial or human, that are in need of it. In Biblical lore, two Virtues assisted in the Son of God's ascension into Heaven after His death, and two others were present at the blessed birth of Adam and Eve's first son, Cain.

Last among The Angels of the Cosmos are the Powers. Ensconced in the mystical borders between the Heavens and the corporeal universe, the Powers are the overseers of all the laws binding the physical realm. They are the guardians of peace, harmony, and order, and are obliged to act as Celestial enforcers as they maintain God's order upon Creation. The Divine energy that they channel down onto Earth is used to strengthen the religious and bolster the faithful against any who would seek to tear down the church. It is known that they keep count of the births and deaths of

God's followers throughout history. They are the gatherers of truth and the keepers of fact, and they hold within themselves all the historical knowledge of the world.

Acting as guardians in a more martial manner, the Powers patrol the borders of Heaven in order to discourage any hellish infiltration or aggression. Samael (later known as Lucifer), before his fall from grace, was the ruler of the Powers, and he shaped them as the most resolute and hardened of warriors. It is perhaps due to their station at the very edge of Heaven, and their proximity to the temptations of the outer worlds, that more members of the Powers than any other angel order were among the Fallen when Satan rose up and challenged God. Physical descriptions of the Powers mark them as the highest of the Celestial Host to possess what is basically a human form, though they are still perfect specimens and have wings.

THE ANGELS OF EARTH

The final house of angels, called The Angels of Earth, or The Angels of the World, resides primarily within the plane of Heavenly spirituality. They are, however, intricately involved with all the affairs of mankind. Their presence is almost a constant in the everyday lives of humans as they weave in and out of our reality, listening and influencing. As those who are chosen to come into direct contact with humanity, these three orders are charged with tasks such as revelation, diplomacy, and retribution.

The initial wing of the last triad is the Principalities. They are the bearers of the social mores necessary for successful politics and administration within the Earthly realm. To various degrees, they have been known to become patrons of entire cities, and even countries. The Principalities specialize in working with large groups and creating positive, symbiotic energies so that acceptable relations can flow.

Principalities are also said to be arbiters of taste and inspiration. They affect humans by bringing structure to the abstract, and vice versa, pushing the boundaries of what is possible in the corporeal realm. As the highest order of this final grouping, the Principalities are allowed more freedom to interact with mankind than the lower orders of Archangels or Angels, and they also determine the assignments of the others. In the physical sense, there are not many traits that distinguish the three orders of The Angels of Earth. They are, like the Powers, essentially a perfect representation of the human form, with sets of wings arising from their backs.

The Archangels comprise the second level of The Angels of Earth, and are the best known of the angelic orders. As is clear from their appearances in Holy Scripture, the first and foremost duty of these large, imposing angels is to carry out the will of God as it relates directly to humanity. They bring the answers to prayers, which is the primary reason why so many people are aware of them. Often, the presence of an Archangel is a signal that a great change is

signal that great change is imminent.

imminent. The actual number of Archangels and their position within the Celestial hierarchy has been a source of controversy and heated debate for thousands of years. Much of the confusion arises from the ancient Hebraic tradition of defining angels as simply "angel" or "archangel."

The final order of the Host is called, simply, Angels. Their focus is the guardianship of humanity, and indeed the entire world, in the literal sense. They exist within and without the material worlds, floating invisibly in the ether, or just out of sight as they keep watch over us. Although these beings rank as the lowest among their brethren in terms of power and proximity to God, the actual divisions that separate the orders are thin, and these angels have an important place in the Celestial Host. They are powerful, magnificent beings who radiate a perfect grace and spirituality. Guardian Angels are members of this lowest tier of angels, and are assigned to every individual person, place, and thing on Earth. There are innumerable angels who watch, record, and influence the happenings of the infinite worlds of Creation.

THE SEVEN HEAVENS

Angels dwell with God in Heaven—which is also home to the souls of the just. In traditional depictions, Heaven is the firmament above Creation. The Book of Enoch (or Henoch), an apocryphal book of the Bible, describes Heaven as seven realms, each with a distinct appearance and character that corresponds to angelic duties.

The First Heaven is named Shamayim, or Shamain, and is ruled by the Archangel Gabriel. It is called the lowest of the Heavens because it is connected to Earth, existing in both the spiritual and material planes. It is the home of hundreds of angelic astrologers who keep watch over all the stars of the universe. Shamayim, with its borders running along the Earth, most closely resembles the material world and has a natural atmosphere and surface water. In the Apocalypse of St. Paul, an apocryphal book of the Bible, it is described thus: "...every tree bore twelve harvests each year, and they produced various and diverse fruits, and I saw the fashion of that place and all the work of God, and I saw there

palm-trees of twenty cubits and others of ten cubits, and the land was seven times brighter than silver."

The Second Heaven is named Raquia, or Raqia, and is ruled by the Archangel Raphael. According to Enoch, not all of the Fallen Angels are exiled to Hell, as some are held here in a prison chamber. The cell is in total darkness, and the angels within wait until the day of final judgment to answer for their betrayal. Raquia is also the eternal resting place of the prophet John the Baptist.

The Third Heaven is called Shehaquim, or Sagun and, as explained within the Book of Enoch, is unique in that its northern border touches upon the realm of Hell. The Archangel Azriel presides over this densely populated realm, but he does so in name only, as the notoriously taciturn Archangel is rarely seen, allowing business to proceed chiefly of its own accord.

The northern lands are filled with icy, jagged mountains and their winds can strip flesh from bone. The border between Heaven and Hell is separated by a river of holy flame that causes any demonic or devilish creature attempting escape agonizing pain. The rare denizen who is able to survive the river crossing must then contend with the multitude of angels who patrol the pathways.

Conversely, the southern lands are a lush, fertile paradise, thought to be divinely connected to the Earthly Garden of Eden, as the Tree of Life also grows here. Two rivers, one of milk and honey and one of oil and wine, wind through the lands. This bountiful, celestial garden is where the souls are taken initially after the death of their physical bodies, to make for a softer transition between the worlds. These souls are carried along the rivers to the eternal afterlife.

The massive gate that leads into Shehaquim is carved of solid gold and 300 angels are in constant procession around the entrance. They shine the divine light from within themselves upon the entrance, which reflects out over the entire region.

The Fourth Heaven is named Machanon, or Machen. The Archangel Michael rules over this region, which is so similar to the southern reaches of Shehaquim, the Third Heaven, that they virtually are the same lands. The Apocalypse of St. Paul tells us that the actual Garden of Eden exists here, flourishing after its removal from Earth. Machanon is also said to be the native seat of the angels.

The Fifth Heaven is named Mathey, or Machon, and in some traditions, this is where God resides. The Creator holds court with his ministering angels who eternally sing hosannas and hymns in the southern half of the region. The very different northern boundaries are the home of Samael, who lives in an expansive corona of fire and smoke with no firm ground above or below his domain. The Watchers, a group of Fallen Angels, are kept bound here in the void until their final judgment.

The Sixth Heaven, called Zebul, has no single Archangel as its ruler. Seven powerful Cherubim and their seven phoenixes reside here, as do legions of other angels who specialize in the study of every science and art

form in existence. They mark the time and breadth of the universe from here, and consider their home a font of celestial knowledge.

The Seventh Heaven is called Araboth and, in some traditions, is ruled by the Archangel Samael. Other traditions maintain that this is where God dwells. Most of the heavenly host resides here, and the Seraphim, Cherubim, and Thrones choose this area of Heaven almost exclusively as their own. This is also the location of The Guph, the gigantic hall, which holds the souls of all those who have yet to be born.

$$\int_{a}^{b} f'(x)\, dx = f(b) - f(a)$$

THE SEVEN SPHERES

The angels, in a further division, are placed within seven spheres of influence, each of which directly affects mankind. They are as follows:

1. Angels of Power: These servants of God teach humans how to channel and release their spiritual energy. Prayer is the essential act of transforming mankind's raw spiritual power from its unfocused, nascent energies into a channeled, accessible step between God and man. The angels who are responsible for this usually stay with one person throughout their mortal lifespan, constantly teaching their charges to expand their soul's consciousness and refine their relationship with God.

2. Angels of Healing: These angels assist men and women in avoiding illnesses and disease, and in healing them when they

Building Angels

Angels of Healing

Angels of Music

contract a sickness. Working closely with a person's Guardian Angel, the healing angels are able to discern a person's emotional, mental, and spiritual malaise as well as physical sickness.

3. Guardian Angels of the Home: These angels protect the home and hearth against dangers, disasters, and ill fortune. The spiritually minded who accept the influences of these guardians seldom find their families or their properties at risk.

Angels of Beauty and Art

Angels of Nature

4. Building Angels: These angels serve as inspirations and help to perfect feelings and thoughts. Humans are still learning to separate themselves from their base emotions and instincts, and this sphere of angels attempts to build mental bridges within people's psyches so that they may one day overcome the fears and pain that prevent them from becoming truly enlightened beings. They also help to inspire humans to treat their bodies as temples, continually striving for a perfect integration of the physical, the mental, and the spiritual.

5. Angels of Nature: These angels oversee the elemental processes of earth, air, fire, and water. They monitor the relationship

Angels of the Home

Angels of Power

between nature and mankind, and simultaneously help to educate humans about that balance. In their relations with mankind these angels are more organic than spiritual.

6. Angels of Music: Music has always been an important facet of angelic existence, and it is only natural that an entire wing of the Host concerns itself with the infusion of music into human cultures. Though they serve to assist in the perfection of every single note of musical composition, these angels do not focus solely on religious, or spiritual, music. The Angels of Music lend their inspiration to all musical creations of mankind.

7. Angels of Beauty and Art: This group of inspirational angels is concerned with artistic creation and the appreciation of beautiful things. Much like the Angels of Music, this legion of muses is concerned with mankind's relationship with the arts, rather than simply the religious aspect of paintings, writings, sculpture, and other artistic creations. The constant proliferation of angelic beings appearing in man's

inspiration to all musical creations.

artistic creations is no coincidence, as these angels have been the sources of inspiration for many of mankind's greatest works. The number of these angels is relatively small compared to some of the other spheres, owing to the much smaller percentage of humans able to create inspired works of art.

TRADITIONS & CUSTOMS

Food and Drink

A fascinating aspect of all angels in general, and Archangels and Angels specifically is that like humans they eat and drink. Manna is the Hebrew name of the foodstuff that angels consume. The literal translation of the word forms an odd question: "What is this?" While the exact type of food the word represents is still a mystery, it is thought to be a rich, earthy, bread-like substance. It is not only consumed by the angels, but it is also at times given to God's loyal human subjects. Elijah was fed manna by ravens during his forty days in the desert, and the exiled Hebrews led out of Egypt by Moses were also given manna by God as they crossed the wilderness to Mount Sinai.

The Archangels are marked

The Angel Alphabet

Another facet of angels that is much akin to human beings is that they are able to read and write languages. There have been a handful of alphabets discovered throughout the ages that have been considered to be angelic, or heavenly, in origin. The Archangels and their regalia are marked with certain sigils, symbols, and runes, all using a specific alphabet. The "letters" that make up that alphabet, known as Angelic Script, do not conform to the rules of any Earthly script other than the basics—the runic marks are strung together

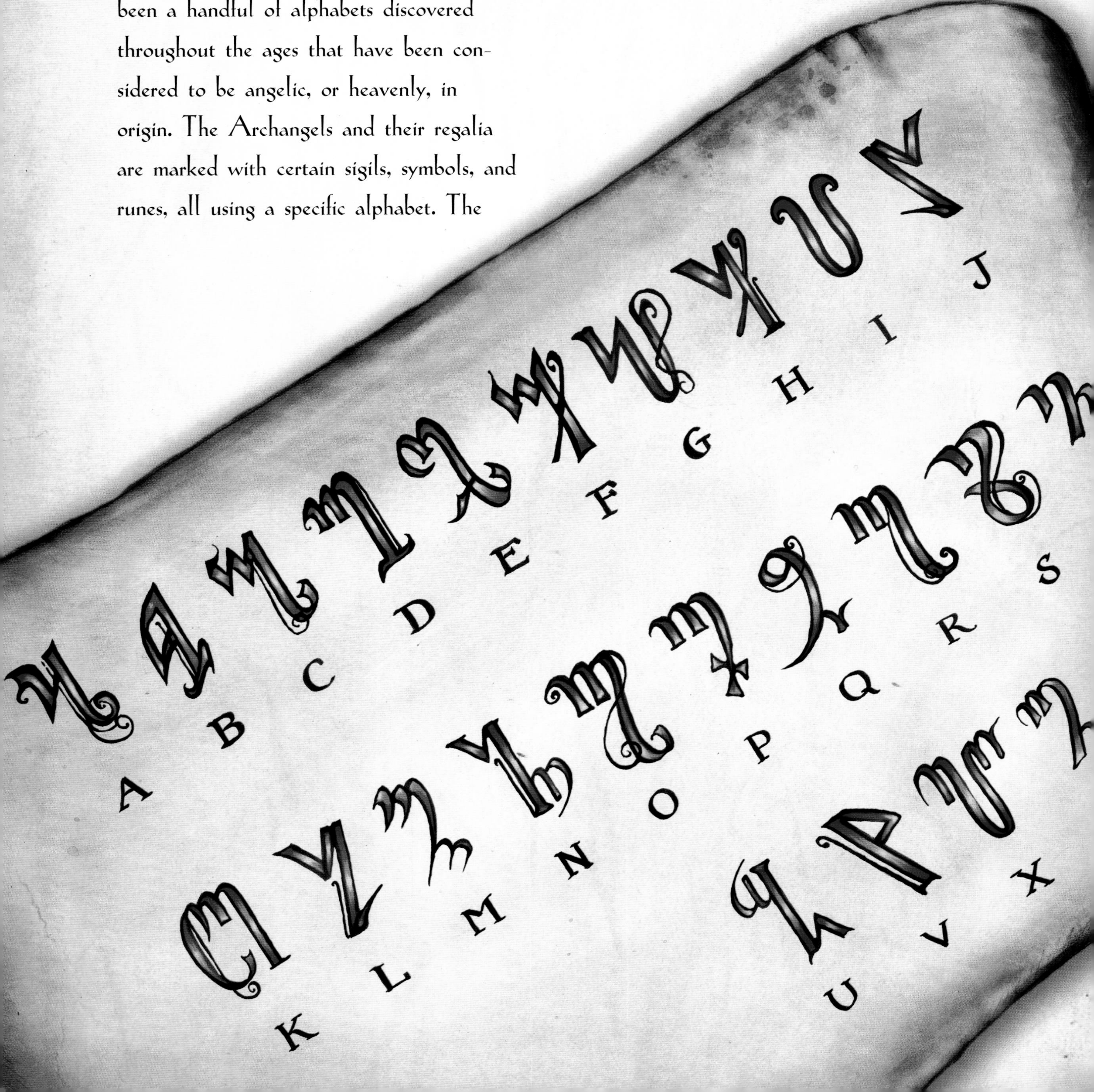

A B C D E F G H I J
K L M N O P Q R S
U V X

to represent an ideal, and moreover, a vocal sound.

This Angelic Script is presented in two versions, informal and formal. The primary difference between the two is that, in the informal, runes are kept separate but placed close together to form a word—while in the formal state, the sigils are intertwined and tend to form beautifully intricate symbols. The Archangels are all marked with symbols that are formed from formal Angelic Script. Some have their names inscribed in their skin and on their weapons, while others prefer to have Biblical or Divine scripture emblazoned on their bodies.

Cultural Influences

Angelic beings have been spoken of, in many different forms, and in dozens of varied cultures for thousands of years. Angels have been seen by prophets and shepherds, as well as by priests and farmers. They have even been seen by those who do not have any religious beliefs. In the majority of those cultures, the ideals of angels are very different than in the three faiths previously mentioned, and some depict angels as more mythical creatures than man-like servants of a higher power.

In ancient Egypt, the Pharaoh Akhenaton winnowed a very large pantheon of powerful gods who were generally the equal to each other down to a single supreme ruler, Aten the sun god. Akhenaton decreed that all the other gods of the Nile were now subservient to the one god above all, and bade the priests of the altered religion to begin describing the other gods, such as Set, Isis, Geb, and Osiris, as being diminished in stature. As was the usual standard for those times, when Akhenaton passed away, his successor restored the pantheon to its former glory, but kept the imagery and ideal of these winged servants of the gods.

Similarly in Persia some time in the sixth century, the prophet Zoroaster declared that only one god was worthy enough to send prayers to, and he would be Ahura Mazda. However, as the local people and government protested, Zoroaster relented and brought back the other members of the pantheon—albeit in diminished roles. The holy man assigned the old gods a new level of power, one that was lesser compared to Ahura Mazda. He then renamed their stations as "bounteous immortals" and "good spirits," depending on the power level of the original god or goddess.

When Alexander the Great marched through Asia Minor and destroyed most fractal religions and their offshoots, Zoroaster and his followers were on the verge of extinction. A tiny number of Zoroastrians survived and fled to India, where they renamed themselves the Parsees. Their religion has barely survived into modern times, though it has been virtually assimilated into the Hindi religion. They consider their primary god, Ahura Mazda, to be dead, but his assistants and brethren in the great sky carry on his legacy.

Angels are also found, in trace forms, in the Asiatic religions that comprise Buddhism and Taoism. These primal, winged beings bear little resemblance to the angels that we consider canonical today, but they certainly influenced many people's imaginations as word of these strange creatures traveled across Asia and down into the Middle East. These early angelic beings were later transformed in ancient Assyrian cults and Mesopotamian invocations, becoming an ideal. Told and retold they gained prominence as their legends traveled through different lands eventually finding their way into Manichaean, Judaic, Christian, and Islamic lore.

Among Native Americans, who generally practice shamanism, winged beings that act as messengers and assassins for the gods are a common theme. Their "angels" always have bird-like aspects, like those of the eagle or the raven, and some of their spirits are helpful to the tribes, while some are evil and steal away their lives. The tribal shamans of the Native Americans are considered to be holy men and generally set the religious philosophies for each different tribe, yet it is an incredible coincidence that tribes from opposite ends

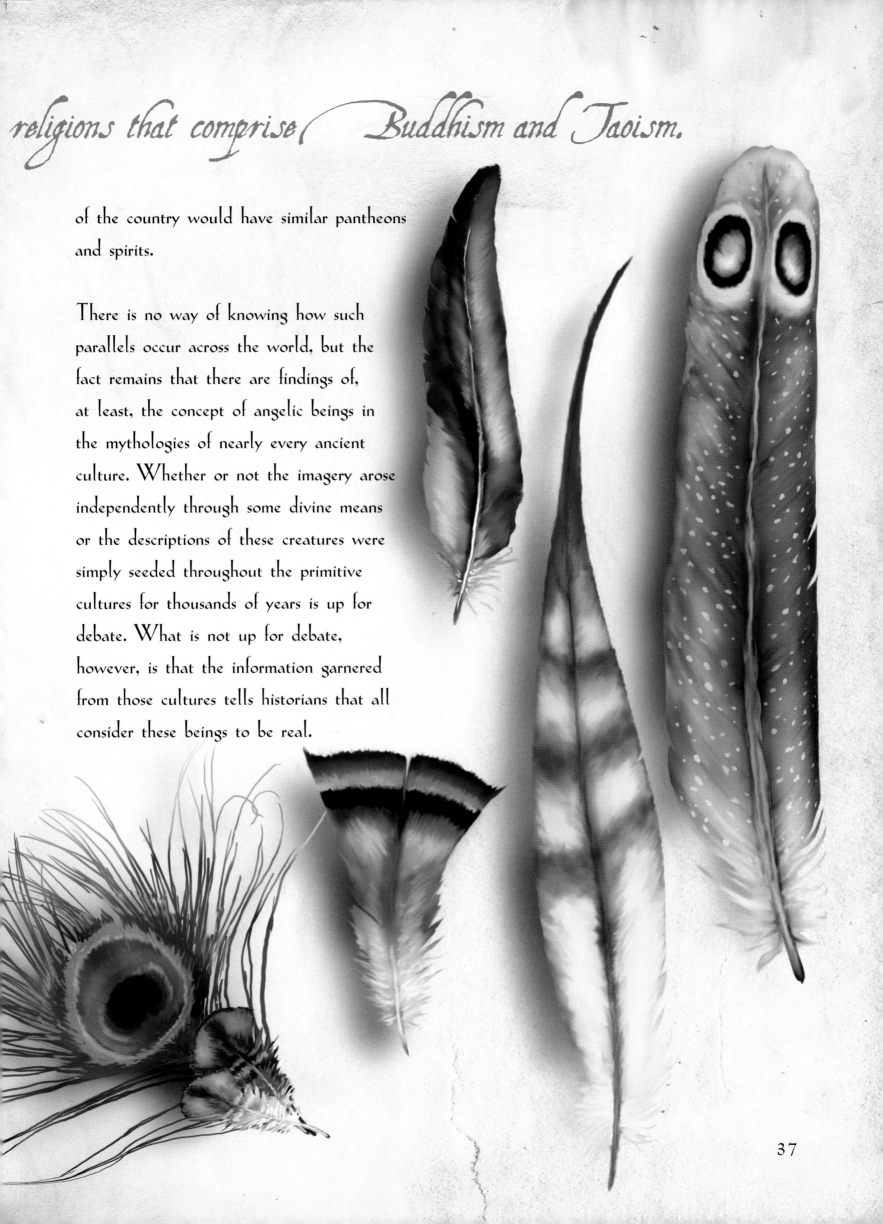

religions that comprise Buddhism and Taoism.

of the country would have similar pantheons and spirits.

There is no way of knowing how such parallels occur across the world, but the fact remains that there are findings of, at least, the concept of angelic beings in the mythologies of nearly every ancient culture. Whether or not the imagery arose independently through some divine means or the descriptions of these creatures were simply seeded throughout the primitive cultures for thousands of years is up for debate. What is not up for debate, however, is that the information garnered from those cultures tells historians that all consider these beings to be real.

Archangels

MICHAEL

> HEARKEN WHEN MICHAEL SPEAKETH,
> FOR I AM HE THAT STANDS
> IN THE PRESENCE OF GOD
> —APOCALYPSE OF PAUL 42

The Archangel Michael has the distinction of being only one of two angels written about in both the Bible and in the Koran. The other named Archangel, Gabriel, is mentioned before Michael in both books, but that is the only instance in which Michael is subordinated.

His common, modern name derives from an ancient Sumerian spelling, Micha-el. The "-el" suffix has two differing but related definitions—"brightness" or "shining"—ending the names of every other Archangel.

He is also sometimes called Sabbathiel by the Israelites, Beshter by the Persians, and Mikael by the Mesopotamians.

Michael holds the key to the gates of

Michael is depicted as the leader of the Celestial Host. His name translates as "Who Is As God," and in Christian literature he is described as the greatest Holy figure aside from God Himself and His Son.

Michael's role as the foremost servant in Heaven is clear from episodes in which God sends Michael down to act on His behalf.

One passage from the Bible relates a conversation between the prophet Daniel and God, wherein God tells Daniel that Michael will come to him in The Lord's stead, as Michael is the one, over all, whom God trusts with such a task. That trust also extends to Michael holding the key to the gates of Heaven and the gates of the Abyss at his belt.

silver shield

Heaven and the gates of the Abyss.

Originating out of Chaldean legend, wherein he was worshipped as something of a minor deity, Michael evolved throughout the years as a Christian staple. The Chaldeans were the original, primitive sect of the Semitic religion, who emerged from the area that was then known as Babylon around 575 B.C.

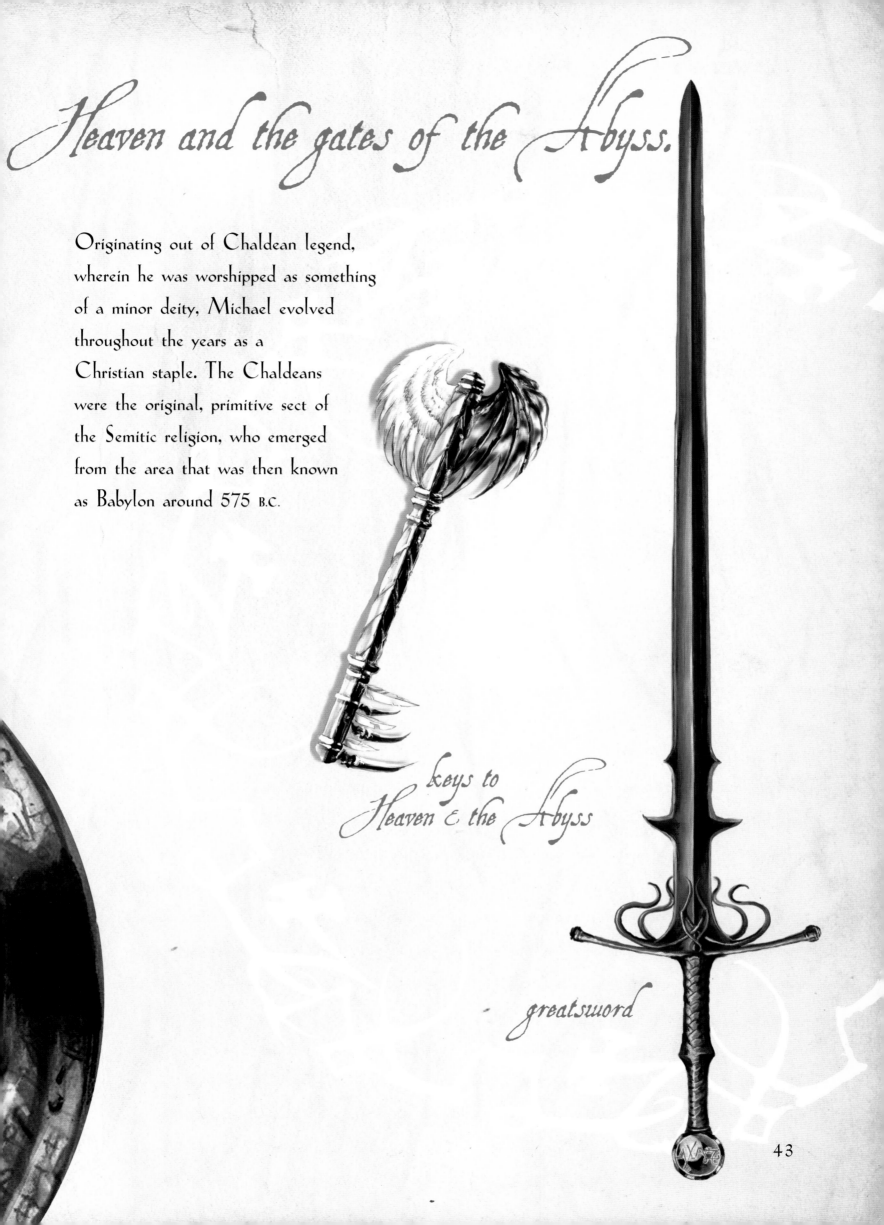

keys to
Heaven & the Abyss

greatsword

43

Michael's singular standing in Heaven affords him great domain, and he is known by many titles. He is called:

Chief in the Order of Virtues
Chief of Archangels
Prince in the Presence of God
The Angel of Repentance
The Angel of Mercy
The Angel of Righteousness
The Angel of Sanctification
Ruler of the Fourth Heaven (Machanon)
Tutelary Sar (Angelic Prince) of Israel
Guardian of Jacob
Conqueror of Satan
Viceroy of Heaven (the station given to Samael, also known as Lucifer, before his betrayal)
Deliverer of the Faithful
Warrior of God
Slayer of the Dragon

He is named as the author of the entire Psalm 85, a unique distinction, as no other Archangel is given sole credit for a Biblical passage.

Known to be the most passionate and tempestuous of the Archangels, Michael is always depicted powerfully in literature and shown dramatically in artwork. His deeds are often described in glowing excess to emphasize their importance, no matter how small the true act. Engravings, drawings, and paintings of Michael throughout history idealize his physical beauty and showcase the traditional trappings of his station: silver armor, round shield, and unsheathed greatsword.

The origin of the sword reflects the lore of its wielder, and is defined in Chaldean myth. The ancients of that religion saw Michael as an instrument of vengeance, and bestowed upon him an artifact that would well serve his justified wrath.

The greatsword tapers up from its set of notches to a perfect point. Michael's

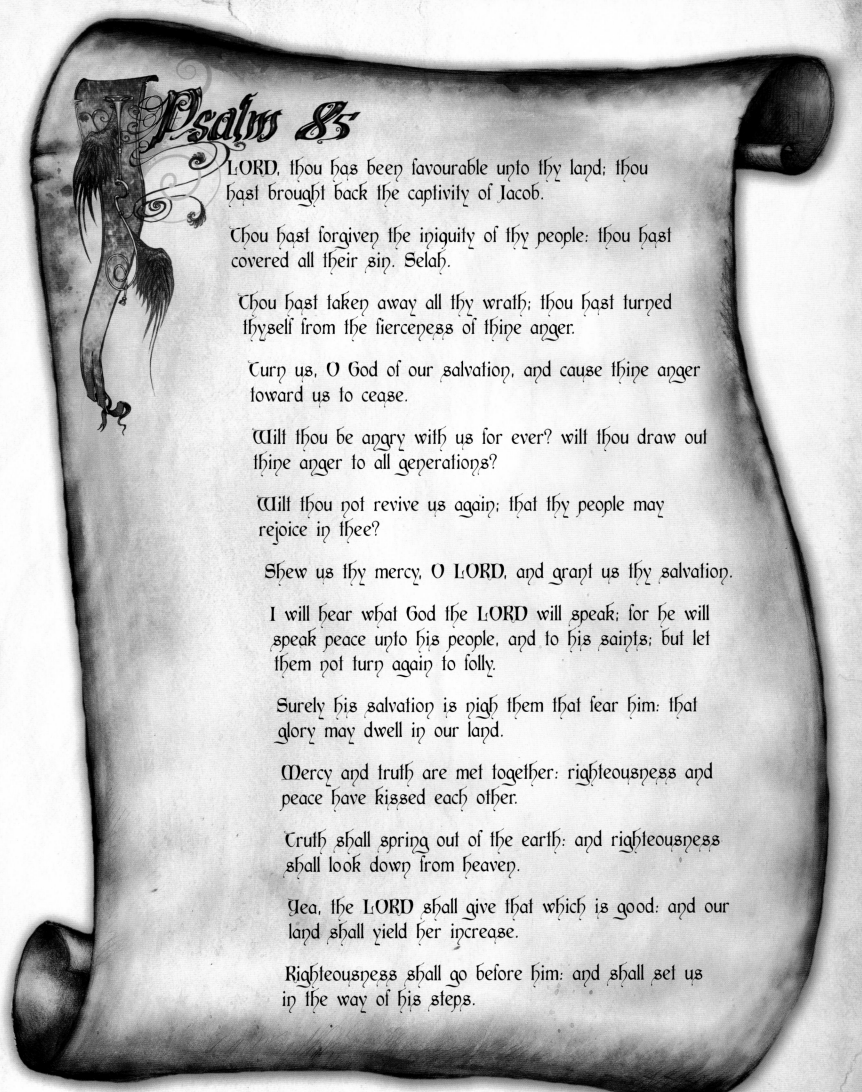

Psalm 85

LORD, thou has been favourable unto thy land; thou hast brought back the captivity of Jacob.

Thou hast forgiven the iniquity of thy people: thou hast covered all their sin. Selah.

Thou hast taken away all thy wrath; thou hast turned thyself from the fierceness of thine anger.

Turn us, O God of our salvation, and cause thine anger toward us to cease.

Wilt thou be angry with us for ever? wilt thou draw out thine anger to all generations?

Wilt thou not revive us again; that thy people may rejoice in thee?

Shew us thy mercy, O LORD, and grant us thy salvation.

I will hear what God the LORD will speak; for he will speak peace unto his people, and to his saints; but let them not turn again to folly.

Surely his salvation is nigh them that fear him; that glory may dwell in our land.

Mercy and truth are met together; righteousness and peace have kissed each other.

Truth shall spring out of the earth: and righteousness shall look down from heaven.

Yea, the LORD shall give that which is good: and our land shall yield her increase.

Righteousness shall go before him; and shall set us in the way of his steps.

greatsword is four-and-a-half feet long. The composition of the sword is unknown, but many have speculated that the material is, like Michael himself, not of Earthly origin.

At the very bottom of the sword, a perfectly round pommel is engraved with formal Angelic Script that translates as "Who Is As God." The cross-hatched hilt of the sword is long and thin, accepting the tang of the blade gracefully.

The choice of a longer hilt gives Michael more options in combat. More often than not, Michael will wield his sword with one hand in order to use his shield in battle. However, the advantage of a longer hilt is that, if he so chooses, Michael may forego his shield and wield the sword with two hands. This particular fighting style gives his strikes greater momentum and impact.

Just as his greatsword is a standard feature of Michael's depiction across cultures and history, so is his silver armor. The exact number of pieces of armor varies, from the minimum—a constant pauldron upon his right shoulder—to a full suit of heavy plate when going into battle.

His large silver shield is engraved with a prayer to God, along with Michael's name in formal angelic script. The paired metal greaves are simple but elegant, with a dark patina and gold trim. The script again reflects the "Who Is As God" name of Michael. His belt carries his seal on the golden, circular front crest and is fashioned of hardened, gilded leather. The keys to Heaven and to the Abyss both hang from the belt on leather straps. His leather kilt is studded with large emeralds at the bottom of each strap.

translates as "Who Is As God"

Michael's warlike nature and loyalty to the Creator have provided writers and artists with an endless source of inspiration. He helped the children of Israel escape from their tyrannical foes, and he also protected the church's armies against their heretical enemies.

metal greaves

pauldron

golden belt

He was the patron of every Christian knight.

He was notably the patron of every Christian knight, who called upon his name in battle. Michael's protection was so absolute and prevalent that even Christian women would pray to him while going through the trying act of childbirth.

Michael's responsibilities as the protector of God's children were not always revealed as a show of detached power. When the Holy City of Jerusalem was under siege by the Assyrians, the warlike Archangel responded with a direct, brutal hand. The massive army of more than 185,000 soldiers was being led by their despot King, Sennacherib, who planned to raze the city from existence. The whole of the city cried out to Heaven for assistance. Michael streaked down from the sky and destroyed the whole of the Assyrian army in a single night, saving their ruler for last and executing him without mercy.

One of Michael's domains is the Last Judgment. He holds the Scales of Justice to weigh the souls of all men. It is he who delivers each immortal spirit to its resting place in the eternal light. The extraction of

Templar shield

49

He engages Satan and binds

a human soul can happen in one of two ways. If the person was wicked and cruel, the soul is ripped from the body, causing the person to endure the rest of existence in excruciating pain. Conversely, if the person was good and kindly, the soul is removed with a care and grace that allows the ascension of the spirit without trauma.

Michael is also known as the benevolent angel of death. He sheds tears over the souls of the pious dead, and as he cries their sins are washed away.

In The Book of Revelation, it is Michael who leads the armies of Heaven against the legions of Satan, who is often depicted at the time of the War in Heaven as a serpent or dragon. At the pinnacle of the great battle, Michael descends from the highest point in Heaven, holding the key to the Abyss and a great chain. He engages Satan and binds him tightly with the chain, which will hold the monstrous dragon for 1,000 years. Michael then casts the betrayer down into Hell and locks the gates.

him tightly with the chain.

There are two instances of Michael interacting with the denizens of Hell after the first War in Heaven. In the first, he warns the betrayers at the Gates of Hell of the imminent Great Flood, or Deluge. He weeps as he speaks, saddened by the immense wave of death which will soon be bringing so many souls to him. As the fallen angels jeer Michael's uncharacteristic softness, they see their jailer's tears turn to precious stones as they strike the unholy ground.

It is also written in the Dead Sea Scrolls that, some millennia after the Fall of Satan, a second deadly skirmish takes place in the skies above Heaven. Michael, the Prince of Light, leads the Celestial Host against legions of demons who through trickery, escape through the Gates of Damnation. Using unparalleled strategic skills and sheer power, Michael and the Heavenly Host return the renegades back into exile.

GABRIEL

> I AM GABRIEL, WHO STANDS
> AT THE LEFT HAND OF GOD
> —LUKE 1:19

The Archangel Gabriel has the distinction of being the only other angel, besides Michael, who is written about in both the Bible and the Koran.

The translation of Gabriel's name is "God Is My Strength," and in every instance where he appears in religious literature, that epithet is justified. Whereas those who came before him, Samael and Michael, had specific attributes that they could focus on their provinces, Gabriel serves as the intermediary between God and Man. This duty is the foundation of both his greatest triumphs as an Archangel, and one noted failure.

Gabriel is the only Archangel who is also viewed by some cultures as a woman. Variations of his name, such as Gabrielle, lend themselves to this interpretation, and many religious scholars point to numerous instances in oft-translated Biblical texts where acts and descriptions would designate Gabriel as female. Traits that lend strength to this argument are Gabriel's mild personality and tolerant manner, which contrast greatly with Samael's brash pride and Michael's passionate, aggressive character.

Other variations of Gabriel's name include Gabri-el (Sumerian), Gavriel (from the Tiberian—an offshoot of Hebrew), Gabril (from the Arabic), and Jibril (from the Islamic).

As with Michael, Gabriel originates wholly out of Chaldean lore, but once he was introduced and tales of the mild-mannered winged demi-god spread, Gabriel was accepted and promoted eagerly by a wide variety of religions. Muslims (Mohammedans), Talmudic Jews, and Arabs all took the attributes given to him by the Chaldeans and built upon them heavily. Gabriel is also notably the angel who receives the most prayers from mankind.

viewed by some cultures as a woman.

Among many religions that acknowledge him, Gabriel is named as the Governor of Eden and Chief of the Angelic Guards who are placed over Paradise. He is also known as:

The Angel of Birth
The Angel of Death
The Angel of the Annunciation
The Angel of the Resurrection
The Angel of Mercy
The Angel of Revelation
The Angel of Humanity
The Angel of the Incarnation
The Angel of the Consolation

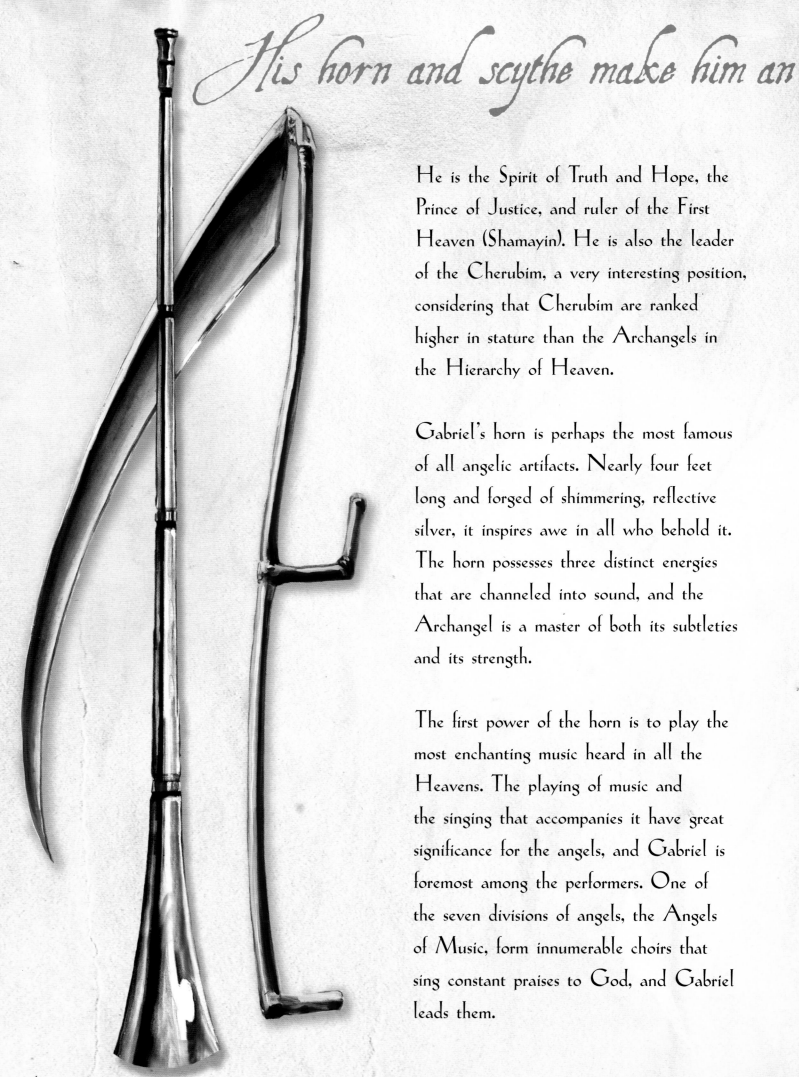

His horn and scythe make him an

He is the Spirit of Truth and Hope, the Prince of Justice, and ruler of the First Heaven (Shamayin). He is also the leader of the Cherubim, a very interesting position, considering that Cherubim are ranked higher in stature than the Archangels in the Hierarchy of Heaven.

Gabriel's horn is perhaps the most famous of all angelic artifacts. Nearly four feet long and forged of shimmering, reflective silver, it inspires awe in all who behold it. The horn possesses three distinct energies that are channeled into sound, and the Archangel is a master of both its subtleties and its strength.

The first power of the horn is to play the most enchanting music heard in all the Heavens. The playing of music and the singing that accompanies it have great significance for the angels, and Gabriel is foremost among the performers. One of the seven divisions of angels, the Angels of Music, form innumerable choirs that sing constant praises to God, and Gabriel leads them.

intimidating sight on the battlefield.

The second power of the glorious instrument is to lull all those who hear its soft, lush tones into a blissful sleep. Gabriel will often use this aspect of the horn when he makes a visitation to a single person and wishes the encounter to be private.

Through the third, and most potent, of the horn's inherent powers Gabriel channels his celestial might into waves of unimaginable strength and destruction. In the first War in Heaven, Gabriel used the horn's ultimate might to keep the legions of betrayers away from the battlefield as Michael defeated Lucifer.

In the rare instances when a more visceral show of power is necessary, Gabriel will use a huge scythe that possesses an awesome sharpness. This vicious weapon is described in The Talmud's Sanhedrin 95b as being "ready since Creation" to spill the blood of those who have declared their enmity with God. Though scythes are thought of as mere farming implements used to cut down stalks of wheat and other grains, they make surprisingly effective and dangerous weapons—especially in the case of Gabriel's

scythe, whose wooden ash handle spans a full seven feet in length and whose iron blade is nearly five feet long. Gabriel girds himself in either heavy, burnished armor, or he wraps his body with thick layers of heavy cloth, which is surprisingly effective against attacks. In flight, he appears as though surrounded by a corona of stunning white, which whips wildly around his body. His unique, daring look and overwhelming power with either his horn or scythe make him an intimidating sight on the battleground.

The wide belt at his waist is composed of leather and gold and the epithet "God Is My Strength" is carved into the soft metal. Being the Angel of Revelation and the foremost messenger of the Word to mankind, Gabriel is fluent in all the languages of men. This also includes the secret languages of Syriac and Chaldee, which were only spoken by sacred priests and holy prophets of those religions.

A mighty linguist, Gabriel taught Joseph the seventy languages spoken at Babel. The Tower of Babel was intended to be the highest monument to God, one that dared to reach all the way to the Gates of Heaven. Far from impressed by the efforts of the audacious men who built it, God decreed that the workers would all speak different languages so that they could not understand each other. Chaos fell upon them, and the tower was abandoned. Gabriel, in his ministrations to Joseph, taught the young prophet all of the languages spoken that day in order for Joseph to keep a truer record in his passages.

One of Gabriel's longest terms upon Earth accounted for his most personal experience with mankind. Over a span of twenty-two years, he appeared at regular intervals to the prophet Mohammed in order to dictate to him the whole of the Koran. Mohammed, in his personal writings, described Gabriel as regal and compassionate. There are 114 sourates, or volumes, that comprise the Koran, and the prophet was careful to take down the Archangel's words verbatim.

During one of the last points of the transcription to Mohammed, however, Gabriel came to a very harsh passage and felt a moment of concern in the telling; unintentionally misspeaking the Word. As a result, upon his return to the realm of Heaven, Gabriel found the gates impassable. For an unknown span of time, the Archangel awaited his return to Grace as he witnessed another, lesser angel, Dobiel, act as his proxy. At the end of his exile, Gabriel felt a call from beyond the curtain and returned to his station. No word was ever spoken of the incident by Gabriel or his winged brethren.

Gabriel's other memorable interactions with humankind include two encounters with the prophet, Daniel. Daniel had a dream in which a ram and a "he-goat" engaged in a lengthy, awesome battle. The Holy Man prayed for guidance to unravel the mystery, and Gabriel appeared to explain to Daniel the meaning of the vision. The Archangel described to him the coming of the Greeks, led by one called Alexander, who would conquer the Persians. That prophecy would come to pass in the year 331 B.C., when after three years of war Alexander defeated King Darius III and became ruler of

was abandoned.

Persia. This was the second occurrence of Gabriel playing the role of divine oracle for Daniel, although it was the first in which the prophet personally entreated the Archangel. The first meeting between Daniel and Gabriel was some time earlier, when Gabriel came down from Heaven to announce the birth of the Messiah—a full 500 years before he would repeat the same information to the Virgin Mary. Many theologians speculate that Daniel was chosen to hear the divine decree because of his great intensity for prayer and loyalty to God.

Gabriel is called The Angel of the Annunciation, which is the formal term for such holy and ceremonial messages. In what Christians mark as his most important appearance on Earth, the Archangel brought down to the Virgin Mary the decree that she would bear the Son of God.

As an intermediary between the divine and humankind, Gabriel oversees the Treasury of Souls, also called the Guph. One of his primary responsibilities is to select, from this divine chamber, the order of souls to be born upon the Earth. To facilitate the transmigration, Gabriel sends a sparrow to escort each soul. The birds sing a constant song while in transit, and continue singing until the new soul is born. (The number of souls is finite, and one of the signs of the Apocalypse is the emptying of the Guph.)

Not only is Gabriel assigned as deliverer of souls to each newborn child, but he is also given the task of watching over the unborn as they come to term. While still growing within their mother's womb, the Archangel whispers all the knowledge of Heaven to them so that they will know their Lord. As each baby is born, Gabriel seals the secrets within the child until their souls return to their Creator. He presses his finger to their lips, leaving a soft mark that appears as the cleft beneath the nose.

There is one instance of a person who disputed the prophecies borne from Gabriel's grace. The priest Zacharias of Alba encountered Gabriel as the cleric prayed at an altar burning with golden incense. Gabriel declared that Zacharias's

sparrow to escort each soul.

wife, Elisabeth, would give birth to a Holy Man who would be called John the Precursor. The priest told Gabriel that the Archangel must be mistaken, for his wife was long in years and could not possibly bear any more children. Enraged by the man's audacity, Gabriel struck him mute until such time as the child would be born. On the day of the baby's birth, Zacharias wrote upon a tablet "His name is John" and opened his throat to sing praise to God. This baby would one day grow up to become John the Baptist.

In a well-known story, Gabriel interceded on behalf of Joseph, youngest son of Jacob. Jacob had given his son richly ornamented robes, signaling the family heritage, because he felt Joseph was worthiest. Jealous at being passed over, Joseph's ten older brothers stripped the young prophet bare and sold him into slavery to traveling Midianites. Unwilling to let such a righteous young man be so humiliated, the Lord took pity on the boy and sent the Archangel Gabriel to him. Gabriel saw that Joseph, though naked, wore an amulet

around his neck, and transformed the bauble into a long, fine garment so that the future Viceroy of Egypt would regain some of his dignity. It is said that Gabriel appeared as a stern, winged man cloaked in a scintillating blue aura.

Though it is the Archangel Michael who usually holds the standard of God's divine retribution, there have been a number of significant occurrences in which Gabriel's battle fervor outshone his fellow angels in conveying the Lord's wrath. In perhaps the most awesome display of Celestial might against man, Gabriel was charged to raze the brazen, sinful cities of Sodom and Gomorrah to the ground. Amidst storms of

lightning and fire, a rampaging Gabriel came screaming down from the Heavens to deliver the ultimate message. Wielding his huge scythe, he cut a bloody swath through both dens of iniquity, leaving complete destruction in his wake. The devastation was so thorough that it left no trace of the people or their buildings. After the cataclysm, the Dead Sea was poured in to cover the ground so that no man would be able to exist on the tainted land.

In the early days of man's existence on Earth, God dispatched angels called Watchers, also known as the Grigori, to teach humans simple tasks and show them how to worship. This they did, but they also taught Man forbidden lore, such as warfare and magic, and incurred God's retribution.

The Creator denied them Heaven and made them to stay upon Earth, where these descendant angels eventually began to interact with humans and produce offspring known as the Nephilim. The Nephilim became crazed giants, hunting and eating

any who fell in their path. In a rage, the Lord cast down into Hell the fallen Watchers, and then dispatched Gabriel to kill the Nephilim. The Archangel used cunning and stealth to turn the massive creatures against one another, and they almost murdered themselves all. The giant Goliath, killed by David, was said to be the last in the true bloodline of the Nephilim.

Gabriel is also the Archangel who awakened the desperate inspiration of the French heroine Joan of Arc. His urgings led her to the magnificent heights she attained while battling for her country's final independence from England. In 1424, the young woman began experiencing visions of the Archangel, along with various saints

Joan of Arc

68

and prophets, who all pleaded with her to force the reinstatement of the Dauphin in Reims. At the time of her execution, it is said a white dove leapt from her chest and was escorted to Heaven by an angelic being who carried a long silver horn.

And as to the Archangel Gabriel's famous instrument, it is written that he will sound his horn on the day of Armageddon, when the Rapture will take place. All the souls of the faithful will arise that day and join each other in eternal peace with the Creator, as the prophecy that foretells the second coming of the Messiah is fulfilled. The triumphant blasts of the Celestial horn will tear down all walls, break all chains, and bend all bars in order to allow all who will serve the Lord, access to Him. Gabriel's unfettered spirit will flow through the world and serve as a beacon for all those who wish to follow it to their final destination.

RAPHAEL

HE WHO PRESIDES OVER EVERY
SUFFERING AND EVERY WOUND OF THE
SONS OF MAN, THE HOLY RAPHAEL

–1 ENOCH 40:9

There has always been a curiosity surrounding Raphael. Though his inclusion in the highest angelic station is accepted and understood in virtually all religious lore, he is never actually mentioned by name within the main text of the Bible. The first named reference to Raphael as an Archangel, and indeed the majority of what we know of him, is written in the Book of Tobit, a volume of the Apocrypha. The Apocrypha is a large set of books that was completely and officially excised from original Biblical text in 1901. While these canonical volumes are not technically books of the Bible, they are important enough to be considered sacred text by Hebrews, Protestants, and Catholics alike.

As with Michael and Gabriel, Raphael's origins lie with the Chaldeans, who originally named him Labbiel. His name

translates to "God Has Healed" and it is written in Enoch that he is "one of the four presences, set over all the diseases and all the wounds of the children of man." The Hebrew term *rapha* means doctor (surgeon), or healer, and it is likely that the name Labbiel was abandoned to illustrate the given role of Rapha-el (his original Chaldean name) as a Healer of Man. Raphael's relationship to mankind is considered a reflection of the paternal bond between God and man.

Raphael's Heavenly and Earthly titles include:

Regent of The Sun
Chief of the Order of Virtues
Governor of the South
Guardian of the West

He is known as the Ruler of Raquia, the Second Heaven, and Overseer of the Evening Winds.

golden shield

Among his Domain titles are:

Angel of Providence
Angel of Repentance
Angel of Prayer
Angel of Love
Angel of Joy
Angel of Light
Angel of Healing

He was named the Guardian of the Tree of Life in the Garden of Eden after the expulsion of Adam and Eve.

no limits to its range when thrown.

Unlike most of the other Archangels, Raphael is also included in other orders of the Celestial Hierarchy. He holds marked places with the Seraphim, the Cherubim, the Dominions, and the Powers. This is because he is the head of the guardian angels and that sphere of duty is spread out over many of the other segments of angels. Raphael oversees the duties of these angels as they watch eternally over the innumerable souls within Creation, and they report their findings to him exclusively. He displays a patron's sense in dealing with mankind that does not extend to his fellow Archangels.

Raphael's left arm is tattooed with informal Angelic Script that reads "God Has Healed." He is frequently depicted in artwork as a powerfully built, winged man walking along a road holding a staff, his dozens-of-sets of wings shining brilliantly with golden light.

He is also often shown in the guise of a man who is holding audience with one or more unsuspecting humans.

Though fighting is not his strength, when the horn of battle sounds, Raphael will answer as is his duty. In combat, he wields a magnificent and terrifying spear that has no limits to its range when thrown. The primary blade of the nearly nine-foot-long iron-sculpted spear is emblazoned with the Archangel's name, written in formal angelic script. Raphael does not enter combat joyously or often, and he always seeks to end the conflict as quickly as possible. Fortunately for him, the powerful and vicious spear in his hands makes a brief fight certain.

In preparation for war, Raphael eschews the heavier armor types that his brother Michael wears, preferring to attack at a greater speed. Over his golden, full-plate armor he wears a gilded leather battle kilt. Forged of iron and mounted with golden sun icons, Raphael's bracers and greaves provide protection, without sacrificing maneuverability.

His golden belt also carries a striking sun display and is inscribed with "The Shining One Who Heals" in formal angelic script. This stunning design is capped with numerous sun-shaped rondels, attached to the belt, which encircle the bottom.

Raphael also carries a large golden shield that resembles a blazing sun. The shield can reflect pure sunlight from its face, even in times where there is no light source. Runes inscribed along the inner rim of the shield echo the phrase engraved on his belt.

In his first appearance in Biblical history, Raphael acts as a boon companion and

greaves

Raphael will answer as is his duty.

guide to Tobit's son, Tobias, as the two travel from Media to Nineveh. Calling himself "Azarias, son of the great Ananias," during the journey, he displays both his divine power and his protective nature by defeating and binding the devil Asmodeus (the commander of Satan's armies) in the upper Egyptian desert. The demonic presence had been sent to plague Sarah, Tobias's fiancée, and threaten their life together as man and wife.

On the journey home, Tobias attempts to catch a monstrous fish that threatens to devour the young man. Raphael assists him in pulling in the giant fish, then instructs Tobias on how to use every part of the fish not only for food, but for medicinal purposes as well. At the end of the long trek back to Media, Raphael heals old Tobit's blind-

ness with parts of the fish and then reveals himself to be an Archangel, while blessing them both. This illustrates two of Raphael's main duties, that of a healer and that of one who watches over travelers on the road to God.

In Jerusalem, there existed a clear pool of untainted water at the small town of Bethesda. The infirm and chronically ill knew that the Archangel Raphael would often visit the spring and infuse it with a healing power. They would then immerse themselves in the mystic waters and become healed through the merest touch of the angel's divine grace.

When God asked his servants for a contingent to stay upon the Earth for a time to teach mankind a

belt with sun-shaped rondels

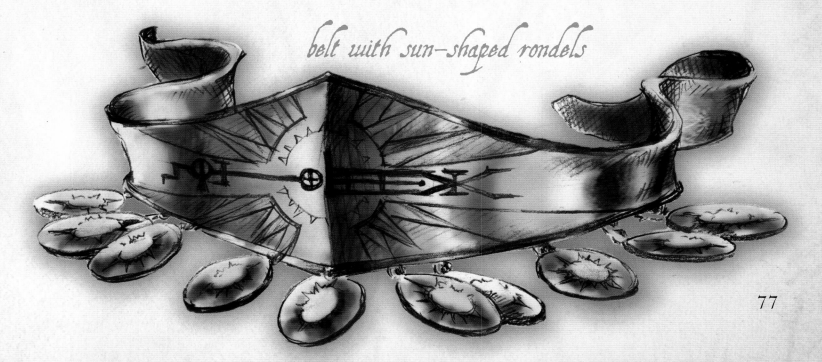

civilized manner, Raphael was the first to volunteer. The Watchers, as they were later known, spent many years alongside the humans, and some gave up their divinity in order to experience procreation. A madness struck deep into these fallen Watchers—a madness that was then passed on to their monstrous progeny, the Nephilim. Raphael, grieving over his lost comrades, helped keep the former angels at bay while Gabriel was charged with destroying the murderous giant children. Raphael asked for leniency when the judgment of the Watchers was passed, but his plea was denied.

Before the Great Flood, Raphael delivered to Noah a divine book that contained many advanced techniques in medicine and physics. Noah did not know it at the time, but most of the book's knowledge was to be employed only after Raphael charged him to build the great Ark. The construction of the massive boat would have been impossible without the architectural expertise held within the book.

78

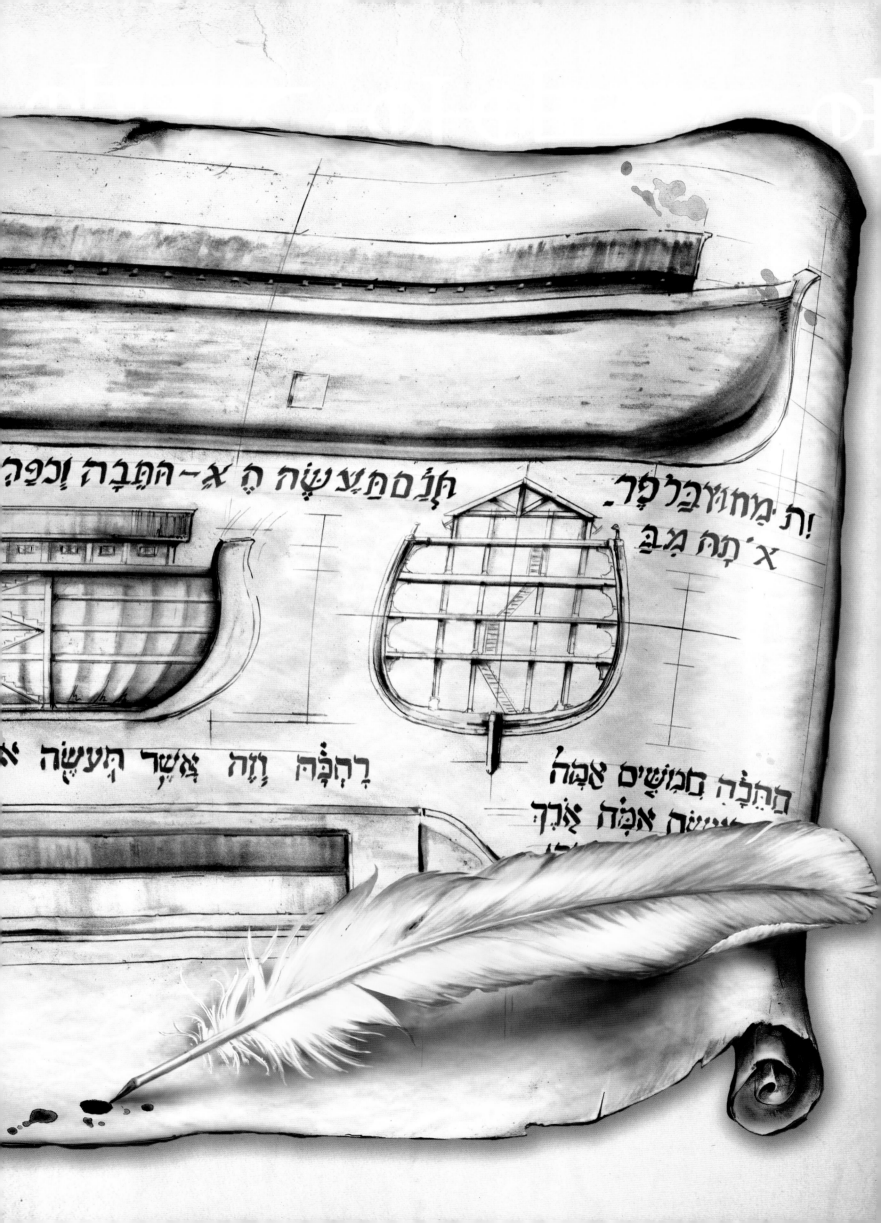

Not only did it allow Noah to correctly build the Ark and survive the Deluge, but afterward, it greatly increased the level of care-giving around the world. As proper healing methods were spread, many lives were saved that would have previously been lost due to medical ignorance.

When wise King Solomon, the son of David and Bathsheba, prayed to the Holy Father for assistance in building his famous Temple that united all the king-doms under one God, Raphael was sent down to Jerusalem in order to person-ally deliver a gift to the king—a magical ring in the shape of a five-pointed star, or pentalpha. The amazing gift had the power to subdue all demons, so Solomon sent out his armies, led by priests instead of generals, to capture dozens of the evil crea-tures to be used as slave labor to help finish, ironically, this holiest of holy build-ings. As a tribute to God, Solomon took the now-famous pentalpha symbol as his own and had it carved into the very pin-nacle of the Temple where it could be seen from every point of the city. This symbol became known as the Seal of Solomon.

as the *Seal of Solomon.*

The massive temple was also the resting place of the Ark of the Covenant, but when the Babylonians eventually invaded and conquered Jerusalem, the temple was destroyed. The temple was rebuilt nearly sixty years later, but by then both the Ark and Solomon's ring had been lost for all time. The powerful artifacts had each been placed in separate, secret chambers deep within the temple's lower halls, but the Babylonians were thorough in their destruction. Afterward, they denied any claim to either treasure.

Raphael is not the perfect warrior that Michael represents, or even an equal to Gabriel, yet in the first War in Heaven, he possessed the presence and initiative to strike down the very first of the Fallen Angels, crystallizing the moment when their paradise was lost. When those who would betray the Lord unveiled their intentions and began to rebel openly, Raphael took up his spear and slew Leviathan, one of Lucifer's strongest allies. Her body and nature had been transfigured horribly by her defiance, twisting her divine, perfect form into a huge draconic serpent.

He takes on the form of a dragon-like beast.

Their brief clash took place over an ocean of ice-blue water, and as Leviathan's massive, still form slid down through the depths, the water turned to red.

In a duty that seems, at first, to be out of his specialty, Raphael also serves as a guide through Sheol, a horrid passage through the underworld that the Hebrews call "The Pit." While he is in the underworld, he takes on the form of a dragon-like beast to more easily traverse the dangerous paths. Jagged obsidian rock juts out from the dark, waiting to cut into flesh and bone to allow the demonic larvae living at the edge of the path to sup on fresh blood. Jets of boiling, poisonous steam erupt from festering pools of muck, threatening to smother all who pass. Raphael once brought the prophet Abraham through these Hellish wastes in order to show him the fate that would befall man should the servants of God fail in their tasks.

It is thus Raphael's unenviable position to heal those around him, even as many tasks he must undertake on Earth compel him to spill blood.

URIEL

BEHOLD THE ANGEL WHO WATCHES
OVER THUNDER AND TERROR, AND
HE IS URIEL

—ENOCH 1

Uriel's name translates to "The Fire of God" and it is widely accepted that, while Michael is God's most formidable servant, Uriel is His most fanatical and pitiless. In the majority of his appearances, he is depicted as a punisher of those who defy the Will of God.

Uriel's name has been spelled many ways and translated into many different meanings, including Suriel ("God's Command"), Phanuel ("The Face of God"), Sariel, Zerachiel, and Sarakiel.

He is the angel of storms, and all manner of hail, fire, thunder, and lightning are at his command. He exercises powers frequently and revels in his domain. According to the Apocolypse of St. Peter, a book of the Ethiopic Bible, "Uri-el, the angel of God,

His name in Angelic

will bring forth in order, according to their transgression, the souls of those sinners. They will burn in their dwelling-places in everlasting fire. And after all of them are destroyed with their dwelling-places, they will be punished eternally. Those who have blasphemed the way of Righteousness will be hung up by their tongues. Spread under them is unquenchable fire so they cannot escape it."

longbow

Among his titles, he is called:
The Angel of Repentance
The Angel of the Presence
The Archangel of Fire
The Archangel of Salvation
The Prince of Lights
The Angel of Vengeance
The Angel of Thunder and Terror
The Presider over Tartarus

Script is "The Fire of God."

Uriel's fiery red hair matches his temperament, and the piercing stare of his eyes causes human, angel, and demon alike to quake. He is one of the tallest angels, eclipsed in height only by The Metatron, the voice of God.

Like his brothers, Uriel also adorns himself with a broad golden belt. His name is transcribed on the belt in Angelic Script as "The Fire of God." Uriel wears only lightweight copper chain mail into battle, as he rarely engages in singular combat. While the other Archangels carry heavy weaponry to wade through enemy lines and cut down opponents, Uriel uses a longbow and soars above the chaos of the battlefield. His tactics are brutal and as simple as an assassin's: he unerringly locates his enemies and slays them with deadly force and accuracy.

On the very rare occasion when he enters into hand-to-hand combat, he will use a huge sword that he imbues with his divine flame. He believes that one's actions are more important than words, thus he rarely speaks. Unlike the other Archangels, who are often seen without their weaponry, Uriel's longbow never leaves his hands.

belt.

The Guardian of the lost Garden of Eden

There is only one Heavenly sound that strikes the legions of Hell with a palpable fear, and that is the war-cry of Uriel, the Archangel of Vengeance. When Uriel announces his presence on the battlefield, he does so with righteous authority. Streaking through the skies as one of his own flaming arrows, he rends the air with a thunderous bellow that crescendos to a jagged shriek of lightning striking steel.

Uriel is charged with being the guardian of the lost Garden of Eden. Standing at the gate of a shattered paradise, he brandishes his fiery sword and allows entrance to no one. His brother, Raphael, is always within sight, as the Healing Archangel stands guard at the Tree of Life. Lost wanderers or seekers of the past will occasionally breach the thick, surrounding forests and approach the Gate to Eden, only to be driven off by Uriel's war-cry and the flash of his blazing longsword.

When Abel, Adam and Eve's first son, was slain by his brother Cain, Uriel appeared to the grieving couple and took up their son's dead body. He carried the murdered young man back into the Garden of Eden and buried him beneath a plum tree. Uriel allowed Adam and Eve to cover the grave with flowers, and this was the only time that they were allowed to set foot back into Eden after their expulsion. Years later, when Adam passed away, Uriel again appeared and brought the body of the first man back home to Eden. Eve was not allowed into the Garden this time, so she gave Uriel a flower to place on Adam's grave in her stead. The Archangel buried the father's body next to his son's and set the single flower upon the grave.

The Archangel of Fire will break

When the prophet Ezra asked God for insight into the visions he was having, the Lord sent Uriel to translate. During these visits with Ezra, in which he appeared over several nights, Uriel disclosed the mysteries of the Heavenly Arcana, The Kabbalah. The Kabbalah is an interpretation key, an "insight to the soul" of The Torah. It is the traditional, mystical explanation of Judaism itself, and more than that, the ways of God himself and the secrets He holds.

Uriel came down to Noah and warned him of the impending Deluge, but did not offer any assistance when Noah asked for his help. He believed that God had already been too lenient with mankind, and felt that a retributive act such as the Great Flood was long overdue. When Noah persisted in his plea, Uriel told the old prophet of his vengeful feelings toward humans and again resisted Noah's urging. For a third time, Noah petitioned the Archangel for a boon, and Uriel streaked back into Heaven without a word of reply, relief, or rebuke.

When Abraham was told by God to "go from your country" to escape the Babylonians and their idolatry, the Archangel Uriel appeared to lead him and the Hebrews out of their homes in the country of Ur to Canaan. When Abraham and his people finally reached Canaan after the desperate trek, they hailed the Archangel from the sky to deliver a message of thanks to the Lord. After that, the pilgrims set about making an altar to worship God.

The primary reason for Uriel's stern countenance and reproachful gaze is that he, along with the angel, Remiel, maintains the Everwatch at the Gates of Damnation, keeping a constant vigil over the hordes of Tartarus (another name for Hell). Uriel is the sharpest-sighted of all the Archangels, and this allows him to see and keep track of any treachery the betrayers might attempt—and to punish any who directly challenge him with his longbow.

Demons and devils rarely wreak havoc directly upon Uriel because many have caught his unblinking, intimidating eye and felt the sting of The Fire of God's longbow. Legend tells of an altercation that served as an example to the other betrayers that Uriel's attention was to be avoided. While attempting to escape from Tartarus, a demon was pinned to the gates by the Archangel's arrows and then disemboweled. As a further punishment, Uriel left the foul creature to hang there, screaming in agony, for one hundred days.

Uriel's final task comes on the day of the Apocalypse. When he hears the Horn of Gabriel sound Armageddon, the Archangel of Fire will break apart the whole of Hell and cast it down onto the jagged rocks of the Abyss, shattering the whole of it—the gates, walls, and bars of the infernal prison. He will then collect all the souls of the damned, including those of the fallen angels, and lead them back into Heaven to prepare them for their final judgment.

AZRIEL

Azriel is the most enigmatic and mysterious of the six Archangels, thus stories and sightings of him are as rare as his actual tasks. He is a solitary figure who does not hold many offices or titles compared to his heavenly brethren, and this serves his ultimate purpose. He is the least utilized, but most feared of the Archangels, for he holds the power of life and death over all, even those who call him brother.

Arabic lore is the first to name Azriel as the Angel of Death. The literal translation of Azriel is "Whom God Helps," although the true meaning may be "Whom God Helps On Their Way," as the souls of the slain ascend to Heaven. The Hebrew translation is "God's Command."

Many cultures through the centuries followed the Arabic example when the founders of differing religions gave names to the Celestial Host. Those names include Azrael (Hebrew), Azra'il (Islamic), Ashriel (Syriac), and Azaril (Aramaic), among others.

Azriel is the ruler of Shehaquim, also called Sagun, which is the third heaven. He is the Angel of Death, and of Destruction. He is considered a *kameoth*, a protector against Evil. The Book of Protection, a collection of *paritta* (protection against evil) discourses (also known as the Buddhist Bible), mentions Azriel, along with Michael and Gabriel, as the Archangels to be invoked in Syriac charms. These prayer chants, originally practiced by priests in Syria, call upon the power and strength of the named patrons to protect the faithful and ward off evil spirits.

The finely tattooed runes on Azriel's face are in formal angelic script and translate, as his name, to "Whom God Helps." These symbols inlaid upon his skin are a combination of the marks of Death and of Destruction twisted into one effigy.

When the time came for God to create Adam, Azriel was one of four Archangels selected for a special task. Within Eden, there existed a tree that held the knowledge of the Universe, and the ground that the tree was planted in was sacrosanct. The Lord bade them all to bring him seven handfuls of earth from the base of the tree, for this new creation, which he called mankind, was to have the ability to learn and know more than any other that He had yet made. Michael, Uriel, Gabriel, and Azriel all made their way down to the new world, each intending to be the first to succeed in this mission.

As they stood at the base of the Tree of Life, each angel scooped up two handfuls of earth and realized that only one of them would be presenting their Lord with a single handful instead of two. As their competitive natures took hold, Michael and Uriel began to argue as to which three would provide two handfuls and who would only provide one. Gabriel attempted to adjudicate the argument, but was soon drawn in as well. As the *scythe*

bickering continued, Azriel, who had declined to join the argument, moved away from the others and quickly filled a sack with seven handfuls of the sacred dirt. He then quietly returned to Heaven and presented the Lord with His commission.

Because Azriel succeeded where the others failed, he was given the duty of separating body from soul at the time of death. And the Lord designated Azriel the Angel of Death.

The Arabic religion holds that Azriel is a deliverer of spirituality who is for-ever writing in a large book and for-ever erasing what he writes. What he writes is the birth of a man; what he erases is the name of the man at death. He follows the thread of a man's life to its end, and then appears at the time of death to collect the soul.

Azriel is able to choose how the transmigration of spirits from the deceased is han-dled. For those who have led a faithful life, he holds an apple from the Tree of Life under their nose to gently entice the soul from the body. For those who have left the path of righteousness, he plunges his hand into their lifeless bodies and rips out their souls. He then delivers the spirits to Michael so that his brother may channel them to their final resting places.

Azriel carries a black scythe inscribed with golden runes that he uses to store the souls of the dead. Written in gold on the scythe is a quote from Exodus in formal angelic script: "And he shall pass over your door, and you shall not suffer the Destroyer to come in and smite thee."

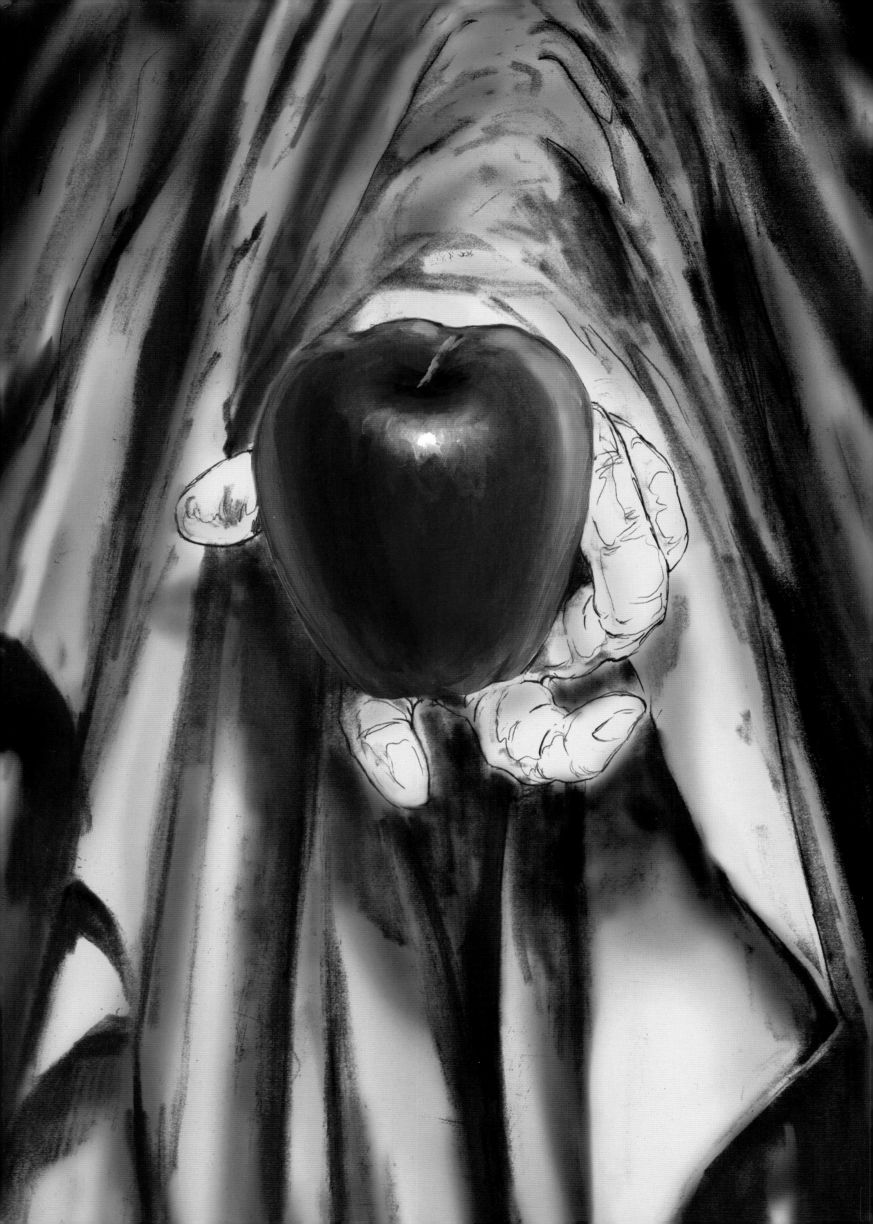

It is not intended as a weapon, but as a channeling device for spiritual energy. Azriel travels from soul to soul, collecting them for their eventual restoration in Heaven. When he returns to the Guph to deposit the souls, Azriel pours them out of the scythe and back into their original resting places. Afterward, the souls are judged and sent to their respective afterlives.

Azriel wears no armor and uses no protective devices because he does not enter into combat. He did not take up arms against Lucifer and the other betrayers during the Revolt in Heaven. The Angel of Death will not stand against any that he has not been instructed to take as part of his domain.

While Azriel is not named specifically as the Angel of Death in the Bible, it is he who slaughters the first-born of Egypt in the tenth plague recorded in the Book of Exodus.

Moses had entreated Pharaoh Ramses II to allow the Hebrews passage out of slavery in Egypt, but the proud ruler refused him, believing that Ra, Osiris, Isis, Horus, and other Egyptian deities were more powerful than Moses' God. In response, the Lord turned the waters of the Nile to blood, and followed each refusal of the Pharaoh with another plague: frogs, gnats, flies, death of livestock, boils, hail, locusts, and darkness. For the last of the plagues, Azriel stole away the souls of the first-born of Egypt, an act so devastating that the Pharaoh finally was forced to let the Hebrews go.

The Angel of Death is the final image all individuals take with them as they begin the crossover to eternal life. The raw fear mortals feel in those last moments of life so shapes perceptions of this Angel as to distinguish him from his heavenly brethren.

LUCIFER

> AND HE IS NAMED THE
> MORNING STAR, THE GREAT
> PRINCE OF HEAVEN
> —Perkei Avoth 6:12

Lucifer was the first, most beautiful, and mightiest of the Archangels, with intellect and pride the primary traits in his creation. Given the name Samael (sometimes translated as Sammael) originally, he was not known as Lucifer until after his fall from grace. The name Lucifer translates to "The Morning Star" or, in a more direct sense, "The Bringer of Light." Both definitions serve as a reflection of his original standing and a reminder of what he lost.

The name Samael is Sumerian in origin, and means the bright and poisonous one, translating literally to "The Venom of God." In his time among the Archangels, Samael's titles included Viceroy of Heaven and Regent of God. He was the ruler of the Seventh Heaven, Araboth, and one of the

"in grace surpassing the angelic mass to command,

seven regents of the world, where he was served by a host of two million angels. His domains included being an Angel of Death. The Kabbalah names him as "The Severity of God."

The highly respected theologian and author Gregory of Nazianzus wrote in *The Moralia* that Samael was at such a higher level of grace than the other Archangels that he "wore the others as a garment, transcending all in glory and knowledge." The sage Ambrosiaster confirmed this when

he wrote that Samael's place in Heaven was almost equal to God's. He claimed that the Archangel was "in grace surpassing the angelic mass to command, in grace subordinate to only his father."

In the traditional sense of theological examination, it is widely accepted that the Archangel Samael led a revolt in Heaven against God's will. The reasons given for his treasonous behavior are few and generally focus on Samael's pride overcoming his reason and his demand to be considered an equal to God.

in grace subordinate to only his father"

Samael gathered his loyal contingent of angels and confronted God, demanding to be set above the other Archangels and to receive equal standing with The Lord. It was not initially Samael's intention to supplant God, but to have Him recognize the Morning Star's obvious superiority over his brother Archangels and allow him a station commensurate with his ability and power. Samael hoped that, by winning in battle against overwhelming odds, God would reward him with such a position. As the battle lines were drawn, however, Samael realized that nothing less than an outright deposition of The Lord would gain him the respect and awe of those he sought to rule from on high.

God sent his loyal angels against the rebellious, and the insurgence escalated into a war, which culminated in Michael casting Lucifer down into Hell.

After his rebellion, Lucifer's names are plentiful, with translations of each one suggesting depraved corruption and the evils of betrayal. Among the more recognized names are Abaddon ("The Black Sun"),

Belial ("Without Worth"), Beelzebub ("Lord of the Flies"), Mephistopheles ("Hater of the Light"), and Satan ("Enemy").

The name Satan has, over the years, become the most common of the vile names attributed to Lucifer, the Betrayer. In Hebrew, the term "satan" translates as "adversary," which is exactly how Lucifer is represented in Biblical literature. However, the word satan also refers to a large group of angelic law enforcers of which Samael was the commander during his time as an Archangel. The formidable group, which administered God's law among the multitudes of angels, was greatly respected and known to be fervent in its domain. In this instance, at least, the term satan and the name Satan possess a common meaning that has become confused over the centuries.

However, the revered St. Jerome contends that Samael, as Lucifer, may be playing a role for God. From his study of the scriptures, Jerome posited that becoming the being known as Lucifer was a monumental task that God assigned to Samael, as he was the only Archangel strong enough to survive the ravages of a Hellish station. This burden, to live as an exile within the flames of Perdition until the End-time, will be revealed when, as a reward for his service, God will accept him back into the ranks of angels and reinstate him to his full power and station as Archangel. St. Jerome was not alone in this belief, as famed religious scholars including Gregory of Nyssa, Origen, St. Augustine, and Ambrosiaster all agreed, in principle, with his theory.

In the Old Testament, in biblical literature, and in theological lore, Lucifer is portrayed as a tempter and seducer. Only in the New Testament, and works relating to it does Lucifer take on a decidedly devilish aspect.

In the Old Testament, Satan is only mentioned in a handful of instances. In his first, and arguably most important, appearance to humankind, he encounters Eve in the Garden of Eden. In the oft-told tale, Lucifer either transformed himself into a serpent or gained control over one, and then spoke honeyed words to Adam's wife so that she might break God's Law and eat from the Tree of Life. The temp-

Lucifer as a serpent

111

tation was successful and began the tragedy of Man's sinful existence upon Earth.

In the New Testament, and especially in Revelations, Lucifer appears in large, intimidating shapes and begins to take on traits such as horns, a tail, and hooves. It is also in the New Testament that he is described as being reddened and having control over Hellfire.

Lucifer's attempts to sway those from God's Will are, for the most part, thwarted by humankind's faith and strength of will. The Devil usually succeeds only in playing the weak foil against followers of The Lord.

Lucifer is unique among angels insofar as his pride demands that he rely exclusively on his innate powers rather than weapons or armor. He does not use any outside force to overcome his opponents in battle, save for his strength, speed, and unparalleled command over fire and light. After his expulsion from Heaven, however, it was God's decree that Lucifer would lose the ability to control light. The Lord did allow

after his fall from grace.

Lucifer to retain control over flame, though, mocking the Archangel by leaving him with such a superfluous power in Hell.

Although he does not ordinarily wear armor, Lucifer donned an extraordinarily polished breastplate of purest gold before the revolt in Heaven. The mirror-like surface reflected the powerful light that emanated from his body, transforming him into a miniature sun. He still wears the breastplate after his fall from grace, which now is blackened and charred by Hell's inferno. It is a constant sign of his defeat and strengthens his resolve to return one day to Heaven triumphant.

When Lucifer was cast out of Heaven, Hell already existed. The iron gates of the nine layers of The Abyss were open and awaiting the fallen Samael when he landed upon the harsh, rocky ground of Perdition. The infinitely deep planes of Damnation are divided into nine separate domains, each overseen by a faithful lieutenant of Satan, who rules over all.

Angelic lore

HISTORICAL TALES

Washington's Vision

Before George Washington became the first President of the United States, he was a general of the American army in the Revolutionary War. In the midst of a brutal winter at Valley Forge, Pennsylvania, Washington received a most mysterious visitor.

An angel came to him that winter and showed him three visions. The following is an account Washington told to a fellow soldier:

This afternoon, as I was sitting at this table engaged in preparing a dispatch, something seemed to disturb me. Looking up, I beheld standing opposite me a singularly beautiful female. So astonished was I, for I had given strict orders not to be disturbed, that it was some moments before I found language to inquire the cause of her presence. A second, a third and even a fourth time did I repeat my question, but received no answer from my mysterious visitor except a slight raising of her eyes.

By this time I felt strange sensations spreading through me. I would have risen but the riveted gaze of the being before me rendered volition impossible. I assayed once more to address her, but my tongue had become useless, as though it had become paralyzed.

A new influence, mysterious, potent, irresistible, took possession of me. All I could do was to gaze steadily, vacantly at my unknown visitor. Gradually the surrounding atmosphere seemed as if it had become filled with sensations, and luminous. Everything about me seemed to rarefy, the mysterious visitor herself

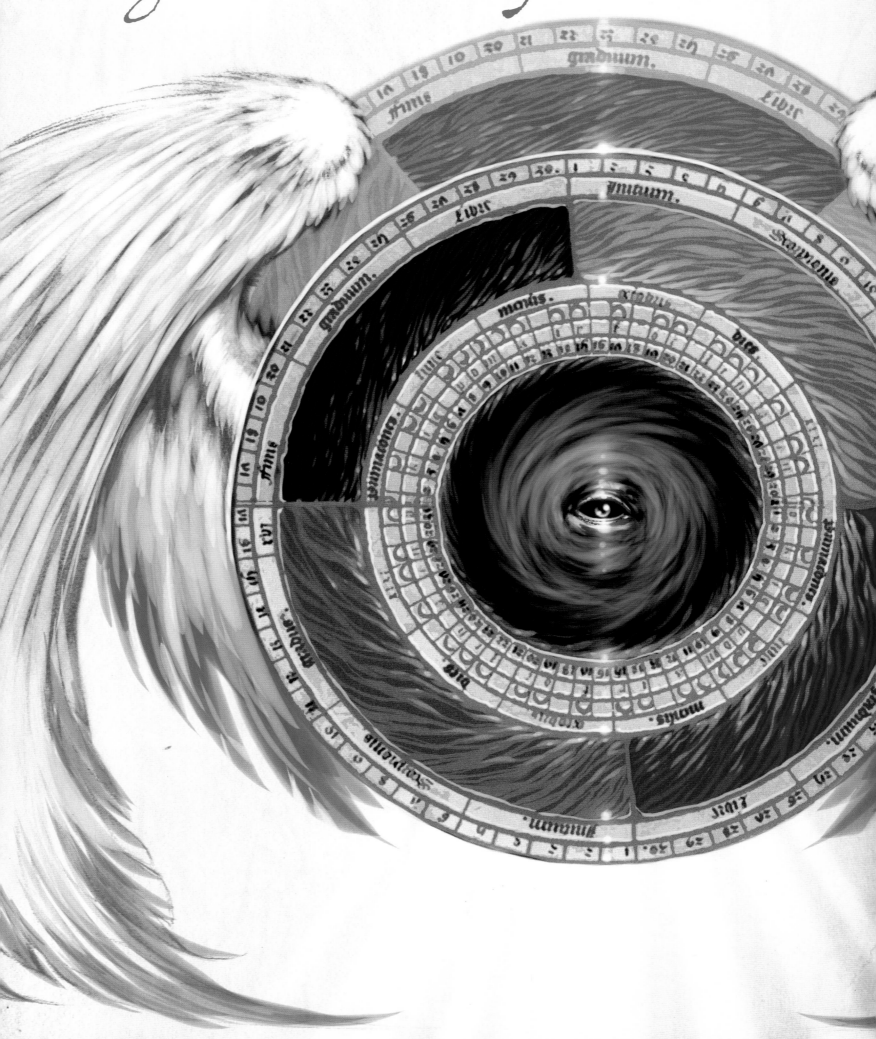

becoming more airy and yet more distinct to my sight than before. I now began to feel as one dying, or rather to experience the sensations, which I have sometimes imagined accompany dissolution. I did not think, I did not reason, I did not move; all were alike impossible. I was only conscious of gazing fixedly, vacantly at my companion.

Presently I heard a voice saying, "Son of the Republic, look and learn," while at the same time my visitor extended her arm eastwardly, I now beheld a heavy white vapor at some distance rising fold upon fold. This gradually dissipated, and I looked upon a stranger scene. Before me lay spread out in one vast plain all the countries of the world—Europe, Asia, Africa, and America. I saw rolling and tossing between Europe and America the billows of the Atlantic, and between Asia and America lay the Pacific.

"Son of the Republic," said the same mysterious voice as before, "look and learn." At that moment I beheld a dark, shadowy being, like an angel, standing or rather floating in mid-air, between Europe and America.

Dipping water out of the ocean in the hollow of each hand, he sprinkled some upon America with his right hand, while with his left hand he cast some on Europe. Immediately a cloud raised from these countries, and joined in mid-ocean. For a while it remained stationary, and then moved slowly west-ward, until it enveloped America in its murky folds. Sharp flashes of lightning gleamed through it at intervals, and I heard the smothered groans and cries of the American people.

A second time the angel dipped water from the ocean, and sprinkled it out as before. The dark cloud was then drawn back to the ocean, in whose heaving billows it sank from view. A third time I heard the mysterious voice saying, "Son of the Republic, look and learn," I cast my eyes upon America and beheld villages and towns and cities springing up one after another until the whole land from the Atlantic to the Pacific was dotted with them.

Again, I heard the mysterious voice say, "Son of the Republic, the end of the century cometh, look and learn." At this the dark shadowy angel turned his face southward, and from Africa I saw an ill-omened specter approach our land. It flitted slowly over every town and city of the latter. The inhabitants presently set themselves in battle array against each other. As I continued looking I saw a bright angel, on whose brow rested a crown of light, on which was traced the word "Union," bearing the American flag, which he placed between the divided nation, and said, "Remember ye are brethren." Instantly, the inhabitants, casting from them their weapons became

friends once more, and united around the National Standard.

And again I heard the mysterious voice saying "Son of the Republic, look and learn." At this the dark, shadowy angel placed a trumpet to his mouth, and blew three distinct blasts; and taking water from the ocean, he sprinkled it upon Europe, Asia and Africa. Then my eyes beheld a fearful scene: From each of these countries arose thick, black clouds that were soon joined into one. Throughout this mass there gleamed a dark red light by which I saw hordes of armed men, who, moving with the cloud, marched by land and sailed by sea to America. Our country was enveloped in this volume of cloud, and I saw these vast armies devastate the whole county and burn the villages, towns and cities that I beheld springing up. As my ears listened to the thundering of the cannon, clashing of sword, and the shouts and cries of millions in mortal combat, I heard again the mysterious voice saying, "Son of the Republic, look and learn."

When the voice had ceased, the dark shadowy angel placed his trumpet once more to his mouth, and blew a long and fearful blast. Instantly a light as of a thousand suns shone down from above me, and pierced and broke into fragments the dark cloud, which enveloped America. At the same moment the angel upon whose head still shone the word Union, and who bore our national flag in one hand and a sword in the other, descended from the heavens attended by legions of white spirits. These immediately joined the inhabitants of America, who I perceived were well nigh overcome, but who immediately taking courage again, closed up their broken ranks and renewed the battle.

Again, amid the fearful noise of the conflict, I heard the mysterious voice saying, "Son of the Republic, look and learn." As the voice ceased, the shadowy angel for the last time dipped water from the ocean and sprinkled it upon America. Instantly the dark cloud rolled back, together with the armies it had brought, leaving the inhabitants of the land victorious!

Then once more I beheld the villages, towns and cities springing up where I had seen them before, while the bright angel, planting the azure standard he had brought in the midst of them, cried with a loud voice: "While the stars remain, and the heavens send down dew upon the earth, so long shall the Union last." And taking from his brow the crown on which blazoned the word "Union," he placed it upon the Standard while the people, kneeling down, said, "Amen."

The scene instantly began to fade and dissolve, and I at last saw nothing but the rising, curling vapor I at first beheld. This also disappearing, I found myself once more gazing upon the mysterious visitor, who, in the same voice I had heard before, said, "Son of the Republic, what you have seen is thus interpreted: Three great perils will come upon the Republic. The most fearful is the third, but in this greatest conflict the whole

angel with a huge flaming sword

world united shall not prevail against her. Let every child of the Republic learn to live for his God, his land and the Union." With these words the vision vanished, and I started from my seat and felt that I had seen a vision wherein had been shown to me the birth, progress, and destiny of the United States.

The Angel of Mons

In August 1914, during World War I, French and British troops were in the midst of a full retreat as the German juggernaut threatened to overrun the southern half of Western Europe. When the order to retreat reached the soldiers of the French and British armies at Mons in Belgium, they all knew that many of them would perish in the attempt.

Many of the soldiers reported seeing strange figures and lights on the field that night during the retreat, but they did not stop to take a closer look. When these troops stopped to gather themselves after the withdrawal, they realized that not one of them had fallen. Although the British ultimately sustained over 1,500 casualties these troops had escaped the bombardment without a single death. They were close enough that they could still hear enemy guns and feel the bullets whizzing by, but somehow, they all survived unscathed.

Some of the British troops later reported that they saw a fully armed and armored angel, while French soldiers claimed to have seen Joan of Arc astride a huge white charger, bolstering their defense. Other English soldiers reported that they saw St. George emerge from a shining, golden mist while mounted upon a huge white horse. Still other troops claim to have seen a golden-winged angel with a huge flaming sword. Also, many of the German soldiers later said that just as they were about to rout the overwhelmed Allies, their horses all bolted and fled the battlefield, while a sense of powerlessness overtook the men. Some among the Axis troops reported seeing a wall of thousands of enemy forces rising up to stop them, holding the line so that their comrades could safely escape.

BIBLICAL TALES

Jacob's Ladder

The prophet Isaac's first and favorite son was Esau, and Isaac planned for his eldest to receive his blessing to oversee the family's inheritance when the older man died. However, his wife Rebekah favored her youngest son, Jacob. One day Isaac asked for some food and Rebekah covered Jacob with furs and sent him to his father with the meal. Isaac, old and blind, touched his son on the shoulder and, thinking it was the older and hairier Esau, gave his blessing. When he discovered the ruse, Esau flew into a murderous rage. Rebekah, realizing that Jacob was in mortal danger, sent him away to live with her brother Laban in the town of Haban.

While on his way to take refuge with his uncle, Jacob had an amazing dream that proved to be a blessing from God. Jacob envisioned a remarkable celestial ladder that stretched the height of the massive gulf between Heaven and Earth. Upon it he saw a perfect procession of thousands of angels who ascended and descended the golden span for an untold amount of time. The blessing bestowed upon Jacob and his descendants wealth, long life, and a place in Heaven.

When Jacob awoke the next morning, he vowed to build a shrine on the very spot he slept, in honor of his providence. The elaborate shrine made of ash and softwoods, along with a large altar elegantly carved with scenes of God's angelic messengers, was soon finished and christened Bethel.

Daniel and the Lions' Den

Daniel, one of the more famous prophets of God, had been instructed by the Lord that a day would come when he would be spared by the Lord's servants.

While traveling through Babylon, Daniel found himself in trouble with certain resident religious sects. The majority of the people in the city worshipped the god Bel, whose likeness was engraved on a statue outside a grand temple. Daniel mocked the false deity and proved that the food and wine set forth daily by the priests as a sacrifice to the statue were in fact, consumed by those same priests and not by Bel. The Babylonian king, Cyrus, was outraged and embarrassed by this interloper, but could not find fault with Daniel—so he executed the priests instead.

A few days later, Daniel learned that a dragon lived within the city walls, and vowed to destroy the creature. He tricked it into eating poison cakes, which placed him back in trouble with the king, as the Babylonians worshipped the dragon. An angry mob called for Daniel to be thrown into a den of seven lions, and Cyrus complied. An unrepentant Daniel felt he had done God's will by destroying an evil creature. The Lord sent seven angels to protect the defenseless prophet. They held closed the jaws of each lion, and Daniel was spared.

And there came a great voice out of the temple

The Final Judgment

Angels serve many important functions in events recounted in the Bible, but perhaps none more dynamic than their role as the emissaries of Armageddon. St. John the Divine describes a vision of seven angels bearing "seven golden vials full of the wrath of God" which must be emptied before the souls of the faithful can enter the temple of Heaven. Each vial contains a devastating plague and each angel is charged with pouring it out in fulfillment of the Divine will.

The pouring out of the first vial causes sores and boils to erupt on all those who carry the mark of the beast (the Son of Satan), and who worship him.

The pouring out of the second vial turns the waters of the ocean to blood like that of a dead man, killing every living soul in it.

The pouring out of the third vial, likewise, turns the rivers of the land to blood.

# of Heaven, from the throne, saying: "It is done."

The fourth vial is poured out on the sun, giving it the power to scorch and burn humankind.

The fifth vial is poured out on the kingdom of the beast, plunging it into darkness.

The sixth vial, when poured out, dries out the River Euphrates and coaxes three unclean spirits out of the mouth of the beast, who gather the kings of the world together for battle.

The seventh angel pours out the seventh vial when all on earth are gathered together in a place called Armageddon: And there came a great voice out of the temple of Heaven, from the throne, saying: "It is done."

LITERARY TALES

The Tales of Faust

There are two primary dramatic versions of the legend of Faust and his encounter with Satan. Both Christopher Marlowe's *The Tragical History of Dr. Faustus* (1588) and Johann Wolfgang von Goethe's *Faust* (1832) are based on actual accounts of Johann Faust, a practicing alchemist known for his brilliant work and dubious moral character. Born in Germany in the late 1400s, the doctor was a greatly educated man who traveled far and wide to further his alchemical studies. He was reputed to have trafficked in the occult, and was quoted in 1535 as calling the Devil his devoted friend, or "schwager." When he died in 1540, his controversial life immediately became fodder for the literati.

Marlowe's tale portrays Faustus as a greedy intellectual who strikes a deal with Satan in the person of Mephistophelis to receive great wealth and success for twenty-four years. Faustus seals the pact with Satan by signing his name to a contract in his own blood. Although the Devil keeps his part of the bargain, Faustus attempts to renege when the twenty-four years are complete, but to no avail. Satan drags Faustus off into Hell at the end. The physical depiction of Satan in the story conforms to the traditional image of the Devil with red skin, horns, a tail, and bat wings.

Goethe's *Faust* varies significantly from Marlowe's story. In Heaven, Mephistopheles boasts to the Lord that he can win the soul of Heaven's favored scholar, Faust. Faust seeks knowledge of the universe, but is frustrated and unfulfilled. He seals a bargain with a drop of his blood, agreeing to do the Devil's bidding in Hell if Mephistopheles will do his on Earth. Most of what Mephistopheles offers Faust are poor and tawdry temptations that distract him from his purpose and blacken his soul, especially his seduction of the innocent maiden Gretchen who dies for his indiscretions. But Faust does gain an ennobling wisdom from his experiences, and at the end of his time on Earth, as Mephistopheles arrives to claim his soul, a host of beautiful angels appear to guide his soul heavenward instead, where the forgiving Gretchen awaits him.

The Circles of Hell

Dante Aligheri's epic poem, *The Divine Comedy*, features one of the most frightening and detailed depictions in all literature of Satan reigning in Hell. In the first section or book known popularly as "Inferno," Dante tells how, on one Good Friday evening, he became lost in the woods and found his every effort to escape thwarted. From Heaven, his lost love Beatrice sees him and asks the Roman poet Virgil to escort her lover through this spiritual wilderness and bring him to her. Virgil tells Dante that their path to freedom will first take them through Hell.

After entering the gates of Hell, which are emblazoned with the warning "Abandon All Hope, Ye Who Enter Here," Dante and Virgil are brought by the ferryman Charon across the River Acheron to the nine circles of Hell, each of which serves as a prison for the souls of sinners. The greater the sin the higher the number of the circle, which corresponds to a lower depth.

The first circle is a limbo for pagans and others who willfully forsook the Son of God and thus are denied His grace.

In the second circle, the souls of the lustful swirl around eternally in a storm so violent it prevents lovers from ever touching each other again.

The third circle is a prison for the souls of gluttons. These damned are mired in its mud and endure a steady rain of filth and excrement while being gnawed on by Cerberus, the three-headed dog.

In the fourth circle, the greedy and those who indulged them are tasked with pushing large boulders away from one another.

Cerberus

Abandon All Hope, Ye Who Enter Here

The fifth circle is reserved for the wrathful. Their punishment is to struggle with one another in the polluted River Styx and choke on its mud.

The sixth circle is the first within the City of Dis, which is circumscribed by the River Styx. Here, heretics struggle to escape from flaming tombs.

In the seventh circle, also in Dis, violent criminals are trapped in a river of boiling blood. Suicides transform here into thorny black trees, and the profligate are chased through the trees by vicious dogs.

Frauds, hypocrites, liars, and sycophants all occupy the eighth circle, where punishments range widely with the sin and include: whipping by demons; burial head-first in holes while flames are held to the soles of the feet; entrapment in a lake of burning pitch; pursuit by venomous snakes; having one's head removed and put on backwards; having to wear lead cloaks; and having one's body repeatedly ripped apart and reconstructed.

The ninth circle of Hell is reserved for traitors and betrayers of all kind. Its lowest level, Cocytus, is a vast lake frozen by the flapping wings of Satan. As rendered by Dante, Satan is a three-headed monster who is partially trapped in the ice. The mouth of each head bites down on one of the three greatest traitors in history: Judas Iscariot, the betrayer of the Son of God; and Brutus and Cassius, both of whom conspired against Julius Caesar.

Dante and Virgil make their way out of the ninth circle, and emerge in Heaven on Easter Sunday.

lock and key to the Abyss

ADAPTED FROM JOHN MILTON'S
Paradise Lost

So stretched out huge in length the Arch-fiend lay

Chained on the burning Lake, nor ever thence

Had risen or heaved his head, but that the will

And high permission of all-ruling Heaven

Left him at large to his own dark designs,

That with reiterated crimes he might

Heap on himself damnation, while he sought

Evil to others, and enraged might see

How all his malice served but to bring forth

Infinite goodness, grace and mercy shown

On Man by him seduced, but on himself

Treble confusion, wrath and vengeance poured.

Forthright upright he rears from off the Pool

His mighty Stature; on each hand the flames

Driven backward slope their pointing spires, and rowled

In billows, leave in the midst a horrid Vale.

Then with expanded wings he steers his flight

To reign is worth ambition though in Hell:

Aloft, incumbent on the dusky Air

That felt unusual weight, till on dry Land

He lights, if it were Land that ever burned

With solid, as the Lake with liquid fire;

And such appeared in hue, as when the force

Of subterranean wind transports a Hill

Torn from Pelorus, or the shattered side

Of thundering Ætna, whose combustible

And fewel'd entrails thence conceiving Fire,

Sublimed with Mineral fury, aid the Winds,

And leave a singed bottom all involved

With stench and smoke: Such resting found the sole

Of unblessed feet. Him followed his next Mate,

Both glorying to have escaped the Stygian flood

As Gods, and by their own recovered strength,

Not by the sufferance of supernal Power.

   "Is this the Region, this the Soil, the Clime,"

Said then the lost Arch-Angel, "this the seat

That we must change for Heaven, this mournful gloom

Better to reign in Hell, than serve in Heaven

Who now is Sovran can dispose and bid

What shall be right: farthest from him is best

Whom reason hath equaled, force hath made supreme

Above his equals. Farewell happy Fields

Where Joy forever dwells: Hail horrors, hail

Infernal world, and thou profoundest Hell

Receive thy new Possessor: One who brings

A mind not to be changed by Place or Time.

The mind is its own place, and in it self

Can make a Heaven of Hell, a Hell of Heaven.

What matter where, if I be still the same,

And what I should be, all but less than he

Whom Thunder hath made greater? Here at least

We shall be free, the Almighty hath not built

Here for his envy, will not drive us hence:

Here we may reign secure, and in my choice

To reign is worth ambition though in Hell:

Better to reign in Hell, than serve in Heaven."

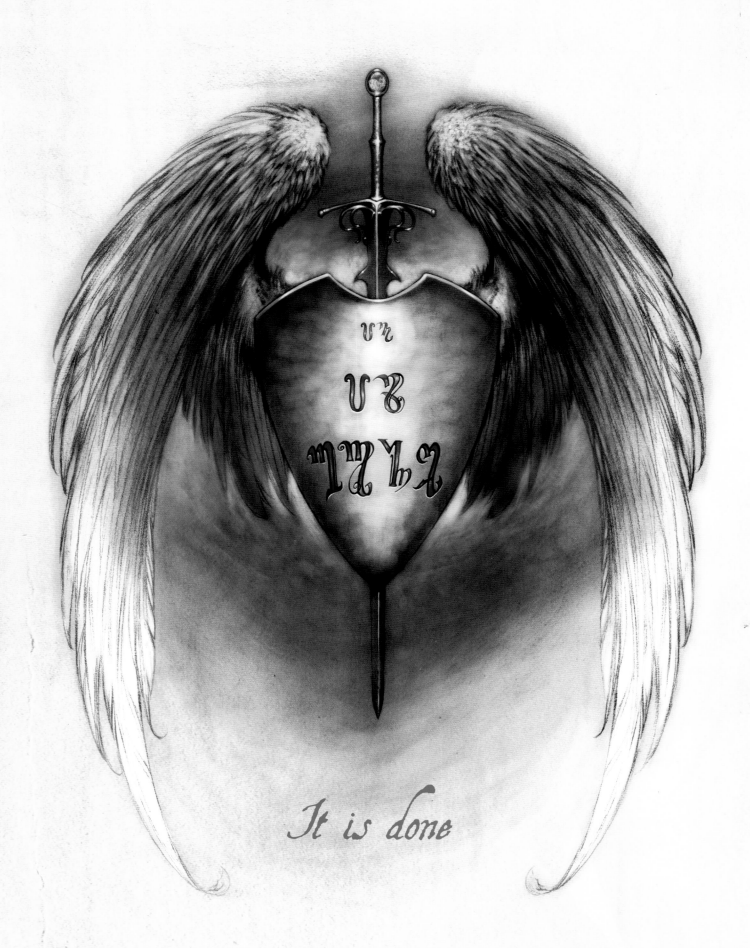

It is done